Prison Cultures

Prison Cultures
Performance, Resistance, Desire

Aylwyn Walsh

intellect Bristol, UK / Chicago, USA

First published in the UK in 2019 by
Intellect, The Mill, Parnall Road, Fishponds, Bristol, BS16 3JG, UK

First published in the USA in 2019 by
Intellect, The University of Chicago Press, 1427 E. 60th Street, Chicago, IL 60637, USA

Copyright © 2019 Intellect Ltd

All rights reserved. No part of this publication may be reproduced, stored in a retrieval system, or transmitted, in any form or by any means, electronic, mechanical, photocopying, recording, or otherwise, without written permission.

A catalogue record for this book is available from the British Library.

Copy editor: MPS Technologies
Cover designer: Aleksandra Szumlas
Production manager: Mareike Wehner
Typesetting: Contentra Technologies
Cover image: Production Shot, *Sweatbox*. Produced by Clean Break, 2016.

Hardback ISBN: 978-1-78938-105-4
Paperback ISBN: 978-1-78938-863-3
ePub ISBN: 978-1-78938-106-1
ePDF ISBN: 978-1-78938-107-8

Contents

Acknowledgements		vii
List of Figures		ix
Introduction		1
Chapter One:	Prison Cultures: Habitus and 'Tragic Containment'	23
Chapter Two:	Genealogies of Prison as Performance: Towards a Theory of Simulating the Cage	49
Chapter Three:	Trauma, Strategies and Tactics: Problems of Performance in Prison	79
Chapter Four:	Race, Space and Violence	113
Chapter Five:	Prison Lesbians: Screening Intimacy and Desire	141
Chapter Six:	Performance through Prison: Institutional Ghosts and Traces of the Traumatic	171
Conclusion:	Paradoxes of Prison Cultures	201
Bibliography		211
Filmography		255
Live Performances		257
Index		259

Acknowledgements

Dedicated to Arlene and Tony Walsh – with love and thanks for your consistent and generous support. I am in debt for the depth and extent of love I am lucky to have enjoyed throughout my life. I should like to offer my gratitude to my primary mentors and inspiration in the field of prison and performance: Alex Sutherland and Caoimhe McAvinchey who both exhibit integrity and vision in their practice with people in prison, and commitment to social justice in scholarship.

Much of the work has been informed by and threaded through with affect, fervour and inspiration that comes from former experience as an artist working in criminal justice with the Writers in Prison Network, National Criminal Justice Arts Alliance, as well as in prisons in South Africa. For work that was informative but not explicitly referenced here, I offer thanks to Mary Fox and women at HMP Drake Hall with the support of the National Offender Management Service (now HMPPS). The company Clean Break has enjoyed a longstanding reach in relation to women in the criminal justice system and has also been significant in my professional life. Thanks to Clean Break Theatre Company – especially Anna Hermann and Lucy Perman – for generosity and access to production images. Open Clasp Theatre Company and Geese Theatre Company also offered support in the form of publicity materials.

Gratitude to my Ph.D. supervisor Patrick Duggan, who was unwavering in his support of the project that led to this monograph. Thanks also to Victor Ukaegbu and the graduate school from University of Northampton. Early versions of the work were awarded the Helsinki Prize (IFTR) and the TaPRA PG essay prize, which enabled conference attendance and development. The University of Lincoln's research leave enabled me to disseminate much of the work and explore new avenues, and I thank Dominic Symonds and Karen Savage. My current workplace has continued to offer outstanding support. From the University of Leeds' School of Performance and Cultural Industries: Alice O'Grady, Joslin McKinney, as well as Sarah Bartley, Emma Bennett, Rebecca Collins, Leila Jancovich and George Rodosthenous for modelling collegiality. I was given support for research assistance from the able Kelli Zezulka.

Some of my thinking developed through working on collaborative performance with students at the University of Leeds in the production *Held* (2017) and *Stand to A Count* (2018), including collaborators WY-Fi, the Probation Teams at Ripon House, Cardigan

House and Magistrate's Court, Leeds. Thanks to Tanja Schult and her careful engagement with practice in working through trauma and performativity for a piece on *Painful Pasts*. For engaging with earlier drafts with precision and care, Marissia Frakgou, Marilena Zaroulia and Sita Popat, my appreciation.

Friends and companions are due love and respect too: Ananda Breed, Robert Dean, Tobi Moss and Siobhán O'Gorman. My family has been constant and generous in their support. In addition to my parents, devotion and thanks to my brother, Aidan and my grandmother, Love. I take such delight in Anna Davidson – thanks for adventures in love and learning.

I would like to acknowledge the importance of developing work through presenting at Quorum, QMUL; International Federation of Theatre Research IFTR; TaPRA Performance, Identity and Community working group; Rhodes University Drama Department; and the University of Roehampton's seminar series for inviting me to present work. At the University of Lincoln's seminar series Critical Encounters, Justin Hunt helped me work through the formulation of prison as performance. I was honoured to deliver the keynote presentation at the Manchester Metropolitan University PG conference (2017). My collaborator Andrea Zittlau at the University of Rostock invited me to her seminar series – an outing for some of the ideas presented here.

Some small extracts from chapters have been extended from essays published in Chapter Three as 'Staging women in prison: Clean Break Theatre company's dramaturgy of the cage' (Walsh 2016). Some ideas from Chapter One are based on '(En)gendering Habitus: Women, Prison, Resistance' (Walsh 2014). The initial ideas for Chapter Two were developed in 'Performing prisons, performing punishment: The banality of the cell in contemporary theatre' (Walsh 2012a).

Thanks also to Intellect editors and reviewers for their comments and engagement that have undoubtedly improved the work.

Finally, my respect and solidarity to all the folks I have collaborated with behind bars throughout the years – practitioners and prisoners: *Aluta Continua*.

Figures permissions

Helen Maybanks and Donmar Warehouse
Clean Break Theatre Company
Open Clasp Theatre Company

List of Figures

Figure 1: Cycle of tragic containment / Cycles of Incarceration.
Figure 2: Panopticon. Ahrens, L. (2008), 'Prisoners of a Hard Life: Women and their Children', *The Real Cost of Prisons Comix* (Artist: Susan Willmarth), p. 75.
Figure 3: Production Shot: *Sweatbox*. Produced by Clean Break, 2016.
Figure 4: Production shot: *There are Mountains*, 2012 HMP Askham Grange. Produced by Clean Break.
Figure 5: Keith Pattison, Open Clasp *Key Change*. Performers: Jessica Johnson and Christina Berriman Dawson.
Figure 6: Production shot: *This Wide Night*, Moss, 2009. Produced by Clean Break.
Figure 7: Production shot: *PESTS*, Franzmann, 2014. Produced by Clean Break.
Figure 8: Ensemble in *Julius Caesar* (Donmar Warehouse Shakespeare Trilogy). Photographer, Helen Maybanks. Reproduced with permission.

Introduction

Introducing Prison Cultures

Many of the memories I have of working as a creative artist in prison swing between sensory overload, moments of joy and the triumph of pedagogic success when connecting with someone unexpectedly. These stimulating times were often matched by sheer frustration at the complexity of managing expectations. My endeavours to use performance, creative writing and filmmaking with prisoners were underscored by a desire to stimulate imaginations beyond institutional rhythms. The impetus for thinking through *Prison Cultures* emerges in between these sometimes oppositional forces – between the desire to create something and the resistance to institutionalization.

Likewise, any search through my viewing histories or record of attendance at performance would confirm a certain relish for popular media that is about prison – including crime drama, detective fiction and stories that make accounts of containment and freedom, desire and resistance. I seek out cultural productions that account for wider social understandings of crime and justice. My thinking in this book is inflected by my own experiences of prison as a theatre practitioner and researcher, though my analysis primarily works through accounts of representations on TV and on stage. In recent times, the imagery of criminal justice as a set of processes that can be captured and mediated in order to draw attention to its operations has been foregrounded by documentation such as dash-cam footage, mobile phone video documentation of police brutality. Performance, in this context, becomes valuable as a method – not merely for disseminating ideas *about* prison but for working through embodied experiences, affects and events.

There has been a wealth of artistic material that testifies to the significance of prison as a cultural construct. Visual representations include the urgent and exhaustive documentary about race and criminal justice in the United States by Ava duVernay *The 13th* (Netflix 2017). These are counterposed by fictional works such as the playful novel *Hag Seed* by Margaret Atwood (2017), which narrates *The Tempest* as a revenge tale staged in a prison to hilarious effect. Historical works and sites of incarceration are being dynamized in artworks such as Artangel's (2016) re-staging of Oscar Wilde's *De Profundis* on the site of Reading Gaol, read by celebrities including Patti Smith (Gormley and Monzani 2016). In the late 1970s, artist Tehching Hsieh produced several durational performances that included incarcerating himself in a cage for a year in his series of *Year Performances* (Heathfield and Hsieh 2015). In a wide-ranging project on medical histories called *Disorder Contained*, UK theatre company Talking Birds contributed new work on histories of confinement (Talking

Birds 2017a, 2017b). In eastern Europe, the interplay between the law, crime, the state and representations is explored in contemporary art exhibitions such as *Extravagant Bodies: Crime and Punishment* (Bago et al. 2016). In the context of North America, Lois Ahrens produced an inspiring graphic novel that contextualizes incarceration with socio-economic contexts. It was produced with graphic novelists who render conditions in *The Real Cost of Prisons Comix* (Ahrens et al. 2008) in different graphic styles. Considering how prison cultures are reproduced beyond the inside, Mimi Nguyen provides a critique of carceral chic in fashion (2010). Bliss et al. (2009) produced a moving curated exhibition called *Prison Culture*, while Pete Brooks (2017) curates an award-winning web-collection on prison photography that draws attention to how visual cultures are produced in – and by – prison. Extending to arts used to rehabilitate, museums contribute inside/out collections to their community-based education (Museums Association 2017). Non-profit UK arts organizations such as Fine Cell Work use approaches such as needlework (Emck 2017), the production of music by Music in Prisons/Irene Taylor Trust (Digard and Liebling 2012) as well as visual arts exhibited in annual awards by the Koestler Trust (Zoukis 2017) and performance (Babetto and Scandurra 2012).

Moving away from the participatory arts world, there has also been a resurgence of visibility of prison tropes in popular culture. Some of the most popular streaming on Netflix includes the series *Orange Is the New Black* (2013–ongoing) that has undoubtedly opened up conversations about women's incarceration in the United States. This wide range of events, productions and stagings signals a critical moment for cultural criminology. My initial introduction of the terrains of cultural criminology augments the terminologies of cultural criminology by also claiming performance methodologies are productive when considering how justice is staged. I consider the impacts, effects and implications of certain representations of criminal justice in the precarious balancing between 'the public' and 'the incarcerated'. In doing so, I am interested in exploring the surrounding discourses that seek to make sense of crime, justice and incarceration, and consider how performance and popular culture disrupts, and, in some instances, reinforces, those discourses. In the context of crime and justice, it is both necessary and valuable to identify existing power structures so that we might ask of representations whether they reinforce, obscure or challenge how power is distributed. In addition, this line of enquiry heeds Lucy Nevitt's call to examine 'how [such power] is used in contexts beyond the performance' (2013: 39).

To that end, the book furthers two means of engaging with prison cultures: first, by theorizing prison through understandings emerging from popular culture representations; second, by analysing performance (theatre and applied performance) as well as analysis of popular screen-based media. Although there are different informing principles about spectatorship that relate to liveness and replicability, I am not looking to construct a hermeneutic that is totalizing, but to offer a series of different perspectives on different modes of production that can tell us more about prison and experiences of prison. In doing so, I am developing the project set up by cultural criminology, and in particular by Michelle Brown (2009), whose work on spectacle considers the location of prison in the public imagination. Eamonn Carrabine's conception of visual criminology as constituting a public understanding of crime through photography (2012, 2014, 2015) has also informed my awareness of how images and popular media form an imaginary of prison. My own interest in contributing to cultural criminology signals the importance of performance in constituting the carceral imaginary. Its significance is its concern with the body in relation to spectatorship and meaning making as valuable when understood against and through how crime and punishment are scripted, enacted and received.

In her incendiary one woman show, *Notes from the Field* (first staged in 2016), Anna Deavere Smith plays out the stories of how minority youth in the United States seem propelled out of the school classroom and towards prison in what has been called the school-to-prison pipeline. In the wake of Black Lives Matter, this subject matter makes for compelling performance, and, as she shifts characters between teachers, administrators and witnesses, Smith is in dialogue with excessive brutality, police violence and young people who are maligned and misunderstood. Throughout, she channels the voices of people affected by mass incarceration whose testimonies explain how it affects people of colour in particular. It is a devastating performance that, by working through these different perspectives gathered from over 250 interviews in the field, shifts locations across the country to depict a wide-scale travesty of justice. Smith's show (adapted into a TV film by HBO, 2018) exemplifies all of the three core themes in the book: first, the characters express desire for a world in which institutionalized racism would not be an adequate excuse for systemic exclusion and marginalization. Second, many of the people interviewed by Smith participate in resisting the state institutions that discriminate against them, target them for abuse and perpetuate racist violence against them. The monologue format enables Smith to use performance to conceive of how both state operatives and criminalized people perform, drawing particular attention to race.

A formative experience of performance in and of prison from my own South African context was seeing a stage production of Athol Fugard's (collaboratively written) play *The Island* (1974) – in which two political prisoners on Robben Island perform *Antigone*. The promotion of gender as both a victimizing category of punishment (the emasculation of male prisoners in this case) and their performance across genders mark this play as particularly rich for staging how the bodies of the incarcerated repeat and reflect the historical, cultural, mythic and political spectres of prison.[1] This notion of repetition that is performed to sadistic ends in *The Island* raises questions about who is incarcerated and why, although this line of questioning is relevant to criminology, and as such functions as an underlying – rather than a central – concern throughout the book. Nevertheless, the sociopolitical context of women's 'offending' and pathways through prison are important to this argument. *The Island*'s play within a play shows how performance can be used as an element of protest and resistance against the stultifying Apartheid regime. These two examples of different approaches of performance – the testimonial monologue and the physical style of South African protest theatre – start the work of how forms in performance lead us towards particular understandings of prisons.

The aims of the book include how theatre practice can be used to explore the performative ontological states of women in prison by analysing contemporary performance and popular media. Underlying this is the consideration of the problems and possibilities of representation. The forerunner to the book is a feminist practice-based project that engaged with women in prison to explore to what extent, how and why modes of performance can be seen as a means of 'survival'. Although originally part of research on *Performing (for) Survival*, this book serves to further my abiding interest in feminist inquiry, containment and sites of contestation. I am positioning this work as feminist because it draws attention to gender's structuring forces in the field of prison, which has long been at the centre of criminological analysis about women, crime and punishment. More pressingly in my own field is the way feminist thinking helps make sense of experiences, histories and contexts for prison's performance that is particular for women. In this, I draw from feminist criminology (Bosworth 2000; Chesney-Lind and Pasko 2004; Davis 1981; Gelsthorpe 2006; Hahn-Rafter and Heidensohn 1995; Heidensohn 1996) as well as feminist spectatorship (as discussed by Jill Dolan 1989, 2005, 2007). The particularities of feminist criminology are not only related to the sense that women are criminalized for spurious reasons or that criminal justice institutions are designed for men. Instead, feminist thinking about how certain bodies are disciplined and punished is important for understanding what that means for normative modelling of gender and the implications for those who deviate from such norms. In turn, then, this helps to offer a productive means of critiquing structural inequalities in prison.

The book does not only focus directly on women, but sets up the parameters for thinking about the intersections of experiences and representations that I then proceed to analyse through specific productions, TV series and events in the second half of the book. Although it might seem theoretically promiscuous, the intention is precisely to move between experiences and representations of women in prison. Theorizing about prison cultures is a means of examining both experiences and representations as porous. In this way, I develop materials that do something to disestablish the foreclosed meanings of 'crime', 'offending women' and 'justice'.

This positions the work as interdisciplinary – drawing on cultural criminology as well as performance and cogent disciplines to offer a means of understanding institutions, agency and how these are disseminated beyond the prison in cultural productions (Brown 2009; Cecil 2015, 2017; Ferrell et al. 2008; Ferrell and Sanders 1995; Hayward 2004; Hayward and Presdee 2010; Ogletree and Sarat 2015; O'Neill 2004; Presdee 2000; Schept 2013; Yar 2010). I see this as a critical contribution to performance studies and cultural studies, in that it is necessary to move beyond a deconstructionist/Foucauldian analysis, or a strictly psychoanalytic analysis of representations of crime and criminal justice. This is because what I demonstrate is that the frame of the institution and its impacts and implications for women need to be called to account. In performance, film and television, representations of prisons and prisoners have a great impact in terms of serving the public imaginary about what prisons are for and what they do to people. For that reason, thinking about prison cultures needs to include a sense of how representational strategies result in feelings and tropes. In my analysis, characters are analysed not simply in relation to their motivations – as if they have agency – but must be considered in relation to how they speak to narratives of power, agency and resistance. In this, I take the cue from scholars such as Ann Cvetkovich (2003), Jill Dolan (1993a, 2005), Jack Halberstam (2001, 2011), Nicholas Mirzoeff (2011, 2017) and José Muñoz (1999, 2009) in order to inflect cultural criticism with a politicized agenda. That is, that the cultural items that I analyse are considered not in isolation, but in terms of how they inform and are informed by wider social,cultural and political understandings about carceral conditions. Representations found and experienced as cultural artefacts are, as performance studies scholar Richard Schechner claims, 'evidence of the violence of desire, its twisted and dangerous possibilities' (Schechner 1988, cited in Presdee 2000: 5).

The understanding of the complex interrelations between culture, imagination and social problems draws on the work of C. Wright Mills' *Sociological Imagination* (2000) whose approach signals the structures and forms in society. To attend to cultural production through such a lens is to be assured of the relatedness between specific examples such as characters, plot points, films or performances, and how they reflect or influence wider cultural meanings. Criminologist Carrabine (2012) offers a detailed engagement with the imaginary of prisons through a range of artistic forms, including fine arts, literature and film. His approach offers a deeply historical sense of prison and the functions of representation for how the public consumes the tropes of crime and justice, and what that might then mean for attitudes related to criminality and punishment. Jon Frauley (2015) takes up this point for an approach to criminology that seeks the challenge of enquiry and also of the imagination. He demonstrates the need to consider contexts, theories and influences as well as provide instances that illuminate how to understand prison as both an institution and experience that is inflected by history. Carrabine's offer, in theorizing a visual criminology in particular, enables a means of considering how prison imaginaries circulate over time (2012, 2015).

Prison's Performance

Performance and prison may, as performance scholar Caoimhe McAvinchey notes, 'appear immiscible' (2011a: 60): at a superficial level we might understand the pleasures associated with theatre and performance as being in opposition to what Graham Sykes (1958) calls the 'pains' of imprisonment. This book contributes to the critical and troublesome genre of analysis that disrupts the neat, compelling stories of 'success' of performance interventions in and of prisons and other sites of conflict (Thompson 2011a). I aim to recuperate performance, both theoretically and methodologically, through examining how it functions in relation to the theatrical presence of the law. This is not a perpetuation of what Jonas Barish (1985) termed 'antitheatrical prejudice'. Rather, following Diana Taylor (2002), a focus on the wider sense of performance enables me to move beyond the logocentric, colonial, Eurocentric boundaries hitherto associated with text-based 'theatre' criticism. The context of this study coincides with an instrumental turn in applied theatre[2] (Thompson 2011a), in which performance practices serve an ameliorating purpose that inevitably conform to funding agendas. In addition, the fraught contexts of arts funding and the resultant conservatism are evident in companies that mount productions that do not challenge the status quo but prioritize entertainment and market their performances as 'experiences' rather than as 'theatre' (White 2013). For these reasons, this research turns away from merely analysing theatre: I am more interested in the sociopolitical function of the work rather than making a case for a specific aesthetic model. As such I am drawing on a provisional and strategic definition of performance instead of 'theatre'.

Performance is a contested term, the limits of which are tested through the book. Sociology and criminology have found tools and vocabularies for translating lived experiences into theories and models in order to explain the world. Performance translates lived experiences into aesthetic encounters while research in prison insists on an ethics of encounter. I view the lived experiences of incarcerated women through the models and metaphors offered by performance. Thus, the institution itself is examined as the performance context or, to use Pierre Bourdieu's term, 'field', of the research (1990). In this argument, then, I define performances as the framing of a set of practices and behaviours in conscious aesthetic and ethical relationships between bodies, in which space and location provide a specific context through which meanings are generated and understood. Drawing on Gareth White's recent formulation (2013: 2–5), attention to 'performance' allows me to analyse practices that occur outside of what has a defined economy and set of values associated with formal 'theatre'. Yet, I also pay close attention to the responsiveness of theatre and popular culture to the cultural and social performances of prisons.

Thus, although the book draws on feminist criminology, sociology and criticism of dramatic literature, the informing discourse is from performance studies. In foundational texts in performance studies, scholars have developed a set of complex explanations for the problems of visibility (Diamond 1997; Phelan 1993), harnessing the worth of Derridean notions of performativity and Austin's Speech Act Theory (Diamond 1997; Miller 2007; Sedgwick and Parker 1995). Performance studies has moved beyond considerations of what is and is not seen in the study of the ephemerality of the theatre – or the always already disappeared (Phelan 1993). Rather, the force of performance as a mode of understanding is in its relation to what remains as traces and in the collapse of separation between the real and representations (Davis 2003; Diamond 1997; Phelan and Lane 1998; Schneider 1997, 2011). These arguments often centre on the value of theatre and performance itself, and there is a wider, methodological implication to the process of applying performance analysis to non-performance sites and contexts. It is in this specific arena that this research is located, amongst scholarship that points towards the need for performance to dismantle what otherwise appear to be inviolable apparatus of the state – such as borders (Nield 2006a, 2008, 2010a), courtrooms (Wake 2010), political leadership (Schmidt 2010) and in war (Schneider 2011; Thompson et al. 2009). The need for critical and radical deconstruction of power and its representations is well explored, and has become more acute since the events

Introduction

9/11, in which concepts such as 'nation' and the 'Other' were highlighted in a spectacular event that collapsed the real (of the terrible destruction experienced by civilians in the United States) with the mediation of cycles of retribution in the 'war on terror' (Taylor et al. 2002; Taylor 2009). I maintain that critical investigation of all state apparatus is necessary in order to better contribute to the wider debates about human rights, safety and security, and global and local futures. As such, this multi-layered performance analysis of and about prison intends to add to these debates.

Director Brett Story's 2016 feature-length documentary *Prison in Twelve Landscapes* ventures towards imaging territories of prisons in the United States. Her film does not approach the micro-level imagining of daily lives, routines and regimes of incarceration, like most other documentaries of prison. Instead, she zooms out to the macro-level perspective of how prison sits within wider social structures, by scoping the landscapes of prison – usually rural locations and de-industrialized towns. The film proposes a means of understanding where prison fits (as site, workplace and temporary home) within the contexts of economic deprivation, unemployment and where the convergence of issues related to global capitalism in the United States in the twenty-first century. Story makes visible issues that are not merely relevant to the United States, though the film helps to make manifest the place of prison in contemporary North American life (Story, 2016).

The rising importance of cultural criminology looks to the need to unravel the public/private dyad made manifest in fictional or documentary representations of prison (Brown 2009; Ferrell and Sanders 1995; Ferrell et al. 2004, 2008; O'Neill and Seal 2012). In part, the value of this scholarship lies in considering how visuals, trends and the dissemination of prison stories in a range of forms impact public understandings of prison life. While Story's evocative film offers site, place and wider social structures as its visual narrative, much of the material in this book looks towards how conceptions of site and structure are carried across prison's perimeters. Thus, although the theoretical lens of analysis focuses on detail, it is important to conceive of the films, productions and artworks I discuss to be understood as operating within the wider field of prison cultures. That is, on the scale that is beyond nations or specific criminal justice systems. I am not proposing that there is a universal experience of how prison functions: any critical engagement with people incarcerated in South African prisons (Dirsuweit 1999; Dissel 1996), India (Cherukuri 2008) or Russia (Moran et al. 2013a, 2013b; Schuler 2013) demonstrates how distinctive regimes, conditions and outcomes can be.[3] *Prison Cultures*, therefore, are to be understood as multiple: forming within and between the interplay between daily performances and structural fields of meaning. For this reason, chapters are structured in such a way as to draw on detailed criminological research as well as cultural productions to consider how they interrelate. My focus for much of the book is on women in prison, how they perform identities and are represented through performance and popular culture. Performance, resistance and desire are productive because they form responses to incarceration that move beyond affect. Indicative examples are considered for how they are produced by prison and in doing so, resistance and desire become analytical categories.

Performance, Power and Patriarchy: Defining the Paradox

Most scholarly work on theatre in prisons tends to fall within one of two camps: cultural or literary analysis of tropes and prison thematics within play texts, or accounts of applied theatre processes with prisoners. Both rely on a preponderance of prison imagery (walls, fences, journeys to and from prison), concern time and explore the interpersonal dynamics of prison and its characters. Literary and dramaturgical analysis is helpful in articulating the ways the panopticon frames and forms the subject of inquiry. By contrast, the applied theatre approach positions the work as 'doing' something, claiming transformation by examining behaviours 'before' and 'after', as well as describing the processes of creative participation 'during' workshops and rehearsals. While cultural studies, literary analysis and applied methodologies are valuable in order to view the multiple ways prison becomes an imagined site, in isolation, such approaches can fix the prison as architecturally and temporally rigid, reinforcing the view that the institution's impact remains as an inevitable traumatic trace or spectre even after leaving it.

By contrast, my vision is for a critical consideration of a broad spectrum of prison cultures: performances *in* and *of* prisons. The prison itself is seen as a character and a site with its inhabitants and workers as extensions of the site (both extending and subverting its operations). The work is informed by over fifteen years of professional artistic practice and is structured as through and around the institution – subject to the tensions, regulations and controls of bureaucratic power – as well as opening up spaces of radical possibility within the prison imaginary. In pursuit of this methodological and theoretical animation of prison *as* performance, I interject with an example of how literary encounters with incarceration enabled me to reflect on my own processes of navigating prison research.

Fictional Release

I'm reading a short story by Italo Calvino. Short stories are all I can hold onto at this time, because longer works make me feel guilty, but I'm gasping for a fictional release from the grips of theory. Only, Calvino's story has drawn me back in to the prison. He conjures a character, Edmond Dantés, who has been incarcerated in a fortress for years, who addresses the reader directly as if confessing his obsession with imagining his position within the prison.

It's a writing experiment – such that the description of the character demands that the reader also imagine her way inside and outside – attempting to remember the many facts, half-memories, postulations and lies told by Dantés – in relation to the second layer of information we are given about the notorious escapee Faria, whose scratchings and regular rhythmic breakouts/break-ins form the soundtrack to Dantés' time.

> Everything that is unclear in the relationship between an innocent prisoner and his prison continues to cast shadows on his images and decisions. If the prisoner is surrounded by my outside, that outside would succeed in bringing me back each time

> I succeeded in reaching it: the outside is nothing but the past, it is useless to try and escape.

In the manner of a Calvino reader, I pause in the story and try to fathom whether he has succeeded in turning the inside of my head into a page in his story. Time passes as I try and get to the end of a sentence just to affirm that my reality is indeed, outside the prison. The prison is outside me.
(Research Diary, April 2012, quoting Calvino 2002: 287)

When it comes to how we understand cultures produced in prison, scholarship on theatre in prison often highlights the paucity of available data on assessing 'impact' after interventions (Hughes 2005a, 2005b; Miles and Clark 2006; New Philanthropy Capital 2011).[4] As a result, most studies focus on the moment of incarceration – relying on the neat containment of theatre interventions in particular times and carceral spaces. They are inevitably focused on documenting the more spectacular, convincing 'stories' of what works (cf. Cheliotis 2012b; Cohen 1985). However, these studies then limit and contain their own value within the values of the surrounding institutions.

In the United Kingdom, there is a rich tradition of arts in prisons with men that seeks to engage in identifying, articulating and then re-framing offending behaviour through performance exercises, explored in more detail in Chapter Three (Baim et al. 2002; Balfour 2003, 2004; Heritage 1998, 2002, 2004; Peaker and Johnston 2007; Thompson 2003, 2004a, 2004b; Watson 2009; Walsh 2017). Men in prison are discursively framed as violent, angry, often addicted and with poor interpersonal skills. Their crimes are symptomatic of aggressive masculine claims of territory. Many men do not feel thwarted by prison, but, on the contrary, characterize their 'time' as part of a passage towards more 'successful' expressions of masculinity (Balfour 2003; James 2003). By contrast, theatre-based programmes with incarcerated women tend to engage with their identities as partners and mothers, or with cognitive behavioural approaches concerning their vulnerability, dependency (on the state or on patriarchal figures), poor mental health (Lawston and Lucas 2011; Kilby 2001) and addictions (Clark 2004; Fraden 2001; Hughes 1998). They are characterized as having chaotic lives and their crimes are very often attributed to the influence of men. Accounts of women's incarceration rarely valorize their bravery, but rather tend to position women as helpless, hopeless and unable to cope with the cold and hard institution (Lamb and The Women of York Correctional Institution 2003; Lamb 2007; Levi and Waldman 2011).

Both views are clearly based on outdated thinking that engages biological determinism by stating that excess testosterone results in crime, and presupposes that women only commit crimes because they are too weak to resist men's dominance. In other words, women in prison are doubly victims of patriarchal oppression; first for engaging in law-breaking at the behest of men; and second for being incarcerated in a patriarchal system, as Helena Kennedy (2005) posits. In addition, where women are not drawn as weak caricatures lacking will, violent women – or what Lynda Hart (1994) calls 'fatal women' – are demonized for being unwomanly.[5] For instance, Susan Sered and Maureen Norton-Hawk's excellent study of resistance offers the following narratives as tropes that inflect women's experiences of incarceration:

> [W]hen women abandon normative Woman identities, alternative symbolic language turns out to be even harsher: crack whore or unfit mother, powerful labels that become embodied through incarceration and loss of one's children to 'the system'.
>
> (2011: 323)

There is a sense, then, in popular culture and media (film, books, television and performance) that Western women in prisons are considered 'acceptable' if they are repentant victims. Bosworth and Carrabine (2001) particularly outline this in relation to a turn to religious 'transformation'. There is a further thrill at operation in the characterization of criminal women as 'monsters' (Hart 1994).[6] Should a woman, upon release, be seen to have 'transformed', she is called a survivor.

Feminist criminology suggests that by definition, women in prison are triply marginalized; first, by their status as women in a phallocentric society; second, by being in prison (having been judged guilty of crimes); and third, by being marginal in relation to other factors that lead to criminalization (such as race, ethnicity and class as well as poverty and education attainment). Such marginalization, and the de facto inscription of performative cycles of (re)offending this implies, is critically questioned in the research. I do not wish to perpetuate the currency of women in prison as victims of circumstance, nor do I wish to engage in the frenzied debate on women's crime and behaviour (both of which reduce and erase agency in favour of banal cause/effect argumentation). Rather, I make use of the time/space caesura of incarceration as a means of moving away from the above stereotypes to the untold stories of a marginalized group.

Prior to McAvinchey's edited collection (Walsh 2019) on applied theatre with women in the criminal justice system, there had been no UK-focused book-length studies of arts with women in prisons. Perhaps this is due to the relatively small number of females in prison in the United Kingdom – there are just over 4000 women in prison in the United Kingdom (Ministry of Justice 2017). The only book about theatre with and by women in US prisons is by Rena Fraden (2001) about the US-based theatre company Medea Project for Incarcerated Women, which is renowned for engaging with how women's testimonies invite witnessing through radical re-positioning of their marginalization (Billone 2009; Fraden 2001; Warner 2001, 2004, 2011). Prior contributions to the area of theatre and women in prison have been in practice-led research, although these tend to be chapters in edited collections (Clark 2004; Herrmann 2009; McAvinchey 2006a; McKean 2006; Weaver 2009). These accounts engage with practitioners' particular models of practice that are defended and tend to relate to the practical and pedagogical implications of conducting theatre-based interventions in an institution.

Introduction

By contrast, this project develops a theoretical model of analysing prison through performance in the model of what I call 'tragic containment'. This model is drawn in order to develop thinking about desire and resistance that is specific to prison and how institutions attempt to contain both. The analytical materials draw on play texts (the documented archives of performance events), but are largely related to experiences of live events, performances and spectatorship of popular TV. Behind this is a wealth of experience in prisons as a theatre practitioner and writer in residence, so that much of the understanding of prison, institutionalization and the critiques of claims for authenticity emerges from experiences I carry from being a creative practitioner – fundamentally different to the experiences of those being punished, but nonetheless still subject to the rhythms, routines and deadening of institutional life. Criminologists Coretta Phillips and Rod Earle suggest that

> [i]n popular culture the spectacular 'othering' of prison and prisoners substitutes for, and obscures, its banality and its grinding dullness, distancing people from responsibility for its more mundane realities. This is not to suggest a simplistic political solidarity with men and women 'behind bars' is either possible or necessary for criminological researchers, but registers the profound ethical ambiguities of conducting such research.
> (2010: 20)

Thus, although I do not include materials on practice-led research in this book, the disciplinary frame of the institution(s) I have worked in over many years marked out pathways for the research that had not been planned, but that became productive in my understanding of carceral spaces, strategies and tactics. The prison habitus is also understood from the embodied perspective of the insider/outsider. This ambiguity I experienced as queer, foreign, practitioner that was granted access to keys but who did not wish to see herself as an employee of Her Majesty's Prison Service. For the people I worked with, however, I held keys and was, in some ways, indistinguishable from gaolers. It is thus fitting that I introduce this strand of argumentation with a confession.

Starting from the Fence

I am profoundly ambiguous about prison theatre. I feel unsettled by the majority of work that moralises, often imposing a particular perspective that privileges narratives of 'victims' or casts prisoners as 'survivors'; or those that demonise institutions entirely without contextualising the social function of prisons, neglecting the question of crime and criminality.

When I am in the audience, I become anxious that theatre's attempts to aesthetically frame prisoners' experiences slip past the desire for 'authenticity' that I can't quite escape (not only in realist modes, but site-responsive and promenade performances too). As a practitioner, I am silenced despite feeling I have something to say. I am bewildered by my expectations for representation – but sense that is not because I believe 'authentic' accounts are possible – but rather because that is how so many prison performances are framed. I am disappointed that so many examples of theatre that include prison do not seem able to function outside binary characterisations of victim–survivor. I am also concerned by performance work that is not in the public realm (as much applied theatre remains process-based). Some of this work seems to me to perpetuate a benevolent approach that, despite 'good intentions', can often end up perpetrating silencing, exclusions, and even co-option by the authorities. I am also guilty of perpetuating that kind of strangulation.

I am more infuriated by the barriers to accessing prison than ever before (and I have been doing theatre in prisons for the last fifteen years). I have no doubt that this is because prison, in the UK at least, has become even more restrictive, more bureaucratic, more risk averse and more tied to cost–benefit analyses than before. In other words, it has become further stripped of its potentiality for humane rehabilitative measures. I'm still trying to get in though. Perhaps this is a productive state to attempt to define a model of reflexive critical research on performance practices in and of women's prisons.

The fence seems to be a good place to start: neither entirely inside the field nor entirely outside, but straddling both. To evoke Minh-ha (2011), the allure of the walls and fences demands a breach.

(Research Diary, May 2012)[7]

Prison Architectures: Concepts and Frameworks

One feature of accounts of research and practice in prisons is the ubiquitous description of entering prison walls and navigating the gates (Kershaw 2004; Williams 2003). These reflections of the outsider's entry into the alienating world of restrictions and sanctions are often then counterposed with detailed descriptions of the 'liberating' experiences of freedom attained through creative pursuits. They are, very often, inspiring stories of the transformative power of the arts (Heritage 2004; Peaker 1998; Rymhs 2012). Indeed, most accounts of arts in prisons rely on a sense of distance between the aesthetics and the 'real' of the prison as the ethical and juridical cages in which the activities occur. Yet, all too often, these narratives do not trouble the very structures of fences, security and surveillance that mark prisoners as captives. At best, the critical examples offer a sentimental gloss that relies on empowerment (Lopez 2003), and in some cases they may reinforce a distinction between 'us' and 'them' (Clark 2004; Cleveland 2003; Davis 2004).

The theories I adopt provide vigour to entering and 'reading' prison as a location or 'field' and provide ways in which to consider the women prisoners' everyday performances, desires and resistances (discussed as 'habitus'). Bourdieu's habitus is analysed in relation to prison as a set of durable dispositions that are informed by the context or 'field', forming the core contribution to performance, criminology and sociological fields. This understanding means that I draw on real experiences to consider the popular cultural representations. This breaks open the fairly fixed ways theories have responded to prison by analysing discipline-specific concerns of deviance, desistance or otherwise the defence of a specific model of artistic practice in prisons. By contrast, the structure I have developed provides a sense of the competing discourses that operate in relation to the topic. What the book does is offering a platform for the contestation in these fields, providing a provocation to how we engage with popular media, contemporary performance and applied theatre.

In the chapters, I navigate a shift between arguing a theoretical position and providing close analysis of screen representations, play texts as well as participation as audience in events. Readers familiar with ethnographic writings will be aware of the jostling of voices in contested terrains. Readers familiar with prisons or other criminal justice institutions will understand the need for multiple strategic deployments of convincing arguments: initially for why the arts can and should be practised in prisons; and second, for the ethical obligation to critique and offer novel insights into how participation, representation and empowerment can move beyond platitudes. The conscious engagement with multiple disciplines is not merely customary, but necessary for developing a robust argument against the limiting discourses about women in prison. In this, I am drawing on geographer Dominique Moran's proposition that spaces of incarceration can be understood '[a]s "texts" which can be "read" as they form "palimpsests" of identity and culture, which both validate and authenticate consensual notions of […] justice, whilst simultaneously inviting alternative readings' (2015: 130).

As such, the questions that drove me during this research, which are interrelated, are: what does theatre/performance and popular culture offer to the subject of women in prison to challenge stereotypes of 'the cage'? And to what extent and in what ways does performance in (and of) prison challenge/subvert/augment/transform our understanding of the institution? These questions raise further sub-questions that are explored in relation to both empirical observation and analysis of contemporary performances. Namely, how do women in prison use performance tactics as part of their everyday performances of desire and resistance? And how are women in prison represented in theatre and popular culture?

The aims of *Prison Cultures* include a desire to address the focus of prison studies to include women's experiences and representations. I do so by considering the specificity and importance of women's stories of criminalization, incarceration and release that are fundamentally different to those of men, and thus deserve specialized attention. By developing a feminist theory of containment that is used to analyse plays, popular culture and television, I aim to maintain a focus on the body and performance as a locus of meaning. In doing so, the book explores how desire and resistance are developed through prison's spaces and performances of punishment. This enables the wide range of examples to contribute to interdisciplinary literature in the fields of cultural criminology, socially engaged/applied theatre and feminist cultural studies.

It is necessary to point towards three caveats that should be considered foundational in the book. I do attempt to identify performance of resistance as 'good' and the institution as 'bad' but works across complexities and conflicts to engage with more nuanced views of the field and the ways women's everyday performances call institutional norms and values into question. However, as its fundamental position, this understanding is placed within a feminist criminology and radical, feminist performance context, which question the structures of power that have led to the sense that the status quo is fixed and irrevocable. Also foundational is that the ideological positioning of criminal(ized) women as 'bad girls/unruly women' dictates the ways they are staged in performance.

The second caveat is that women in prison are not a homogenous group, defined by a community of interests. They are not a collective connected by any particular ideology, history, religion, language or 'nation'. Rather, they hold as many positions of identification, belonging and resistance as women outside of prison. This notion is somewhat refined in relation to the most recent feminist criminology which shows that disproportionate numbers of women from minority groups and poor people are incarcerated, which has led some criminologists to assert that race and poverty do assert a sense of 'community' that is criminalized. I point towards the ways poverty, class and race constitute criminal communities (Loyd et al. 2012). Nonetheless, I am reminded of Jessi Jackson's cogent reminder of the need for activists and activist aligned scholarship to be wary of universalizing claims, and to recognize the significance of different, intersecting locations, identities and experiences (2011). They are considered a 'community of location', and part of what performance can do is explore how the location is mapped across other identifications. Yet, it is a mistake to imagine that women in prison would experience punishment in the same way, or manage pathways towards 'rehabilitation' in the same ways. The complexity of engaging with these multiplicities is evident throughout this book. Women in prison have no discernible common discourse, but they have a current common experience of being incarcerated, which leads to my assertion that their common experiences can be understood through Bourdieu's notion of 'field' and 'habitus'.

The final caveat to address is the preponderance of male theorists whose sociological principles I have animated in relation to concerns of women in prison.[8] I have clearly positioned this work as a feminist project, and thus it would be preferable to engage with existing feminist paradigms, and draw more on works by feminist scholars. I do rely on feminist criminologists whose analyses of the patriarchal criminal justice system are foundational to this project. Yet, I maintain that there is a productive potential in the recuperation of theories (such as Bourdieu's) that are evidently useful for feminist analysis and to consider their value in the paradigm of women's prisons. In part, this serves to validate the theories, but does not, as some feminist perspectives would have it, mirror the experiences of women who must submit to the phallocentric discourse of the institution. Instead of 'reading' women through the hitherto 'masculine' theories, I attempt to 'engender' the theories (see Toril Moi 1991) by attending to the particular potential of gender categories and performances to trouble theory's singular force. The result is that feminist criminology's complaints about women's (re)victimization in institutions designed for men are complemented by the critical theorization of how women's everyday performances can be understood as desires and gendered resistance that perform against a range of oppressions.

The thematic interests sit alongside consideration of how the arguments prove productive for an understanding of both social processes and cultural outcomes as 'performance'.

Introduction

Broadly, Chapters One and Two promote a theoretical contribution to cultural criminology; Chapters Three and Six relate primarily to theatre and performance; and Chapters Four and Five attend to film and screen representations. Chapter One 'Prison Cultures: Habitus and Tragic Containment' articulates the primary theoretical frame for the research. It is predicated on Erving Goffman's influential research on 'total institutions' (2007), and argues for the value of Bourdieu's theory of 'field' and 'habitus' (1987) in prison-based research. The theoretical concerns posited by feminist criminology are threaded through the articulations of 'habitus', since I argue that both site and dispositions are inherently gendered. The research seeks to demonstrate that the operations of power, discipline, punishment and rehabilitation need to consider and acknowledge the ways gender (and other categorizations of race, class and ethnicity) are practised, enforced and performed. The theoretical concerns are indicated in a model that functions in several ways throughout the research; namely to explore the characterization of women in prison as 'victims', 'survivors' or 'heroes'. This model is later used to analyse applied theatre performance, contemporary performances and popular culture representations of women in prison. The chapter offers the theoretical architectural blueprints about habitus, performance and resistance that inform the remaining argument.

The second chapter 'Genealogies of Prison *as* Performance: Towards a Theory of Simulating the Cage' serves to elaborate the ways in which prison operates as both a cultural trope and a performative mechanism in a range of interrelated ways. This chapter takes on Foucault's conception of the panopticon, which sees each cell as a 'little theatre' (1977).[9] By means of establishing a genealogical sense of the prison's function within wider society, I introduce three examples: the Stanford Prison Experiment, conducted by Zimbardo and colleagues (Haney et al. 1973) and the performance art staging by Guillermo Gómez-Peña and Coco Fusco of *Two Undiscovered Amerindians Visit…*, also known as *The Couple in the Cage* (1992). The final example is Rideout's replica cell, which was installed at the Southbank Centre and elsewhere in the United Kingdom as part of the exhibition *Art by Offenders* (2010–ongoing). This detailed analysis of simulations of cells provides an important springboard for the argument as it outlines the public visibility of 'the cage', with the suggestion that simulated cells inevitably return audiences to a conservative, rather than radical, point of view about the function of prisons. Following Joseph Roach (1996) and Diana Taylor (2002), there is value in thinking about the impact of performance genealogies as constitutive of a kind of cultural performance.

> Performance genealogies draw on the idea of expressive movements as mnemonic reserves, including patterned movements made and remembered by bodies, residual movements retained implicitly in images and words (or in the silences between them), and imaginary movements dreamed in minds, not prior to language but constitutive of it, a psychic rehearsal for physical actions drawn from a repertoire that culture provides.
>
> (Roach 1996: 26)

I do not mean to conflate all women's experiences of prison habitus as constitutive of a singular or even coherent 'prison culture', but rather, to propose that prison's performance in the lives of women leaves a trace or scar of its presence.

Taking another line of enquiry, Chapter Three, 'Trauma, Strategies and Tactics: Problems of Performance *in* Prison', introduces the practices of applied theatre in prison, drawing on two main examples from Clean Break Theatre Company and Geese Theatre Company. Both examples are explored in relation to key concerns raised by trauma theory, articulated through an understanding of Michel de Certeau's 'strategies' and 'tactics' (1984). This offers a critical perspective on the ways prison spaces and the functions of prison are enacted through arts programmes that may claim radical intent. In other words, despite appearances of emancipatory intent, when practised within the prison, theatre practice is always already subservient to the hegemonic structures of the institution. This relationship must be articulated, and not subsumed by the ideologies of 'transformation' or 'liberation' that inevitably do not stand up to scrutiny in relation to institutional discourses.

Chapter Four 'Race, Space and Violence' offers an important theorization of prison cultures as defined and delimited by race, ethnicity and prejudice. In her compelling prison abolition work in which Angela Davis (2004) constructs the prison as a border, the collision of race and justice issues is starkly rendered. By developing and extending her characterization of the social performativity of criminalization, her work promotes a reading of prison spaces, violence and the Other. Its focus turns to how and in what ways race and its intersections with gender shape the construction of meaning in popular culture. It draws on the vigour and political urgency of these arguments and aims to develop a distinctly feminist analysis of contemporary media phenomenon – the popular TV series produced by Netflix *Orange Is the New Black* (*OITNB*). By foregrounding race and representations in a mainstream series about prison, I consider what that can offer for debating how institutions perpetuate and exacerbate inequalities for women.

Chapter Five, 'Prison Lesbians: Screening Intimacy and Desire', develops a theoretical understanding of how desire and intimacy are deployed as tactics against the institution. While attending to emerging arguments about how the trope of the prison lesbian has emerged in film in particular, I outline how sexuality is performed in and against the institution. This is particularly important in light of prisons' denial of prisoners' agency. In this chapter, I explore lesbian desire in screen and fictional examples that are about women in prison in particular. I consider how such desire is produced as a fundamental tactic of surviving in prison, and thus forms a core element of prison culture that is not often studied. In turn, I propose same-sex desire as a challenge to the institutional habitus so that it becomes a feature of resistance, forming a series of tropes across a range of genres representing women in prison. The examples I analyse are from the novel *Affinity* by Sarah Waters (also a BBC adaptation), via exploitation films through to mainstream television series *Bad Girls* and Australian television drama *Wentworth*.

The final chapter, 'Performance *through* Prison: Institutional Ghosts and Traces of the Traumatic', seeks to engage with the step away from prison as the site of performance; not as the site of performance of sentences, but as a phantasmagoric repetitive image that maintains a presence after women have been released. I explore how the argument has defined prison as a field, and to what extent the prison maintains a performative function in the lives of women post-release. Incarceration is seen as a process towards successful re-integration in society – a rehearsal for successful performance of citizenship and belonging. As such, prison is discursively framed as a performative process: a space that gathers a group of social actors together to collectively and individually undertake a temporal programme that is intended to lead to rehabilitation, in which the citational preparation for *becoming* is itself a performance.

The chapters collectively engage in telling a multi-faceted story that draws upon several disciplines. *Prison Cultures* thus does not provide clear answers to the 'problem' of women in prison. That would suggest that the question asked how performance could resolve women's relationship with incarceration, which occludes the ways crime and justice are always already socially constructed and culturally mediated. Rather, using performance as methodology and object of analysis allows me to problematize both the institution and the women's responses to incarceration. The throughlines of the argument could be grasped in a number of ways: one reading of the argument relates to spatial relationships and representation; another details a set of challenges raised by feminist criminology and how performance manifests some of these concerns.

What *Prison Cultures: Performance, Resistance, Desire* does that is unique and specific is to develop a perspective of resistance and desire that is particular to performance. The analysis attends to the political and social performance of prisons and thus a theorization of the containment of bodies. This is both novel and important, especially in light of the current era of mass incarceration and what has become known as the refugee crisis drawing attention to issues of punishment and criminalization. This helps to point towards how punishment becomes extended beyond institutional regimes of control – and projected outwards into cultural productions. In addition to working through examples that are Anglo-American focused, the book attends to international trends in representations of women in prison. It includes close readings of contemporary performance (including by Clean Break and Geese Theatre Company), analysis of television series (including *Orange Is the New Black* and *Wentworth*) and works through indicative examples in order to make a compellingly feminist, radical argument about prison's culture as it relates to women. Further work on international representations such as the popular Spanish television series *Locked Up* (Bourdillon 2017) would be valuable.

As abolitionist Davis has said:

The prison is one of the most important features of our image environment. This has caused us to take the existence of prisons for granted. The prison has become a key ingredient of our common sense. It is there, all around us. We do not question whether it should exist. It has become so much a part of our lives that it requires a great feat of the imagination to envision life beyond the prison.

(Davis 2003: 18–19)

Taking up this challenge, the book considers how critical engagement with cultural productions could be one means of avoiding such taken-for-grantedness. It does so by interrogating cultural productions and performance practice to explore alternative tropes and characteristics by considering them in relation to a spectrum of 'victim–survivor–hero'. The aim is not to seek 'authenticity' in representing women in prison to the extent that the public can identify with them. Rather, the analysis serves to expose the ways performance strategies and tactics often perpetuate rigid typologies of women (both in prison and upon release). This points towards the need for radical revision of the potential of performance and popular culture to disrupt hegemonic spaces, to shatter mimetic assumptions and to expand epistemological approaches to the subject of women in prison. In particular, the research articulates the importance of artistic interventions and theatre representations to move beyond characterizing women as merely victims or survivors. In other words, what is needed is to conceive of women as both desiring and resisting in the context of an institution that does much to make both impossible.

Notes

1. I wish to note that the two characters' adoption of stereotypical 'feminine' characteristics is not unproblematic, nor is the insistence on compulsory heterosexuality (see Adrienne Rich 1996). It nevertheless serves a function in the portrayal of the institution's penetrating power over the virility of the political prisoners in the play by Fugard et al. (1974).
2. 'Applied theatre' is an umbrella term that incorporates a wide range of performance practices outside of the formal theatre, usually based upon the perceived benefits of participation, advocacy and pedagogy. What is contestable about the term is the difficulty of adequately representing the distinctions and divergences in practices as diverse as theatre for development, theatre in healthcare contexts, work with young people and those with disabilities (Prentki and Preston 2009). While it is not unproblematic, the term is used in the book, as it is nevertheless the recognized term in this sub-discipline of performance studies.
3. Also see Janina Möbius (2017) on applied theatre work with Mexican juvenile offenders; Woodland on Australian practice; Alex Sutherland (2013, 2015, 2017) and Miranda Young-Jahangeer (2013, 2015) on South African applied theatre practice. Pussy Riot's public prominence highlighted the state of the Russian criminal justice system for women (Schuler, 2013). From a criminological position, Winfree et al. (2002) discuss Mexican and New Zealand contexts; and *The Economist* (2017) and Ugelvik (2014) offer a Norwegian perspective. Sudbury (2002, 2005a, 2005b) draws attention to the global issues of the prison industrial complex and abolition movements.
4. This is not only because companies tend to conduct short-term work in specific prisons, as there are some notable exceptions to this, such as the UK-based Writers in Prison Network Ltd, which situated writers in residence for two- or three-year residencies. It is also because the Ministry of Justice does not provide (or cannot provide) access to onward records of prisoners upon release, or even in the case of moving prisons. This is not only related to

the complexities of re-housing and probation loads, but also draws attention to the ironies of basing rehabilitation on 'pathways' when such routes are not adequately mapped for monitoring and evaluation purposes.

5 Maggie Inchley's exploration of women who kill children circulates on the unspeakable crime. She works up a theorization of how representations perpetuate opportunities to hear the 'unhearable' (2013).

6 See Lynda Hart's description of 'monstrous' convicted murderers Myra Hindley and Aileen Wournos in *Fatal Women* (1994).

7 This diary entry refers to a six-month delay while I waited for full enhanced security clearance from the Ministry of Justice to gain access to the specific institution for Ph.D. research practice.

8 This is particularly relevant in the example of Raymond Williams (1977) who has been critiqued for his obliteration of 'female' subjectivity through the use of the obligatory masculine pronoun, demonstrating a patriarchal bias. I animate his 'structure of feeling' in relation to Elaine Aston's (2003) feminist re-appropriation.

9 I have worked with the 1977 translation by Sheridan.

Chapter One

Prison Cultures: Habitus and 'Tragic Containment'

Theorizing Prison Cultures

Prison is commonly understood as an impermeable location in which 'unruly women' (Faith 2011) are held while they are stripped of their civic function in society (Billone 2009) for (presumably) 'offending' that society. This view suggests that the looming structural force of the panopticon obliterates the women's narratives. Jeremy Bentham's notorious architectural innovation when designing the panopticon allowed a central watchtower (and a single officer) to maintain surveillance over a large number of prisoners by rendering them constantly visible. Foucault characterized each cell as a 'little theatre' (1977: 200; Kershaw 2003).[1] Panoptic surveillance makes little allowance for the accrual of many imperceptible shifts of attitude that collectively become 'change'. Rather, 'transformation' is a stated aim of incarceration. In light of this, it is worth considering Erving Goffman's characterization of 'front' as a performance, which, if successfully executed, can lead to freedom.[2] First, transformation itself is problematic when understood as operating according to hegemonic normative structures. In addition, from a feminist perspective in relation to criminal justice, it is necessary to question the utopian ideals of 'freedom' for women who have offended, considering that upon release, women may well continue to experience multiple vectors of oppression, marginalization and discrimination. This theoretical chapter explores different disciplines to cover the ground that leads to the emergence of novel ways of viewing women in prison, their daily performances and theatre and popular culture *about* these women.

The intent is to articulate a feminist structure of feeling (Aston 2006) in relation to Pierre Bourdieu's (1990) notion of 'habitus' in order to form a frame through which to consider performance and popular culture. This is done by developing an argument for a gendered habitus as an empirical and theoretical tool, and is further specified by exploring habitus in the context of women's prison. Bourdieu forms the backbone of this theoretical approach, and therefore a specified and micro-social analysis is preferred. For this reason, Goffman's notion of the performance of everyday life remains important. My agenda in constructing this theoretical approach is to re-appropriate the work of male theorists by extending their terms to fulfil the needs of a feminist project: habitus is (en)gendered. Every thread of my later arguments is pulled through the frames I propose here; and thus, since one of my fundamental critiques relates to how women in prison are ontologically and epistemologically framed by a phallocentric system of criminal justice, my theoretical frame needs to question inherent hegemonies. I argue that performance itself and the theoretical and methodological tools wrought in relation to researching such performance are a means of redefining subjectivities and re-animating material conditions that are taken for granted in other epistemological approaches that are prevalent in criminology.

In this, I am furthering Mary Bosworth's important 1999 study of resistance, in which she promotes an understanding of women in prison as highly individualized and by necessity holding complex and intersecting identities. For feminist criminologist Bosworth, 'women in prison are caught between competing expectations of values and behaviour that [are] centred upon an implicit valorization of passive feminine subjectivity' (1999: 120). These must be disputed and challenged as women begin to assert agency – which occurs, as Bosworth demonstrates in her ethnographic material, through diverse choices of manifesting identities and acting on responsibilities. However, rather than being de facto positive, Bosworth also shows that 'practices of resistance are often "read" in different ways by individual women concerned, by the inmate community and by staff' (1999: 152). What she is referring to here is the sense of diversity, divergent codes and practices that code power and resistance differently according to roles, subcultures, prison's enculturation and pre-existing cultures and beliefs. This is most obvious in an example of resistance that for one group may dictate lesbianism is a resistance of passive feminine behaviours on the one hand, while for other prisoners, this could be a threat (as theorized by Dirsuweit 1999). Similarly, political prisoners may garner support for a wider cause by relying on the harms and deprivations of prison life as a means of resisting. For authorities, this can serve to justify harsher treatment and separation from other prisoners.

The study of women's resistance, theatrical tactics and the use of performance as resistance (discussed by Bosworth and Carrabine 2001; Boyle and Bogad 2015; Butler et al. 2016) are highly important areas for further research. Jenny Hughes and Simon Parry's warm online collection (2015) about the influence and legacies of Ireland's notorious feminist activist Margaretta D'Arcy signals this remarkable woman as staging her personal story of activism, resistance, by seeking visibility and renown for the political struggles she wages. The octogenarian had participated in many feminist protests – most recently being incarcerated in 2014 for protesting against the military industrial complex (specifically, the US military being permitted to use the airport in Shannon). Hughes and Parry consider her interventions in relation to 'gestures of protest developed by contemporary activists [that] draw on the potent figures and forms associated with historical struggles' (2015: n.pag.). In D'Arcy, we see the figure of a charismatic woman activist who draws attention to state coercion on the bodies of its citizens – an argument taken up in performance by the performance group 'Speaking of IMELDA' who agitate for abortion law reform in Ireland. By promoting this lone figure here, it is evident that there are strata of resistance, and that the gestures proffered by D'Arcy when she resists the state are multiplied when she is incarcerated for the crime of resistance. Her imprisonment becomes a gesture that results in outrage, garnering visibility for her activist intent. It is obvious that prison is not the end point of her activist gesture, but a core locus of the lengths states go to when women do not comply. While public personae such as D'Arcy perhaps know best how to stage incarceration as state coercion, and draw visibility to wider oppressions and injustices, prisoners who are not incarcerated for their political activism but criminal activity are also subjects of the state's control.

I want to broadly engage with the subjects of desire and resistance, and consider how these interact in the context of prison to produce certain types, tropes, images and representations that the later chapters will analyse further. Some of the questions thrown up by theorizing prison cultures engage with disciplinary borders and boundaries, for example considering how to challenge/critique applied theatre models in criminal justice. Other concerns relate to the categorization of 'victim' and 'survivor', in particular to how we can further understand the complex negotiation of identifying as/rejecting the label of 'victim'. To this end, future research ought to consider to what extent and in what ways 'survivors' in prison are victimized, as well as engaging with how prison itself operates along the dialectic of victim–survivor. The four main criminological categories used for exploring how prisoners cope with incarceration are: regulation, deprivation, adaptation and resistance (Goffman 2007; Sykes 1958). I consider how performance cuts across these four categories of meaning to animate, trouble and distress fixed understandings of women's incarcerated bodies.

Within criminological narratives, offending and crime are seen as repeated cycles – borne out by data from the United Kingdom showing that the average re-offending rate for women leaving prison is 37 per cent.[3] At a policy level, most research engages with the problem of re-offending; in practice, prison programming reflects the pressure to reduce these cycles by following 'Seven pathways to reducing re-offending' (Rumgay 2012). The notion that a short-term custodial sentence would adequately engage women in programmes that effectively 'transform' their behaviours without simultaneously addressing their material conditions seems flawed, especially since incarceration itself is seen as a significantly destabilizing factor on housing, and whether children may have been taken into care. Even if women do not lose their homes, it is likely that family ties have been strangulated as a result of the long distances between women's homes and where they end up being incarcerated (Corston Report 2007; Kennedy 2005; Prison Reform Trust 2011a; Rickford 2011). These cycles and 'failures' carve a deep groove of repetition from custodial sentence to further crime. From this basis, I draw a model of what I call 'tragic containment' in which I describe the cyclical narratives of crime and punishment in juxtaposition with a model of tragedy developed through re-working the traditional cyclical notion of tragedy. My working through of tragedy is largely based on Terry Eagleton (2003) and Diana Taylor (2009) using more recent thinking on tragedy's relationship to trauma (Duggan 2012; Duggan and Wallis 2011). The purpose of this model is to open both cycles to alternatives that may begin to dismantle the sense of an inevitable repetition for women and in relation to representations of women's offending. After a brief overview and critique of the main tenets of feminist criminology, I move towards viewing women in prison as operating on a victim–survivor spectrum, which is problematized with the addition of a third vector of 'hero'. Several themes emerge in mapping the theory in relation to performance and representations, such as how women's everyday performances sit on a shifting spectrum from docility to resistance. Women who 'resist' in various ways are said to be 'acting up' or seeking attention, raising questions about the role of audience in relation to women's prisons. 'Acting up' is further explored in trauma theory, in particular in recent works relating performance to trauma (Duggan 2012; Duggan and Wallis 2011).

A key dramatic theme that is taken up in many films and television as well as plays is of prison as a space of excess time – a caesura in real life – offering a space for reflection. This space – presented as a poetic encounter with the self, memory and desire in plays such as Rebecca Lenkiewicz' *An Almost Unnameable Lust* (2011) – promotes a key problem when viewing prison on stage or screen. That is, how to attend to the real impacts and implications of incarceration for people in prison without romanticizing their experiences, diminishing the pains of incarceration, nor making simplistic causal links between inside and outside.

The book attends to performance representations that aim to share women's stories, and to this end I concentrate on the themes and ethical concerns of 'witnessing'. The underlying project of prison is ostensibly to effect a 'transformation' from 'offender' to civilian – itself a cycle that suggests a logic existing within social structures. Alongside Bourdieu and my feminist re-appropriation of his theory of habitus, I engage with trauma studies for some valuable concepts that add to the criminological frame. I pull apart the multiple theoretical threads that inform the study before weaving them together in the form of two models that are then used to engage with performance *in* and *of* prison. Throughout, I signal the theoretical approaches by offering examples that will later be taken up as part of the critical analysis project, and, in each section, the modalities of performance are prioritized.

In Foucault's development of the theory of panopticism, punishment of prisoners produces the effect of a 'docile body'. For Foucault, docility equates to a lack of agency. In this chapter, I position resistance and a particularly gendered habitus against such a notion. This is done by showing that the agency displayed may result from and be inscribed by traumatic past experiences (such as abuse/violence/incest) but nevertheless disrupt the hegemonic discourse through expressions of resistance (hunger strike, dirty protest, destruction of property, insurrection). As a theoretical framework, it generates an understanding of how a gendered habitus becomes a means of women asserting agency in the terms they define for themselves: desire and resistance. The two driving considerations are, first, that popular culture, theatre and performance can provide an aesthetic frame through which to consider prisons and the performativity of punishment; second, that engendering habitus becomes a means of framing women's performances of transgression and resistance of domestication or docility.

Prison Terms: Avoiding 'Offence'

I have elected to use the term 'prisoners' in order to refer to the collective group of people who reside, work and perform everyday tasks in prisons because they have been incarcerated there as a result of committing crimes.[4] This is a somewhat unusual choice, since most recent literature from the United Kingdom refers to 'offenders' (Cabinet Office Social Exclusion Task Force 2009; Hedderman et al. 2008), whilst the US terminology is most often 'inmates' (Alexander 2012b; Laughlin 2017; Levi and Waldman 2011). Whilst I can recognize the need for institutional uniformity in nomenclature, and as such it is sensible for all government and third-sector publications and directives to use the same term, it is troubling that cultural criminology and cultural organizations have adopted the terminology without problematizing it sufficiently.[5] This choice of terminology positions this approach (or, indeed, other arts practices) within a specific methodological frame, since the research subjects are named according to their community of place, rather than attempting to define people in prison as 'offenders' or those who have left prison as 'ex-offenders'.

On the one hand, it is important to acknowledge that prison's purpose, activities and ethos in the United Kingdom is (nominally, anyway) concerned with 'rehabilitation' of those who have committed crimes.[6] On the other, the title 'offender' implies that the subject is *still offensive*, that is, still actively participating in the activities that are deemed offensive to society, which seems to run counter to the conception of prison as a rehabilitative site in which behaviours and attitudes can be 'corrected'. Goffman's view of 'rehabilitation' is that it claims to reset 'the inmate's self-regulatory mechanisms so that after he [sic] leaves he [sic] will maintain the standards of the establishment of his [sic] own accord' (2007: 71). However, he maintains that the changes made by incarceration are often not those intended by the institution. It is possible that departing from the term in this research does not adequately challenge the latent moralizing implicit in the term, since its use is not restricted by those operating within the institutional field. Nevertheless, this choice points towards the critical overlap of institutional and so-called interventionist discourses. I also see this choice of terminology as a performance of resistance on my behalf against characterizing all prisoners as 'offensive'.

Performativity of Punishment: Goffman's Frames and Moving Beyond the Total Institution

Goffman's 'frames' and Bourdieu's habitus may be re-appropriated and applied to the analysis of performances in prison. Goffman (2007) contributed to the performative turn in sociology by investigating the ways in which everyday life can be read as social performances.[7] In addition, Goffman's investigation into the social functioning of asylum inmates and staff became a means of defining a 'total institution', which is defined as a place of residence and work in which individuals in the same situation who are removed from the wider society for a period of time and who 'lead an enclosed, formally administered round of life' (Helmreich 2007: xxi). Other total institutions are prisons, boarding schools, residential homes and orphanages. Characteristics of these sites are that everything occurs within one place under one authority; that individualism is erased as all are treated alike; time and activities are governed by strict rules and sanctions; and that these are enforced in order to maintain the order of the institution.[8]

In his detailed analysis of such institutional spaces, Goffman suggests that surveillance is a critical operation, so that uniform compliance enhances the visibility of any infraction of rules and regulations. During their time within the institution, inmates undergo a process of 'disculturation' (Goffman 2007: 13), in which everyday habits are 'unlearned' in order to better acclimatize to the new structures (including timetables, rules and regulations, and restricted personal agency). This process can serve, in the long term, to render inmates incapable of managing certain features of daily life if and when they are released (2007: 13). The shock of release from confinement to 'freedom' is richly mined in popular culture (*Buffalo 66*, Vincent Gallo, 1998; *Sherrybaby*, Laury Collyer, 2006). This is also the main thematic thrust of Chloë Moss's play for Clean Break, *This Wide Night* (2008), which characterizes Lorraine as a naïve and confused woman unable to navigate the complexities of finding the office to validate her housing plan, or successfully engage with strangers in the pub. Her time in prison has 'institutionalized' her, and her re-integration into society is painful and difficult. The chasm between incarceration and freedom is wide, traversed with difficulty; often it is so difficult that ex-prisoners would voluntarily return to the institution rather than continue to struggle with daily life that includes accessing accommodation, organizing benefits, facing stigmatization and the explicit difficulty in finding work as an ex-prisoner (Gelsthorpe 2010; Goffman 1963; Opsal 2011). These challenges are wonderfully evoked in the performed monologues in Clean Break's *Joanne* (Bruce et al. 2015). Goffman's work on stigma may help explain how ex-prisoners are tinged with negative perceptions, with a tendency to engage a partial view 'from a whole and usual person to a tainted, discounted one' (1963: 2–3).

For Goffman, one of the main accomplishments of total institutions is 'staging a difference between two constructed categories of persons – a difference in social quality and moral character, a difference in perceptions of self and other' (2007: 111).

His words point towards a troubling tendency – despite centuries of prison reform initiatives – of a strong social imagery of the transformative power of institutions. Such an agenda seems to underlie many of the work-based, educational and therapeutic interventions in custodial settings, and marks many prison arts activities with cloying grammars of hope and change. In other words, instead of challenging the institutional norms and values, 'transformation' as a discourse positions the institution and its activities as benevolent, charitable and in pursuit of 'the public good'. Rather than being radical or resistant, this discourse actively supports and reinforces the oppressive structures of the prison.[9] This is particularly problematic in connection to arts activities that otherwise lay claim to a radical agenda, discussed later in relation to two UK theatre companies, Clean Break and Geese Theatre.

I am aware that there are shifts away from Goffman's thinking in criminology, yet it is productive to use Goffman's terminology, since he conceives of everyday habits as 'performative'. In particular, he writes of the 'fronts'[10] employed by inmates:

> [M]anaging the guise in which [he] appears before others […] for this he [sic] needs cosmetic and clothing supplies, tools for applying, arranging, and repairing them, […] In short, the individual will need an 'identity kit' for the management of his [sic] personal front.
>
> (1997: 20)

Here, Goffman is referring to material objects that can help prisoners feel secure, but the psychological armoury developed as coping strategies are also considered 'fronts'. For Goffman, fronts can be intentional or unwitting, and involve 'setting' through the use of spatial and material objects 'appropriate to the performance', such as a 'uniform' or 'props' (Goffman 1997: 97–101).

Applied theatre scholar Jenny Hughes, for example, recounts the ways 'fronts' and veneers of toughness impacted on her long-term drama project with women in HMP Styal. Incarcerated women have been considered a 'more resistant, volatile and less predictable group' than men (1998: 49). She describes the vulnerabilities of participants, and admits that drama can intensify the 'dangers of prison' by destabilizing or calling into question the 'general deadening routine and intrusiveness of prison life' (1998: 49). In other words, if the drama serves to dislodge the 'fronts', it can expose vulnerabilities and insecurities. In practice, this has meant that institutions are suspicious of any activity that might arouse or stimulate psychologically painful memories. It is clear that there are many contextual considerations for prisoners, including anxieties about their cases, uncertainties about prison life and their futures, and there can also be issues relating to drug dependency, and for women, in particular, potential worries about children and their ability to maintain family ties (Hughes 1998; Rickford 2011). I engage with some of these tensions in later chapters, particularly in connection with the risks of performance, failure and participation in group activities.

Goffman insists that the daily strategies of the inmates are related to the staff and the wider institution; and thus, his analytic framework sets the ground for detailed consideration of how each impacts on the other. I endeavour to consider prisoner 'performances' within the wider setting – not just the drama that occurs within theatre-based workshops, but the narratives of hopes and desires, fears and anxieties that permeate the atmosphere between classroom, gym and wings; or performances of everyday life within the context of the institution. These routines and ruptures in routine relate closely to Bourdieu's conception of field and habitus (1990). In order to develop a more concrete frame for analysing the prison and its inhabitants, I turn to Bourdieu in order to explicate the theoretical thrust of my approach to prison cultures.

Setting out to review how the micro-sociological theory of habitus can be re-appropriated through both feminist concerns and through analysis of performance is done in order to engage with how gender in performance is both informed by, and resistant to, the institutional field. I model a theoretical approach to performance, through which further (everyday) performances in prison might be productively explored. The chapter posits that both formal theatre and everyday performances in prison provide a means of foregrounding the slippage between articulations of 'equality' or 'gender neutral punishment' (Opsal 2011) and practices that remain fixed in discursive binaries of how women in prison are seen as good/bad; chaste/whore; compliant/deviant. It is necessary to revisit social theories such as Bourdieu's habitus in order to examine how gender is performed. In doing so, I explore how the 'criminal field' and the 'institutional field' are interrelated; and also, from the analytical side, how the feminist field interrupts the phallocentric one. Furthermore, I propose that habitus needs to be re-articulated in the wake of these 'fields' that appear to be in conflict.

(En)gendering Habitus: Introducing Feminist Criminology[11]

The intersection of fields I mention here – institutional, criminal and discursive fields that are feminist and phallocentric – suggests that I adopt a somewhat complex theoretical approach. On the contrary, although there are several weighty concepts discussed here, I consider habitus to be a valuable approach for the subjects in the book, considering what is to be investigated is located in and between institutions and representations produced in popular culture. While initially, this theorization seems to be located on the level of the everyday, it is productive for the analysis of fictional examples too.

As I outline the value of this theory for *Prison Cultures*, I am extending work I explored initially in relation to gender, sexuality and prison (Walsh 2014). In an article on (en)gendering habitus, I demonstrated how the roots of Bourdieu's conception of 'habitus' are seen in ancient philosophy, in the Aristotelian notion of *hexis*, which concerned a consciously acquired yet entrenched 'state of moral character that orients our feelings and desires in a situation, and thence our actions' (Wacquant 2004: 315). For Bourdieu, habitus is a social aptitude arising out of specific situations and milieus, and is thus variable, transferable and not static. It is a set of practices and behaviours that produce patterns that replicate the social structures in which they are more widely located, at the same time differentiating between individual and societal principles. In '(En)gendering habitus: Women, prison, resistance' (Walsh 2014), I demonstrate that the concept is useful for exploring the multiple vectors operating within a prison. Even while we suppose prisons are immutable (McAvinchey 2011a), unique and bounded places, the lives of their inhabitants are also contextualized by race, class, gender and economics, as well as, increasingly, mobilities and migrations. Habitus becomes productive precisely because it makes allowance for traces, dispositions and practices from 'before' prison to be understood within the new 'field'. By extension, this posits that the routines, embodied behaviours and attitudes of prison may well remain as traces and tropes upon release. As a means of explaining specificities on a micro-level, habitus is located within a trajectory of past events as well as structuring present representations and actions. Yet, it is not meant to be a fixed description archiving a single social structure, but rather to reflect the multiple dynamic intersections of the many spheres of influence (personal, economic, political, etc.) that constitute a life. As a theory, then, it pays heed to performances, both tacit and implicit, by seeking to locate them within a wider social context. It also allows us to conceive of prison cultures not as fixed and particular to place, but as constituted by and through the informing habitus of its inhabitants (prisoners and workers), as well as its regime and structuring principles.

In her feminist discussion on agency and resistance, Lois McNay points out that for Bourdieu, habitus incorporates the social into the corporeal, making a distinction between his system of durable, transposable dispositions, and Foucault's sense of 'discipline', which she reads as deterministic (McNay 1999). On the contrary, for McNay, Bourdieu's habitus is 'a generative' structure because there is a relationship between individual habitus and the social circumstances or 'field' (1999: 100). Bourdieu says that

> an institution can only be efficacious if it is objectified in bodies in the form of durable dispositions that recognize and comply with the specific demands of a given institutional area of activity; the *habitus* is what enables the institution to attain full realization.
> (1990: 57, original emphasis)

Applying this concept to the prison, the institution is only read as efficacious if it produces docile bodies that are in service of whatever contemporary socio-economic political field makes necessary. In the wider discourse of criminal justice, 'efficacy' is considered to be the attainment of reduced re-offending (which is where much policy and research attention focuses) and successful re-integration (which is closely related but less of a priority, in terms of programming and budgeting). Also relevant in terms of efficacy is security of the public and safe custody of prisoner. This is where Bourdieu's thinking relates to Foucault's formulation of biopolitics, and where the intersection with feminist critique becomes valuable. For Foucault, the inevitability of biopolitical mechanisms signals the need for complex resistance tactics. A feminist view reiterates the need to undermine the phallocentric assumptions and discourses that circumscribe the institutions. In other words, glossing Judith Butler's critique, what is needed is a theory of prison culture that resists the prevailing objectivity of the field (McLeod 2005). Importantly, in this conception of habitus, an individual may have a predisposition to act in specific ways but there is potential for innovation and creative action. This provides a productive measure for the specific site of prisons that contain bodies for a certain present, as punishment for past behaviours, with the intention to rehabilitate (or transform) prisoners' behaviours for their future return to society. In other words, if transformation is the rhetoric behind rehabilitation, it becomes valuable to see habitus as a model of exploring and understanding what behaviours are carried into and through prisons; which 'performances' survive the corrections regime; and furthermore how habitus is engendered by the processes of incarceration. Running alongside such questions, then, is the consideration of how performance gives an insight into these temporal processes and dispositions.

Bourdieu's conception of habitus as the 'intertwinement of corporeal being and agency [...] transcends the opposition between freedom and constraint characteristic, for example, of liberal conceptions of the subject' (McNay 1999: 104). The related notions of 'habitus' and 'field' offer a way of ensuring that multiple subjectivities are considered, and particularly reviewed in relation to gender. Indeed, exploring the performative practices of prisoners serves to dismantle the traditional views of outside as synonymous with freedom and inside as synonymous with constraint, for example. Such refusal to play to these distinctions is, in several of the plays and cultural productions I discuss, specifically circumscribed by the characters' gender. Yet, as theatre scholar Maria Shevtsova points out: 'habitus survives contingencies and, by sheer dint of its survival, becomes institutionalized' (2002: 58). Since immanence is a productive concept for performance studies, implying an embodied readiness, rehearsal and preparedness for performance, an engendered habitus becomes a useful means of examining performances and performativity in (and of) prison.

Toril Moi offers her view that gender as a social construction is inscribed by differing contexts (1991); and in the context of women's prisons, prisoners' habitus is (en)gendered by the roles, rituals and rules of the institution. Further, this shifting spectrum of personal habitus and institutional habitus becomes foregrounded when analysing how women are characterized primarily in relation to gender norms. Whilst I am not trying to claim that all women in prisons are victims and therefore blameless (clearly, arguments about how crime and justice are performed are wide-ranging), analysing performance provides ways of exploring how women's habitus is informed and delimited by prison as an extension of patriarchal hegemonic structures of society in general. This argument is also taken up in Mary Bosworth's feminist assessment of resistance (1999), in which victimization is critically interrogated.

Feminist criminology can be put in conversation with a feminist re-appropriation of Bourdieu's habitus (1977, 1990). Bourdieu has been critiqued for setting gender aside in his conception of habitus, but feminist theorist Moi finds that 'appropriating' Bourdieu's microsociology animates the potential for undoing or overcoming 'the traditional individual/social or private/public divide' (1991: 1020; see also Lovell 2000 and McLeod 2005). For Moi, the two interrelated concepts 'field' and 'habitus' each generate power games. Field is seen as a competitive space that functions according to its own specific logic, and habitus is a 'system of dispositions adjusted to the game of the field' (Moi 1991: 1021). Furthermore, conceiving habitus in relation to critical feminist theory, Lovell states that what Bourdieu 'offers that is most powerful is a way of understanding both the arbitrary, and therefore contestable, nature of the social, and its compelling presence and effectiveness' (2000: 15). Moi's analysis explores how these two concepts of habitus and field rely on often unspoken rules or norms, and thus a feminist appropriation must unpack the ways in which phallocentric discourses continue to inscribe them. In order to make a full account of how habitus should be re-imagined in relation to gender, Moi shows that Bourdieu's focus on embodiment offers a way to insist that embodied practices, gestures, movements and ways of looking at the world form important challenges for research (1991: 1030–31).

With a shift to consider the sociology of theatre, Shevtsova highlights a further concern about the slipperiness of habitus, since one must account for individual and 'group' dispositions as well as

> to the dispositions incarnated in or interiorized by the practice of a field in its distinction from another field – a distinction that is only possible because it is relational, that is, always defined in respect of something else that it is not.
>
> (2002: 57)

Applying these concepts to performances of punishment, then, is to explore the ways in which the spaces and dispositions of the institution are perpetuated by both explicit and tacit forms of power that legitimate them. I suggest that docile prisoners comply with the disciplinary field because they have been habituated to do so: they perpetuate the institutions' norms, values and rules by enacting the relations of prisoner/officer, by engaging in programmes and by following its timetables. Such 'habituation' is clearly not voluntary, but inflicted, or enacted, through punishment, deprivation and other violences. I suggest that such (symbolic and actual) violence is not gender neutral, but on the contrary serves to highlight specific issues and vulnerabilities ascribed to gender. Susan Sered and Maureen Norton-Hawk's discussion of overdetermination considers how gender forms a network of performative norms that inflect how women in prison are regarded.

> Women who, for a variety of reasons, do not or cannot comply with symbols of the good Woman run the risk of having symbols of bad Woman forcibly imprinted onto their bodies: they may be beaten, raped, burned, sterilised, denied their own children.
>
> (Sered and Norton-Hawk 2011: 323)

Compliance also correlates with increased privileges, so women may submit to a lesser form of punishment to be granted a privilege (such as a family visit).[12] Departing from the compelling work of Sered and Norton-Hawk (2011) also requires understanding resistance as inherently gendered.

One of the core aims of the book is the modelling of theory re-appropriated for feminist concerns. Having argued how habitus is re-appropriated for a productive approach to performance, I turn to a critical feminist perspective. Feminist cultural critic de Lauretis is instructive here, saying that female 'is what is not susceptible to transformation, to life or death; she (it) is an element of plot-space, a topos, a resistance, matrix, and matter' (de Lauretis 1989b: 251). According to de Lauretis, the insistent emphasis of a feminist approach to criticism is that gender must be accounted for, not only as a biological difference, or a 'problem' of signification, nor even as a cultural construction of masculine desire, but 'as a semiotic difference' (1989b: 255).[13] In the case of arts arising from and with women in prison, then, it is important to ensure that analysis does not merely extend to describing 'difference' arising from gender (such as how women's behaviours are different to men's, or how women's institutions differ) but to construct gender-specific models that incorporate and problematize the ways in which women perceive and perform their gender within the site. This provides an ontological position from which to consider how gender becomes a means of being-in-the-world, and then considers gender from an epistemological point of view – or how gender shapes and determines the ways in which women (and the researcher) construct prison-specific taxonomies of knowing. The kinds of issues these suggest are, for example, the codes and habitus of the institution and the adaptations women make whilst in prison; or, to re-position that statement in relation to performance studies, the ways women's pre-existing habitus in relation to institution are informed and contained by the field as much as improvisations within the carceral landscape. The following chapters analyse how plays, artistic productions and popular culture account for how gendered epistemologies are produced in the field of prison.

Butler's work on 'gender trouble' explains that gender should be overthrown or rendered 'fatally ambiguous precisely because it is always a sign of subordination for women' (1999: xiv). Her influential approach demonstrates (alongside Foucault), the ways in which juridical powers serve to produce the subjects they require, so feminism has ascribed woman as 'subject' by virtue of applying the linguistic and political categorization it seeks to dismantle. In other words, there is an inevitable cycle of signification (through language and policy) that impacts practices (Butler 1999: 3). For Butler (see Derrida), this signals the political need to interrogate the 'subject' even while acknowledging that the 'subject' is constituted by systems that are being called into question. Whether it is possible to 'perform' outside of the discursive limits of gender, and if 'woman as subject' is foreclosed by law are the kinds of questions addressed by interdisciplinary research. Within the context of prison, we might question how gender ambiguities are 'read', especially with regards to the claim feminist criminology lays at the feet of the statue of Justice – that she is blind to 'difference' but nevertheless founded upon and entirely committed to upholding phallocentric ideals about what a just and fair society is. Indeed, most feminist criminologists maintain that, in practice, gender-neutrality is not helpful in punishing or rehabilitating women. On the contrary, gender-aware penology is needed (Corston 2011; Gelsthorpe 2010).

If a feminist model of prison cultures is to be functional, then it should rupture the gender assumptions in its own structuration – particularly in relation to participatory arts (or applied theatre) practices in the criminal justice system that I discuss later. We can see the difficulties feminist critics have identified by returning to de Lauretis' claim that 'woman' serves a specific function in mythic (and all narrative) structures (1989a). Her view then serves as a challenge in this research to imagine beyond 'woman' in prison as more than *topos*, or boundary, but as protagonists with agency. Yet, de Lauretis would undoubtedly return readers and audiences to the question of how agency is manifest in the wider context, and as Nina Billone (2009) points out in relation to The Medea Project, incarcerated women do not simply 'gain' agency from participating in performance (or education) programmes.[14]

The value of such a conception is that it serves to locate the work as critically reflexive of the context of prison as a performance of punishment and arts activities – including exhibitions, installations, performances and research outputs as implicated within those narratives. The prevailing discourses in arts in criminal justice are generally lacking sufficient criticality of the complexities of power imbrications, and thus discussions of prison cultures can seem oddly apolitical. *Prison Cultures* attends to this by prioritizing a politically inflected approach to cultural criticism.

Feminist criminology asserts that criminal justice institutions discriminate unfairly against women at the level of criminalization (arrests), in the process of trial, during sentencing and whilst in prison (Kennedy 2005). The primary argument is that women's dispositions and material situations (both in the commission of 'crimes' and during incarceration) need to be understood and responded to in gender-appropriate ways. Frances Heidensohn explores the sociology of imprisonment and its relation to gender. Her argument poses that female criminality is not in itself distinctive. She highlights the ways in which public and private behaviours are limited and controlled in gender-related ways (1996: xi). Furthermore, she asserts that women are doubly punished, not only for wrongdoings, but also for 'not keeping to their proper places' (1996: 83). Her critique of criminal justice lies in its definition of deviant or transgressive women in sex-stereotyped ways. She suggests that incarcerated women are often seen as 'not-women' or as 'masculine, unfeminine women' (1996: 96). She goes on to demonstrate that the ways in which dualisms of good/bad, chaste/unchaste, virgin/whore are reiterated in popular media, as when public portrayals of 'bad' women are made, there is always reference to the 'possibility of good' (1996: 99). For Heidensohn, such stereotyping is inevitably tied to the enormous amount of advice, moralizing and guidance offered to women 'on how to be good women – that is, good wives and mothers' (1996: 103). Conformity, then, does not just mean complying with the rule of law, but obeying the multiplicity of patriarchal structures of society (Carlen 1983, 2002).

This insistence on gender role normativity is a startling feature of contemporary punishment, but is geared towards supporting the view that women are inferior in society. Carol Smart asserts that the prevailing normative discourse sees 'femininity [a]s the antithesis of criminality' (1977: 182). Foundational to her view is that women commit less crime, 'since their performances of identity are over-controlled, and that when they do, they commit them within man-made frameworks of controls' (1977: 199). Baroness Joan Corston's reports have persistent calls for 'gendered' institutions in the United Kingdom. This was the primary finding in home office reports commissioned to concentrate on women's experiences of criminal justice (Corston 2007, 2011). Despite this, Gelsthorpe shows that 'the treatment of women in the criminal justice system in general, and in prisons in particular, has continued to reflect a curious mixture of "hard" and "soft" measures – punishment and "re-education" or moral tutelage' (2010: 380).

Performance and popular culture can play a role in the explication of such 'tutelage' by exposing how hegemonic rules of the field can be resisted and re-imagined. The emphasis of this study as a whole reflects the need to engage with both micro-level and wider contextual controls. By choosing to frame the theoretical concerns through feminist criminology, I point towards the functions of theory to specify the field of study.

To be a woman in prison is to be excessive, to have excess affect, with the performative result that prisoners are constantly seeking connection, alliances, comforts – many criminological analyses call these 'kinship ties', and are used synonymously with lesbianism. In my own practice, many of the workshops I conducted in prisons with women required managing dynamics of relationships that would spill across the room, result in people sitting in each other's laps, and sometimes to want to stage desire and overt sexuality (seemingly) in order to provoke responses from the assembled audience of officers and outsiders. As I encountered this difference in being with one another in the two contexts of male and female prisons, I realized that it was not a matter of identification, or community, that I was encountering in these workshops, but a concentrated form of what prison *does*. Prison produces particular subjectivities that shift performances of sexuality into understandings of prison lesbians, rather than lesbians who are in prison.

These experiences from when I was navigating my own multiple identities as a queer, foreign artist working in prisons in the United Kingdom alerted me to the intricacies of desire and the centrality of the body in contexts of containment. And these differences were gendered. My own simultaneous struggles to understand what is so taken for granted as a freedom of self-expression in the outside world became complicated further by how prison structures, spaces, regimes and rhythms are enacted for those inside. What I hope to do in my work is to avoid the tendency to explain lesbian sex and desire as *pseudo-families* as often characterized in criminology (Dirsuweit 1999; Giallombardo 1966; Hensley et al. 2002; Owen 1998; Ward and Kassebaum 2007), not least because it constitutes lesbian attachments as contingent, or performative rather than real. For example, for some studies, lesbian pseudo-families are read as those women who form alliances with a compatible partner as a marriage unit. The inmates maintained that 'to engage in homosexuality as duplication of the outside world, makes times go by faster and (furthermore) that no one can do time alone' (Giallombardo 1966: 136).

I do not want to position desire here as merely related to sex and sexuality. Instead, I hope to further how desire is a relational affect that operates through the imagination. Throughout, what I am explicating is how this imagining and yearning for something other than material confinement can in itself be a form of resistance.

Towards a Model of 'Victim–Survivor–Hero'

Prison populations tell important stories about who is criminalized and why. Recent UK newspaper articles have claimed that conditions in women's prisons are not fit for purpose, whilst highlighting the high rates of poor mental health in women's backgrounds.[15] Yet, reform campaigns and feminist criminology seem to reiterate that the 'problem' of women in prison is their inevitable 'victimization', marginalization and exclusion from alternative pathways in society. The result is that both discourses maintain an outraged tone while being unable to find other ways of speaking about (and for) women in prison. In order, then, to propose a productive means of theorizing beyond moralizing, I attempt to prioritize a sense of agency in generating the spectrum beyond victim–survivor as is common in much criminological literature. The model I discuss is underpinned by the foreknowledge that women in prison have been tried and found guilty of crimes – a consideration that emerges as a theme or trope throughout this book, but which is not intended to be the focus of investigation. The question for audience members and, more directly, for cultural producers creating work about prisons, is how to escape moralizing, and indeed, whether that is necessary, or possible, in the forms and genres available.

In related work that explicitly attends to trauma and survival, I discuss this model and how I developed it in fieldwork with women in prison (Walsh 2018a). In that work, I aimed to engage with performativity and how different categories of behaviour and identification can be used to imagine shifts to habitus, or the hopefulness of transformation that is central to narratives in and of prison. For women, the conscious adoption of structures and identifications may appear fixed, and perhaps be controversial. The three categories of the victim, the survivor and the hero I consider are animated in relation to one another as lenses through which performance and performativity are analysed. I propose they work as temporary lenses rather than fixed labels to identify women whose narratives are not singular, but often complex and chaotic. In the context of ethnographic fieldwork in prison (Walsh 2018a), it is clear that these are not categories that are foreclosed or fixed, but rather they interrelate. Nonetheless, this triad of identifiers is productive in analysis of cultural production too. Rather than strictly operating as categories for others to identify women, this model could apply to women's own understandings of their potential to transform or re-focus attention from repetitious narratives of victimization that appear to be inevitable and are tied to offending behaviour. The model

> animates how self-concept within the institution does not need to cement women's behaviors or predicate their future deeds. As such, the model offers a way of troubling categories in order to consider the issue of prison's performative potential – how women might attempt to rehearse conventions and norms of behavior for the future.
>
> (Walsh 2018a: 223)

As several examples of testimonial and life writing with women in prison proffer (Graney 2006; Lamb 2007; Levi and Waldman 2011), there is the need for women to rehearse alternatives, and to be able to perceive themselves as having agency beyond the limited offering of prison life. However, as I move towards utilizing the model to analyse cultural productions, I need to inflect a complex and iterative relationship between the positions of the model 'victim–survivor–hero' rather than to replicate moralistic assumptions that are often, as feminist criminologists demonstrate, about what Lynne Haney calls 'successful' performance of gender roles (2010: 30–35). At this stage, then, a more explicit link back to performance and the aesthetic is in order.

Theatre scholar Elaine Aston has written about a Clean Break production, *Yard Gals*, in which she investigates how the writer Rebecca Prichard constructs girl gang identities as nihilistically seeking to create 'girl power' (2003: 72). Aston's consideration of feminist structures of feeling (2003) is a useful way to consider how the victim–survivor–hero tropes are negotiated aesthetically in plays such as Rebecca Lenkiewicz' *An Almost Unnameable Lust* (2011) and *Her Naked Skin* (2008) (Walsh 2014), Lucy Kirkwood's *it felt empty when the heart went at first but it's alright now* (2009) (Walsh 2016) and Chloë Moss's *This Wide Night* (2009) (Walsh 2018a). Victim–survivor–hero provides an important and original contribution to thinking through performances because it is a means of reflecting on how simultaneous positions can be used to reflect on the multiple subjectivities of women in prison, in contrast to many theatrical representations of women in one of the three lenses. Shifting identification can occur through discovery of a new set of behaviours (as proposed by Geese Theatre, for example).

Yet, women in prison may make conscious choices to deploy one or more 'categories' of identification for specific purposes. For example, if the mode of 'survivor' is valorized within the current system, women may choose to model behaviours that highlight or present their survival in order to achieve something. They may, for example, be more likely to access interventions such as mandatory courses relating to drug and alcohol abuse if they adhere to the perceived 'correct' attitude to addiction, rather than maintain an attitude of victimization or blaming others. While here I am referring to women's real-life adoption of role, it is worth considering how dramaturgical means of reflecting shifting identifications is framed. Later, I explore the potential for playwrights to experiment with chronology, multiple sites and the relationship between women's feelings and experiences in prison alongside the structural socio-economic contexts that give rise to public opinion (Walsh 2016, 2018a, 2019).

The feminist criminology frame offers a means for understanding how women in prison are described in terms of their victimhood, closely intertwined with women as survivors of traumatic pasts (often with lives characterized by deep poverty, lack of education, alongside structural inequalities in relation to employment, drug addiction, sexual abuse, domestic abuse and violence) (Prison Reform Trust 2011b). Chesney-Lind (1997) explores the ways in which victimization of women 'offenders' is often related directly to their gender, for example through sexual abuse, incest and rape. In addition, such 'victims' often conform to societal gender role expectations relating to aspirations and relationships (prioritizing motherhood, domesticity and care over alternatives), with the result that 'the victimization related to their gender continues into their adult relationships with both pimps and customers' (1997: 142). The gendered view of punishment and the concomitant roles legitimated by the criminal justice system has resulted in a limited spectrum of behaviours for women who have 'offended'. This can be seen in a complex dynamic triad of victim–survivor–hero, whereby women may be seen in one frame predominantly, but a change of lens or discourse may move her towards another of these labels.

The literature about why women commit crime tends to highlight the wider conception of women as oppressed, while largely avoiding the complex task of viewing multiple contingencies of understanding human agency as including both victimizing narratives of marginality and exclusion as well as the perceptions of female criminals as active perpetrators of crimes (in other words agents of transgressive meaning). Such ellipsis is telling because it discursively insists on placing women's agency as inherently 'good', and the 'system' as patriarchal oppression, or 'bad'. Lynda Hart reflects on the preoccupation with the '(im)morality of women and the ever-present paranoia that women possess an inferior sense of justice'. She goes on to state that psychoanalysis 'obsessively reproduces "women" as implicitly dangerous' (1994: 25). This relates to the discursive characterization of all women as dangerous, modelled by formative scholar Cesare Lombroso (Lombroso and Ferrero 1895). These factors are reflected in the ways in which the model victim–survivor–hero is analysed in relation to performance.

I have demonstrated that criminology in the first instance, and feminist criminology in retaliation, both maintain and confirm 'woman' as a problematic signifier, to be grounded by means of further identification, namely by assessing and articulating how 'good' or 'bad' she is vis-à-vis prevailing laws. Rather, there is the need to determine a third possibility whereby binaries are re-positioned as fluctuating. Performative models provide an alternative to thinking in terms merely of subject vs oppressor, if developed in such a way as to disrupt victimizing narratives without denying their impacts. In other words, instead of functioning in a simple two-dimensional operation (subject/object or survivor/victim), the characterization of a woman (her habitus, her stories) shifts between nodes of potentiality that are specific in time and space. This supports the value of cultural analysis in order to conceive of how culture (performance, TV and mainstream representations) might reproduce or challenge such signification. Baz Kershaw considers prisons to be inherently theatrical because they 'stage the absolute separation that society seeks to impose between good and evil – or […] between acceptable and unacceptable forms of subjectivity' (1999: 131). Performances, in turn, can work towards unpicking the threads of what 'unacceptable subjectivity' might be, by, for example, engaging the audience in a new relationship in which affective witnessing predicates the literal meanings of the text. Hans-Thies Lehmann's notion of postdramatic theatre posits that theatre's promise of being together invokes a sense of community (2006). In relation to the concerns of women in prison, performance thus opens up spaces for dialogue, creativity and belonging that transcend the fixed categories of the institution. Thus, thinking alongside scholars of performance such as Dolan (1993a, 2007, 2011) as well as Duggan and Muñoz (2009), it is productive to consider how theatre and cultural productions relate to wider politicized movements. In my project, that is how performance on stage and screen can serve to challenge the intersecting structures that serve to criminalize women. Cultural criticism considers how work can 'be articulated in terms of politics: representation, ideology, hegemony, resistance' (Reinelt and Roach 2007: 5). Such an approach makes it possible to consider how representations and experiences are co-produced.

Locating Habitus in a Prison Context: The Cycles of 'Tragic Containment'

Institutional research must make account of its informing discourses as a means of unpacking the dynamics of power implicit within it. My approach is grounded in a profound sense of the difficulties of incarcerating women in this milieu, many of whom have repeatedly been characterized as not 'belonging' in prisons. In recent years, the United Kingdom has been shown to have incarcerated a record number of women with multiple and complex needs, especially mental health needs (McAndrew and Warne 2005; Rickford 2011). This awareness fuels my own desire to explore performance practices that challenge and subvert the insidious characterization of women as 'unacceptable' or 'unruly' (Faith 2011). In this context, then, power is evident in the institution itself (its informing discourses, and the socio-economic context); in the relations between staff and prisoners; the prisoners' activities in the institution (both sanctioned and unsanctioned); and in their progression out of the institution. It is thus necessary to examine not only the formal or legitimate narratives, but to explore how resistance, rule-breaking and transgression operate as performative ruptures of the prison habitus. The framework of analysis is then both institutional habitus and personal habitus. In this regard, I do not perceive ruptures to be positive and docility necessarily negative – for example, self-harm may be a woman's means of rupturing the institutional regime, but has obvious negative effects for her and others.

Below, I outline a simplistic model of a cycle of crime and punishment by expressing the 'stages' (though not necessarily discrete and sequential) through performative terminologies, specifically utilizing the terms of tragedy, as outlined by Eagleton (2003). I use this as a starting point – an extended metaphor – rather than a predetermined lens, because tragic structures more or less fix and thus limit the subjective potential for demolishing its cycles. Ideally, from an activist/abolitionist perspective, such as the charity Women in Prison, the frame needs to be dismantled at policy level and through the various practices in order for the notion of 'inevitable' consequences to be dispersed. Yet, since this research is placed in a critical feminist perspective, it is important to note that wider structures of inequality and oppression are not dismantled, and thus oppressive cycles are maintained.

Eagleton's view of tragedy is that it involves a protagonist being trapped in 'irreducible dilemmas, coerced into action by daily compulsive forces' (2003: 62). He cites Barthes:

> Tragedy is only a way of assembling human misfortune, of subsuming it, and thus of justifying it by putting it in the form of a necessity, of a kind of wisdom, or of a purification. To reject this regeneration and to seek the technical means of not succumbing perfidiously (nothing is more insidious than tragedy) is today a necessary undertaking.
>
> (in Eagleton 2003: 70)

Taylor furthermore explores the notion of 'containment' as central to the tragic form, since, she argues, it 'orders events into comprehensible scenarios' (2002: 95). For her, the potential for destruction of tragedy is inherent to the form itself, which is miniaturized and complete, reassuring spectators that 'the crisis will be resolved and balance restored. The fear and pity we, as spectators, feel will be purified by the action' (2002: 95). The tragic model thus forms a practice of containment intended to 'warn' witnesses (audiences) of inevitable consequences, in the same way as punishment is used as a means of deterring the wider public from disobedience (Foucault 1977; Kershaw 1999). Recent scholarship has begun to explore the ways in which trauma, tragedy and witness become cultural 'tropes' by virtue of their proliferation (see Wallis and Duggan 2011; Duggan and Wallis 2011).

We may see the two fields of performance and prisons as interlocutors, and in reading carceral spaces as sites of performances (both transgressive and docile), consider the values of catharsis as a means of working through the emotions inevitably raised in such performances. Such a view proposes that the performance is framed as tragedy, which is a limited but productive view of prisons and those imprisoned within them. Ford argues that tragedy's special pleasure arises from 'pity and fear through imitation that the tragic poet is obliged to reproduce' (1995: 110). He traces the multiple definitions of catharsis from the medical sense of purging, restorative 'pill' through to the sacred moral refinement of the spectator's soul (both notions resonate with a Foucauldian sense of prisons historically as restorative). Yet, Ford rejects the notion that tragedy could be merely a physiological purging of painful emotions, as this reduces the value of the art form to the status of emotional orgy (1995: 111–12). It is not necessary to be purged of the feelings arising from tragedy, since 'to feel pity we must first judge the suffering to be undeserved; to feel fear, we must calculate that a given disaster is such as might happen to us' (1995: 112).

Arts practices in prison are crystallized around the notion of incarceration as potentially transformative, or, to use the language of tragedy, cathartic. Such a view exposes the burden on punishment to change prisoners' future performances of self. Furthermore, it points to the public response to stories of incarceration – if the point of presenting theatre dealing with these stories is for public catharsis, then how are we to transform the protagonists' experience from always already 'tragic' into something that can be transformed? The tension here is that tragedy might be seen to 'fix' or 'sediment' the categories of identification – such that women in prison find their repertoires limited (in particular, considering the ways in which women's characterization as 'criminal women'/'offenders' remains a trace that continues to delimit their identities).

The model I propose below is a theoretical tool that maps criminological concerns of context, habitus and institutional habitus and the inferences for cycles of re-offending. By means of introducing the concerns of criminality through cycles of tragedy, I propose that there is a dramaturgical structure that can be seen in individual acts of crime and pathways through prisons. It remains to be seen how tragedy as a model can be productive for the exploration of the empirical participatory research in prisons. Yet, it serves as a valuable tool for the consideration of key plays from Clean Break, as well as providing structures for the analysis of popular culture, seen in Chapters Four, Five and Six.

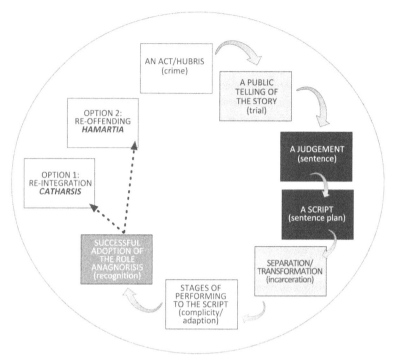

Figure 1: Cycle of Tragic Containment/Cycles of Incarceration.

By examining the cycles of incarceration alongside a structure of tragedy, I intend to put the structures in conversation with one another. The purpose of the model is to provoke questions on the structure of feeling that emerges from mechanisms of crime/punishment/rehabilitation. I explicitly return to this model at various points in these chapters. As such, the model provides the theoretical and methodological dimensions for subsequent analysis. In that respect, the model points forward to the repetition of offending cycles, and also to the individual nature of women's cycles and stories even though there are obvious collective experiences that form a sense of common experiences, impacts and outcomes for women in contact with the criminal justice system.

Play, Pause, Repeat

The first time I watched This Wide Night *in the Soho Theatre (August 2008), I was struck by my resistance to imagining the residue that prison can have upon women's lives after release. I struggled to accept that the two characters Marie and Lorraine could hold so tightly to their mutual experiences of prison without being able to articulate them. I suppose I maintained that freedom from prison meant a freedom from its insistent repetitions. Later, when I was touring with the performance to women's prisons, I heard over and over how the traces of prison continue to affect women insidiously, often returning them to a cycle of re-offending. I came to see the characters' struggles not merely as representing women adapting to post-release circumstances, but as examples of women navigating complex interpersonal concerns.*

(Research Diary, January 2012)

The model of tragic containment links most directly to the concerns of trauma theory, in which the traumatic event re-plays the original event through embodied or psychological repetition (Caruth 1995, 1996). One of the common conceptions of trauma, particularly in the medicalized view of Post-Traumatic Stress Disorder (PTSD), is to what extent psychological repetition impacts on the sufferer's ability to function in the world. Repetition of the traumatic event, in various ways, functions as 'proof' of the original trauma, and so the complex functioning of repetition and continued harm exposes the iterative workings of time for a traumatized psyche (Caruth 1996; Fassin and Rechtman 2007; Leys 2000). Women affected by criminal justice (and the ways in which they are represented in Clean Break's plays, as well as Open Clasp's work) are engaged in the processes of responding to traumatic events (often sustained domestic violence) through psychic repetitions. I am concerned with how aesthetics reflect the transformative nature of trauma where the traumatic event serves as a moment of change for the subject – such that the world is not phenomenologically experienced in the same way thereafter. The traumatic moment remains as a 'trace', a repeated memory. Our assumption as consumers of popular culture may be that incarceration is highly dramatic, but its overwhelming state is banal repetition. In coming to an understanding of prison cultures, I am interested in repetition as a not only behavioural but also aesthetic strategy for women in prison.

Having glossed the value of trauma theory to the models I propose, it is valuable to explore the role of time more deeply by considering how the model of repetition and the shadows cast by trauma are reflected within the dramaturgies of the plays and popular media. The model articulated above becomes a touchstone to which I return in subsequent chapters; first, in order to consider the implications of a (feminist) criminological view of women that perpetuates their victimhood; and also to consider the limitations of arts projects that are predicated on the cyclical (value-driven) agendas of rehabilitation or 'transformation'.

Performance provides articulations for subject positions not always possible in other ways within the prison (in other words, seeing performance as making possible translations across discourses). This is done within applied theatre workshops by engaging body, affect and imagination (discussed further in Chapter Three). My own experience as an artist in prisons has convinced me that small ruptures within creative workshops provide spaces for participants to reflect. Creative improvisations are embodied in different ways from the routines and habits of prison work, education and the cycles of legal processes. The creative workshop is seen as a space in the prison somehow set apart from its reality through re-framing. Unlike the rules and regulations that govern the institution, the laws of performance can bend and shift. However, as later analytic chapters demonstrate, this 'setting apart' is not always productive in the pursuit of transformation of institutions.[16] In the wider examples of popular culture and performance practice, desire and resistance are core points of analysis that drive the understanding of prison cultures as produced within and between prisoners (habitus) and the institution (field).

What is important to note at this point is that 'resistance' is the tactic I am most concerned with, first because resistance positions actions as choices with potential impact on the field or environment, and therefore resistance holds more political and social potential for the re-visioning of the institution. However, this also raises the need for questioning how resistance is understood, on whose terms and with what repercussions. My specific understanding of resistance emerges forcefully in later chapters, whereby I am not merely concerned with a normative model of resistance to the regime (in the form of damage to property or rioting, for example), but also more personal, embodied acts of resistance that disrupt the prison's functions (such as self-harm or hunger strike) as well as the risky choice of developing friendships, kinship or romantic relationships within the institution.

This thread applies Bourdieu's sociological concept of habitus to the concerns of feminist criminology. Its fundamental purpose is to outline an argument for 'engendered habitus' that enriches and anticipates findings in later chapters. Conceiving of habitus in this way led me to construct a model of victim–survivor–hero, since the rich criminological literature and performances about women in prison alongside my own experiences working in prisons suggest that fixed and deterministic categories were both inaccurate and unstable. The material in the book is thus located within a critical discourse that engaged with shifts and changes even while acknowledging prisons as seemingly monolithic, impenetrable and immutable institutions of control. Ruptures to the institutional habitus, and departures from fixed cycles, are explored in the opening half of the book as the performance of desire and resistance. Habitus provides the tool for conceiving of these as performance; and furthermore, it expands the ways in which we can understand the institution (or field) itself. Finally, in relation to the predominance of 'resistance' in the research of women in prison, the model 'tragic containment' is put forward as an analytic touchstone. The theoretical grounding here provides an understanding of the field as productive of durable dispositions. Next, the analysis considers more explicitly the ways in which prison constitutes an institutional field for the performances of women; and as such, it proposes that prison itself must be understood *as* a set of performances.

Notes

1 I further this argument in Chapter Two as well as in relation to the spectral presence of the institution post-release in Chapter Six.
2 Goffman's earlier work on 'line' and 'face' describes the ways social actors adopt performative tactics or roles according to specific situations. See Goffman's work on 'interaction rituals' (2005). However, my main point of interest is in Goffman's close analysis of social behaviours within an institutional setting, and thus his term 'front' is used. In addition, 'front' implies a

degree of artifice that is productive in the analysis of social performances. I also explore this in discussion of line and face in applied theatre practice (Walsh 2018a).

3   Reconviction data are complex; the charity Women in Prison state 37 per cent is the average rate in the United Kingdom for women; while for men, the rate stands at a much higher average. Elsewhere, however, Women in Prison (2013a) cite a figure of 51 per cent reconviction rate. See the media report on the Ministry of Justice re-offending data (Travis, 2010).

4   'Work' here refers to the everyday work of institutions (such as cleaning, laundry and cooking), which are done by prisoners, as well as prison industries that are run as factories for various industry contracts such as dog food packaging, fixing wheelchairs and assembling badges. Prisoners in the United Kingdom get an average of £10 a week for their labour, which allows them to purchase items from the canteen. Some female prisoners have reported getting less than £1.50 a day. In a 2011 article, a journalist discusses a law that deducts 40 per cent of earnings to be put towards victim awareness causes (Scullion 2011). James Thompson has produced a compelling critique of prison work (2000), and Mary Bosworth's consideration of women's resistance in prison accounts for the specifically gendered notions of work (1999). I have engaged with this and the affective and gendered dimensions of work elsewhere (Walsh 2019).

5   The Arts Alliance (now called National Criminal Justice Arts Alliance), for example, is the umbrella organization that provides resources, training and lobbies government for continued support of the arts in criminal justice. It has used the term 'offenders' in all publications, in line with government policy terminology (Arts Alliance 2011).

6   The vision and values of what used to be called the National Offender Management Service was:

> Our role is to commission and provide offender management services in the community and in custody ensuring best value for money from public resources. We work to protect the public and reduce re-offending by delivering the punishment and orders of the courts and supporting rehabilitation by helping offenders to reform their lives. Our Vision: We will work collaboratively with providers and partners to achieve a transformed Justice system to make communities safer, prevent victims and cut crime.
>
> (NOMS 2011)

7   See Goffman's seminal work *The Presentation of Self in Everyday Life*, 1990; *The Goffman Reader*, 1997; and *Asylums: Essays on the Social Situation of Mental Patients and Other Inmates*, 2007.

8   I occasionally use the term 'inmates' since Goffman's study was concerned with the total institution in general, extrapolating from intensive fieldwork with asylum inmates. While my own applied theatre work in psychiatric wards signals certain commonalities, there are numerous differences across the secure estate.

9   An important exception to this is the work of the Prison Reform Trust (see Prison Reform Trust 2010, 2011a, 2011b; Rickford 2011).

10 In both the United States and the United Kingdom, Geese Theatre Company has developed a mask-based practice to explore prisoners' uses of 'fronts' to cope with criminal activity

initially, and then different 'fronts' for managing prison life. Some of the fronts or masks they have developed include 'Mr Cool', the 'Stone Wall', 'The Joker', 'The Rescuer' and 'The Victim' (Mountford and Farrall 1998: 113). Each mask is used in workshops to explore habitual destructive practices in order to provide prisoners with self-awareness of their choices, responses and affect in high-risk situations. Their techniques are strongly underpinned by drama therapy, and are often integrated into therapeutic programmes (Watson 2009). A criticism is that thus far their work has tended to be delivered in male prisons, and that their understanding of female prisoners' 'masks' and 'fronts' is limited.

11 Parts of this section have been published in a slightly different form in *Contemporary Theatre Review* (Walsh 2014), in which the notion of engendered habitus is modeled explicitly in relation to Rebecca Lenkiewicz' plays.

12 In the United Kingdom, these are called Incentives and Earned Privileges (IEP) and are governed by Prison Service Orders. Also see Kennedy (2005), Heidensohn (1996) and Gelsthorpe (2010).

13 De Lauretis draws on Derrida's concern with difference, but, as with other feminist scholars, she resists the implication that Derrida could speak 'from' the position of women. She would invoke Kristeva and Irigaray alongside Derrida for a particularly nuanced feminist sense of 'difference' (de Lauretis 1987: 32).

14 See Billone (2009), Fraden (2001), Son (2006) and Warner (2001, 2004). The Medea Project is run by Rhodessa Jones with women in US prisons. It is explicitly framed as transformative and empowering and has, of all the prison programmes in the United States, received the most favourable response from criminal justice bureaucrats who often authorize temporary release for women to present productions in public.

15 The former UK chief inspector of prisons, Nick Harwood, is cited in this article by Paul Peachey (2012) as saying 'Prisons, particularly as they are currently run, are simply the wrong place for so many of the distressed, damaged or disturbed women they hold […] I think the treatment and conditions in which a small minority of the most disturbed women are held is […] simply unacceptable. I think, I hope, we will look back on how we treated these women in years to come, aghast and ashamed'. A former governor of HMP Styal reflects the conditions women endure in articles by Mark Townsend (2012a, 2012b).

16 One of the only prison theatre programmes that deliberately engaged with the institutional frame in pursuit of wider systemic change was conducted by researchers at Queen Mary, University of London. People's Palace Projects' five-year 'Staging Human Rights' (People's Palace Projects 2013) was led by Paul Heritage (Heritage 1998, 2002, 2004; McAvinchey 2006b; Weaver 2009).

Chapter Two

Genealogies of Prison as Performance: Towards a Theory of Simulating the Cage

Prison as Performance

In order to further a theory of prisons *as* performance, I undertake a genealogical exercise that considers how spectacles of punishment are specific, local and historically informed. This is necessary in order to argue that it is in the conscious, aesthetic framing of prison's performance that the relationship between politics and the apparatus of the theatre and performance can be understood. The central proposal in this book is that performance (understood broadly in relation to performance of the everyday and theatrical performance) offers a way of knowing about and a means of relating to prison as institutional frame. I attend to the ways aesthetic choices become foregrounded in the discursive repetition of prison as a cultural inheritance of how (certain) bodies are punished. In particular, here, I am concerned with some of the preoccupations of carceral geography – that is, how spaces of incarceration reveal and conceal the implications of punishment. First, prison *as* performance enables a focus on emotional and affective engagement with carceral spaces in studies conducted with prisoners through empirical research on site. This offers an understanding of carcerality as a social construction that is replicated beyond the prison estate in numerous ways, as discussed by scholars in geography, sociology, criminology and visual studies (Allspach 2010; Brown 2009; Carrabine 2011, 2016; Moran 2012a, 2015; Turner 2016, 2017). Second, by considering how spaces are produced and received through cultural products, we attend to how incarceration is embodied and experienced. This kind of approach enables critical engagement with issues of representation and the mediation of how prison cultures are disseminated through both performance and popular media.

The three events I identify as genealogically valuable are: the Stanford Prison Experiment, and two performance installations; one by US-based artists Guillermo Gómez-Peña and Coco Fusco, and the other by UK theatre company Rideout. My provocative reading of these three events sets the modes of analysis that I bring to bear on applied theatre practice, theatre and fictional television representations from the United Kingdom, United States and Australia. Cultural criminology calls for a prolonged critique on prisons as sites of cultural imagination. This chapter approaches such critique by exploring the spectacle of their surveillance functions as well as considering the relationship between the prisoners' bodies as objects of a punitive gaze by a perceived 'public'. As Moran proposes in an approach from carceral geography to the study of prison museums:

The commodification of the macabre at prison sites erases as much as it reveals in relation to the communication of meaning and purpose of contemporary imprisonment and punishment to visiting audiences (Moran, 2013, Walby and Fiche, 2011). Where prison heritage sites *do* articulate a consciously and intentionally politicized message through the preservation and interpretation of the site, it is rarely about imprisonment *per se*.
(Moran 2015: 139)

What is thus highlighted as urgent, then, is the need to bring together specific problems of imprisonment and the cultural critique of sites, events and cultural performances about prisons.

This adds to the emerging context of cultural criminology's excellent work on the visual (Brown 2009, 2014; Carrabine 2012, 2014, 2016; O'Neill 2004), film (Cecil 2007b, 2007c, 2015, 2017; Hayward and Presdee 2010; Rafter 2000; Rafter and Brown 2011; Yar 2010), subcultures (Ferrell 2004; Ferrell and Sanders 1995; Ferrell et al. 2008) and popular culture (Carrabine 2015; Mason 2003a; Ogletree and Sarat 2015; O'Neill and Seal 2012). Forging an analytic frame that emerges from performance studies furthers the potential for what is particular in performance that is of value from a feminist criminological perspective – namely, the capacity to analyse spectacle and processes of production of meaning in relation to the body and the experience of being in and encountering prison.

While the book attends to how incarceration, removal, programmes of rehabilitation and re-entry cycles perpetuate distinctions between 'us' and 'them', here I am concerned with the means by which 'the cell' itself performs this function. In doing so, I am concerned with how prisons stage this distinction in spatial, aesthetic and affectual ways. I am interested in the means by which the functions of prison systemically contribute to a moral, ethical and aesthetic separation of certain types of bodies, and to what extent the prison's successful 'performance' demands a particular repetition of the restoration of societal norms predicated on law. I am referring here to the well-rehearsed critique of the neo-liberal milieu (in the West) in which, disproportionately, people of colour, poor people and immigrants are criminalized. This is particularly so in the United States and the United Kingdom (Wacquant 2009b, 2010b). Performance here is understood in the McKenzian (2001) dimension in relation to the operations of the prison as well as critical analysis of prison perform a labour.[1] I have developed this thinking elsewhere in relation to Sarah Ahmed's (2004, 2014) formulation of affective labour (Walsh 2019). Here, what is productive is the particularity of culture in terms of representations, aesthetics and the implications of the production of meaning, rather than the institution itself. The three examples in this chapter serve to articulate the prison *as* performance in a way that deliberately shifts from a focus on national contexts as I attempt to sketch out the ubiquity of prison cultures for a criminological imagination.

The prison's public/private dynamic can be reconsidered through performance. In light of the ways in which criminal justice is concerned with the spectacle of 'successful' rehabilitation, the chapter is concerned with the power of carceral spaces. Prisons are analysed *as* performance. A point to raise here, explored in the models I propose, is about the assumption of a linear progression of the cycles of incarceration, and how such linearity becomes disrupted by performances of resistance. Performance studies offers important tools in this regard by engaging with the contexts, settings and nuances of actions and receptions of the (broadly defined) performances or resistances.

In other work on my own practice in women's prisons in the United Kingdom, I have considered the value of performativity of testimonies of rehabilitation. The examples from performance and practice demonstrate iterative and cyclical functions, norms and conventions that have a forceful effect (Walsh 2018a). This conception of performativity is developed by Parker and Sedgwick, who hope to move discussions of performativity beyond considerations of the gaze and towards a sense of interpellation in which the space of reception involves 'contradictions and discontinuities' (Sedgwick and Parker 1995: 7). Derrida's (1993) work on performativity is glossed here in relation to the means by which the violence of the law serves both as an interruption of time and as a performative promise. 'Justice' functions through promissory demands that an act equals a sentence, and that a sentence equals a predetermined set of processes relating to removal, rehabilitation and transformation before expulsion into the 'real' world.[2] In this view, the appearance of the reformed subject at the end of the sentence legitimates the performative function of the sentence. The maintenance of cultural tropes that highlight dangers and risks of prison also maintains the discursive power of the law.[3] Later chapters demonstrate that the 'public' perceptions of prison life are perpetuated through cultural and mediatized imaginaries. Much of this requires a restoration of harsh, punitive conditions that can reassure the 'public' that justice is being done. This is one of the foundational tenets of cultural criminology (Brown 2009; Ferrell and Sanders 1995; Ferrell et al. 2004).

In a special edition of *Law Text Culture* (Lieboff and Nield, 2010), contributors explored the interaction between performance studies and law in order to consider the theatrical presence of the law. The fruitful dialogue between disciplines suggests ways in which performance can be considered as more than a metaphor or dismissive claim of in-authenticity. Juridical meanings are considered in relation to witnessing (Wake 2010); prison architecture's performance via presence (Branco 2010); and the emergence of the theatricality of political apology (Schmidt 2010). The collection positions juridical processes as needing to be analysed as theatrical problems, or what Schmidt considers 'problems for theatre, but also ideas that theatricality problematizes – such as problems of representation, authenticity and spectatorship' (2010: 55). As Leiboff suggests, 'the theatrical militates against law's insistence that actions and events are rendered according to the narrative and chronological certainties of the Aristotelian well-made play' (2010: 388). While the work is compelling, this academic discourse engaging with (or appropriating) performance demonstrates the promiscuous 'value' of metaphors. Indeed, 'performance' as a term is often used to indicate the success of worth in capitalist terms of a company. This dual sense of 'performance' is also explored in Jon McKenzie's work on disciplinarity and performance (2001). When considered in relation to prisons (some of which are private companies), the idea of 'performance' needs to be robustly problematized. While not explicitly attended to in this book, it is considered in related work I have done on the balance between neo-liberal values of the institution and values in arts-based investigation in prisons (Walsh 2012c). Instead of focusing on performance in this sense, I use three performance examples to model my argument about prisons *as* performance. It is important to acknowledge that two out of the three examples were explicitly staged as performance in public. The other – the Stanford Prison Experiment – was a simulation that was set up as a psychological experiment. Its value in the subsequent understanding of prison spaces and impacts on affects and cognitive functions as well as the bodies of prisoners, and its significance for thinking about prisons, discipline and punishment, leads me to analyse this as a performance. As such, performance becomes a methodological concern throughout this chapter – or to put it differently, performance becomes the research lens.

By means of unpacking what is understood by carceral spaces, I attend to the operations of power and subjectivity before arguing that performance studies provides valuable analytic tools for investigating the aesthetic and cultural work done as prisons perform their functions. The argument is supported by a working through of the genealogies of prison *as* performance, in which three examples of cells in public spaces, or what Dominique Moran calls 'transient carceral landscapes' (2012a, 2013), are analysed.[4] Each of these examples explores the carceral landscape in a sociopolitical context, and through staging, each of them raises important questions about (racialized, sexualized) bodies in relation to the spectacle of suffering.[5] The examples provide scenes of subjection in which the relation between optics, audience presence and the implications of the relations between the two are explored.

Carceral Spaces: Power, Punishment and the Panopticon

In her investigation of the connection between architectures of power and visibility, Patricia Branco investigates the similarities between two historically significant prison and theatre spaces, which she sees as having 'both specular and spectacular functions, in which space acts as a manifestation of power to shape the place or stage where law and theatre come to life and perform their spectacle' (2010: 277).

What Branco's formulation offers is the sense that the panopticon is not merely an architectural structure that renders individuals visible not only to the central authority in the watchtower, but also to each other such that individual punishment is always already co-performed. She offers a description of the ways in which 'space serves the purpose of inflicting the power of law over the prisoners and where each and all are both actors and spectators in the spectacle of oppression that involves them all' (2010: 284).

For Branco, prison architectures provide an understanding of the operations of power from a vertical (top-down) and a horizontal approach, which can be between prisoners. The notion of an external audience/witness (such as a theatre practitioner, or researcher, or theatre audience to a play staged in prison) further complicates the operations of this power dynamic, so that spectating and spatial politics are in conflict.

The architecture of prisons and the ways in which space performs domination and punishment have been well rehearsed since Foucault's history of the birth of the prison (1977). One of his major concerns was the investigation of operations of power and visibility in Jeremy Bentham's panopticon (which literally means 'to see everything'). Bentham proposed a radial design, in which a central watchtower asserts the illusion of being able to see into every cell, effectively turning each of them into 'so many cages, so many small theatres, in which each actor is alone, perfectly individualized [sic] and constantly visible' (1977: 201). Foucault's understanding of the panopticon resulted in a theory of how discipline is meted out through the notion that conformity or docility results from 'eliminating autonomy and reforming the "self"' (Kershaw 1999: 131). One of the main functions of the panopticon was to engage in surveillance for economic reasons – employing fewer staff to oversee many more workers, asylum inmates or prisoners.[6] Foucault shows how Bentham's concept was that power should be 'visible and unverifiable' (1977: 201); and resultantly, there is a dissociation of the 'see/being seen dyad: in the peripheric ring, one is totally seen, without ever seeing; in the central tower, one sees everything without ever being seen' (1977: 203). The panopticon provides valuable structural metaphors for the modelling of visibility and spectatorship, but needs to be considered critically in relation to women. In particular, the women prisoners-as-objects are rendered doubly marginalized in their positions as subjects to the all-powerful (male) gaze.

In order to enter the argument about the prison *as* performance, I begin with a theatrical response to the notion of the panopticon. This brief framing section is intended to not simply acknowledge a formative cultural representation of the spectacularization of the criminal body. It also provides a means of considering the function of the theatre in framing,

Figure 2: Panopticon. Ahrens, L. (2008: 75) 'Prisoners of a Hard Life: Women and their Children', *The Real Cost of Prisons Comix* (Artist: Susan Willmarth).

aestheticizing and reproducing values related to social justice. In turn, I make use of this entry point later in the chapter when I discuss three genealogical examples of the transient carceral landscapes.

British playwright Caryl Churchill's play *Softcops*, written in 1978 (published in a collection in 1990), was intended to be a work about the soft measures of control inflicted by institutions of society. In her introductory notes to the play, Churchill acknowledges the influence of Foucault's *Discipline and Punish* (1977), which results in *Softcops*. It is about the attempt by 'government to depoliticize illegal acts, to make criminals a separate class from the rest of society so that subversion will not be general' (Churchill 1990: 3). The play is set in France in the 1830s, and Churchill stages a conversation between Bentham and Pierre, in which Pierre demonstrates a spectacular performance of punishment by presenting a man stretched out on 'the rack'.[7]

> PIERRE: [...] here you have the shock and at the same time the reasonable explanation of how the crime came about and how to resist any such tendencies in one's own life.
> BENTHAM: But this sight is not giving us a pleasure greater than the man's suffering. I've seen enough. Release the man at once.
> PIERRE: I must devise punishments that will continue to be a novelty and a real attraction to the public.
> BENTHAM: Stop stop. It goes on and on.
> PIERRE: That's the perfection. It can go on all day and every day. Don't worry Mr Bentham, come closer. He doesn't feel a thing. Can you see now? The wheels turn but he is not stretched. It's an optical illusion.
> (1990: 39)

Bentham then tells Pierre about how he has spent years working on a project that was related to increasing the productivity of workers. It comprises, he says of an iron cage.

> BENTHAM: A central tower. The workers are not naturally obedient or industrious. But they become so.
> PIERRE: The workers gaze up at the iron cage?
> BENTHAM: No, no, your idea has to be reversed. Let me show you. Imagine for once that you're the prisoner. This is your cell, you can't leave it. This is the central tower, and I'm the guard. I'll watch whatever you do day and night.
> (1990: 38–39)

Pierre spends some time undergoing a humiliating, drawn-out experience of being watched, and he narrates his sensations. Finally, he begs Bentham to tell him whether he has correctly understood the purpose of the panopticon:

PIERRE: [...] Instead of thousands of people watching one prisoner, one person can watch thousands of prisoners. I've always wanted to affect the spectators. You're affecting the person who is seen. This is a complete reversal for me.
(1990: 40)

Churchill offers an important consideration for the investigation on prison *as* performance, which is the need to analyse the directionality of the gaze (or the intentionality) and the implications of power differentials between bodies staged as and for punishment. Her play stages the danger and violence inherent in even the spectacle of prison *as* performance. The regime's routine along with risk, pain and danger characterizes prison life, and architectures and daily patterns, in turn, reflect such dangers.[8] Having said that, it is simplistic to characterize carceral spaces as merely 'dangerous', and for popular culture, there is some value in unpicking some of these fetishisms of violence and danger.

Popular culture has a tendency to subsume the dangers of surveillance and the powers it grants authorities over the bodies of the incarcerated subjects with the erasure of agency proposed by Foucault's 'docile bodies' (1977). Yet, representations should not oversimplify the spectacle of punishment by reproducing violence or fetishizing the 'cage'. In the examples I consider, there is a much more nuanced exploration of negotiation, participation and the construction of relation that is discussed by Rancière (2009), in which tensions, ethics and politics are staged and forged *as* performances (McGuinness 2016).

Theatre and performance scholars have rarely satisfactorily critiqued the theoretical notion of the panopticon, I contend, because it provides neat and compelling arguments for the relationship between the audience and the performer. Instead, I propose that performance can, rather than co-opting the imagery of the panopticon and its dispersed surveillance, problematize the direction of the gaze, the assumptions about audience homogeneity, and introduce complex affectual responses to the subject of crime and incarceration.[9] What needs further investigation is exactly in what ways power and punishment are performed in and through institutions and their day-to-day apparatus. Kershaw acknowledges that Foucault's view insists on an ethical reading of the performance of power and punishment (1999). Conquergood demands that research should consider the politics of performance, asking for consideration of 'the relationship between performance and power' (1991: 191). The examples in this chapter begin to unpack how understanding prison *as* performance troubles fixed understandings of the functions of juridical systems that are predicated on binaries right, wrong, inside and outside.

In the chosen extracts from *Softcops* (1990), Churchill stages the moral and ethical implications of the aesthetic spectacle in the scenes between Bentham and Pierre. In other scenes, too, prisoners are displayed, marked out with placards stating their crimes, and paraded in chain gangs around France. The play's debt to Foucault is evident in its exploration of the shifting modes of punishment relating to a range of social attitudes to crime. Most importantly, however, the play positions visibility of the criminal body as paramount. The scene above exposes the force of seeing/being seen dyad that is so central to the notion of the panopticon as well as to performance.

The workings of the law offer the separation of criminal bodies as a reassurance of safety. We (the public) are, paradoxically, meant to assume that society is safer when more men and women are locked away. Yet, criminology has offered multiple rebuttals to that assumption, demonstrating that there is increasing criminalization of intersecting social issues such as class, poverty and lack of education. This follows Foucault's assertion that the carceral landscape 'assures, in the depths of the social body, the formation of delinquency on the basis of subtle illegalities' (1977: 301). It is necessary, however, to ensure that there is a robust critique of the assumptions that dictate what makes society 'safe' or what constitutes a 'risk'. These concerns, rather than being objectively true, are culturally informed and contextualized by economic and political milieus. What lies beneath the ongoing redefinition of effective performances of safety and security is a wider concern about nations, sovereignty and belonging, and how these are circulated through cultural production.[10] This accounts for the insistence of markers of inclusion and exclusion that repeatedly coincide with the markers of what is considered criminality. What is worrying is that this mapping of criminality against poverty, class, race and exclusion from the mainstream has not abated since Charles Booth's mapping of the criminal underclasses in London in the nineteenth century.[11]

Criminal justice, in general, and prison, in particular, stage the separation of 'Others' by literally marking out carceral spaces as constituting the punitive inside and the outside as freedom, the protected 'us' against the 'them' from whom we need protection. I propose that performance apparatus is employed to do so, although this reading can be subverted through resistance. Yet, in their hegemonic legitimacy, prisons are physical stages set aside for removing undesirable Others from the society to which they once belonged. Prisoners and staff perform set functions, marked out by deliberate costumes and behavioural scripts (or habitus). Prisoners and staff do not occupy the same spaces, so prisoners' steps are directed by painted lines on the ground, with particular areas marked out as 'out of bounds'. Staff, additionally, have the capacity to navigate through any door, fence or gate. Most importantly, prison staff maintains good order and discipline largely by rigid adherence to rules about when and where prisoners may move, with whom they may associate and what activities are sanctioned.

It is not merely between prisoners and their guards that there is a staged separation between 'us' and 'them'. In visitation halls in the United Kingdom, red chairs indicate prisoners and blue chairs indicate visitors. This is practical for the officers, who spend most of the day correlating the numbers tally, as they can more easily count red chairs rather than become confused when there are many bodies in seats of the same colour. This is particularly the case with sentenced women prisoners who are largely allowed to wear their own sweatshirts and trousers, rather than the representation of the iconic orange or plain khaki jumpsuit seen in popular media (for example, *Orange Is the New Black*, 2013–ongoing), which is discussed later. It also serves as a reminder for those participating in the visit that the prisoner is not merely a member of the family, for example, but is first considered a prisoner. In other words, the personal agency of the subject is subsumed by the role as prisoner. It is this erasure and denial of difference that has inspired feminist scholars to develop critical tools that insist on the placing of subjective, embodied experiences in their analyses. As such, it is necessary to develop research that takes cognisance of the means by which difference, marginality and Otherness are staged by prison apparatus. As a means of considering the performance of prison's disciplinary operations, the next section works towards an understanding of the aesthetics of prison, in which I articulate what I call prison cultures.

Prison Cultures: Performance and Cultural Constructions of the Institution

Against the backdrop of unfettered markets and enfeebled social-welfare programs, when the penal system has become a major engine of social stratification and cultural division in its own right, the field study of the prison ceases to be the province of the specialist in crime and punishment to become a window into the deepest contradictions and the darkest secrets of our age.

(Wacquant 2002: 389)

Conquergood asks researchers to engage with performance and cultural process: 'What are the consequences of thinking about culture as a verb instead of a noun, process instead of product?' (1991: 190). In this section, Conquergood's suggestion that culture may be considered to be in the process of being constructed serves to frame the investigation. Thus, I begin with examples from literature that explore the interrelationship between stages and prisons, and move on to a critique of the dynamic between witnessing stories and participation. The main contribution of this formulation is to set the ground for an understanding of a genealogical understanding of how prisons (and their simulations or replicas staged in public) operate in relation to the social and political milieu.

Prisons perpetuate and rely on a perceived fixity, as explored by McAvinchey (2011a: 60), producing spectacles that serve to further how the public engage with offending, crime and justice, also discussed by Michelle Brown (2009).[12] However, for prisoners, these imaginaries of fixity are consistently undermined by the changing repertoires of discipline and punishment that are inevitably local, specific and embodied. This results in a paradox for prison cultures. Rather than sketching a fixed or already existing prison culture, I evoke three historically located examples of how prison has been 'performed' in the public eye, in order to begin to carve out a lexicon of terms and practices in the realm of performance. Prison, performance, power and punishment are explored alongside one another as a means of thinking through how 'prison cultures' are multiple and variable. The purpose is to consider the powerful narratives that performing the prison and the prison's performance play in shaping wider understandings of the functions of incarceration, both for the 'protagonists' (the incarcerated) and for the 'audience' (the 'public', or society).

In an article about a now-famous performance in prison, Erin Koshal (2010) writes of a noteworthy staging of Samuel Beckett's *Waiting for Godot* in San Quentin high-security prison in the United States in the 1980s. She explores the productive connections evident in the prison-audience responses to the play with their own narratives. Didi and Gogo's existential waiting (2010: 190) becomes aligned with the political and social uncertainty faced by prisoners as they await orders, judgments, or what Koshal refers to as a 'state of exception' (cf. Agamben 2005). Koshal privileges a political reading of the text by examining its staging in prison. For her, the issues of rights, participation and recognition of prisoners as humans are prefigured in the performance space as prisoners in the audience engage with representations of a predicament – of in-between-ness, in which the future is to be determined by an unseen force. She says that in San Quentin,

> the prison was a carceral theatre in which performance became a way for prisoners to negotiate the demands that they make themselves recognizable and also respond to conflicting norms and identities inside and outside the prison.
>
> (2010: 205)

Furthermore, Koshal indicates that the prisoners' need to perform 'according to an institutional norm of "acceptable personhood" as that term was defined legally and by the prison' (2010: 205). Her depiction of the prisoners' responses to the play prefigures the importance of the aesthetic frame through which prisoners could reflect on their own performance: compliance or defiance of prison rules, docility or resistance, recognition of the script dictated by the prison sentence, and the concomitant performance for parole. This example of performance reflects the concerns I have already articulated regarding the apparatus of power and punishment, but more precisely brings into focus the ways in which the aesthetic and moral and social frames are deployed in the understanding of prison itself as performance. This sets up the concept of prison cultures, whereby we may begin to see prison scenes and settings through the focus on the body of the prisoner as 'subject' not only of punishment but also with an aim to be 'rehabilitated' or reduce re-offending, which are the lynchpins of contemporary criminal justice in the United Kingdom.

The volume *Captive Audience* by Thomas Fahy and Kimball King (2003) provides examples of the ways in which the invisibility of imprisonment is challenged by staging concerns in theatres. They suggest that the constraints of theatre sets an (albeit defined) duration of confinement in auditoria. The audiences' witness of stories of and about prison breaks apart the shroud of secrecy of institutions, and the shared experience 'makes us aware of both our role as passive observers and our tacit acceptance of the abuses within the prison system' (2003: 1–2). Theatre, for them,

> [i]ndividualizes the people held captive by telling their stories, and raises questions that are typically ignored: How and why are they in prison? What steps can be taken to

prevent this outcome? In doing so, these works [...] challenge viewers to recognize the social forces that contribute to crime and ultimately, to act.

(2003: 1–2)

Yet, I would claim that these questions point towards an omission in many contemporary plays in which prison tropes are mined. Their overreliance on cathartic models of performance in the book undermine this intention, which is what James Thompson suggests when he argues in his review of the volume that the

> intersection of prison as performance and performances that tackle prison as theme/metaphor is most acutely foregrounded when inmates themselves are invited to the stage. In these moments, the panopticon can be replayed (with the audience now guards) or the gaze be returned (as prisoners are empowered to look back at their captors).

(2005: 466)

By alerting readers to applied theatre practices in prison, Thompson highlights the possibility for a subversion of the gaze: from the controlling and dominating gaze of the panopticon to the (presumed) more empathetic relationship between speaker and witness. Thompson's (2005) critique is directed at the blind spot of Fahy and King's study that ignores a fairly established (though not widely publicized) practice of the arts in prisons, particularly the use of theatre as both an entertainment for prisoners, but increasingly, using acting, improvisation and devising methods in order to engage with offending behaviour in alternative ways to standard psychotherapeutic resources offered to prisoners (Balfour 2003, 2004; Thompson 1998, 1999, 2001, 2004a; Watson 2009). These are what Goffman calls 'removal activities' (2007: 68), which are intended to be sufficiently engrossing for participants in order to 'lift' them out of themselves, making them 'oblivious for the time being to [their] actual situation' (2007: 68–69). What Goffman acknowledges is that while the intention of these activities (such as arts therapies, workshops or crafts) is to alleviate psychological stress, it is in their 'insufficiency [...] that an important deprivational effect of total institutions can be found' (2007: 69–70).[13]

Although limited to mainstream theatre, Kimball and King's study outlines some valuable areas for this investigation since it foregrounds the epistemological poverty of literary or dramatic sketches of prison. However, it is clear that prison as a trope is forged through a range of performance strategies, and not merely 'represented' in contemporary plays. As I proceed in this study, I exploit a wide understanding of performance, and in this chapter, in particular, I evoke performance practices in order to re-imagine the ways in which prisoners as 'protagonists' and audiences as witness can be troubled.[14] I challenge the moment of encounter between audience as witness to prisoners' stories in order to grasp how performance can shift fixed binaries, and have the potential to re-imagine the worlds of prison and beyond.

Prison *as* performance comes into focus by attending to space, apparatus of power and subjectivity. By drawing on aesthetics of prison and punishment, I am able to examine genealogies of prison *as* performance. This furthers an understanding of the ways in which prison simulations project different issues into the cultural milieu as they are framed variously as scientific (The Stanford Prison Experiment), anthropological/artistic (*Two Undiscovered Amerindians Visit…*) and social (Rideout). As such, they are not immediately analogous. Yet, by exploring these three examples together, I reflect on the imbrication of silence, domination and violence in the construction of, first, cages, which offer a particularly transparent view of the bodies within; and, second, cells, which are generally constructed to occlude visibility. 'The cage' demands the visibility of the caged and closely resembles the parade of animalistic power, strength or 'freakish Otherness' of anthropological 'world fairs' of the nineteenth century (Kruger 2007). By contrast, the cell excludes and occludes public interaction, but nevertheless functions as a container that renders a differential of power visible (Walsh 2016).

In the wake of the well-known Stanford Prison Experiment (1973), and the world tour of the couple in the cage *Two Undiscovered Amerindians Visit…* by Guillermo Gómez-Peña and Coco Fusco (1992), there have been other simulations of cells and cages that display performances of and about incarceration and colonial violence (Lindfors 2003; McGuinness 2016; Taylor 1998).[15] Such contemporary performances are generally mounted in order to extend and expand the awareness of the issues of the constructedness of 'the cage' – as embodied manifestations of racist and (hetero-)sexist domination. The simulations demonstrate the perpetuated inequality of how those within the cage are viewed. Performances become a means of articulating the position of the oppressed bodies within wider discourses of social capital, and yet, too often, are implicated in replicating the narratives they seek to rupture.

The desire of the public to experience and encounter 'the caged' is borne out through endless fascination (Brown 2009) with the mediated images and stories of crime and punishment through television, film and other media, often affirming cultural assumptions of a stable notion of the prison (McAvinchey 2011a: 37–38). This desire to locate the workings of justice in a site, and on the bodies of prisoners, serves to mark both the bodies and the prison with a sense of fixity. This limits the potential for both space (cell/cage) and inhabitant of the space (prisoners/specimens) to disrupt the labels and binary narratives of justice. In the same way as colonial encounters with the savage Other exhibited bodies in specific ways that served to highlight difference, there is the desire within popular culture to display prisoners' moral 'Otherness' in an embodied way. Thus, 'most mediated images and stories encountered by the public highlight (and perhaps exaggerate) the divide between acceptable and transgressive behaviours; relying on stereotypes that are inevitably inscribed by race, class and gender' (Walsh 2014: 51).

The public imagination is indubitably conservative when it comes to the ways in which criminal identities are performed (Ferrell and Sanders 1995). In addition, the institution itself maintains an impenetrable allure (Carrabine 2012). This next example was not framed as a public spectacle, and therefore, is one that is being co-opted in this argument for its genealogical value.

'Transient Carceral Landscapes': The Stanford Prison Experiment and the Simulated Prison

The body believes what it plays at: it weeps if it mimes grief.

(Bourdieu 1990: 73)

There is an established history of the simulation of the prison environment that has been used to determine the effects of imprisonment on both the imprisoned and those in control. The intention of the so-called Stanford Prison Experiment was to simulate a fully operational prison environment, with all participants fully aware of their own (randomly assigned) roles of prisoner/officer in an enclosed environment with no external audience and very little contact from the experiment team. In other words, the experiment was intended to be an extended performance of the roles of controller and controlled within a contained environment.

The experiment has captured the public imagination since it was publicized in the 1970s, resulting in drastic reviews of research ethics protocols, participant safety and the insistence of the credo to 'do no harm'. The simulation of prison conditions was designed by psychologist Philip Zimbardo and his research team in order to explore the social psychology of prisoner/officer power dynamics and the 'social capital' brought to each role (Haney et al. 1973; Zimbardo et al. 1973). The intention was to conduct a real-time experiment in which research volunteers were randomly ascribed either role, and in doing so, to explore to what extent the 'officers' manifested control and domination as part of their job, and how the 'prisoners'' liberties were eroded in this role. Zimbardo suggests that it was important to have conducted the experiment outside of a 'real' prison setting, since the institution (a 'fortress of secrecy' Haney et al. 1973: 3) is immune to external observation. The experiment was designed in order to replicate the sensations of imprisonment in an embodied way (inasmuch as that was possible with voluntary research participants who had given consent), with rituals and ploys devised in order to encourage de-individualization, dependence and emasculation under arbitrary control. The team's co-authored account uses theatrical language to describe the effect of the framing of the experiment: '[t]he combination of realism and symbolism in this experiment had fused to create a vivid illusion of imprisonment [...]. It was remarkable how readily we all slipped into our roles' (Haney et al. 1973: 6). In the event, the research subjects mounted a rebellion against the control of the officers, staging what Zimbardo calls a 'riot', which was quelled by the 'officers', who developed incentives and privileges for the good 'prisoners', and a system of punishment for those who resisted. As a result, the researchers reported that there was much greater docility and compliance by the 'prisoners' (1973: 6). For the research team, the experiment highlighted the 'dehumanizing tendency to respond to other people according to socially determined labels and often arbitrarily assigned roles' (1973: 8). The wider implications of the research questioned to what extent 'we' allow ourselves to become imprisoned by docilely accepting the roles others assign 'us', or, indeed, choose to remain prisoners because being passive and dependent frees us from the need to act and be responsible for our own actions (1973: 9).[16]

In their analysis of the experiment, Haney et al. refer to the 'pathological reactions' (1973: 75) of both 'prisoners' and 'officers'. The experiment was terminated after six days rather than continue for a second week, as had been planned, because of the 'intense' affective responses from both subject groups (Haney et al. 1973: 88). Indeed, one of the striking reflections from the researchers is the fact that due to having recruited a fairly homogenous group of young men (all Caucasian and of similar age), several defining features of imprisonment did not surface as indicative behaviours in the simulated prison (such as rape – what they call 'involuntary homosexuality', racism, physical beatings, etc.). Rather, the power differential of role allocation caused the 'officers' to seek alternative 'differences' to justify arbitrary punishments. In other words, rather than remaining de-individualized, the mechanism of control and domination becomes more marked as it focuses on specificities. Subsequent critical explorations of the Stanford Prison Experiment have criticized its approach, and the researchers have been implicated in the psychological harm caused by the effects of domination and control. The simulation of the prison is defended as an example of the importance of status and role, but nevertheless this experiment has been widely castigated for its unethical exploitation of its subjects.

The simulation performs as a model of power and its correlative docility by explicitly connecting power to hyper-masculinity. Its frame as a serious psychological experiment removes it from a public domain, yet its findings have contributed to a wider public sensibility of punishment and incarceration.[17] As a performance trope, the simulation also raises important questions about the responsibilities of observers and audiences witnessing power abuses, psychological degradation and potential trauma. The example is cited here not merely because of its historical value as a formative staging of prison and its effects, but also because of the ways in which it consciously demonstrated the insidiousness of roles that may otherwise be considered determined by social factors such as morality, education and upbringing.[18]

In his study of 'timeless cruelty', Stephen Bottoms (2014) locates the Stanford Prison Experiment and its performance/popular culture offspring as rooted in deeply theatrical trappings. He is particularly interested in how psychology as a frame, authority as an object and submission as an outcome were constituted by a bizarre tension between authenticity and theatricality.

> Zimbardo's experiment sought to abstract human behaviour into 'pure' experimental conditions – to extrapolate generalizable conclusions about human psychology *per se*, that would float above history, while also speaking to it. Another way of putting this is

that Zimbardo was seeking to stage a kind of universalizing dramatic metaphor for the experience of imprisonment.

(2014: 165)

The team at Stanford deployed costumes, a limited time frame, a 'contract' that constituted roles. For Bottoms, both the original experiment and its resulting performance artworks that include Artur Zmijewski's 75-minute video *Repetition* (2005) seek to distil the experience of prison into the components of time, space and behaviour while never matching what is perhaps most obscure about prison: its banality and simultaneous lack of predictability. Bottoms says that the experiment

> represented a kind of hypothetical model made flesh – an attempt literally to *embody* certain pre-formed assumptions about the 'deep structure' of prison relationships. Put another way, the SPE's design was fundamentally tautological: in order to demonstrate that prisons are psychologically oppressive places, this staged simulation had to real-ize [*sic*] the dynamics of oppression.

(2014: 169, original emphasis)

By considering the example through Bourdieu's field and habitus, it is clear that the insidious strength of the field as socially inscribed by power, inequality and domination leads quickly and inevitably to both 'officers' and 'prisoners' improvising new behaviours and strategies in order to fulfil their functions. In other words, the habitus of both groups are defined and delimited by the expectations and possibilities of the field. The findings of the experiment demonstrate the totalizing power of the domain to inform how everyday behaviours are performed. This view recalls Goffman's reading of 'total institution' (2007) roles as mutually interdependent, which suggests the need to question perceptions of privilege and punishment and the means of the institution to implement them.

By way of exploring the cage trope within performance, and its challenges as an object on stage, I turn now to a renowned performance event that intended to foreground the cage as trope, and invited spectators to question their own reactions to the couple who 'appeared' in the cage. The example operated in a wider frame of postcolonial performance, making reference to containment of the subaltern body (Spivak 1988).[19] While it is not a direct performance of a 'prison cell', the cage is invoked as a metaphor of containment and the spectacle of the Other in a staging that foregrounds the performers' ethnicity and gender as a spectacle as well as a product of the performance. It operates as a crucial example of audience/performer relationships in which the audience is always already simultaneously powerful and impotent. This paradox is further highlighted in an article by Caoimhe Mader McGuinness (2016), whose powerful deployment of *The Couple in the Cage* puts forward an argument about the production of agonistic spaces of protesting institutional racism in the United Kingdom in relation to Brett Bailey's *Exhibit B* (2012–13).

The Couple in the Cage: Guillermo Gómez-Peña and Coco Fusco

In 1992, artist–scholars Coco Fusco and Guillermo Gómez-Peña created a touring performance called *Two Undiscovered Amerindians Visit...* in which they remained in a golden cage for three days as specimens of an undiscovered Amerindian tribe from an unknown island. The performance of the 'savages' was staged in galleries, museums and cultural institutions in several locations around the world. Diana Taylor refers to the ways in which the location of the cage in legitimating institutions served to implicate the 'hosts' in the 'extermination or abuse of aboriginal peoples' (1998: 163). The performance attempted to engage with the role of viewer in perpetuating the fetishization of the postcolonial body, with references to the many disturbing historical precedents of 'savages' displayed before the colonial gaze. In her own reflexive account of the performance, Fusco refers to the attempt to create a 'satirical commentary on Western concepts of the exotic, primitive other' (2000: 130), remarking that there were two unexpected outcomes from the performance. Namely, audiences seemed to believe that the fictional identities were real, and that intellectuals and the artistic community began to refer to the 'moral implications' of the ways in which the work used 'deception' precisely because the claims for authenticity were questioned. Furthermore, Taylor's (1998) analysis of the event explores the ways in which the performance highlighted the audience's maintenance of a postcolonial condition: that is, the audience seemed to want to believe that this was an example of 'authentic' savagery (despite the countless ironic references to popular culture that made such a frame impossible to believe).[20] Fusco considers the legacy of 'the cage'.

> Ethnographic spectacles circulated and reinforced stereotypes, stressing that 'difference' was apparent in the bodies on display. Thus they naturalized fetishized [sic] representations of Otherness, mitigating anxieties generated by the encounter with difference.
> (2000: 132)

Some specific examples are discussed by Fusco, highlighting the ways in which the caged subjects became hyper-sexualized, not merely as disempowered objects of a 'gaze', but rather in a more embodied and intrusive way that reinforces racial dehumanization. One incident was when a female audience member attempted to feed the savage male a banana in an overtly sexual manner, insisting on wearing latex gloves to do so. This action foregrounds assumptions about gender, in which the infantilizing feeding is viewed as emasculating, but is particularly marked by the racial difference between the powerful white woman 'agent' and the subaltern body of the postcolonial male Other (Gómez-Peña). The banana becomes a performative object that can disappear – the phallic symbol devoured by the savage caged subject. In this performance moment, the participating audience member re-animated the sexualized dynamic between colonial 'masters' and the racialized Other, whose potency is always already understood as in relation to the dominant white female, as put forward by Frantz Fanon (2008). The cage thus serves to explicate the continuing inequalities, presumptions, essentializing and stereotyped characteristics of the colonial narratives that are perpetuated by neo-liberal regimes.

What is astounding about this performance is the division between the intention of the work as satirical (considering it is framed as ridiculous, contradictory and ambiguous by deploying a mixture of 'native' traditional tropes and artefacts alongside postmodern accoutrements, such as a mini keyboard), and its reception by the majority of spectators as 'authentic'. Taylor goes on to show that the documentation of the event provided a doubleness to the performance as it captured the audience responding to the 'authentic' event. The camera seemed to lend legitimacy to the initial performance that viewers may otherwise have seen through.

> Some viewers clearly wanted to believe in the Guatinauis. They longed for authenticity. One dollar was a small price to pay for an encounter with 'real' otherness. The reassuring notion of stable, identifiable, 'real' otherness legitimated fantasies of a real, knowable 'self'.
> (1998: 167)

Taylor positions the performance in the simulated ethnographic cage as a postmodern test of the public's enduring desire to encounter authentic Others.

> They, like many others including myself, really are from nowhereland, really are Guatinauis of sorts, though not in the way their spectators were being asked to believe. For some viewers, the bars actually protected against that realization, marking the radical boundary between the 'here' and the 'there,' the 'us' and the 'them,' allowing for no inter-, no cross-, no trans-cultural-nada. Precolonial subjects, frozen in static essence, didn't experience today's hybrid ethnic and racial identities. The native body was believable, then, not because it was 'real' but precisely because it wasn't.
> (1998: 168)

She asks readers to consider that the 'real' project was the intent to focus on the audience's reactions – such that the audience's performance is the performance we should attend to in analysing the event. This leads to a multiply-sited view in both time and space: of the original cage; its historical precedents; and of the archival documentation of the event alongside the researcher's empirical observations. Taylor's analysis engages with an important concern of performance – its mimetic function. In her evocative description of the exotic fantasy of the couple in the cage, she is concerned with the ways the rhetoric of authenticity helps reinforce pre-existing prejudices by physically and aesthetically staging the boundaries between 'us' and 'them'.[21]

The final example considers a more recent performance of prison that was staged in the United Kingdom in a range of high-profile arts institutions in recent years. This example reflects the issues raised in the prior two examples; namely, the insidious applications of roles and the importance placed on the encounter alongside considerations of authenticity.

As the only example I have witnessed live, it incorporates ethnographic fieldnotes as documentation of my experience. It thus also offers a different model of analysis that propels the argument in the remaining chapters in relation to my own experiences of prison's performance through carceral landscapes.

Ethnographic Witnessing: The Cell Project at the Southbank Centre

In 2010, the organization Rideout, a pioneering company in arts in criminal justice, renowned for their technological gloss on arts participation in prisons, developed a touring project called *The Cell: 'gotojail' Project*. The project situated a simulated prison cell in public places across the United Kingdom (including pedestrian shopping precincts in Birmingham as well as in London's Southbank Centre) in order to demonstrate the conditions of prison to the wider public. In addition to the replica cell being placed in high-traffic areas, Rideout hired two 'prisoners' to inhabit the cell in order for members of the public to interact with them. After their cell visit, audiences were invited to take part in a survey that explores their attitudes to incarceration, and to deliberate on the 'fate' or sentences of the two prisoners. In other words, based on the audience's experience in the cell, they could recommend a longer or shorter sentence, or choose to remove or reinstate various privileges. Obviously, such a 'recommendation' does not have any real-time consequences for the 'prisoners', since they go home each night, having served their term in the cell each day. The invitation for the audience to participate in the 'punishment' of the 'prisoners' is reminiscent of the role of the officers in Zimbardo's experiment in terms of the ways in which audience members ended up being able to 'decide' the fate of these 'prisoners' – albeit in a safe vacuum, free from any real consequences.

The audience is well aware that the 'prisoner'-performers are able to leave the cell at 7pm, when it is locked up. Their decisions are thus enacted in a space of limited ethics, in which their (perhaps very real) opinions on punishment and consequence are not directly performed on the bodies of the two 'prisoners'. Rather, the audience is led to feel their opinions are valued, but they do not have to carry the ethical burden of the consequences of their decisions, unlike the burden we might expect 'real' prison officers, magistrates and the multiple other purveyors of justice to carry. This, then, is in contrast to the audience experience of *Two Undiscovered Amerindians Visit… (The Couple in the Cage)* in which the actions and reactions of spectators did have real consequences. Perhaps this contrast is due to the framing of the performances: Fusco and Gómez-Peña insisted on implicating their audience with a durational, embodied existence in the cage, and the resultant instability of the authenticity claim of the 'savages' that McGuinness explores as 'destabilizing spectators' expectations' (2016: 216).[22] By contrast, the 'gotojail' prisoners were clearly not 'banged up'.[23] The replica cell was staged in a manner that exposed the agenda of the event explicitly through its programme notes and the pushy attendant (aka 'The Governor'). Moreover, there was a sense of pretence that was patronizing – both to the 'prisoner'-performers and to the audience. These two examples raise questions about representation, authenticity and spectatorship.

The replica cell is not just intended to show the living conditions of prison, but to be a simulation of prison life. Two 'prisoners' are in the cell for long stretches of time reading, playing draughts and drinking orange squash. Every move is recorded by CCTV cameras and streamed live on a dedicated website. By the time I stepped into the cell, there were already two conversations happening: the first between Paddy and an older gentleman, and the second between Wayne and two women. I immediately noticed that there was an interesting dynamic in the discussions. The older man was checking the conditions of the cell, evidently surprised at the neat surroundings. He conducted a lively conversation with Paddy on the similarities of the 2-man cell and his air force barracks. He was also concerned to find out that Paddy could not read, and wanted to know whether Wayne read to him. By contrast, the women immediately asked Wayne what his sentence was, and what he had done to get in to prison. They seemed to commiserate with the length of his sentence, leaning forward, trying to work out what to believe (Fieldnotes: 17 October 2011, The Cell: 'gotojail' Project, Southbank Centre).[24]

The performance is staged on several levels that circulate around what Brown calls the 'penal gaze' (2009: 98); first, the situating of the cell in public is itself a kind of intervention in awareness raising about prison conditions, both physical and emotional. Second, the intimacy of engaging with 'real' prisoners is a performative encounter of authenticity. Finally, the audience interaction with the narratives of punishment and reward is a performance, since it engages in changing the sentences for the 'actors'. But there is another level of performance, in which the organization, Rideout, is representing a counter-hegemonic view about punishment designed to engage and challenge public perceptions. These three levels are further explored below by invoking a related incident that demonstrates wider implications for analysing how justice and performance are intertwined.

My experience of the cell was situated within London's Southbank Centre as part of the Koestler Trust's 50th annual Arts by Offenders programme (2011). It is encouraging that an influential arts institution had chosen to support arts in criminal justice for the previous 4 years, lending credibility and cultural capital to the ongoing debate about the value of arts within criminal justice. Yet, there have also been several instances where narratives of 'public acceptability' and the status of the organization have masked, or even obliterated, some of the valuable ground covered by this sector. One instance was when an artwork that had been bought by the Southbank Centre to display in its foyer was subsequently publicized in tabloid newspapers as having been created by a high-profile criminal, alongside lurid details of his crimes. Rather than maintain its support for the value of arts in exploring debates about crime and punishment, the institution chose to remove the artwork. This 'removal' resulted in much discussion amongst arts in criminal justice practitioners and researchers engaged in observing and evaluating projects (Arts Alliance 2011; Rideout 2011).

This removal also has resonances with wider censorship or moral panic in the realm of arts in criminal justice (Walsh 2017). Alongside The Comedy School's removal from HMP Whitemoor (Thompson in McAvinchey 2011b), Prison Service Order 50 (PSO 50) implemented a 'public acceptability test' in order for prison governors to judge how 'the public' would respond to publicity about arts in prisons. The implication was that media coverage of arts would be detrimental and harmful to further opportunities to conduct work, and that such sentiment would be de facto negative. As a result, there was an enormous negative impact on arts in prisons, with prison governors clamping down on perceived 'luxuries' that included arts education. From this example, it is clear that legitimacy is contingent, and that public sentiment leads the decision making about what is visible, and what must remain hidden. The complex machinations of legitimacy in programming of arts venues must also be considered, since the economics of arts audiences are driven by specific sentiments, which, in turn, are influenced by local and specific policies, microeconomics and funding agendas.

In the '*gotojail*' *Project*, Rideout's accompanying information sheet explained that the installation of the cell was a 'public consultation exercise', providing data about the costs of imprisonment to British society, but what was not clear is to what the consultation was meant to contribute. The intention, it seems, was to ensure that the public are exposed to conditions and stories in order to experience incarceration phenomenologically. Yet, as one audience member reflected, 'I would have preferred to have the door closed, so I could feel the claustrophobia. As it was, I felt I could just leave at any moment, and so could these men' (Personal interview, audience, 2011). If the intention of the performance was to provide an embodied experience of imprisonment, then the framing of the performance could have engaged with the rituals of locking up audience members, getting orders from officers or demonstrated a wider sense of affective responses to incarceration than boredom and docility, according to this interviewee. As it was, the site and subject matter itself were made to claim more than the actual experience of the simulated cell. Similar critique is also offered in Brown's discussion of dark tourism in the form of former prisons as hotels (Brown 2009), in which 'the authenticity of punishment is […] rendered further dependent on cultural imaginings, souvenirs and representations of "going to prison"' (2009: 98).

In simulated cells, performance halts at the level of prison semiotics, and does not attempt to foreground the phenomenological potential of carceral subjectivities for participating audience members. Perhaps, in light of the resulting unrest during the Stanford Prison Experiment, the organizers of *The Cell: 'gotojail' Project* chose to 'play safe' by limiting duration. Furthermore, Rideout did not risk overtly political radicalism by avoiding staging the range of dynamics between prisoners and officers. For me, the installation highlighted the chasm between applied theatre approaches and other modes of performance, where the benevolent intention of the work can obscure or justify the outcome (Walsh 2018b, 2019). Brown offers a perspective on the claims of authenticity produced in prison tourism:

> We can see how the penal gaze lays claim to particular effects of truth, how it produces and disciplines particular kinds of subjectivities and subjects […] it conceals key contradictions, uncertainties and alternatives that might otherwise challenge the current practice of punishment.
>
> (2009: 98)

The second level of analysis concerns the authenticity of the encounter, which was in constant flux, as guests to the cell encountered prisoner/actors and used questions to find out just how authentic they were. This strange and interesting line between 'performance' and 'reality' meant that audiences were compelled to reflect upon whether the men were drawing on 'real' prison sentences to perform prisonerhood. Authenticity here may have undermined the very point the simulation was trying to present, by pulling audiences in to encounters with particular people, rather than consider the conditions of the system more generally.

In performance, it seemed as if the men had been given several factors to mention – like student actors in improvisation; and who were duly fitting in multiple 'facts' about prison (low literacy, unfair sentences, harsh punishments) in order to ensure the audience understood what being in prison is like. Yet, these factors are also a matter of perspective: what is a 'fair sentence'? Who decides? And why would we trust a prisoner to tell 'the truth' about prisons? In relation to the problem of authenticity, I further wondered whether these character histories were drawn from the 'performers' themselves, or whether they were fictional. If the performers were representing their own stories, it would be necessary to re-frame their participation in relation to audience reactions that may fall outside a liberal paradigm precisely because of the 'penal gaze' discussed by Brown (2009). Prison narratives are so often perpetuated through re-telling petty injustices that seem of major importance to the prisoners concerned, but which take on a different hue when interrogated by the wider public who may feel outraged at the thought that prison in the United Kingdom is like a 'holiday camp' (Carrabine 2012; Jewkes 2007), with access to comforts such as toasters, kettles, televisions and play-stations. The presence of the public in the simulated cell raised questions about victims of crime, although these narratives were largely invisible in the staging.

Towards the end of this first visit, another couple entered the cell and started trying to ask many questions about the fairness of the sentence. There was a sense they were 'testing' the prisoners to see whether their responses confirmed the moral position of the questioner. This paradox seemed to me to be at the heart of the project: confirming a pre-existing moral position that punishment is harsh but crime is wrong. However, the project did not pose questions about who decides what crime is, which is a particularly key tenet of feminist and critical approaches to criminology (Brown 2009; McAvinchey 2011b).

When I went to visit the cell for the second time, I met Paddy on the threshold. He was not captured by the CCTV camera's live feed, and felt able to speak frankly/slipping between the 'performance' and his current reality post-release. We spoke of his 8-year involvement with Synergy Theatre Company. When the 'governor' came back after some time, she was carrying take-away tea. She gave an insight into the project, and there was a comic interplay with the tea and the power dynamic of the 'governor' serving the 'prisoners' their tea. I started to feel as if the 5 hours a day spent by these performers is still quite a 'sentence': having to repeat and repeat the banal 'truths' of prison mixed in with semi-autobiographical 'facts' and some fictions is a tough gig for any actor, but for ex-prisoners, there must be more machinations than are immediately visible as they do time in the simulated cell (Fieldnotes: 20 October 2011, *The Cell: 'gotojail' Project*, Southbank Centre).

The final level of analysing how audiences engaged in punishment and reward trickles through the fieldnotes. The accounts of my visit to the cell in the Southbank Centre provoke questions about the ways in which institutions perform within a wider discourse of governmentality, and may be seen within the general performance trend of exploring the dramaturgies of the real (Megson and Forsythe 2009). The first example in the genealogy is a well-known psychology experiment that confirms the cultural expectations that the cell itself performs a function in rendering human natures extreme, violent and oppositional (authority vs subject). In other words, prison cells reinforce their projected meaning by both reinforcing and furthering the performances of prisoners and officers. By working through the three examples, shifting from the decidedly non-public psychology experiment that has nevertheless gained public visibility, through to the ironic postcolonial cage of *Two Undiscovered Amerindians Visit…* and thence to a public awareness campaign that stages a cell, I evoke the repetitious force of the 'cage' as analogous to the cell, in which spectres of slavery, ownership, the spectacle of bodies at labour and the construction of simulation render the prison cell a cage. The accounts reflect a concern with the ways in which transient carceral landscapes hold a powerful iconographic position in the Western cultural imagination. Seen together, the three performance moments open space for arguments about the spectacle of punishment and the ambiguously reassuring comfort (or catharsis) that 'Othering' can offer. In each of the examples, the insidious distinctions of those with agency to view the Others are performed by staging differences between 'public', 'officer' and 'prisoner', between the bodies of those inside and those outside the cage. The performances highlight the implicit and explicit powers granted to those that view and those that are viewed. This reading of the simulations as performance offers a sense then of what is afforded by the labour of the cell or the cage in public.

A further example of a simulated prison cell was created by artist Jai Redman, in *This is Camp X-Ray* (Jai Redman, 2003). The site-based work (simulated cells transposed into a field in Manchester) aimed to get spectators and participants to contemplate conditions in Guantanamo Bay (Shaughnessy 2012; Nevitt 2013: 66–68; Thompson et al. 2009: 298–301). This simulation was explicitly political, and anti-war in intention. In a rather generous view, carceral geographer Moran suggests that prison cell simulations, or 'transient carceral landscapes,' can help to stimulate debate about prison conditions, and the purpose of incarceration, and also about the agency of prisoners in these spaces, and the unexpected and ingenious ways in which they engage with and beyond them (Moran 2012: online).

While opening debates about these concerns through performance replicas is legitimate, my own argument positions the aesthetic framing of the simulated cells as important. For me, the cell performs a cultural function in its context (in the art gallery, or in public space). By inviting the public to constitute an audience to 'prison', and in particular, in the ways in which the bodies of the incarcerated are displayed, the simulated cell enacts a performance function that we might see as cathartic. Such catharsis is inevitably related to conservative public sentiment, and does not provoke radical or revisionist responses. A politicized reading of these three examples might turn on the effectiveness of the spectacle (Kershaw 2003). Cathartic framing diminishes the urgency of such spectacle.

The Aristotelian notion that catharsis restores emotions to their 'correct' place is performed in tragedies with the 'removal' of the protagonist from the stage, allowing the audience to come to some privileged knowledge of the ways in which the protagonist's hubris has led, inexorably, to his/her downfall. The tragic form historically aimed to indicate which behaviours were acceptable and which were not, which people counted as human (*anthropos*) and who did not. In other words, the convention of tragedy sets up clear distinctions between inside and outside, right and wrong.[25] Simulations of prison cells position the public/audience as a homogenous series of witnesses – sharing similar political viewpoints. Such simulations are often more revealing about the audience/public than they are about the 'caged subjects'. Indeed, it is not merely the passive omniscient spectatorship posited by the panopticon that is underway in these simulations, but the very participation in the caging, questioning, observing, and sometimes taking on of roles as officers or prisoners that is valuable in transient carceral landscapes. This suggests that, rather than submit to the critical view I have already posited above, simulated cells allow for valuable representations of how publics engage ethically and aesthetically with the site and the bodies of the incarcerated subjects. The powerful cultural tropes of prison *as* performance set the ground for arguing how and why cultural and aesthetic representations of prison must be attended to, even when seemingly problematic. This promotes a rethinking of prison spaces as producing specific subjectivities, both resulting from architectural operations of power through visibility (see Foucault), and the everyday performances of officers and prisoners. The three specific examples are seen as genealogical. Simulated prison cells not only perform a specific cultural function, producing a public awareness of prison conditions (see Moran), but also reinforce limiting dynamics of 'the public' audience as outside/guest to the cell. The prisoner as subject of the gaze is rendered marginalized.

In turn, the argument seeks to propose alternative, critical and reflexive performance methodologies that consciously unpick such issues in a departure from the examples of always already co-opted applied theatre practices, which are problematized in the next chapter. Seeking to move beyond the panoptic model of spectatorship as the primary critical tool, I have also drawn on the emerging discourse on transient carceral landscapes that provide audiences specific political encounters with the implications of incarceration. Ethics are staged, framed by the aesthetic choices of the artists, and foregrounded when the radical injustices of racialized and gendered discrimination are acknowledged. The examples I analyse offer valuable critical texture for later chapters, whereby the thresholds between viewing, being and knowing about prison spaces are translated into and through performance and popular media.

What is consistent in this investigation is the critical lens on the interplay of power and agency, resistance and desire in order to articulate the consequences of looking at prison *as* performance. I offer a new perspective that shifts the thinking of prison/theatre as merely reflecting performance qualities but actually engaging with moral/spatial/juridical and agential performances brought to bear by the prison. Most specifically, this reading relies on the crossing of interdisciplinary boundaries as I foreground the concerns raised by feminist criminology. It is precisely the critical interest in the production of the subject that is common in both criminology and performance studies. Although these examples from three distinct approaches are not specifically about women in prison, they nevertheless enable a theory of the prison *as* performance to be considered. Later chapters attend specifically to the meanings, impacts and implications for women in prison.

By thinking through prison *as* performance, we can move beyond reflecting on institutional values as a result of a stimulating theatre production, or performance/simulation. What is made possible in the genealogy is a more nuanced consideration of tragic containment, and how that is reproduced in simulations, replica cells that are explicitly staged in public – that is – outside the theatrical framing of stages or arts institutions. Yet, McAvinchey (2011a) has laid out some valuable critical questions relating to the ways we should approach the subject of carceral institutions through performance. She stresses that while theatre about prison has historically encouraged new ways of thinking about incarceration, there are several concerns that arise. She says:

> Thinking about theatre and prison provokes an inquiry into the relationship between the individual and the state, forcing us to consider how prisons perform within the economy of punishment, and compelling us to question narratives of crime, punishment and justice that are believed to be true and effective.
>
> (2011a: 3)

Replicating the conditions, duration and risks of incarceration via simulation provides experiences of the values and economies of punishment, rather than its thematic treatment in contemporary performance. Thus, having analysed prison *as* performance, the remainder of the argument engages with specific practices of performance *in* and *about* prisons. This is done in order to identify existing power structures so that we might ask of performance whether it reinforces, obscures or challenges the 'distribution of power and how it is used in contexts beyond the performance' (Nevitt 2013: 39). These questions about how social or public attitudes to crime and punishment are culturally constructed have been well trodden in relation to (mainly film and television) media.[26] In particular, Jewkes (2007) raises concerns about how fictional representations of institutions reinforce the construction of prisoners as mediated 'Others', and beyond our compassion, by showing which techniques are used to 'make some of the most punitive actions seem both ordinary and acceptable' (cited in Carrabine 2012: 69).

Themes of crime and punishment have been explored in a vast range of genres, most of which perpetuate the imaginary of prisons as a moral vacuum, prisoners as deservedly tormented or surprisingly triumphant in their resistance against the penal 'machine' (Carrabine 2012: 65; Wilson and O'Sullivan 2004). By contrast, theatre practitioners who work within prisons tend towards two positions: the first position is a radical one that seeks to 'apply' the arts as a means of 'empowering' (Digard and Liebling 2012), or 'giving voice' to an excluded and socially marginal group (Caulfield 2010, 2011; Escape Artists 2006). The importance of applied work thus lies in the possibilities it opens up for witnessing and the notion of transformation or even 'reformation' (McAvinchey 2011a: 3). The second position replicates the inscriptions of domination of the institution by targeting the change to the concomitant institutional values. Yet, all too often, the power inferred in claims of transformation is left under-examined by applied theatre practitioners, not least because, in the most part, applied theatre practices are disseminated through project reports about 'successes'.[27] This means that there is an underlying agenda in such sources to gain further access, to acquire more funding and to prove effectiveness.[28] Next, I investigate models of performance in prison (applied theatre) by troubling some of the assumptions that performance in the site of prison can be practised outside of its informing dynamics of control and punishment.

Notes

1. I am grateful to R. Justin Hunt for this formulation that emerged through a dialogue at Critical Encounters at the University of Lincoln, 20 January 2014.
2. I am drawing on J. Hillis Miller's (2007) eccentric unravelling of the differences between Austin's speech act performativity, Butler's notion of performativity and the Derridean. For a further reading of the performativity of the law in relation to speech acts, see Theron Schmidt (2010). A particular theorization of performativity, trauma and rehabilitation is explored in an article entitled 'I've stood at so many windows' (Walsh 2018a).
3. For a particularly rich examination of the performance of punishment, see Thompson (2004a). Paul Khan's evocative account of legal performance and the imagination of sovereignty is also noteworthy (2006).
4. The transient carceral landscape relates to the transportation and mobility of punitive measures of control. See also the edited collection by Moran et al. (2013). Examples include prison vans, temporary holding cells, etc.
5. Throughout these considerations, I have foregrounded a feminist concern with the subjective positionality of female bodies, rather than bodies in general, in order to ensure that women's double marginalization is always attended to in the research. Chouliaraki's (2008) work on the spectacle of suffering has been valuable in this regard.
6. In the surveillance society, the panopticon has been translated into constant surveillance through CCTV imagery and biometric data. Mahjid Yar's (2003) excellent exegesis about the pathologization of surveillance is instructive in this regard.
7. The rack is a torture device that aims to stretch out the body, pulling limb from limb. The person being tortured is tethered to the rack, and the tethers are tightened by turning a wheel. This is discussed in Foucault's discussion on the spectacle of the scaffold (1977: 32–69). The relation to spectacle and spectatorship is furthered in relation to Baz Kershaw's work 'Curiosity or contempt: On spectacle, the human, and activism' (2003), and Conquergood's

excellent engagement with the death penalty in the United States (2002b) 'Performance, punishment, and the death penalty'. See also Lizzie Seal's account of historic imagined communities and the death penalty in the United Kingdom (2014).

8 Several examples of prison literature as well as reflexive practitioner research make account of these rhythms of daily life. Many of them do not escape dualities and perpetuate a victimized narrative of prison life (Graney 2004, 2006; James 2003; Lamb 2007; Levi and Waldman 2011). Throughout this research, I maintain that this tendency returns prisoners to a marginal position. Instead, prisoners writing autobiographical work and artists working in a range of media with prisoners could and should engage with a broader spectrum of focus that engages not merely with prisoner as object and institution as omniscient. The work of Grant and Crossan (2012), for example, serves to decouple discourses of legitimacy from the institution. Carrabine also furthers engagement with narrative (2012) and image (2016) in relation to the criminological imagination. In Walsh and Tsilimpounidi (2016), this is explored in a performance poem about neo-liberalism and institutions.

9 A recent controversial example of this is South African director Brett Bailey's *Exhibit A, B* and *C* series that stage the postcolonial body as object. (See for example Krueger 2013; Larlham 2009; Third World Bunfight 2012; Vlachos 2013.) These scholars appear to support Bailey's claims to be mounting the *tableaux vivants* as human zoo in an apparent attempt to subvert the power of the Western gaze. By contrast, performance scholar Mader McGuinness reads the performance against the *Couple in the Cage* by Fusco and Gómez-Peña as replicating racist ideologies and staging Black pain for consumption by a presumed white audience's gaze. She says, that unlike Bailey, Fusco and Gómez-Peña

> played with historical objectification of colonised bodies while blurring their original meaning through destabilising spectators' expectations completely. Both artists' critique of the form of 'authentic displays' themselves opens up their work in such a way that highlights the broader implications of racist objectification, rather than using Bailey's strategy of displaying its symptoms, however brutal. Moreover, Fusco and Gómez-Peña's playfulness points towards a disidentificatory practice. Following Muñoz's definition of the term, dis- identification is a strategy through which people of colour, and other subaltern people, engage with damaging representations as victims of these representations, which does not elide their 'harmful' [Muñoz, 1999: 12] or contradictory components.
> (McGuinness 2016: 216)

10 In particular, this can be seen in the works about photography and capturing atrocity such as Peggy Phelan's work on Abu Ghraib photographs (2009), following Sontag's (2004) concern with how aesthetic framing reinforces the imaginary of nationhood and civic responsibility. Taylor et al. (2002) reflect specifically on the manner in which performance attends to these matters. The philosophical implications of this are furthered in Judith Butler's works *Precarious Life* (2004) and *Frames of War* (2009).

11 Loïc Wacquant explores ghettoization in *Punishing the Poor* (2009b) and *Urban Outcasts* (2008b).

12 Also fruitfully discussed by Jennifer Turner (2013, 2016, 2017).

13 Chapter One describes Goffman's thinking about total institutions – which include asylums, some special hospitals and boarding schools, for example. However, I am particularly focusing on the impacts he notes about involuntary incarceration in institutions.
14 I am aware that the characterization of prisoners as 'protagonists' is troublesome from a purely theatrical perspective (in which protagonists are always singular and the focus of the dramatic action). Yet, my argument seeks ways of understanding that individual prisoners are of course protagonists in their everyday lives, and that the agency understood by 'protagonists' ought to be restored to prisoners and ex-prisoners so that they are not merely incidental characters in others' grand narratives.
15 For example, Brett Bailey's *Exhibit B*, introduced above, was staged in Brussels, Berlin and Amsterdam. The work staged ethnographic museum exhibits that highlighted the colonial legacies of occupations. It has both received widespread critical acclaim for its empowerment of marginalized 'Others' as well as protests against its replications of racism. For more information, see Third World Bunfight (2012) and McGuinness (2016).
16 I am aware of the problematic use of 'we' in relation to assumed responses, but I am complying with the original formulation of the findings as presented by Haney et al. (1973). Despite 'failing' as an experiment since it was abandoned earlier than anticipated, the findings are presented as if they are generalizable.
17 The Stanford Prison Experiment inspired books and films such as the acclaimed German film *Das Experiment* (2001), based on the novel *Black Box* by Mario Giordano (1999).
18 As Wacquant's body of work shows, there is a contemporary concern with over-representation of racial minorities in prisons (in both the United States and the United Kingdom). The Stanford Prison Experiment's distinct lack of factors relating to race and class means that the experiment was not biased by pre-existing inequalities or power dynamics, and was thus also limited in scope (2002, 2005, 2008b, 2009a, 2009b, 2010b).
19 Antonio Gramsci's use of the term 'subaltern' was originally defined in relation to the proletariat in prisons under fascist rule, and his understanding was that an autonomous political subjectivity should be possible (Gramsci 1971). In this analysis, Spivak's definition of subaltern is considered more apt, since, she argues, 'subaltern' is 'the structured place from which the capacity to predicate is radically obstructed' (Morris 2010: 7). Spivak's seminal essay 'Can the subaltern speak?' sought to rebut the views of theorists such as Foucault and Deleuze, whose thinking presupposed that 'the oppressed, if given the chance … and on the way to solidarity through alliance politics … *can speak and know their conditions*' (1988: 25, original emphasis). For Spivak, this line of thinking results in the problem of essentializing experiences with a normative and homogenizing tendency. Rather, the 'subaltern' is multiple and varied, and can be understood as those who are denied access to both mimetic and political forms of representation.
20 For example, the performers wore hybrid costumes that incorporated 'native' attire as well as boots. They were given laptops and piano keyboards to play with. The hyper-satirical contradiction of capitalist postmodern aesthetics vs re-appropriated traditional ethnic objects and attire has been furthered in the work of La Pocha Nostra (Fusco 2000, 2001; Gómez-Peña 2000, 2005, 2008; Gómez-Peña and Wolford 2002).

21 Such stark divisions recall the argument made by Raymond Williams who writes of 'continuity' (2006: 37).
22 McGuinness notes:

> [W]hile playing with representations of authenticity, such as a form of native dress of their imagined South-American tribe, [they] also made use of sun glasses, cigarettes, a computer, Coca-Cola bottles, and other signifiers of contemporaneity. The doubling up of historical fact with idiosyncratic elements blocked any possible ascription of exotic authenticity to the couple. Rather than simply re-enacting the fact of colonial human displays, however sublimated, Fusco and Gómez-Peña's approach to the brutal nature of the colonisation of the Americas also critiqued, through its idiosyncratic aesthetics, the Western desire to access this type of 'savage authenticity'.
>
> (2016: 216)

23 'Banged up' is UK prison slang that means being locked behind doors/bars.
24 I am using the character names provided in the programme note rather than choosing to anonymize them, since this was a public performance.
25 This deliberately echoes Agamben's formulation on bare life (1998), along with Butler's discussions on whose life counts as grievable (2009). I take forward these notions in relation to philosopher Achille Mbembe's formulation of 'necropolitics' (2003) in Chapter Four.
26 For an excellent overview of the spectacle of punishment and the criminological imagination in contemporary cultural forms, see Carrabine (2012, 2014, 2015, 2016). For other views that develop the field of cultural criminology, see Brown (2009); Carlen (2002); Cecil (2007a, 2007b, 2015); Cheliotis (2012a); Chesney-Lind (1999); Chesney-Lind and Irwin (2008); Ferrell and Sanders (1995); Rafter (2014); Rafter and Brown (2011); Valier (2004).
27 The National Criminal Justice Arts Alliance has made a significant contribution to getting an evidence library archived and accessible to the wider public. Yet, its contents are largely reports and evaluations that disseminate practice outcomes and thus tend to remain reportage rather than critical or informed by research inquiry.
28 McAvinchey writes that the professionalization of the arts over the past two decades has led to arts contracts that are intended to service 'specific programmes of work which delivered pre-identified aims and objectives aligned to those of the prison service and wider government concerns' (2011a: 77). This is problematic in relation to how projects are valued – see New Philanthropy Capital (2011). I explore this in the 'Critical introduction to arts behind bars' (Walsh 2017). A more politicized consideration of arts, emotional/affective labour in the context of applied theatre practices prison is made in 'What works' (Walsh 2019).

Chapter Three

Trauma, Strategies and Tactics: Problems of Performance in Prison

Applied Theatre in UK Prisons

Having done time as a creative artist and researcher (though never as an inmate), I have come to know prison's regimes, noises, smells and sudden shifts in atmosphere intimately. Despite having my own experiences as a worker navigating the institution, I may never fully appreciate the institution and its impacts on those who reside there. Since I first entered prisons for a community arts project in South Africa in 2002, I have been reminded often that there is a lot that can be learned in institutions and by paying attention to its operations and dispositions. In one freelance project, I facilitated creative workshops with Clean Break Theatre Company, and this vignette serves to introduce some of the key tensions in this practice.

The incident concerns one of the moments of tension between performance and the institution. The play *Missing Out* (Mary Cooper, 2009) is about a young woman who makes a series of choices when she doesn't return to prison after a day release and ends up at her mother's house trying to convince her to look after her child. The performance is staged to about 30 women in the morning, and in the afternoon, I facilitate a theatre-based workshop with cast and prisoners about the themes in the play, in which we develop scenes about making alternative choices at various moments in the story. Most of the women are particularly clear about the protagonist needing to have respect for the mother character, and help her identify alternatives to flying into a rage. They criticize her for stealing £20 from her mum's kitchen. They seem to have internalized all kinds of tactics for solving conflicts. The team seem pretty smug when we are told that one of the women who engaged brilliantly in a scene with the daughter character is extremely 'hard-to-reach' with severe mental health problems. After we have done a congratulatory ceremony with participation certificates, the women go back to their dorms, and the company prepares to dismantle the enormous set and get back on the road. As we are ticking off every bolt on our inventory, I realize that the (fake) £20 note has gone. One of our participants had decided to take it back to the dorm, even though hard currency has no purchasing power in prison. I am obliged to report it as a breach of security (Practitioner Fieldnotes: 2008).

In order to render some of the issues related to performance in prison more visible, I view prison *as* performance since it stages the separation and reformation of characters judged to have offended the public. Its presence in the public imaginary reinforces the social need for order, security and the restoration of 'good' over 'bad'. Such plot points are overly simplistic, rendering social and political inequalities as backstories rather than structural informants of plot, characterization and the aesthetics of performance praxis. If, as proposed by cultural criminology (Carrabine 2012; Presdee 2000), prison cultures are so fascinating to the wider public because of the allure of what remains hidden and invisible, then a focus on the kinds of applied practices that occur within prisons is valuable. This allows a focus on what problems are raised when theatre in particular (concerned with seeing, and making evident) is applied in the context of prisons.

Although I am drawing on over fifteen years of my own theatre and writing practice in prisons, in both South Africa and the United Kingdom, I am not discussing my own theatre practice here. There are several reasons for this, including a growing ambivalence about claims for efficacy in the arts in criminal justice (Walsh 2017). Since radical practice would seek to dis-articulate power structures, the demands of sanctioned entry into a secure institution invites complicity with its narratives. This places a certain pressure on the project to maintain awareness of the multiple ways in which its own formulation and practices embody and apply coercion, domination and erasure. Kershaw writes that 'anyone who ventures into prisons to "do" performance is, initially at least, bound to seem to the inmates to be party to the authorship of their oppression' (1999: 133). The examples discussed here are thus from two established significant UK organizations Clean Break Theatre Company and Geese Theatre Company. This research develops from the understanding that there is an epistemological potential in analysing performance *in* and *of* prison, and so, in this chapter, my analysis of performance in prison considers the operations of ethical and aesthetic framing of the prison, prisoners' agency and the socio-economic context in which arts in prisons are conducted.

It may be understandable that artists and writers create songs, plays and write scripts or novels about prisons, due to the pleasures or enjoyment of transgression (as discussed by Presdee 2000), or the particular drama of life inside. The use of the arts inside prisons is not a new phenomenon, even though it is not often as visible in terms of cultural production. The term 'applied performance' or 'applied theatre' when it is used here is deployed precisely because it is an umbrella term that does not, in itself, signal a particular aesthetic mode. It is merely a means of signalling an intent that practitioners are creating within a particular context, and often with a focus on the artistic processes rather than outcomes for the wider public. As Mojisola Adebayo (2015) points out, the term 'applied' erases the specificity of intentions in different modes of performance making. Applied theatre's claims often also circulate around 'change' and 'transformation', in which the practitioners use theatre-based processes in order to rehearse or articulate desires for change.[1] Thus I often use 'prison theatre' to distinguish the particular expertise managing both aesthetic and institutional demands required in the context.

The arts in criminal justice is a growing field, with practices across artforms in a range of countries – some focused on offending behaviour (Balfour 2003, 2004; Mountford and Farrall 1998; Thompson 1999), some aligned with education and literacy (Trounstine 2004; Young-Jahangeer 2013), or on self-expression (Hughes 1998; Sutherland 2013, 2015). Other practitioners focus on producing performance outcomes (such as Curt Tofteland's

'Shakespeare Behind Bars'; 'The Medea Project', Warner 2001, 2004), or Paul Heritage's 'Staging Human Rights' project (1998, 2002, 2004). I have explored elsewhere (Walsh 2017) how the arts behind bars are usually driven by a belief in the arts as a unique way into education or else the particular value of arts-based processes as a therapeutic methodology.

In the preceding chapter, I put forward that prisons perform their functions in relation to society, under the remit of interpretations of the law. Incarcerated women may well be guilty of crimes, but they are also disproportionately punished for transgressing norms of appropriate feminine behaviours. Prisons in the United Kingdom attempt to address this inequality by (at least in principle) creating gender-sensitive programmes in order to 'succeed' in reducing re-offending. This turn follows the Corston report's findings that women's prisons were characterized by inappropriate conditions and programmes that did not adequately address the needs of women (2007, 2011). There is much more that can be done to address the particular needs relating to housing, maintaining familial bonds, engaging with addictions and ensuring there are intersectional programmes that enable women to build resilience for resettlement.

This chapter provides an account of performance processes in prisons by making the link between often-hidden experiences of aesthetic process and the wider political conditions that sometimes get erased when discussing specific interventions. In my reading of two examples of applied theatre practice from the United Kingdom, I depart from the status quo in scholarship about applied theatre practice, in that I do not attempt to explain or justify the relevance of a particular methodology of praxis, but rather, construct a critical argument about prison cultures that is rooted in a feminist criminological approach. That is, the analysis re-positions the women participants as the focus of investigation, rather than as explanatory reference points about a practice or intervention.

Before turning to the specific values of applied theatre practice, it is worth reiterating the politicized function of theatre and performance. Janelle Reinelt says that theatres might be considered spaces that are

> patronized by a consensual community of citizen-spectators who come together at stagings of the social imaginary in order to consider and experience affirmation, contestation, and reworking of various material and discursive practices pertinent to the constitution of a democratic society.
>
> (1998: 286)

In the case of performance processes in prisons, such 're-workings' of the various practices relating to the development of a functioning society happen within a tightly controlled environment, in which the material and discursive practices are always already marked out by prevailing logics of 'good behaviour' and 'readiness for the community'. While Reinelt's point is about the role of formal theatre in constituting part of the public sphere (a point also made by Balme 2012), the applied theatre examples discussed here are nevertheless contested practices.[2] This is due to their uneasy 'siting' between discourses of 'healing', 'transformation' and 'catharsis' that tend to fit alongside whatever funding agenda gains prominence in shifting cultural and economic landscapes (see Hughes 2005b; Thompson 2011a, 2011b). There is nevertheless an important consideration of performance processes as a production of social imaginary, in which, as Reinelt has asserted, the relevance of performance is as a site 'of democratic struggle where antagonisms are aired and considered, and where the voluntary citizenry, the audience, deliberates on matters of state in an aesthetic mode' (1998: 289).

This necessitates a turn from the wider context in which we understand prisons *as* performance, to consider some of the arts-based programming in prisons that often contributes to the institutional agenda. As such, applied theatre practices are considered from a critical perspective, while recognizing that their impacts and benefits may well be meaningful for women participants during and immediately after the sessions. However, my critique is largely predicated on the unstable and un-sustainable practices that characterize performance in prisons. It is worth noting that my intention is not to solely critique these projects but to use them as cultural productions that help clarify some of the wider theoretical considerations in the book. My own background in the arts in criminal justice contexts and particular focus on practice in the United Kingdom serves as a basis for the tensions I explore in this chapter.[3]

Without neglecting the wide range of applied theatre practices within prisons in the United Kingdom, it is important to note the significance of the two companies I discuss here, both of which have sustained different modes of practices over decades. The discussion centres on two main examples, namely Geese Theatre's *Journey Woman* (2009) and Clean Break's *There are Mountains* (2012). Both are significant forms of applied theatre practice that can nonetheless be examined critically in service of the book's main argumentation about desire and resistance. These two examples are chosen as a means of illustrating the major problems I identify in the practice of performance work in the context of the institution. These are the problem of 'giving voice', the problems of testimony and of witnessing and the problem of evidence. While I have termed these 'problems' this does not mean I am signalling critical issues in the practices, but productive issues that reflect some of the wider discourses in applied theatre. In other words, the examples protrude outwards offering a means of problematizing wider practice, rather than being, in themselves, problematic. These interrelated problems form the structure of the chapter; and I engage with some of the key concepts of trauma theory in order to respond to these concerns. Yet, while trauma theory provides valuable terminologies for interrogating these problems, I engage them critically, as Thompson (2011a) does. This is necessary in the field of a penal institution, because the therapeutic or rehabilitative aim of catharsis through testimony is not unproblematic (Adebayo 2015).

By means of placing performance practices into conversation with theoretical concerns, the bulk of the chapter examines applied theatre practices in relation to the model 'victim–survivor–hero'. A Bourdieusian concern with habitus and field proves productive in working through how performance practices operate in prison. The notion of 'durable dispositions' that are nevertheless malleable corresponds with the sense that theatre processes in prisons are often used in the service of what Jenny Hughes (somewhat simplistically) defines as a number of benefits, or impacts. These range from 'increased self-confidence to transferable skills – which can help divert people away from pathways to crime or break the cycle of re-offending' (2005a: 8). In order to consider the measures that are integral to performance practices in prisons, it is necessary to unpack some of the troubling elements of 'measurement' in relation to criminality.

Resisting 'Measures': Refusing Legibility

Cesare Lombroso's nineteenth-century anthropometric investigation into what constitutes 'female offenders' serves as an opening trope to this chapter in order to assert the trouble of research in prisons. Lombroso's scientific research aimed to construct a taxonomy of criminal bodies by learning how to read the 'living documents' contained in prisons as what he called 'palimpsest in reverse' (cited in Horn 1995: 113). His claim, according to Horn, was that if 'read correctly' the body-as-text 'yielded up its submerged truths: the signs of degeneration and atavism' (1995: 113). His methodology, underpinned by biological determinism, included pictorial representations of criminals' characteristics as well as detailed measurements of facio-cranial details. The study of female criminals was constructed against imagery of 'normal women' (with no such counterpart in his taxonomy of male criminality), in order that the 'female offender might become distinct, visible, and legible' (1995: 115). Horn's insight into Lombroso demonstrates the 'difficulty, if not impossibility, of any reliable readings of the deceptive female body' (1995: 120).

Lombroso and Ferrero write 'the child-like defects of the semi-criminal are neutralized by piety, maternity, want of passion, sexual coldness, weakness and undeveloped intelligence' (1895: 151). Seen together, their images of deviant women do not form a coherent story about what constitutes a female criminal, instead suggesting that *all* women demonstrate some of the characteristics they identify in the deviant bodies. Horn shows that Lombroso merely pathologizes women in general, remarking that 'the normal [sic] woman […] embodied potential criminality […] [and was] constructed as both normal in her pathology and pathological in her normality' (1995: 121). Horn continues to suggest that such a construction reinforced women as suitable objects for continued surveillance and 'corrective interventions that, in an effort to restrict 'opportunities' for criminality, blurred the lines between penal practices and social work' (1995: 121). While criminology has certainly moved away from biological determinism, its legacies can be felt in the enduring arguments that seem to hold that certain women commit certain types of crimes (Kruttschnitt and Gartner 2008; Richie 2004).[4] The remnants of the measures of control are still evident in the United Kingdom's current system and pervade both practices and research in prisons. This rather condensed overview of the historical study of women in prison is positioned at this point in the chapter in order to raise a warning against the tendencies in research studies to attempt to develop neat taxonomies: lists of characteristics that define and delineate what constitutes 'offenders'. This same tendency arises in several of the documents of theatre practices in prison – a danger that it seems to me relates to the desire for arts practices to assert their legitimacy in the space of the institution (Balfour 2003; Kanter 2007a). Lombroso's investigation re-surfaces later in the chapter in order to trouble the dominant scholarly practices in the field of applied arts in criminal justice settings. By means of introducing some of the methodological implications of arts-based programmes in a prison context, I sketch out some overlapping fields of concern in both performance and research practices in the criminal justice system.

The Bromley Briefings reported that the prison population is approaching the highest annual figure ever recorded in England and Wales – at 85,556, having risen 82 per cent in the last 30 years (2017: 12).[5] The Anne Peaker Centre's *Handbook for Artists* (Peaker and Johnston 2007) draws on this context of overcrowding and poor conditions. It explores the practicalities of working in custodial and correctional settings, particularly providing arguments for a variety of art forms as methods. Hughes' overview of arts practices in prisons in the United Kingdom examines the many issues identified as threats to arts delivery in prevention, in secure settings and in re-integration contexts, namely the lack of professional best practice and standards in the sector, and the 'roles within the administration and implementation of the intervention' (2005a: 51). She also considers the need to justify the use of arts in a system aimed towards reducing offending, and the issues of 'proof of effectiveness' that have elsewhere been shown to be difficult to quantify (Belfiore 2002; Matarasso 1997). This has particularly been the case within the system of attainment targets that pervades education and correctional services, under stress from government to respond to reduction of numbers, and without budget or resources to support the facilitation of 'soft skills'. Hughes' contention is that the research practice around theatre in prisons is weak, and asserts the need for technical and conceptual review, but acknowledges that the reflexivity of many theatre practitioners working in prisons is valuable in developing theories of change within this context (2005a: 9–11).[6] She also sees criminal justice as a foundation for the UK (New Labour) 'government's drive to tackle social exclusion' (2005a: 13). She says:

> The arts are seen as an effective response to the need to innovatively engage offenders, many of whom have had negative experiences of formal education, in learning experiences. The arts are seen as an effective means of re-engaging disaffected groups and bringing about a state of 'readiness to learn' through the development of self-esteem and basic personal and social skills.
>
> (2005a: 39)

Interestingly, Hughes' study of arts practice in the criminal justice settings includes a section of 'impact on the institution' (2005a: 38–39). She suggests, having reviewed the sector, that arts provision reduce 'disciplinary problems and violence in prisons' (2005a: 39). However,

Figure 3: Production Shot, *Sweatbox*. Produced by Clean Break, 2016.

as in Heritage's view, the focus is not on how the art form may seek to transform the institution, but how it may collude within its structures of power, 'reducing rule-breaking' (2005a: 38) and institutionalizing inmates further by making them compliant – more 'docile' (Foucault 1977). This view is rarely considered in a critical way by artists writing about their own practice – perhaps because of the precarity and marginality of arts discourses, which seem to be concerned with positivistic accounts rather than reflexive accounts. Yet, this raises some important points regarding the ethics of arts practice in prisons, particularly in connection to the expansion of considering representation beyond what Phelan calls the 'traps of visibility' (1993: 10) in relation to performance. Similarly, but from a sociology of imprisonment perspective, Matthews writes of the spectacle of suffering that historically warned the public of the hellish connotations of crime. He says 'culprits were expected to show repentance and to confess their crimes before the assembled crowd. Public confessions were often the route to a quick and relatively painless death' (1999: 2). He claims that after the public forms of torture and humiliation of the eighteenth and nineteenth centuries, outlined by Foucault, 'punishment was required to be more universal and to penetrate more deeply into the social body if it was to create a docile and responsive workforce' (1999: 12).

In light of the relationship between spectacle and punishment, James Thompson (2003) entreats practitioners to avoid the performance of punishment that pervades the context of prisons, and thus casts a shadow on any performance-based project in prisons asking for whom is the performance intended, and how will the prisoners be viewed? He says that we need to examine 'how our performances relate to other performances of punishment and check that they do not display prisoners to the further delight and voyeuristic pleasure of the crowd' (2003: 57). Sketching the morally ambiguous terrain of arts practitioners working in prisons, Heritage asks, 'in entering the prisons, do we seek to create that tranquillity or inspire the rebellion?' (1998: 234). In a further provocation, he says that

> [t]heatre has never had an easy time within the prison system and yet it seems very appropriate to prison. Perhaps the performative nature of punishment and the necessary tension between the hidden and the public, which prisons depend on, makes them natural sites for theatre interventions.
>
> (2004: 97)

It is precisely this compelling interplay between performance, power and the public that informs this theorization of prison cultures.

Mapping the Problems of Applied Arts in Prisons[7]

Arts behind bars are not immune to the pressures and tensions faced by other charitable endeavours, and in the United Kingdom, arts have faced increased scrutiny on their intentions and outcomes. This is in light of both controversies (such as PSO 50 discussed in the preceding chapter) and increased demands for 'results'. In criminological research in the United Kingdom, the focus has turned to an assessment of 'what works', in recent years and, under the current government, a programme of 'payment by results' (Arts Alliance 2011; McNeill et al. 2010). In a discussion elsewhere on the affective labour of applied theatre practices (Walsh 2019), while the question 'what works?' makes sense in relation to overcrowding and the rates of recidivism,[8] it nevertheless means that institutions are compelled to engage in more stringent measuring and accounting of every programme. This means that the wide range of projects that had proliferated in the United Kingdom under the Labour government's 'social inclusion' (Matarasso 1997) policies now need to justify themselves in order to maintain resources.[9] In lieu of a widespread acceptance of the arts, then, arts interventions in criminal justice contexts are analysed as one strategy that 'works'. This burden, and the problem of assessing value, means that the arts are often called upon to justify themselves in terminologies and with outcomes that seem unlikely, and inordinately burdensome.

Some of the claims furthered by practitioners are that arts programmes are seen to offer a

> non-traditional, non-institutional, social and emotional environment; a non-judgmental and un- authoritarian model of engagement; and an opportunity to participate in a creative process that involves both structure and freedom.
>
> (Peaker and Vincent 1990, cited in Bamford and Skipper 2007: 14)

Furthermore, McNeill et al. state that engagement in the arts can help to develop new relationships (with peers, and with the prison regime). On a wider level, they suggest that the arts often provide the means of imagining different future pathways in which (ex-)prisoners form different social identifications and rehearse different lifestyles. However, they point out that arts interventions are not likely to deliver concrete and realizable sentence plans in light of the complexities of resettlement needs, but that they 'may help foster and reinforce motivation for and commitment to the change processes that these formal interventions and processes exist to support' (2010: 10). Both sets of claims hint towards the difficulties of the 'place' of the creative arts in institutions. In the majority of evaluation reports and research papers about arts practices in prisons, the romanticized terms 'imagination', 'creativity' and 'freedom' rub uncomfortably against 'concrete' and the restrictions of the prison environment. The artistic dimensions of the work, although central, serve as tensions instead. Michael Balfour suggests that the debate on applied performance turns on a telling point:

> [N]ot that the tension between the aesthetic dimension and the utilitarian is not experienced by most practitioners, but that the articulation of that practice often eschews a discussion about the value of aesthetics. Caught in the habit of writing too many field and evaluation reports, the concentration is on proving the social efficacy of the work, rather than analysing the affect of aesthetics. The artistic dimension therefore is often relegated to the second division, a footnote to the value or purpose of the project.
> (2009: 356)

In the same vein, James Thompson's volume *Performance Affects: Applied Theatre and the End of Effect* (2011a) argues for a critique of languages of impact and 'effect'. McAvinchey says he 'proposes new models of theoretical engagement which re-frame the political and aesthetic possibilities of affect' (2011b: 233). He urges those involved in the commissioning or development of programmes to consider how this work is influenced by trauma studies, particularly ideas about the healing possibilities of narrative recall, and how these may support 'an aesthetics of injury' (2011a: 9), an idea that draws on Julie Salverson's (2001) writings on the 'erotics of injury' in testimonial-based performance. His exploration of several examples of performance practice in sites of extreme conflict outlines a critique of the ways most work is influenced and framed by trauma studies. In particular, he argues against the assumptions that narrative recall, testimony and witnessing presuppose a result of 'healing' that fits neatly into the agendas of commissioners, or funding agencies (Thompson 2011a: 33–35). Rather, he 'calls for an ethnographic approach that acknowledges culturally specific performance practices and how they support a negotiation with or resistance to crises' (McAvinchey 2011b: 234). *Performance Affects* argues that clear articulations of purpose are required in order to make explicit the tensions that may arise in oppositional contexts 'because the private never remains completely private, we must be fully engaged with how the work is refigured, co-opted or put in service of diverse public discourses' (2011a: 34).

The concerns raised by Thompson reflect Didier Fassin and Richard Rechtman's (2007) critique of the over-medicalized industry of trauma, in which they argue that trauma is rendered banal in its ubiquity. In other words, while sites of conflict (including prisons) undoubtedly contain narratives of trauma, and concomitant spillages of uncontainable memories, repetitions and seepages, we must attend to the ways in which 'traumas' are taken for granted, and to what extent the narratives of 'healing', 'catharsis' and 'transformation' are operationalized by institutions. This is crucial because institutions are not exempt from also perpetuating traumas through their own performance of surveillance, discipline and punishment.

Trauma is thus seen as a transferable framework – a justification that Alan Feldman refers to as 'the facile fusion of trauma-aesthetics and testimonial display' (2004: 186). Thompson goes on to demonstrate that theatre makers have employed the terms of trauma studies 'because they already use quasi-theatrical terminology that emphasizes the repeat and the staging of that repeat: because they emphasize the importance of telling a story in front of an audience' (2011a: 61). He demonstrates that such a model is simplistic, since it denies the potential that traumata are mediated, are experienced by individuals and are contextualized in very specific ways. He continues: 'an understanding of the relation between a performance by a person or community in crisis needs to be reconfigured beyond this medical contagion model' (2011a: 61). As such, the examples of practice explored in this chapter aim to consider how, and to what extent, performance processes in prisons rely on articulations borrowed from trauma studies; and to what extent these methods then reinforce and maintain practices that are un-productive in the aesthetics, framing or dissemination of the artistic materials.

Thompson's critical writing (2001, 2003, 2004a) explores the ethical framing of work in prisons, and can be seen alongside Heritage's (1998, 2002, 2004) for its rigorous attention to the movement of power and shifting dynamics of the capacity of theatre to mimic narratives of exclusion and domination. In addition, there are several core texts that are concerned with the practice of theatre making within prisons, some of which provide practical advice and outline strategies for coping with excluded participants (for example Andy Watson's discussion of Geese Theatre and their use of masks as psychological defences, 2009). Others reflect on the placing of theatre within the prison setting, for example Kershaw (2004) on the pathologies of hope in prison theatre. Michael Balfour's edited volume (2004) alongside Thompson's (1998) formed the primary texts for the kinds of practices that were practised in the United Kingdom. US theatre in prison programmes have been explored by Rachel Williams (2003), and Jonathan Shailor (2011). Yet, many of these practices have been critiqued. For example, Balfour suggests that the cognitive-behavioural approach favoured by institutions, and which underlined the TIPP Pump! and Blagg! Programmes, is constrained by its disconnect from informing 'grand narratives'. He says that

> the personal construction of the world becomes more than something that is learnt and unlearnt; it is something influenced by common ideologies held by different groups of people determined by social formation like class, gender, race, and age.
>
> (2003: 15)

By combating the perceived market-driven prison industrial complex (Rusche and Kirchheimer 2003), the arts offer a means of understanding the 'affect' of incarceration. There is the desire to engage with novel means of limiting harm whilst in custody, which the arts have been 'proven' to do (Miles and Clarke 2006; Hughes 2005a; Peaker and Johnston 2007). Nonetheless, Baz Kershaw says that

> in any disciplinary system designed by some to control others [...] there will probably always be a 'space' for resistance, a 'fissure' in which the subject can forge at least a little radical freedom [...] We should see them as crucially *constituting* the dramaturgies of freedom because they represent an absence that creativity seeks to grasp.
> (1999: 156, original emphasis)

Kershaw sees theatre as determined by power, class and hierarchies and radical theatre that which disrupts or de-stabilizes. He specifically refers to how received notions of 'good' and 'evil' are blurred in radical theatre practice. Specifically useful to an analysis of institutions is the performance of absence, aligning prisons to a postcolonial space, or a space of exile (1999: 153). Performance can, for Kershaw, open up opportunities for radical resistance in the fissures appearing in even the most oppressive sites and contexts (1999: 156).

One of the foremost practitioners of prison theatre, Heritage writes of projects he conducted in Brazil, highlighting this tension: 'prison is a world where survival is tested at its limits. Performance is [...] that which does not survive' (2002: 169). Heritage frames his concern with performance and prison by drawing attention to the ways in which staging theatre within prisons engages 'in a bizarre act of negation: denying something essential in both the institution of prison and the activity of theatre' (2004: 200). He goes on to say that '[t]he survival of performance in prisons has for me become a form of resistance and negation of the system itself' (2004: 200). There is a complex relationship between the discourses of arts (as border crossing, boundary breaking and liberating) and prisons (as containing, punitive and limiting). Yet, this relationship can be obscured by the ways in which arts projects are framed, without necessarily exposing the complicity of organizations choosing to situate work within prisons as engaging on the terms of the institution. McAvinchey, drawing on Kershaw, points out that the site itself does not make the practice of theatre within its limits radical, but rather the methodologies of such practice do (2011a: 59).[10] Arts practices in prisons can be a means of disrupting the surveillance and discipline of the institution, and the following section suggests how de Certeau's concepts of 'strategy' and 'tactic' can offer a means of thinking alongside practice towards how performance in prison works.

Prison Repertoires: De Certeau's Strategies and Tactics

De Certeau's influential exegesis on the practice of everyday life conceives of strategies as canonical, institutionalized and 'objective', while tactics are miniscule, reactionary and determined by informing strategic principles (1984: 35–37). In this view, criminal justice institutions, for example, are governed by the claim of objectivity through the law. They enact certain strategies in order to maintain order, prove the efficacy of the law and generate a wider sense of security – that is, encourage a sense of management of threats to stability. Strategy, for de Certeau, is always a means of managing a 'Cartesian' attitude that delimits its own place from an exterior threat (1984: 36). By contrast, tactics are 'calculated actions' that emerge within the discursive and practical field of the given power. A tactic, in de Certeau's view, 'is an art of the weak' (1984: 37). The notion that tactics form obstacles to the rationalization of institutional power has been widely adopted by performance practitioners and scholars, who have tended to take up de Certeau's (1984) formulation as a means of describing arts processes as 'resistant' tactics that interrupt the smooth operations of the strategic field (de Certeau 1984: 35–38; Thompson 2011a: 1–42).

Performance processes in prison claim to create 'spaces' for creativity and (an often uncritically assumed) concomitant liberation from institutional norms of the field of the institution. Susanna Poole asserts that precarity 'is always an issue in the ephemeral space of the prison' (2007: 142). She describes how prison life turns around uncertainty and the deprivation 'of key fundamental civil and political rights, but [prisoners] also lose control over their time and space' (2007: 142). Yet, as geographer Nancy Duncan (1996) has suggested, temporality also needs to be reawakened in the understanding of practices. However, she asserts that thinking of strategies as space or established power and tactics as temporal

> is based on a false opposition, between space and time, and the consequent misleading characterisation of space as the immobile realm of established power. All this from understanding representation as spatialisation [...] Indeed, the very equation of representation with spatialisation might be questioned. What is at issue in representation is not in fact the spatialisation of time but the representation of time-space.
>
> (1996: 135–36)

Duncan's formulation suggests that it is the mutual imbrication of both space and time, or the established powers and the resistant tactics that are worth investigating. In light of applied performance, then, we can consider her approach as insisting on the awareness of how both concerns need to be viewed together. Initially, however, it is important to consider how the understanding of strategies and tactics points towards a wider concern between public and private spheres. Furthermore, Marxist geographer Doreen Massey considers the domains of public as being defined by transcendence – the realm of production; and private as defined by immanence – or the static realm of reproduction (1994). Such a conceptualization not only turns around her understanding of spaces as gendered (1994), but also offers productive terms for performance itself. In the context of prison, it is tempting to see the spheres as distinct, in which the temporal present 'here' is considered separately from a potential future 'there'. Using Massey's formulation in relation to the space/time of prison, the notion of stability of inside/outside is contingent upon the ways space-identities are understood through the assertion of boundaries. 'The identity of a place does not derive from some internalized history. It derives, in large part, precisely from the specificity of its interactions with "the outside"' (1994: 169). In relation to prison, then, the immanence of the private is somehow eclipsed by the 'transcendence' of the public.

Using Massey's argument about space and time in relation to performance practices is instructive. Thompson (2011a: 15–41) highlights this oppositionality in performance in places of conflict that trouble the distinctions of immanence/transcendence, here/there, now/then. Practices that seek to disrupt or at least question these dualisms by asserting the relevance of both time and space to identities have the potential to unravel the sense that 'past' actions are foreclosed, for example, by having served a prison sentence. In performance in prison, the narratives of both immanence through detention and transcendence through 'rehabilitation' or 'correction' are prevalent. This results in neat and generalized practices that do not make allowance for the messy contingency of the social context in which performances of 'corrections', rehabilitation and recidivism occur. In the examples of practice in this chapter, then, it is my intention to demonstrate how these binaries collapse and become troubled by the process of performance tactics. Such tactics are not merely aesthetic moments provided in the safe spaces of a workshop facilitated by an arts practitioner, but may be personal, private attempts to resist discursive, logistical and legal imprisonment.

From Private to Public: What Happens When Performance Is Staged Inside Prison? Clean Break's *There Are Mountains*

Clean Break Theatre Company is amongst the most well-known companies in the field of arts in criminal justice in the United Kingdom. Since 1979, their focus has been on women at risk and with experience of the criminal justice system. For over four decades, they had two strands to their work, including a robust and enduring education programme (Herrmann 2009) that introduces women to pathways of learning, as well as an artistic programme that regularly features at festivals as well as mainstream theatre venues. In 2018, Clean Break's operations shifted to a different delivery model that exemplifies the challenges faced by funding and sustainability for applied theatre in the United Kingdom (Walsh 2018b). However, this does not diminish the significance of its scope in the arts in criminal justice sector. A recent high-profile collaboration includes several women graduates who performed alongside professional actors in the Donmar Warehouse Shakespeare Trilogy (*Julius Caesar, Henry V, The Tempest*) set in prison, directed by Phyllida Lloyd (2012–ongoing) (Abraham and Busby 2014).

There Are Mountains by Chloë Moss (2012) at HMP/YOI Askham Grange was the first production by Clean Break to present, to the public, a work with a 'mixed cast' with one professional performer and seven serving prisoners.[11] The play was written by Moss after a series of residential workshops with women at Askham Grange (an open prison near

York, UK), directed by Imogen Ashby (*The Economist* 2012).[12] The play demonstrates some of the complexities of the journey of women in prison from incarceration to release. The script explores women's anxieties about the potential pathways they face leading up to release. My critical analysis of the play offers a reading of the ways the institution's values are strategically articulated through its public performance. The model of practice is a rare example of performance work that occurs in and through a prison residential process and then is staged for the public on the prison grounds. The performance invites a reading in which I position myself as a member of the audience. Thus, where I use the term 'we' I am not claiming a homogeneous audience reaction to the performance, but asserting a particular experience invited by its dramaturgical framing. I attempt to avoid totalizing assumptions about audience responses as argued in Elin Diamond's critique of the violence of 'we' (1991).

Most literary and performance narratives about prison maintain an idealistic distinction between inside/outside, here/there, then/now. In this play, however, Moss crafts an ensemble work that deliberates on the tenuous threads between these dichotomies. The characters (five prisoners and one officer) present a series of prison dorm scenarios leading up to a home visit for two of the characters. The casting choices were instructive: the prison officer was played by one of the women still serving a sentence, while the professional actor played a woman prisoner. The other women in the dorm present a range of emotional counterpoints to the anxiety of the 'release'. The protagonist, Brenda, struggles to gain access to her daughter, and when she does, she brings the teenage girl a 'Hello Kitty' gift perhaps more appropriate for the little girl she had been when her mother went to prison. Another character struggles to articulate her fear at being out of touch with the world, and, rather than maintain her hard-as-nails 'mask' from the prison dorm, her confidence is shattered as she feels exposed, vulnerable and uncertain on her town visit. When she returns to the dorm, she is able to trade on the 'capital' she has gained inside.

The performance I saw was staged in HMP/YOI Askham Grange's biggest room – a large hall of the converted manor house, with a full lighting rig and a professional set showing a cramped five-bed dormitory, a family kitchen and a rundown diner. The majority of the action occurs in the dorm, with the women negotiating their various concerns about impending release in the insistently communal environment. Brenda faces disciplinary action after her daughter rejects her and she trashes the dorm by throwing the all-important television set to the floor. However, the story concludes with the reconciliation between mother and daughter that seems trite in light of the years of separation. The other four prisoners, the audience is left to assume, continue to struggle with their impending 'release'.

In the post-show discussion, I noted that the audience was a supportive one, comprising families, friends and some local dignitaries looking rather out of place with mayoral chains. I realized that there was no opportunity to concentrate on some of the more difficult concerns the performance raised, as the forum suggested a celebratory, if superficial congratulation to the participants for their hard work. One audience member asked the women about the theme of release, and the answer revealed that most of the performers had

Figure 4: Production shot: *There are Mountains*, 2012 HMP Askham Grange. Produced by Clean Break.

no experience of release. They were merely reflecting the *potential* for hopefulness despite the fear raised by the play. Their position was from 'inside', reflecting on their imminent release to 'outside', as yet contingent on their successful performance of their sentence. It struck me that the performance reinforced a distinction between inside/outside and private/public that, for me, was eroded by the institution as field. The play positions the characters as unable to transgress the institutional habitus they have internalized during their sentences, and indeed, as needing to develop new dispositions in order to cope (or survive) in the outside community. These new dispositions are as yet unarticulated, but revolve around the hardships of maintaining loving supportive relationships, feeling bonded to a community, and the ability to navigate expectations as well as cope with practical real-world demands of getting jobs and keeping appointments. By contrast, the performers were presented as having developed new skills in relation to their participation, as reflected in an article by staff writers in *The Economist*.

> Helen Cadbury, the creative-writing tutor at the prison, thinks that the production offered real industry experience, involving work with professionals and deadlines. Women's institutions often find it hard to recreate the sort of workplace environment – car-maintenance workshops and the like – that Chris Grayling, the justice secretary,

wants prisons to offer, both to improve discipline and to help inmates find work when they leave. Two of those involved in *There are Mountains* say they may try for a theatrical career. Another is keen on events management.

(*The Economist* 2012: online)

However, practitioners need to be cognizant of the bias reflected in the 'public' that has entered a prison in order to support a performance presented by prisoners. There is no doubt that, as Reinelt asserts, a 'consensual community' is created, but this could erase some of the value of having a stage that 'consider[s] and experience[s] affirmation, contestation, and reworking' of the issues (1998: 286). Part of the danger of applied theatre programmes is the hearty gloss of benevolence, 'success' and self-perpetuating presence in the sites of conflict (Thompson 2011a).

It is not my intention here to offer a critique of the aesthetic value of the performance, despite the fact that it was framed by theatrical trappings. Perhaps, in light of the 'success' of the performance, it is more important to reflect on the ethics of such performance. First, see trauma theory, it is valuable to present stories for 'outsiders' to witness, as prisoners' stories of struggle do not become erased when they leave prison. As such, the 'private' journeys of women's incarceration need to be witnessed by a wider public. Yet, the question raised for this research is how the framing of performance processes (applied theatre) in semi-professional or public performance alters the ways such witnessing is attended to. Second, intentions of process-based projects tend to have different claims to those that have a public 'face'. The ethical encounter of a public with the result of prisoners' labour requires a sense of the framing of such labour. In the case of this performance, the site was framed as progressive, supportive and beneficent. The prison staff members were praised for their support of the project, and the institution was 'cast' as a rehabilitative haven in which freedom of expression is prized. However, the moment of 'liberation' offered by the performance is transient while the disciplinary functions of the prison are permanent (even though they are applied randomly, as Goffman [1990, 2007] has shown in discussions on total institutions).

By contrast, Grant and Crossan (2012) write a moving account of a performance project in a Northern Ireland prison that never happened. Unlike most accounts of prison practice that tend to focus on 'success', their framing of 'failure' to perform is under investigation. Their reflection outlines a process that was due to lead to a public performance in a nearby Young Offenders' Institute, but which was inexplicably cancelled when one of the performers was refused clearance for, the prison service claimed, security reasons. Such 'random' decision-making, following prior 'successful' performances to the wider prison community highlights for the authors, 'the inconsistency between the prison system's ostensible commitment to the effective resettlement of released prisoners and the way in which enforced conformity with the prison regime suppressed the very autonomy on which successful re-integration into society depends' (2012: 98), and hence it is worth reflecting that one of the authors is a serving prisoner; and there is thus a claim for representing the responses of the performance participants. Borrowing heavily from Goffman's research into 'total institutions' (2007), they claim that 'success in adapting to prison life is therefore often the equivalent of a failure to retain a necessary sense of self' (2012: 98). As a result, the entire group decided to pursue a tactic of solidarity with their ensemble member and also refused to perform. Such a tactic was a means of asserting self/group in relation to the institution. For these men, refusal to 'perform' became their means of resisting the institutional field. I would add, too, that such refusal is also gendered in relation to the power of masculine refusal or non-compliance (Ashe 2007).

We might see this contrasting example as a counterpoint to the gloss of public 'success' offered by the public performance at HMP/YOI Askham Grange. By staging the prison as 'successful' at creating women who appear to be ready to re-integrate into society, the prison is operating at a strategic level, in which public support in the wake of politically motivated cuts has become important.[13] The performance provided a stage for the institution to present its supportive and rehabilitative 'face' to the public. This was particularly evident in the jolly uniformed women who operated the registration desk, ushered us to our seats and served snacks in the reception.

In light of these concerns, I return to the model 'victim–survivor–hero' in order to offer an analytic perspective on the practices discussed above. In HMP/YOI Askham Grange, the women's performance is analysed as a means of perpetuating the institutional narrative of 'good order and discipline'.[14] *There are Mountains* demonstrates that the women's ability to successfully perform their sentence plans is about, first, learning the 'correct' language and, second, adopting a prescribed 'habitus' that indicates whether they can be judged 'fit' for release into the community.

In the play, Brenda is patronized by a member of staff for failing to understand why her daughter rejects her, suggesting that her release date is dependent on having close relations with support networks. As audience, our experience of Brenda's excitement at the reunion with her family, and her enthusiastic consideration of which gifts to buy her teenage daughter, can lead to a sense of her as a victim when her mother and child appear to reject her. Her ability to cope with her prison sentence is paraded as a virtue, but is undermined when she smashes the television set. We may realize that her confidence of upcoming release is a 'front', and what prevails is the erosion of sense of the capital she has in the prison. This is further reinforced when she is disciplined and removed from the dormitory. In these sequences, we feel Brenda is a victim of the faceless institution. If we can understand her devastation at the rejection, the prison staff not similarly understanding her reactions is foregrounded? The play offers no through-line for how Brenda makes the steps from being 'sanctioned' to being released in a later scene. The play does not indicate what the sanction is, but we are led to assume that Brenda is placed on 'the block' (otherwise known as solitary confinement, or SHU) as a means of punishing her for her destructive behaviour. However, we are meant to accept that she has 'learned her lesson', and discovered the performance needed in order to convince the parole boards that she is fit for release. In other words, she has needed to develop a habitus that is deemed by the prison service to be acceptable for coping in the 'field' beyond the institution. Yet, this new set of dispositions has been inscribed by prison rules and enforced by its regulations, and does not guarantee how such a habitus might transfer from inside to outside.

The value of this example is that the performance models the complex interplay of the spectrum from victim–survivor–hero. The performers (serving prisoners) and their characters (facing release) shift between subjective positions on the basis of institutional whims, as a result of violent arguments, or medication levels, or even on the basis of status games played by the women in the dorm. In the performance I watched, I sat next to a member of the Independent Monitoring Board, who was quick to introduce himself, claiming that the 'difficult one' was perfectly pitched, and that the prison was full of women who are both hurtful and hurting. He wanted to assert the 'truthfulness' of the performance in creating a taxonomy of 'types' (see Lombroso and Ferrero 1895). His words suggested, what much of the current literature confirms, that many women in prison are survivors of multiple forms of abuse (by others, by drugs and alcohol, and themselves).[15] Yet, there was no hint within the play that the strategic performative operations of surveillance, power and control exerted by the officers were also victimizing. Rather, the play suggested that women themselves perpetuate performances of themselves as 'victims' of the system.

There are Mountains aimed to present the issues relating to release for the wide range of women sharing living and working space in prison. The reception of the performance highlighted the willingness to cast participants as 'heroic' for gaining the confidence to perform in front of strangers; they were praised for finishing something. In some cases, working together was posited as heroism. The tone of the work, and its public staging suggested that its performance was an advocacy tool, presenting the pathways of women as a struggle for survival, but more so, as a complex narrative of obstacles – both institutional and 'real-world'. What was perhaps missing in the work was the sense that recidivism is a problem, and thus the cyclical sense of women as 'performing' but failing to convince a wider societal 'audience' that they are fit to belong to their community. Yet, to return to Thompson's plea that we must acknowledge the ways in which public and private are folded together in the staging of applied performance work, it was evident that the performers in this work too, alongside the prison staff and supporters of this work, had all staged a 'publicly acceptable' model of women's rehabilitation. The successful staging of the play was only one level of the performance at operation. It was supported by the welcoming hosts at the conference centre who signed us in; and in the cheerful 'residents' who greeted people without any (apparent) anxiety, shame or shyness. This contrasts with the reversal of the performance of outsiders entering the prison, facing disciplinary surveillance alongside the knowledge of being spectated by prisoners and officers.

There is also a more complex view of what performance studies can offer to the example of women in prison, through employing the frame of habitus.

> Just as habitus informs practice from within, a field structures action and representation from without: it offers the individual a gamut of possible stances and moves that she can adopt, each with its associated profits, costs, and subsequent potentialities.
>
> (Wacquant 2008: 8)

Wacquant's characterization of habitus and field here might be seen in relation to both prisoners preparing for release and the practices of making performance in prison. That is, women's individual habitus determines the 'affect' of the day-to-day operations of the prison, while the institution shapes and determines the possibilities open to women upon release through its structuration of their 'pathways'. In similar ways, the structure of feeling offered by (often inevitably short-term) performance processes is structured and delimited by institutional norms and values. Both are evident in the example of *There are Mountains*, with a suggestion that the performance was in fact a preparation for something else – in which time and the potential result of the action are deferred.

In this example then, the performers metonymically refer to all other prisoners, and their playing through or working out of the issues they might face upon release alludes to the potential for performance to prepare for 'the real'. In other words, the process bears a mimetic relationship to their potential futures. Lynda Hart, drawing on performance theorist Elin Diamond's formulation of 'mimesis-mimicry' (1989: 49), asserts that mimicry 'repeats rather than represents; it is a repetition that is non-reproductive. Mimesis operates in the order of model/copy. Mimicry performs its operation in the realm of simulacra' (1996: 64). Furthermore, she deploys postcolonial critic Homi Bhabha's understanding of colonial mimicry that is expressed as a 'desire for a reformed, recognizable Other as a subject of difference that is almost the same, but not quite' (1984: 318). The characterization of women's performance of readiness for release as mimetic is also understood as one that measures the believability that the prisoners are indeed ready. In other words, once the women are 'read' as reformed, they are judged ready for re-integration into the 'real' world. Yet, as Bhabha's quote suggests, this desire maintains a distance between a 'real' performance of well-adapted citizenship, and a satisfactorily mimetic performance.[16]

It is precisely this awareness that the women's multiple mimetic realms are complex to decode that has given texture to this study. It would be hubris to choose any singular intervention to 'read' success or failure in a woman's pathway through the criminal justice system. However, the arts in prisons have taken on too large a burden with the need to prove efficacy. Rather, I propose that performance, in the example of *There Are Mountains* ought to be analysed as a form of mimetic rehearsal. This rendering of applied theatre performance positions the women participants as rehearsing their future release and the audience as working through the possibilities offered by this performance in the realization of that rehearsal. Such a view chimes with Duggan's conception of 'mimetic shimmering' that emerges in the spectatorial state of not quite 'deciding on the images as reality or mimesis' (2012: 73).

Performance studies provides tools to critique the forms of cultural manifestations precisely because public events are predicated on specific relationships between theme, spectator and performer (Freshwater 2009; White 2013). This positions the themes and subjects of performances as processual, and under construction during the performance event (and sometimes afterwards).[17] Performance – whether it is seen as a specific theatre event or a social performance event such as a protest – has a set of aesthetic and logistical frames of investigation – it occurs in a specific place and time, and is framed by particular aesthetics and the material conditions of the event, spectacle or action. When dealing with performance processes (such as actor training, devising and applied theatre), it is necessary to consider how researchers gain access to the work. This forms one of the primary challenges of applied theatre as sub-genre in performance studies because projects do not always have public outcomes, nor do they all have the resources to develop extensive documentation.[18] While many projects produce reports and evaluations of their work, there is generally an imperative to 'prove effectiveness', rather than disclosing challenges too candidly. Nevertheless, applied theatre projects can indeed offer insightful documentation and critically relevant reports that can prove productive in the issues they raise. The methodological consideration is foregrounded here because the second indicative example of applied processes with women in prisons has been accessed through secondary sources. Nevertheless, it provides an important counterpoint to the experience of viewing *There Are Mountains*. In particular, I analyse this example of performance in prison by Geese Theatre in light of its stated concern with authenticity and offer an understanding of 'giving voice' through mimetic reflection. It forms a brief counterpoint with the prior example in order to demonstrate a range of applied theatre practices in prisons in the United Kingdom.

Trauma, Masks and Mimesis: Geese Theatre's *Journey Woman*

Stephen Bottoms' account of *Journey Woman* (2010) provides an important insight into the performance practices of this well-established company, which began in the late 1980s in the United States. Practitioners in the United Kingdom developed the methodology over the last 30 years (Baim et al. 2002). Geese Theatre's method generally involves a structured improvisation style performance, in which actors wear half masks and in which the stock characters, such as 'The Wall', 'The Joker' and 'Mr. Cool', are presented in scenarios the participants (in this example, female prisoner) may have experienced (Bottoms 2010: 484–86). The company facilitates participation by asking audiences to give suggestions for how the characters might 'lift the mask' (Watson 2009) in order to reveal the thought processes and possibilities for alternative choices that might lie 'behind the masks'. Michael Balfour demonstrates that the company 'began as radical practitioners working with the marginalized in prisons in the USA, to become a company specialising in the use of theatre to focus on an individual's responsibility for their offending behavior' (2009: 349). Balfour sees this shift as firmly rooted in the prevailing socio-economic discourses that define the funding agendas that support (or reject) this kind of arts-based intervention.

Journey Woman is the first work by Geese Theatre that was created specifically for a female audience. Bottoms reveals the shifts in methodology needed in order to ensure the work held relevance for the participating audience, which is achieved through using full mask.[19] The performance is constructed as flexible and open enough for a wide range of audience to connect with the protagonist, Ellie, which is then worked through in what they term 'groupwork' sessions after the performance. Louise Heywood, one of the longstanding Geese Theatre facilitators, is cited at length:

> [...] our experience has told us that if you do too much pushing and challenging with women, they'll back off. Also what happens with the women is they're more ready to 'lift their mask' from the start, anyway. They tend to go to the heavy, internal stuff fairly quickly, so you can't just go in and say, 'right, we'll keep this surface level, talk about acquiring skills and what you need to do when you get out'. Whatever you do has to have an element of allowing them to go to the internal stuff, and to find a safe way of doing that. If you don't go there, it just sits on the sideline like a little ghost in the room.
> (in Bottoms 2010: 490)

Heywood's remarks point towards an interesting difference in Geese Theatre's approach between working with male and female prisoners.[20] Her claims that affect is more evident in women's prisons is well rehearsed in criminological literature (Gelsthorpe 2010; Heidensohn 1996; Smart 1977; Ramsbotham 2003) but also reveal the instrumental turn in theatre practice needing to answer to skills acquisition, and practicalities of resettlement.

Rather than rely on re-telling the narrative of *Journey Woman* as related by Bottoms, I have elected to engage with the theoretical problems raised by these practices before returning to the examples. The following section thus shifts from the close reading of the examples to posit an analytic frame that will engage these examples in service of the wider argument of this research, namely, whether and to what extent performance tactics can be seen to challenge, subvert or support the strategies of penal institutions.

The examples have raised several pertinent points that will be analysed in relation to one of the theoretical strands running through the book, since, I argue, the terms and 'symptoms' (cf. Duggan 2012) of trauma theory relate to performance practice in their spatial and temporal appearance within the context of the prison. This is necessary since the site as 'process' of rehabilitation or corrections suggests a 'working through' of past events and the creation of new or future potential identity narratives. Trauma theory informs this section, as I return to several of the concerns that relate explicitly to the problems raised by the examples of applied theatre practice above (Duggan and Wallis 2011; Duggan 2012; Stuart Fisher 2011). Trauma theory provides a framework through which we might thread some of the practices of applied performance in prison, to address some of the common practices of performance making in prisons.

Applied theatre practice is often informed by the notion of 'salve', as Thompson (2011a) suggests. It follows that a 'wound' has been identified, to which performance processes have been identified as a potentially ameliorating tactic.[21] This wound might be understood as a primary trauma (such as a war, a refugee's flight) or a feature of the consequences of the primary event (such as the trauma of being detained, or the refugee's dis/appearance at the border). Participating in theatre workshops (and performances) becomes the means by which participants are given the conscious space and creative tools with which to 'work through' these wounds. Of course, Thompson (2011b) demonstrates that there are power dynamics inherent in the definitions of sites, events or personal histories as 'wounds', and also in the choice of theatre or performance as the mechanism that claims to 'heal'. Duggan has also shown that there is a complex interplay between trauma event and repetition that is central to trauma theory (2012: 24). Given that trauma's performativity constructs certain relationships between event, memory, narrative and witness, these structures also need to be investigated in the ways they in turn perpetuate and co-construct their very understanding of 'wounds' and 'salves'.

By means of reaching towards how these two performance examples raise the need for more critical practices that challenge representations even as they rely on them, I turn to Julie Salverson's compelling work on the 'erotics of injury' (2001: 123). In this work, cited at length, she demands thinking through the ways mimesis operates in relation to the 'authentic voice' that is central to applied theatre practices in general, and the examples discussed here in particular.

> How do the participant/performer, the audience member, or the form of the play itself engage the violation that is the event being testified to? What is the range of possibilities for what is known, imagined, or responded to in this engagement with the event? Critical here are possibilities within performance itself, which address distinctions among several notions of mimesis that operate by either 'upholding a model (representation) or improvising a variation (representing).' The latter approach considers mimesis to be a faculty that demands of its audience an active engagement with the story through a kind of 'interpretive labor'.
>
> (Salverson 2001: 123)

She is specifically concerned with the ways a model that relies on the 'traumatic event' seems to privilege an aesthetic of injury (Salverson 2001). Thompson (2011a, relying on Scarry 1985) has further proposed that while ethics are at the cornerstone of performance making in conflict zones, such projects can and should incorporate beauty. In other words, the perceived 'worth' or benefit of arts interventions should not diminish the artistic or aesthetic values.

Geese Theatre's *Journey Woman* provides an example upon which we can consider the role of silence as resistance (cf. Thompson 2011a), as well as beauty to provide spaces for mimetic reflection. The performance method and workshop create a framework for projection of participants' stories onto the protagonists', by, as Bottoms (2010) suggests, engaging with an open storyline and a more neutral mask than their existing male wardrobe of masks.[22] The performance encourages the women participants to make their own connections with the wider narrative, which they do by having women offer explanations of what 'happens next' in certain scenes. This is a well-rehearsed technique used in applied theatre workshops, in order to encourage cycles of action–reflection–transformation (Taylor 1996a). The scene deliberately halts at certain key moments, in order to allude to multiple possible outcomes, such as when Ellie seems to be threatened by her large burly partner. The dramaturgical structure inserts openings and pauses for participants to engage through reflecting on their own experiences. It becomes important for Geese Theatre (as highlighted by Heywood's [2012] comment on the affect that is close to the surface when working with women in prison) to be able to frame affects as symbolic and meaningful, and not merely as risky and dangerous. Performance can be one set of practices that provides articulations of a range of affects in a structured and defined context that is 'safe' both psychologically, as it is located in the realm of the symbolic or aesthetic, and physically, through its careful negotiation within the institutional norms and values.

In a shift to a critical analysis of the applied theatre tactics that have been outlined above, I make explicit the functions of performance in the site of the prison. This enables a better understanding of the cultural work these hidden processes in applied theatre do. Thompson argues that there is an alliance between the curative function of 'telling' and the discourses of 'survival' that is particular to the West (2011a: 45). He suggests that the imperative to 'tell your stories' as individuals can erase other possibilities to be found in performance. Thompson is explicating the need for culturally specific practices that might be different to individual transformations. His work refers to collective or communal modes of aestheticizing change that are influenced by social contexts that privilege collective meaning making (2011a). His argument is that in addition to straightforward testimonies, there is a wide range of performance strategies that move beyond simple frames of staging 'telling' and 'witnessing' that include resistant strategies of 'not speaking'; or indeed, culturally specific modes of performance that resist 'revelation'. I return to the possibilities found in 'silence' in the subsequent section on representation.

It is problematic to assume that performances in prison would or should take the form of testimonial theatre, since there is an interplay between the psychological personal narrative of the prisoner and the wider social narratives that include issues of crime and justice. The imperative to tell one's story as a prisoner suggests that the narrative will include details of crimes and the processes of justice. Often, in literary projects with women, such healing narratives return to 'originating' traumatic moments that might be seen to have 'wounded' the women in some way. The kinds of narrative projects I am talking about circulate on testimony (and include Davis 2004; Graney 2003, 2004, 2006; Lamb et al. 2003; Lamb 2007; Levi and Waldman 2011; Opsal 2011; Rymhs 2012; Warner 2011; Williams 2003). In these examples, the 'story' of the original trauma can be seen in several ways. First, the ability to tell a story reveals the acknowledgement of a traumatic event through articulation. However, the 'wounds' of the trauma are not merely described as symptoms, but causes of further destructive behaviours (such as drug abuse, or a history of violent relationships). Further, the story of the wound can be employed as an 'excuse' for criminal activities. This critique, however, is not intended to diminish the continued presence of trauma symptoms in the lives of those who have suffered personal traumatic events, but to point towards the performativity of trauma in the context of prison, and thus to its potential force in applied theatre testimonies.[23]

In the practices of applied performance, the tendency to victimize participants by insisting on revelations of trauma might in fact fetishize the traumatic. Rhodessa Jones' US-based company The Medea Project routinely creates public performances developed through prison-based processes that engage with 'testimony' and 'witnessing' of supposedly 'authentic' stories (Billone 2009; Fraden 2001; Son 2006; Warner 2001, 2004, 2011). By contrast, Clean Break's public performances tend to gloss over such 'relief', preferring instead to expose concerns related to criminal justice more broadly. This aesthetic choice might be considered in relation to the intentions of their work to straddle public/private discourses. While individual healing from trauma is both laudable and important in private processes, it does not necessarily share the aesthetic form that will result in social change.[24]

In the model from Geese Theatre, spectators are women like Ellie. Bottoms states, referring to *Journey Woman*:

> The play's spectators are encouraged – through its minimising of the kind of individuating information provided by faces or dialogue – to see Ellie as being in some way a reflection of themselves rather than as a fully fleshed-out character (an other). And yet, conversely, if a spectator sees something of her own past experiences in Ellie's journey, she is also able to view these experiences from a spectatorial distance – as a narrative that is in some way occurring to an 'other'.
>
> (2010: 492)

To witness, or to bear witness to a testimony of suffering, places the spectator in a position of responsibility for what has been seen, heard and felt (see Duggan 2012: 89). While some theorists consider the degree of responsibility merely about 'being alongside', others place special emphasis on the embodied experience of the moment of testimony (Fisher 2011). Geese Theatre's performance described by Bottoms positions the prisoners as witness to a story bearing mimetic resemblance to their own. Their groupwork processes reinforce and rehearse different ways of working through the responsibility of seeing, and recognizing ones' self in the other. Duggan's formulation of allowing the traumatic 'without intervening towards cure' (2012: 89) operates as a model of analysis for contemporary performance, but in the context of prison, where 'curative' solutions are prioritized, we should rather seek to understand how and to what extent performance processes can predicate on witnessing as a transaction in order to effect desired responses. Next, the argument departs from the framework of trauma theory, but is related to the concerns raised above, in the sense that criminal justice is predicated upon a sense of the relation between private and public. The cycles of incarceration, explored below, as well as the ways theatre in prisons grapples with public and private concerns by staging them, are of concern.

The UK report 'Unlocking Value: The Economic Benefit of the Arts in Criminal Justice' (New Philanthropy Capital 2011) was commissioned by the National Criminal Justice Arts Alliance on behalf of the charitable sector to explore the 'value' of arts-based programmes in the lives of ex-prisoners. It considers the effectiveness of theatre participation in relation to reducing re-offending, and potential for future employment with the aim of demonstrating that the theatre 'intervention' saves the government over five times what it would otherwise cost to incarcerate recidivists annually. The report states a fundamental disconnect between what arts organizations can do within criminal justice and the system itself:

> While government targets are built around an end (offending) arts organisations tend to focus on the means (personal, social and emotional skills). What is often lacking is a clear theory of change and evidence that links one to the other.
>
> (2011: 10)

The report raises some concerns about how the arts are put in service of the economic savings to the prison service, and what such an intention means for the ethical framing of the arts. In other words, the labour demanded of the arts is always already determined by the institution. In de Certeau's terms then, arts tactics are in service of the strategic aims of the institution. This explicit discursive attempt to align practices with the wider function of the system presents a worrying dilemma for the analysis of performance in prison. Furthermore, the report attempts to consider theatre's cost-benefit analysis in discrete categories (ignoring affect and 'soft outcomes'). There is the need for charities and third-sector organizations to compete in terms of funding for the sustainability of their work, but it is surely not value free. This issue is central to much contemporary work that straddles disciplinary borders between arts and social change interventions. This report highlights an ongoing struggle in the arts – having to justify their terms in the language, and with the values of other paradigms. Although the results may compel future funding of such work, the consideration of return on investment seems to occlude the other, more nebulous values that pervade theatre programmes. This critique is relevant here because it presents the conditions within which performance practices occur in prisons in the United Kingdom – that is, precarious, under suspicion, and necessarily ephemeral in nature. The economic and social pressures I highlight here are important contexts for recognizing the value(s) of the artistic practices.

The examples of the Clean Break performance, and a play/workshop in the repertoire of Geese Theatre, are counter-posed by the opening vignette from my experience working as artist/facilitator with Clean Break several years previously on *Missing Out* (Mary Cooper, 2009). The narrative from my research notes highlights the tension between the intentions of the work, and its apparent 'success' on a range of levels, and the small rupture offered by an improvised moment of resistance when someone stole fake currency. The account asserts some of the ambiguities and complexities of applied theatre practices in prisons – offering a more complex reading of how such resistance is inevitably subsumed by how power circulates in institutionalized practices. Although desire compelled the theft of the paper money, resistance was not emancipatory but resulted in greater surveillance. The applied theatre practice therefore mobilized both desire and resistance but its outcome could not be considered 'success'.

My memory of this 'failure' in the workshop offers a way of understanding the insidious relationship with power concomitant with gaining access to an institution. On the one hand, the 'theft' of fake currency is hardly significant in the ways other more horrifying consequences of performance have been.[25] On another, the rupture, or refusal of complicity that is offered by the 'theft' is another means of improvising. I do not frame their 'improvisation' as de facto positive. Rather, it is a means of harnessing performance vocabularies as one performative tactic amongst several, including 'docility', silence or refusal to cooperate with authority. In any other context, the woman's 'creativity' and 'cunning' would be appreciated, but in prison (as in wider society) such qualities can only be praiseworthy within the rather tightly defined bounds of 'acceptable' behaviour.

This is precisely Mike Presdee's (2000) argument about criminality and the carnivalesque. He notes that what is important in the state's articulation of offending behaviours is how or why transgression could be sanctioned or not. This point returns me to the well-rehearsed description of 'restored behaviour' or 'twice-behaved behaviour' that Schechner (2006) outlines as a defining feature of performance. However, in the context of institutions and their strategic aims, where transgressive 'behaviour' is under contestation, it is important to reflect on how performance practices model and reinforce normativity in the arsenal of behaviours/habitus on offer.

At this juncture it is important to consider what, in the framing of applied theatre processes, is emphasized as 'the performance'.[26] In Geese Theatre's example, Bottoms focuses on both the company's performance of a scene, and the performance of women in a workshop designed to process the themes in the work. The women in those sessions were thus asked to use performative tactics in order to rehearse for future performances of self in which wider repertoires of agency might be possible. My reading of the institutional discourse frames the practices through a normative understanding of 'behaviour'. However, the practice has remained 'private' insofar as it did not have any public presentation of outcomes, aside from Bottoms' mediation of the sessions.

In the example of *There are Mountains*, Clean Break positions a semi-professional product as 'the performance', while alluding to the performative labour that has gone into the creation of the play. Yet, to a greater extent than the Geese Theatre example, this public staging of the women's cycles of 'tragic containment' reinforces and supports the site itself. It does so through the script's repetitions of familiar tropes of helpless females who are unable to define their own terms of 'success' or 'failure', and who must revert to a hegemonic set of practices in order to fulfil their narrative potential (to return to de Lauretis' [1987] view of woman as *topos*). While the ambition to stage such performance asserts the importance of the (mostly) private struggle of re-integration to a wider public sphere, there remains a sense that the 'making public' *is* the performance, intended to have a wider, more politically resonant impact than the process of working together. This can upstage whatever more personal effects/affects women may have experienced in the process of participation. Massey's discussion (1994) of immanence and transcendence is worth recuperating here – as some of the tension in making applied theatre practices public is fundamentally about how 'inside' interacts with 'outside'.

By considering these examples, I do not intend to create a taxonomy of practices, but rather to gesture towards the ways in which both effects and affects of performance practices in prison *are* the currency by which they should be considered. Thus, in a return to the theoretical challenges posed in the beginning of this chapter, I have resisted Lombroso's taxonomic constructions of knowledge of prisoners and their institutional experiences. Rather, see de Certeau, I considered the tactics and strategies of applied theatre in prisons.

The potential of victim–survivor–hero seen in relation to the cycle of tragic containment is that there is the possibility to engage both the personal narratives of injury, loss and trauma (in the victim–survivor–hero model) *and* the narratives of recidivism and desistance that resonate in the realm of the political (seen in the cycles of tragic containment). However, these need to be articulated through the 'interpretive labour' mentioned by Salverson, in relation to both ethics and aesthetics (2001). The position of applied theatre practices as largely outside of the public realm, thus, means that it is important for critical practices to do this interpretation in relation to how the range of narratives become articulated in relation to one another. What is evident from the range of literature evaluating arts projects and sources offering case studies of performance practice is that the terms of effect/affect often become indistinct, and subservient to the dominant discourses of the commissioning agents. 'What works' is articulated in the language of the prison service, reinforcing the generalizing discourse of the regime, rather than carving out productive tools that can be adopted by individuals as 'habitus-specific resources' (Susen 2011: 368). This signals a tension that is characterized by competing discourses that will be recognizable to abolitionist-academics or practitioners of arts interventions in prisons.

Balfour offers a gloss on Neelands' querulous concern about what he calls hero narratives that make claim for change through evoking the language of transformation and revolution. He relies on Neelands' argument that 'it is important to distinguish between localized and anecdotal "miracles" and how these instances are "generalized and theorized or proved in the textual discourses of the field"' (Neelands 2004: 47, cited in Balfour 2009: 353). Taking this argument further, Balfour proffers that it is everything that goes into gaining access that highlights the ideology of the practice. He says the need for

> discharging and advocating for aesthetics [is] central, and of establishing open-ended relationships that hold in tension the quality of the process that participants go through in making theatre and the quality of the work that is created. The point of entry is where competing ideological values interplay with each other, some are articulated, whilst others are deeply subterranean within the practitioner, the institution, or group.
>
> (2009: 357)

The separation of the impact or effectiveness of performances in prison from the wider field, and the affect(s) of such work, is both difficult and counter-intuitive. From a Bourdieusian perspective, the interplay between habitus and field, and the multiple forms of capital that are formed and lost in everyday processes shift constantly in relation to one another. 'It takes the *meeting* of disposition and position, the correspondence (or disjuncture) between mental structures and social structures, to generate practice' (Wacquant 2008: 8, original emphasis). It is short sighted to argue for a purely aesthetic judgment of performance work in prisons, since the very aesthetic is imbricated within the field of the institution, its values and norms. Equally, though, it is reductionist to attempt to calculate the value of 'effects' of such work, as interventions do not happen in a vacuum. Rather, the moral and ethical questions arising from this chapter suggest that the important questions are related to determining the implications of 'good performance', and to working through what such performative signs might be.

The paradoxes and messiness of performance projects in prisons circulate around claims for 'giving voice' and 'representing' women in prison and how they are circumscribed by competing agendas (funding demands, political affiliations and activist intentions alongside permissions to gain access in the first instance). Women's tactical refusals and resistances reveal more deeply the force-field of the institution, its perpetuation of power, domination and control. The companies and our access to their work behind bars enable a means of examining how desires and resistance are performed in participatory projects.

By constructing this chapter around practice, I offer a new perspective on performance in prisons – it does not seek to measure and evaluate 'effects' or 'impacts' of the arts as intervention. It does not position theatre processes as a transformative or ameliorating practice that radically alters the prisoners (or indeed, the institution). Rather it raises questions about what performance in prison claims to *do*. Positioning the practices in relation to trauma theory, 'healing' and catharsis are considered potential, but not inevitable, effects. It suggests that institutional access and gatekeeping always already mark the project with an agenda. Prison theatre must therefore necessarily be seen in the relationship between both these more private, process-based applied theatre projects and contemporary performances about prisons. The possibilities of participation and representation of women in prison are always reflected in both modes of performance practice. This approach resists the discursive and practical boundaries of 'interventions' or 'events', as women's durable dispositions are modelled and re-modelled in light of their experiences both in prison and in the transition to communities upon release. It is this dynamic of inside and outside, public and private that characterizes both thinking in this book and the performance of women prisoners as they navigate their journey(s) between prison and society.

Notes

1. Other important works on the wide range of practices, informing principles and methodologies are foundational to prison theatre practice (Adebayo 2015; Neelands 2004; Nicholson 2005; Prentki and Preston 2009; Thompson 2006a; White 2015).
2. Applied theatre is more fully defined in the introductory chapter – it is used here as a 'hold-all' term, not necessarily as the term used by the practitioners themselves.

3. Also see Walsh (2017) for a general account of arts in criminal justice; Walsh (2019) for discussion on applied theatre as labour; as well as Walsh (2018a) for a specific discussion of my own practice in women's prison in the United Kingdom.
4. These are still described in relation to class and race primarily. However, what emerges strongly in the literature is that crime and criminalization results in a spatialized mapping of risk not dissimilar to the Booth maps outlined in Chapter Two.
5. Peaker and Johnston show that 'this is nearly more than 20000 more than in 1997' – an astronomical rise in just ten years (2007: 17). And in the years since then, the figure has risen to over 86,000. Women make up just 5 per cent of the prison population in the United Kingdom; with the most recent figures suggesting that 'just under' [sic] 4000 women are imprisoned. That figure is contextualized with the incarceration figure of 13,500 women each year, highlighting the 'churn' of women incarcerated for short-term sentences (see Prison Reform Trust 2013b).
6. See, for example, Cleveland (2003), Escape Artists (2006), Johnston and Hewish (2010). The National Criminal Justice Arts Alliance, founded in 2008 by arts organizations in criminal justice, has developed an evidence library as well as training programmes to ensure more robust research is accessible.
7. The opening part of this section has been adapted and disseminated in report form for Ovalhouse's Future Stages network entitled *Creating Change, Imagining Futures: Participatory Arts and Young People 'At Risk'* (Walsh 2013b).
8. Recidivism refers to the rate of return to incarceration, or in other words, the percentage of prisoners who return to criminal activities *and get caught*. It is a word that engages with institutional 'effect' by measuring to what extent prison 'works'. The concept is slightly different from desistance in criminological literature, which engages with affect, in the sense that it is ex-prisoners' agency that is under investigation. See McNeill et al. (2010).
9. The impacts of austerity in the United Kingdom have affected arts organizations of all kinds. The list of arts in criminal justice organizations that have been forced to cease or dramatically reduce activities due to cuts include Escape Artists, Dance United, Writers in Prison Network amongst many other smaller organizations.
10. This point has also been made by Balfour (2003) and Kershaw (1999, 2004). Paul Heritage (1998) writes of a rebellion in a Brazilian prison that was blamed on a high-profile theatre performance, positing that, while theatre can and has encouraged and facilitated 'change' in small and large ways, for example in his ambitious Staging Human Rights Project (2000–05); the 'revolutionary' (1998: 231) impulse that drives many practitioners to make and present work in prisons is necessarily translated in – and determined by – the context.
11. Clean Break's programme of workshops and residencies in prisons cast a professional actor working alongside serving women prisoners. This production staged the 'mixed cast' to a paying public on prison premises. Other companies that regularly present professional/prisoner productions in prisons in the United Kingdom include Pimlico Opera's project that has been running since 1991 (Pimlico Opera 2013), as well as Playing for Time (McKean 2006, 2011).
12. Open Prisons (D-category) are institutions that focus on the resettlement needs of prisoners as they progress towards the final stages of their sentences. Open prisons include training

programmes and often involve community-based voluntary work placements as well as 'town visits' in order to prepare prisoners for interacting with wider communities upon release. Interestingly, HMP Askham Grange was also the prison from which Clean Break was founded by two serving prisoners in 1979.

13 This point was made in conversation with a staff member who was responsible for placing women in community workplaces. She suggested that the work placements are only possible if the local business owners feel able to understand and contribute towards the re-integration processes (Anonymous prison officer, personal interview, 30 November 2012).

14 GOAD (Good Order And Discipline) is one of the underlying principles of the prison service (Loucks 2000). It is a concept that is not clearly articulated, and as such becomes a 'trope' employed by prison staff in order to maintain a subjective set of practices within the institution. This can be seen in relation to the many instances where staff actions in support of 'GOAD' were deemed unacceptable by the Chief Inspectorate of Prisons (BBC 2009).

15 In one of the most compelling forms, Lois Ahrens and her collaborators (2008) present contexts and statistics for the United States through representations in graphic novel-style comic strips. Other sources on victimization and offending are Dehart and Lynch (2013), with the Corston reports (2007, 2011) the most indicative UK policy-related sources.

16 I take up this argument about readiness for release as performative in Walsh (2018a).

17 This is explicitly staged in performances that are predicated on a degree of audience participation or autonomy in the unfolding story. Examples of companies that purport to do this are Blast Theory and Punchdrunk for example. This unfolding, agential relationship to meaning through participation is discussed by White (2013).

18 It is also worth noting that documentation can provoke ethical questions, as safety of participants is paramount. In the case of prisons, security and discipline are considered important, and identifying information, reference to crimes, mention of harms to self or others and glorification of crime is considered a security breach. Any documentation must therefore be considered in light of the potential impact on victims as well as the maintenance of security to the institution. Prisons are thus extremely unlikely to provide access to video documentation or photographs. See McAvinchey (2006b) for detailed discussion on documentation procedures in prison theatre research.

19 It is important to state here that my awareness of the performance comes through Bottoms' publication, as well as from personal conversations with Louise Heywood from Geese Theatre (Heywood 2012); and as such, it is mediated by the documentation choices made by these individuals (which is McAvinchey's concern, 2006a). This is because their work within prison settings is always, emphatically, framed as 'private' and therefore not open to public scrutiny. This raises questions about how and why Bottoms' presence as researcher was admissible, for example. The opening of the sub-section on Geese Theatre addresses this concern more fully.

20 However, further exploration of the differences in approach between methodologies that 'work' with male and female prisoners is beyond the scope of this study precisely because I argue against the possibility of definitive claims that arts projects within the frame of penal institutions can be said to 'work' after release. This is not because I do not believe they could or do have real impacts, but because access to longitudinal research data (on re-offending

rates, for example) is not accessible (Hughes 2005a); and most evaluations do not include follow-up data on participants. In other words, the bureaucracy of prison and the secrecy of records make lofty claims difficult to prove.

21 There are numerous examples to cite in relation to the characterization of a 'wound' and its relief through arts processes. This is distinct from the arts therapy bibliography but some of the vocabularies overlap (see Salverson 2001; Thompson et al. 2009; Thompson 2011a; Wake 2009b, 2013).

22 Bottoms reflects on his observation of the groupwork session, in which an older woman, who was serving a life sentence, had made some important connections with the story, despite acknowledging differences in Ellie's narrative and her own as she discussed the ways in which life circumstances can conspire to lead one into trouble. 'She seemed to be speaking as someone who had now been reflecting critically on her own past for a long time, and for whom the play offered further confirmation of lessons learned' (Bottoms 2010: 487). In other words, the participant in the workshop recognized a mimetic representation of herself in the character of Ellie.

23 I discuss performativity and trauma elsewhere (Walsh 2018a). Prison is performative in the reiteration or cyclical repetitions that produce an effect (rather than effecting transformation as others understand the concept). In the context of prison, performativity is thus considered not as signalling 'real' transformation, but as a citational repetition (Caruth 1995: 90) of what transformation looks like so that women can progress through sentences and be released into society.

24 I am distinguishing here between two forms of practice because I argue that Clean Break's 'public' facing performance work 'performs' in a different way to its education work. I do not wish to make the distinction too stark since they inform and interrelate, but to highlight a divide in the efficacy of 'advocacy' focused outcomes and personal development outcomes and how both intentions interrelate with aesthetic considerations.

25 For example, Thompson talks about a massacre of 27 boys and young men at Bindunuwewa rehabilitation centre in Sri Lanka in 2000 as having direct links to a performance-based intervention (2011a: 15–42). This account of ethical impacts and implications is part of applied theatre research (Hughes 2005b; Thompson 2006b; Wake 2013), but also of course relevant to criminological research interventions (McLean and Liebing 2007; Lyng 2005). Other disciplinary approaches that consider representations and research in and of marginalized communities have been informative (Bharucha 2007; Conquergood 2007; Fitzpatrick 2011; Frank 1995; Gluhovic 2012; Madison 2012; Read 1993; Routledge 2009; Wade 2009).

26 What counts as 'the performance' in applied theatre projects is dealt with in a chapter by McAvinchey (2009) called '"Is this the play?": Applied performance in pupil referral units'.

Chapter Four

Race, Space and Violence

Racism, Cultural Criticism and the Prison Industrial Complex

A Dominican woman in prison is harshly punished for a minor transgression. Her white counterpart, the protagonist of the show, joins her in a standing protest against the regime. The prison's workshop conditions are becoming harder for prisoner/workers to bear, and in escalating tensions, an untrained officer restrains, and kills, a prisoner in the canteen, by crushing her to death. The casual shift from everyday prison routines to inmate murder is unfortunately not only for entertainment purposes, but signals the ongoing correlation with real-life battles over whose life matters. The Netflix series *Orange Is the New Black* (*OITNB*) (Jenji Kohan, 2013–ongoing) is a popular culture phenomenon that has spurred a renewed interest in women in prison. Piper Kerman and the inmates of Litchfield penitentiary allow for an increasingly critical exploration of incarceration – its causes and its effects. It also represents some of the significant issues in criminal justice in the United States and is one of very few prison TV shows that focuses specifically on women in prison.

There is a long history of activist scholarship in the United States that argues for prison abolition – much of it based on critiques of punitive laws that disproportionately criminalize poor people of colour, unjust sentencing (Alexander 2012; Caster 2004; Wacquant 2009a, 2010b), and the school-to-prison pipeline (Giroux 1996, 2003, 2015). In addition, the influence of activist-scholars (Davis 2012; Davis and Dent 2001; Sudbury 2002, 2005a, 2005b; Loyd et al. 2012; Sudbury and Okazawa-Rey 2009) in arguments about women in prison is particularly important for developing criminological critique that moves beyond theories of reform but that drives for policy change, redress and, ultimately, whole-scale abolition (Kandaswamy 2016; Whitehead 2007). In addition to containment and separation, there are specific harms and deprivations caused by prison for incarcerated women. When cultural critiques begin to consider how other elements coincide for criminalized women, including race, poverty and educational attainment, we can begin to see the ways prisons symbolize far more than the logic of law and order.

Angela Davis (2008) makes clear the ways in which race as the determinant of liberal freedom comes to bear on prison populations:

> With the dismantling of the welfare state […] the institution of the prison – which is itself an important product marketed through global capitalism – becomes the privileged site into which surplus impoverished populations are deposited.
>
> (2008: online)

Foundational to many of these arguments is the acknowledgement that race and racism have shaped, and continue to define, experiences of criminalization and incarceration. In a report for the African American Policy Forum, Kimberlé Crenshaw makes the case for a specific forum for gendered activism related to the ways in which Black communities are criminalized.

> In order to comprehend the root causes and full scope of state violence against Black communities, we must consider and illuminate *all* the ways in which Black people in the US are routinely targeted for state violence. Acknowledging and analyzing the connections between anti-Black violence against Black men, women, transgender, and gender-nonconforming people reveals systemic realities that go unnoticed when the focus is limited exclusively to cases involving Black non-transgender men.
>
> (Crenshaw et al. 2015: 6)

Thus, any study of experiences of prison and representations in popular culture must attend to how and in what ways race and its intersections with gender shape the construction of meaning.

This chapter draws on the vigour and political urgency of these arguments to develop a distinctly feminist analysis of the contemporary media phenomenon of the popular TV series *Orange Is the New Black*. I explore how the foregrounding of race and representations in a mainstream series about prison can offer valuable materials for debating how institutions perpetuate and exacerbate inequalities for women.[1] As bell hooks forcefully contends:

> There is a direct and abiding connection between the maintenance of white supremacist patriarchy in this society and the institutionalization via mass media of specific images, representations of race, of blackness that support and maintain the oppression, exploitation, and overall domination of all black people.
>
> (1992: 2)

hooks' reading of a range of examples from film, music and media in 1992 forged a politicized reading of how blackness is constructed and forms a legacy of imagery to which popular culture returns again and again, and which is worth quoting at length.[2]

> The issue is really one of standpoint. From what political perspective do we dream, look, create, and take action? For those of us who dare to desire differently, who seek to look away from the conventional ways of seeing blackness and ourselves, the issue of race and representation is not just a question of critiquing the *status quo*. It is also about transforming the image, creating alternatives, asking ourselves questions about what types of images subvert, pose critical alternatives, and transform our worldviews and move us away from dualistic thinking about good and bad. Making a space for the

transgressive image, the outlaw rebel vision, is essential to any effort to create a context for transformation.

(1992: 4)

hooks' perspective proposes the need for more complex ways of constructing representations, without replicating the trap outlined by Black feminist thinker Patricia Hill Collins (1986), who argues for cultural critiques that are predicated on self-determination, rather than analysis or definition that comes from outside. While my own standpoint is not as a Black feminist, but as an antiracist feminist, my perspective is one that hopes to consider precisely how race performs in the field of representations of women in prison. The aim here is to consider whether Jenji Kohan's *OITNB* manages to construct a space within the wider representational field of women in prison for Black characters whose agency speaks to 'self-valuation' (Collins 1986: 18). More recent cultural criticism of performance and race as put forward by Rocchi et al. who argue for '[a]rtistic performances [that] question the category of blackness so as to locate silences, expound desire, and continuously reconfigure the way meanings are negotiated on the cultural stage' (2013: 2–3). They see this as contributing to an understanding of 'blackness as both the expressions of one's being black and the racializing discourses that generate the otherwise nonexistent category of race' (2013: 2–3).

One of the important possibilities in analysis of *OITNB* is that it screens representations of women in prison that are not entirely fictionalized, nor mediated through the agenda of outsiders, but are based on memoir (see also Collins 1986). There is a large body of prison memoirs (Graney 2003, 2004, 2006; James 2003; Kerman 2010; Lamb 2007; Lamb et al. 2003; Levi and Waldman 2011; Lawston and Lucas 2011). Of these, the prison memoir by Piper Kerman (2010) *Orange Is the New Black: My Time in a Women's Prison* has been adapted into the mainstream streaming series produced by Netflix (2013–ongoing). The production team includes Kerman as an advisor, and is one of very few TV series that includes a majority female cast. What makes it productive for prison cultures is the analysis of race, space and violence. I examine key storylines in the series predicated on two of the main propositions throughout this book. First, prison as a locus of cultural meaning allows for rich human drama in its capacity to produce stories that navigate dualities such as individual vs the system; good vs bad; and inside vs outside. Second, form and genre take on significance in the consideration of how representations are formed. The series resists adherence to a single genre, incorporating both tragic containment and dark humour, which means themes of incarceration that are otherwise usually fixed in morality and genre are refracted through more complex aesthetics. Although I am drawing on the series because of its visibility in mainstream culture, there are several major concerns and critiques to be acknowledged. Despite its incorporation of a multi-ethnic cast, the show's reliance on the privileged white woman encountering the Other in prison forms a large part of the unfolding plotlines (Artt and Schwan 2016; Belcher 2016; Enck and Morrissey 2015; Fryett 2016). Several critics point to some problematic racial stereotyping (Barak 2016; Belcher 2016; Cecil 2015). This suggests that a more explicit focus on race in the analysis of the show is desirable – not least because race is central to the understanding of prison cultures more broadly.

While the series is decidedly mainstream in its popularity and reach as well as its genre-straddling between drama and comedy, it also affords of the kind of visibility not often available to issues related to women in prison.[3] Despite the distinctive and important position of this series in contemporary Anglo-American culture, the approach in this chapter is to problematize its representations of race and violence in prison by engaging primarily with hooks' cultural critique in *Black Looks* (1992), *Outlaw Culture* (1994) and Stuart Hall's arguments about 'new ethnicities' (1996). These foundational works, as well as Crenshaw's (1993) theorization of intersectionality, prove valuable to thinking about how race and its countervalences of gender and class perform against the institutional field. In doing so, I further the politicized project in Black Studies of forging a fugitive method (Harney and Moten 2013: 40), which I explore further below.

Fugitivity and Grievable Lives

Stefano Harney and Fred Moten's (2013) concept of fugitivity deploys a methodology of resisting representations as fixed meanings while at the same time acknowledging the structuring forces of institutions. This suggests a style that deliberately provokes – identifying and acknowledging the existing ways in which meanings are forged and critiquing their limitations. This allows for an opportunity to see characters, storylines and visual tropes as questions posed *of* and *to* the institutional structures of the prison industrial complex. Such criticality sees blackness as a challenge to existing hegemonic knowledges that reinforce white supremacy as well as uphold institutional norms. This approach aims both to further the understanding of how prison cultures reflect existing oppressive structures and to inflect how academic discourse and cultural production form a counterpoint to the policies and everyday practices of carceral institutions. It is important to reflect here that while I deploy the logic of fugitivity, I am also aware of the limitations of my own white feminist epistemologies, and thus hope to avoid closure in my reading of how race, space and violence interrelate in the chosen examples.

Fugitivity flees the containment of the here and now, and moves towards a concept of futurity. While some of the examples I put forward here are about how the characters breach the perimeter, Harney and Moten (2013) theorize fugitivity beyond mere escape, understanding it as an unfolding, processual, perhaps elusive, resistance of authority, which feminist thinker Tina Campt (2015) calls a 'decolonial rejection of partial subjecthood'. Harney and Moten's (2013) fugitivity is a methodology of resisting representations in popular culture as fixed while at the same time acknowledging the structuring forces, and incessant *presence* of institutions. Fugitive methods allow for an opportunity to see characters, storylines and visual tropes as questions posed *of* and *to* the institutional structures of the prison industrial complex.

The reading of *OITNB* serves to foreground the necessity for radical challenge to representations of blackness and ethnic diversity in prisons as a matter of political urgency. In a filmed public discussion about the series, hooks critiques the series and its ghettoization of the ethnic groups but highlights a desire to engage with affirming, nurturing representations of a non-normative family structure in the form of Sophia Burset (a transgender woman played by actor Laverne Cox) and her wife and mother of her child, Crystal Burset (hooks and Cox 2016). hooks' commentary reflects her stated interest in representations of blackness that transcend dominant imagery of Black characters as transgressive and unruly – defined as such by being different from the norms and structures of white supremacist capitalist patriarchy.[4] However, what this critique misses is that the entire prison industrial complex can be examined as one of the formative institutions of white supremacy and its imbrication with what Wacquant calls 'workfare' (2010b).[5] Drawing on hooks' perspective (1992, as well as hooks and Cox 2014), the chapter proceeds in relation to some of the more recent criticisms of criminalization, blackness and the spectacularization of Black bodies in relation to everyday life (Mirzoeff 2017). The intent here is to construct a fugitive visual culture of blackness (Harney and Moten 2013) that can serve to critique the otherwise taken-for-granted coupling of blackness and unruliness that prevails in the United States and also in the United Kingdom as a legacy of the racist state and its operatives.

In order to do so, I will briefly rehearse some of the recent political philosophy theorization on grievability and whose lives matter (Butler 2004, 2009) that take as a starting point theories from Agamben (1998) related to 'bare life' (1998). His thinking about the notion of agency of those otherwise not recognized as integral to the body politic is mirrored in Butler and Athanasiou's work *Dispossession: The Performative in the Political* (2013). Their work seeks to position resistance within wider political and ethical questions about the limits of agency, sovereignty and responsibility. Agamben's argument in *Homo Sacer* is cogent on this point:

> Behind the long strife-ridden process that leads to the recognition of rights and formal liberties stands the body of the sacred man with his double sovereign, his life that cannot be sacrificed yet may be killed.
>
> (1998: 10)

In his important essay 'Necropolitics' (2003), philosopher and political scientist Achille Mbembe argued that Michel Foucault's concept of biopolitics is no longer sufficient to explain contemporary relations of power. Unlike biopolitics that governs from the perspective of the production and regulation of life, necropolitics regulates life from the perspective of a production and regulation of death. Mbembe observes how life is actually regulated within the extreme conditions of a war machine and of global capitalism. The notion of 'necropolitics' refers to life reduced to its bare existence, in other words, to life at the verge of death. While Foucault's biopolitics as mode of governmentality can be described in an axiomatic way as 'make live and let die', in Mbembe's necropolitics this expression is rephrased as to 'let live and make die'. Mbembe's working through of the notions of biopolitics via Hannah Arendt (1969), and Foucault draws particular attention to the ways in which state violence and sovereignty are enacted as an explicitly racist ideology: that is, it functions as a regulation of the distribution of death, by regulating whose lives count. Mbembe's necropolitics considers the 'capacity to define who matters and who does not, who is *disposable* and who is not' (2009: 27, original emphasis), a point taken further by Butler in *Frames of War: When is Life Grievable?* (2009).

Such thinking has arguably become ever more pressing in relation to the range of social crises of dispossession, precarity and state violence. This is particularly acute when we begin to consider how the state authors certain people as regulated, controlled, surveilled and subject to violence. Movements that respond to Black deaths resulting from police brutality, as well as protests against prison brutality signal an opportunity to make visible the ways in which policing, the carceral state and necropolitics render Black deaths a spectacle of corrections and control. As cultural theorist Alexander Weheliye defines it, 'blackness designates a changing system of unequal power structures that apportion and delimit which humans can lay claim to full human status and which humans cannot' (2014: 3). For Nicholas Mirzoeff, this makes the case for a visual culture of 'appearance', in which the effects, impacts and implications of the real events are multiplied, disseminated and solidified.

> To appear is to matter, in the sense of Black Lives Matter, to be grievable, to be a person that counts for something. And it is to claim the right to look, in the sense that I see you and you see me, and together we decide what there is to say as a result.
> (Mirzoeff 2017: 17)

The force and value of popular culture that attends to the questions of lives that matter is not underestimated when the setting is prison and that means that the range of intersecting issues from class, race, sexuality and gender are present in one setting. It is not merely that prison draws stark lines between privilege and legacies of oppression, but that the institutional field provokes particular habitus that fundamentally enables surviving the system.

OITNB begins by introducing Piper Kerman, a white, middle-class woman, into the prison system. The audience's experience mirrors the naïve, privileged outsider as she comes to terms with her new environment. By Seasons 4 and 5 of *OITNB*, the focus of the series shifts from the multiple intersecting stories of women incarcerated in Litchfield Penitentiary, and storylines relate to race-inflected protests at the prison industrial complex. Women form alliances to protest against worsening labour conditions, which shifts into some racial gang incidents (that are bizarrely represented as accidental, even though the living conditions are segregated into 'Spanish Harlem' for Latinx women, 'The Ghetto' for Black women and 'The Suburbs' for white prisoners). Finally, however, although racial tensions remain acute, the women form a series of protests against officer brutality and the lack of trained staff with a particular focus on the antagonist, Captain Desi Piscatella, whose backstory includes having been investigated for inmate murder in a male facility.

These increasingly more dramatic resistances correlate with the peaceful protests that are congruent with social justice movements. They include hunger strikes (in Season 2 where college student Brook Soso protests poor conditions), and then a more widespread strike that is initiated by Flores standing on dining tables. The escalation of the protest reaches a peak at the end of Season 4, where a poorly trained officer restrains Poussey, who suffocates and dies as a result (Season 4, Episode 12 'The Animals'). Poussey's death has direct resonances with the death of Eric Garner (2014), and her phrase 'I can't breathe' reflects his last words that were documented and disseminated widely (Mirzoeff 2017). Her death sparks a riot in the prison when the privately owned company does not acknowledge culpability. Several uniformed officers are taken hostage, and the riot (lasting several days) is the focus for the entirety of Season 5.

The gloss of grievable lives and its precedents suppose that representations of squalor, exploitation and distress position prison cultures as borderlands, or as spaces outside of legitimate civic existence. This correlates with Mbembe's necropolitics (2003). The formulation of some lives counting while others do not also reflects the constructions of borders, nations and identities. Prisons contain and separate 'us' from 'them' in similar ways to nation states drawing borders and building walls to protect land and peoples. This is also true of representations of prison in film and media, in which 'we' are the spectating public viewing the stories of the incarcerated Other. As Trinh Minh-ha highlights,

> a conversation of 'us' with 'us' about 'them' is a conversation in which 'them' is silenced. 'Them' always stands on the other side of the hill, naked and speechless, barely present in its absence.
>
> (1989: 67)

In his important work on new ethnicities, Stuart Hall (1996a) proposes that

> events, relations, structures, do have conditions of existence and real effects, outside the sphere of the discursive; but that it is only within the discursive, and subject to its specific conditions, limits and modalities, do they have or can they be constructed within meaning. Thus [...] how things are represented and the 'machineries' and regimes of representation in a culture do play a *constitutive*, and not merely a reflexive, after-the-event, role.
>
> (1996a: 443, original emphasis)

This view signals the importance of working through how popular culture constitutes the wider understanding of prisons and their populations. The obvious resonances in Season 5 with Black Lives Matter and the ways the series represents current material conditions for people institutionalized in the United States is one way *OITNB*, despite its problematic glib tone at times, puts forward a sense of prison culture. Similarly, the casting choice of trans actor Laverne Cox to play a trans woman prisoner (Sophia) is at once unusual in mainstream media representations and highly valuable for foregrounding the specific representational trope of trans identities in prison. For the most part, Sophia's trans identity is unremarkable, and her story is about her desires, alliances and struggles for recognition, as well as her desire to keep her family safe.[6] However, the character makes the particularities of institutional life for trans prisoners visible for a wide audience of spectators for whom otherwise, assumptions about gender, agency and offending might remain fixed. While this is important, it also erases the specific difficulties trans women face being recognized as women in sentencing – with many who end up incarcerated in men's facilities (Jenness 2010; Kandaswamy 2016; Lees 2017; Stanley and Smith 2011).

Writing about prison in the United States, Angela Davis says:

Women's prisons throughout the country increasingly include sections known as security housing units. The regimes of solitary confinement and sensory deprivation in the secure housing unit (SHU) in these sections within women's prisons are smaller versions of the rapidly proliferating super-maximum security prisons. Since the population of women in prison now consists of a majority of women of color, the historical resonances of slavery, colonization, and genocide should not be missed in these images of women in chains and shackles.

(2003: 77)

In Sophia's storyline, she is sent to the SHU on several occasions – ostensibly for her own protection. This tactic is used by prison officials when the existing mechanisms of security are inadequate and can often be deployed illegally.[7] In Season 4, Episode 4 ('Doctor Psycho'), Sophia floods her SHU cell by blocking the toilet and flushing it repeatedly, to try and get the attention of Governor Caputo.

CAPUTO:	Burset.
SOPHIA:	I never thought I'd be happy to see that moustache. You gotta get me out of here.
CAPUTO:	Well, turning your cell into a Russian bath is not helping your case. Flooding is a punishable offense. You should know that.
SOPHIA:	How else was I supposed to get your attention?
CAPUTO:	Well, you can ask for me.
SOPHIA:	Are you kiddin' me? I've been shoutin' your name for months.

(Season 4, Episode 4 'Doctor Psycho')

The scene proceeds with the governor lying to Sophia about how long she will remain segregated. Caputo has lied to Crystal about Sophia's whereabouts.

SOPHIA:	I wanna talk to my wife. Tell her where I am.
CAPUTO:	I've already spoken with Crystal.

SOPHIA: What? What? What'd she say?
CAPUTO: Well, she agrees with me. We need to wait for the right time to return you to gen pop.

(Season 4, Episode 4 'Doctor Psycho')

Caputo resorts to lies because his regime under the private company cannot guarantee Sophia's safety. He is aware that his badly trained staff employed by MCC are likely to perpetrate the kinds of prejudicial treatment Sophia face, rather than offer protection.

Sophia's storyline promotes thinking through the limits of prison representations on TV – we must imagine beyond gendered assumptions (related to which prisoners are placed in institutions appropriate for their genders). By focusing on placing her in the SHU, the audience must consider the implications of solitary confinement for prisoners. This signals the attempts of the series to raise conditions of survival in prison, and is one instance of the condition of the prisoner as one of bare life is highlighted. It also enables audiences to consider the diversity of people's experiences in women's prisons, drawing parallels across time. For Sophia, her experience of the deprivations and uncertainties of solitary confinement means that her connection with her family is untethered. This radical uncertainty and complete denial of agency on the Black subject is reminiscent of past mistreatment under slavery.

Having discussed the need for positioning and some degree of pluralism in cultural understandings of blackness, Hall says that 'categories and divisions and are constantly crossed and recrossed by the categories of class, of gender and ethnicity' (Hall 1996a: 444). Hall's point signals the importance of exploring how narrative choices and genre allow for the articulation of pluralism. This suggests the need to engage with women in prison as a genre, before considering specific examples of *OITNB*.

Resisting Genre Shackles: Women in Prison on Film and TV

The cultural turn in criminology attests to the growing importance of the interplay between representations and meanings for how we might understand prison (Ferrell and Sanders 1995; Ferrell et al. 2008). In particular, there has been a marked increase in the desire to define and unravel how meanings of prison are deployed in visual media – especially in film (Mason 2003a; Rafter 2000; Rafter and Brown 2011; Wilson and O'Sullivan 2004). Nicole Rafter's claims about the genre of prison on film is that they are

> essentially fantasies, films that purport to reveal the brutal realities of incarceration while actually offering viewers escape from the miseries of daily life through adventure and heroism [...] prison movies enable us to believe, if only briefly, in a world where long-suffering virtue is rewarded.
>
> (2000: 117)

Paul Mason (2003b) suggests that there is a more complex understanding of how genre of the prison film (and also by extension television) is constructed. His volume (2003a) offers a wide-ranging analysis of the range of genre-straddling that are to be found in prison films. However, as Wilson and O'Sullivan admit, the academic study of the genre of women-in-prison films has a bad reputation, dominated by accounts of exploitation films (2004: 120). What is relevant for the argument in *Prison Cultures* specifically is how the focus on women in the genre seems to trouble the neat narratives of virtue and fantasies of the 'normal' subject of prison representations – the male hero who overcomes prison's harms and deprivations to teach the spectators about how binaries of good and bad can be thrown into relief by fighting 'the system'. The primary examples of this for men are of course *The Shawshank Redemption* (1994) or *I am a Fugitive from a Chain Gang* (1932), discussed by Mason (2003b). By contrast, Walters sees the women-in-prison film as 'not one unitary genre but rather an odd and eclectic pastiche of many sub-genres – from melodrama to teenage trouble to exploitation to protofeminist' (2001: 107). Wilson and O'Sullivan account for the oddly shifting genre in many prison films and television between deeply serious (in which case, they argue, they can replicate the imagery and forms of exploitation films), or else resorting to 'camp', 'cartoonish' representations in what they call the 'pleasure/purpose bargain' (2004: 124). Partly, they suggest, there is the need to exhort viewership with eclectic juxtaposition between the serious intent of giving voice to the 'harsh realities' of prison, but also to entertain with comic relief in revealing status being undercut, exposing injustices and revealing the constructedness of power (2004: 128). For them, stories about women in prison have the ability to bring attention to the 'irrationality of prison' (2004: 121) to the wider public.

What is specific about women in prison on film is the distinction between the women and their diverse experiences. Viewers' personal political beliefs might span liberal to conservative responses to incarceration. There is no singular perspective then on the encounter with characters and narratives in film and television. However, in terms of genre, there are several tropes that are evident in overturning the often-hegemonic ways in which we understand women – angel and whore; wife and mother; or single woman as threat to stable family life. A feminist approach to stories that include women's crime and incarceration would seek to destabilize these binaries.

Queer theorist Jack Halberstam (2001) offers an impressive exploration of representations of violence and proposes a queer reading of Black violence as resistance. Their examination of violence fundamentally offers a means of resisting categories such as victims, and demands new imaginings about the morality, assumptions and outcomes that are upheld as hegemonic. This reading takes on a renewed urgency in light of police brutality and everyday violence perpetuated by the state as seen in places such as Ferguson and the Black Lives Matter movement (Mirzoeff 2017). In Halberstam's reading, there is an explicit connection between the solidarity of women behind bars against their oppressors:

In its problematizing of femininity and its simultaneous exploration of female violence as female bonding, 'the prison film makes clear links between poverty, female masculinity, female criminality, and the predatory butch'.

(Halberstam 1998: 202, cited in Walters 2001: 121–22)

Halberstam excavates violence and how popular culture links with intersecting vectors of marginalization. While the focus of much of the study of women in prison on film is most often on the problematics of gender and sexuality, it is also necessary to consider how the critical apparatus of analysing the tropes of women in prison draws attention to how race, ethnicity and violence are characterized.

In a similar vein, Schwan draws on Mayne (2000) and Mulvey (1975), saying that '*OITNB* exploits generic tropes to open up a debate around relationships and differences between women, differences to do with ethnic, racial, and sexual identity' (2016: 5). This reading is critical of *OITNB*'s consideration of Piper's claim for 'colour blindness'. The show does not sufficiently draw attention to the structural issues that lead to racial profiling, inequalities that result in criminalization, and the differentiation between sentencing for Black and minority ethnic people. This is precisely the issue at the heart of Alexander's criticism of mass incarceration (2012), and as such demands specific attention to how race is performed in relation to the prison industrial complex, and what this means for the notion of genre. Colour blindness in relation to the prison industrial complex is inappropriate, unethical and enables the perpetuation of racist structuration that continues to be more punitive to people of colour in the United States.

Performing Race, Resistance and Agency: *Orange Is the New Black*

In one of the most significant sociological studies of race, space and criminalization, Loïc Wacquant develops an understanding of ghettoization and systemic means of punishing the poor (2008b, 2009a, 2009b, 2010a) via institutions and growing insecurity. Wacquant's analysis of space, structural racism and the sociology of marginality seeks to theorize the means by which ghettos, the cycles of welfare dependency and the sense of precarity coagulate in the construction of pipelines that criminalize people. For Wacquant, these social conditions mean that lack of opportunity, stigma, lack of financial security and fractured sense of civic belonging result in urban outcasts (2008b).

Wacquant's later theorization of workfare[8] draws attention to how both welfare and prisons become people processing institutions, which, he says

has been facilitated by the transformation of welfare in a punitive direction and the activation of the penal system to handle more of the traditional clientele of assistance to the destitute – the incipient 'penalization' of welfare matching the degraded 'welfarization' of the prison.

(2010b: 203)

Using Wacquant's criticism of workfare to explore the re-rolling of Litchfield Penitentiary as a state institute to being managed by the private corporation MCC, it is obvious that the driver of profit over the welfare of prisoners is paramount.[9] This is particularly evident in the figure of Linda Ferguson, the Director of Purchasing, who promotes cost cutting to include cheap restraints, affordable pre-cooked meals and scrapping the education programme to 'vocational courses' that are rather free manual labour. Governor Caputo is shown to be almost powerless in how he implements these decisions, which is made especially galling when he realizes that Linda has never entered a prison, yet holds all the decision making purse strings. He also critiques the implementation of methods that are appropriate for men, asking for consideration of women's needs and differences. As discussed elsewhere, this is one of the primary issues noted by feminist criminology: that women's needs are distinct and require tactics and programmes that are fit for purpose, rather than imported from a male estate. This definition of workfare and the brief overview of the institution depicted in *OITNB* serve to introduce the section on the relationship between the prison, agency and resistance.

Thinking through women prisoners' subjective agency demands awareness of the ways in which such agency is always already framed by institutional norms and values. Thus, a focus on resistance-as-agency is valuable. In recent literature, criminologists have begun to explore creative resistance as an important area for research, because it demands rethinking the ways in which power, punishment and its effects are performed, or otherwise mediated through popular culture (Carrabine 2012; Cheliotis 2012a; Liebling 2004). From a feminist perspective, resistance is important because it asserts a countervailing force that may be able to disassemble the monolithic power structures once conceived of as inevitable. Resistance in everyday life is not only evident in large-scale refusal or denial of power structures, such as riots, revolts and revolutions; rather, an everyday resistance is an embodied reclamation of agency that causes a re-framing of the original (oppressive) status quo. Halberstam says:

> [t]he scenes of rebellious women in prison films always allow for the possibility of an overt feminist message that involves both a critique of male-dominated society and some notion of female community.
>
> (1998: 201)

Media and cultural studies scholars Householder and Trier-Bieniek collated a range of feminist articles (2016a) on *Orange Is the New Black*. The contributors suggest there is a need to understand the importance of a mainstream show with the subject matter of life in prison. The volume also seeks to develop critical materials on the effectiveness of representations, the problematic associations of sexuality, predation and race and the tropes and narratives that are replicated despite the stated stance of activism by the show's creator, Kohan (cited in Householder and Trier-Bieniek 2016b: 17). Many of the contributions in this volume and critical articles on the show develop critical vocabularies around issues of representation and identity politics, focused on the degrading tropes of lesbianism aping heteronormative 'conquest' (Fryett 2016; Hunting 2016); race and ethnicity (Artt and Schwan 2016; Enck and Morrissey 2015; Fryett 2016) and class (Schwan 2016).

These analyses seem to suggest that a mainstream television series should develop responsible narratives that represent these categories effectively and appropriately. Yet, what is not adequately accounted for in this scholarship is the ways prison effectively re-inscribes damaging and degrading representations of brutal sexual dominance (especially between uniformed officers and prisoners such as between Tiffany/Pensatucky and Charlie Coates), the devaluation of agency and the use of sex as currency, as well as fickle alliances related to existing power structures that are often inscribed in racial terms. Thus, for critics of *OITNB*, the series either succeeds merely because it 'stages diversity' (in terms of race and class in particular, but also because of its diverse representation in terms of age, body type and sexuality); or it fails because it does not adequately offer the identity categories transformative potential beyond prison.

What I hope to further here is that it is a matter of genre, not simply of familiar women-in-prison tropes, that is productive in *OITNB*'s representation of prison culture. Fernández-Morales and Menéndez-Menéndez say:

Even in their hostile, potentially destructive context, the show's protagonists still fight to improve their plight, initiating a series of 'transformative actions' that, in Susan Sered and Maureen Norton-Hawk's (2011: 328) terminology, can be dubbed 'resistance' […] We adopt this label of resistance to counteract the tendency to conceptualize women in prison as victims.

(2016: 4)

Resistance becomes particularly relevant in Seasons 4 and 5, where we witness agency beyond individual tactics to get access to extra food from commissary, or indeed, to maintain a sexual relationship with each other. In prior seasons, these tactics were part of what enabled the genre to develop as a blended comedy of tragic containment. The stakes for women were fairly low, and their tactics reflect a low-grade comic perspective on life in an institution. The tactic for how to avoid getting athlete's foot in the unsanitary showers was to devise flip-flops out of sanitary pads; one way to get high is to stick a head into a bucket of bleach supposedly intended to clean the floors. Though the wit and snappy dialogue as well as a cast of supporting characters allow for continued one-liners about the harms of prison life, the overriding merit of the series is that it offers representations that unsettle as they straddle comedy and tragic containment. The rest of this chapter engages with how the shift in the series moves away from individual stories and begins to consider how group solidarities render the prison narrative more politicized. Speaking from a perspective of global resistance, Amoore says:

Though resistance is characteristically understood to be expressed through the politics of protest, demonstration, public statement or declaration, then, the more mundane gestures of everyday life reveal significant sites of political struggle.

(2005: 7)

The examples that I analyse here are a small range of the possible storylines or moments in the series that are particularly selected as they offer a means of understanding some of the complex intersections of living and surviving in the context of prison. It is precisely this that is the core of my analysis of this series – that although problematic, it offers representations of mundane/everyday actions of survival rather than heroic narratives – they correspond to forms of activism that highlight this idea of life (such as Black Lives Matter).

In her chapter on the series, Kalima Young offers a nuanced view of racialized trauma of the prison system using dual concepts of trauma and spectacle to explore how violence and dehumanization in the prison can serve to 'erase' victim status (2016: 48). By contrast, Young says, *OITNB* deploys the device of flashbacks as a means of humanizing the characters, largely in relation to how agency is navigated in youth and on the outside. While this works well in earlier seasons – particularly as a means of offering up intersecting vectors of marginality for the people of colour in the story – in later seasons, the flashbacks become longer and often serve as social commentary (such as Red's youth in Soviet conditions, which serves to dilute the politicized focus on present oppression in the rioting prison throughout Season 5).

A fugitive reading of some of the scenes in *OITNB* that stage race, space and violence offers a viable opportunity to consider how desire and resistance are interlinked. This is important in relation to the issues that I foreground in the earlier part of this chapter – namely the struggle to appear, and to count as human. For cultural producers the challenge is thus to inflect representation with the sometimes-competing discourses of victimhood, oppression and the heroics offered by resistance. A cogent example of this is in the final episode of Season 3 ('Trust No Bitch'), where a security breach enables women in Litchfield to escape the perimeter fence and to swim in a nearby reservoir. The sequence (straddling Seasons 3 and 4) depicts women's joy at experiencing freedom while simultaneously demonstrating the ways the prison regime disciplines and delimits women's capacity to enjoy themselves. This is one narrative example of the series positioning desire and resistance as mutually constitutive, but nonetheless always circumscribed by carceral logics.

This is particularly clear in one storyline that is traced from the breach, in which Suzanne and her friend and love interest, Maureen, stay out rather than return, when the officers notice the situation and return the prisoners to their wings. This opportunity could offer them a chance to be together, as Maureen tries to convince Suzanne to stay with her. However, Suzanne becomes concerned about missing the regime's routines, and returns voluntarily, to prison. Throughout the series, the performer Uzo Aduba's ability to represent Suzanne's struggle with mental illness is notable.[10] In this sequence, however, what is depicted is not so much an indication of Suzanne's inability to desire a different life, but rather a dependency on the systemic structures that help make her feel safe. The ramifications of the escape, however, mean that the prison regime becomes even more punitive, and it is in the context of the stronger security systems, the privatization of the spaces of incarceration and the intolerance of the regime that is not fit for women that much of the politicized force of the series is reflected. Desire, for Suzanne, is unknown. Despite feeling attraction to Maureen, and enjoying the momentary freedom offered by the escape, Suzanne's story arc returns to a narrative of tragic containment. Resistance, evident in her regular resorting to violence, is often a result of seemingly feeling vulnerable.

The flashbacks that run throughout the series explicate Suzanne's story as a Black child adopted by white parents and whose naivety and mental health resulted in her sentence. Much of the focus on Suzanne explores a sense of dissonance between blackness and her childhood experience of whiteness and privilege (as compared to some of her friends in prison, for example). In terms of her role, Suzanne's character typology forms much of the darkly comic material, largely in relation to the tactics used by her fellow inmates to help, or ignore, her shifts in symptoms of mental health crisis. This is acute in the example of Suzanne's fight with Maureen that she is goaded into by an officer, discussed below.

The focus on Suzanne's struggle with mental ill health becomes much more nuanced in later seasons, especially when fellow inmates become responsible for administering (and withhold) medication – as they claim medication becomes another form of discipline. Kathleen Kendall considers the interconnectedness between gendered expectations, deviance and criminal lunacy. She suggests that overreliance on medicalizing women has historically meant that even though women 'were not merely passive actors [...], they were not able to direct the scenes either' (Kendall 2005: 55). In Suzanne's case, her trajectory in the story is initially having been isolated and typecast as 'Crazy Eyes' where her mental illness is coded as 'beyond reason' (Kendall 2005). In later seasons, as characters learn to navigate her outbursts, she gains popularity when she creates a fantasy adventure that is sexually explicit. Suzanne represents the capacity of desire to resist the prejudice she faces in daily routines by writing the 'Time Hump Chronicles'. Her science-fiction adventure forms a fan club, in particular garnering the amorous attentions of Maureen. Her project had offered her and others a creative release, but is ultimately quashed by the counsellor as inappropriate. Prison writing as one form of prison cultures is routinely censored under waves of moral panic about the need to limit creative freedom.

OITNB offers some of the means of understanding the experiences that lead to incarceration, but it is particularly notable that there are no direct examples of women of colour who have been incarcerated in the so-called 'war on drugs'. Michelle Brown's important work explores race and the entrenched attitudes of prejudice that operate at every level of criminalization through the courts, via sentencing and into prisons. She says:

> What is painfully obvious when one steps back from individual cases and specific policies is that the system of mass incarceration operates with stunning efficiency to sweep people

of color off the streets, lock them in cages, and then release them into an inferior, second-class status.

(2012: 103)

For Alexander, the war on drugs is the most significant area in which the 'colour of justice' in the United States is to be seen (2012: 98–139), chiming with Wacquant's analysis of workfare (2010b) and punishing the poor (2009b). The limitations of the series are evident in the roughly equal representation of women from different ethnic backgrounds, which is not representative of the statistics (The Sentencing Project 2015). The choices of narrative and fast-paced shifts initially circulate on tropes of Piper as the white outsider (in class, status and experience – despite being sentenced for drug trafficking) entering a new world to the tropes of gangs and alliance building of a range of outsiders against 'the system'. Yet in the first seasons, this means that some of the elements of women's prisons are left out. As Belcher claims:

The show eschews overt racism by representing a diversity of bodies and cultures, but the structural racism that lands a skewed sample of black and Hispanic women in prison is ultimately left without much interrogation.

(2016: 4)

Some of these omissions are arguably due to the stultifying boredom of prisons, as well as the predominance of medicated individuals as decidedly not spectacular. Perhaps a difficulty that is posed for representations is the causality of some of these issues. It is obvious that Suzanne's mental health is constructed as a spectacle and that it needs management. For women with mental illness in prison, the impacts of low-level medication on women's energy levels, their abilities to remain alert to dangers or cope without medication are more pressing for the regime when multiplied. Similarly, women whose addictions mean they maintain behaviours that seek narcotic highs mean that there is an importance in managing access to substances, what responsibilities they are given and an understanding of how people might attempt to access highs. These are two examples of how energies and motivations of women in prison might need management for their own safety. But these rather more banal understandings of safety are less about individuals' own agency and reflect on the wider sociocultural phenomena that code Black women as unruly and are likely to over-medicate Black women.

Suzanne's character serves a valuable purpose in the series, becoming one of the stable storylines that drives many of the plot points. As demonstrated, though this is initially light hearted in the semi-comedic seasons, the focus on Suzanne's dependency on medication and her treatment by officials draws attention to one of the most significant problems faced by women in prison. An important report on the misuse of jails in the United States for the Vera Institute makes the following point about consequences of jailing people with mental illness:

The lack of treatment in a chaotic environment contributes to a worsening state of illness and is a major reason why those with mental illness in jail are more likely to be placed in solitary confinement, either as punishment for breaking rules or for their own protection since they are also more likely to be victimized.

(Subramanian et al. 2015: 12)

The link between lack of care and victimization (both by fellow prisoners and officers) is evident in the following scene from Season 4, in which there is a violent fight that renders the loser hospitalized. The series largely avoids excessive violence, relying instead on women using scare tactics or minor bullying between prisoners. This fight moves beyond threat and results in actual bodily harm. The violent incident occurs between Suzanne and Maureen, and in some ways could be seen as personal vendetta. Yet, what is offered by the imagery of the scene is that Suzanne is clearly an unwilling participant, is struggling with understanding the conflict and is overwhelmed by the crowd, when an officer goads her into beating Maureen, who is frustrated with how their potential romance/escape ended.

MAUREEN:	Because you never gave me the chance.
SUZANNE:	Please don't push!
MAUREEN:	Well, then fight me. Fight me!
SUZANNE:	I, I don't wanna do this!
OFFICER:	Well, you might as well.
MAUREEN:	You don't know how romance works. You don't even know how people work.
OFFICER:	Get back in there.
SUZANNE:	Be quiet. Be quiet!
MAUREEN:	And you never will. You'll always be the person that everybody laughs at.
SUZANNE:	Shut up!
MAUREEN:	The same pathetic loser virgin!

(Season 4, Episode 11 'People Persons')

The brutal beating is presented as inevitable – a logical outcome to humiliation by the officers, the confusion of the crowd baiting her and as retaliation against Maureen for making her feel vulnerable. Suzanne's violence can also be read here as a further representation of how unruly Black women are coded as violent and expected to behave by authorities. This visual representation of the Black woman as excessive, and thus as inevitably justifying excessive force and pre-emptive surveillance is reminiscent of the policing of Black women in the United States, including Sandra Bland and many more (Lazare 2015; Mirzoeff 2017). It also pre-empts the force used by Officer Bayley against Poussey in the following episode – which might signal how Black violence is fugitive – when Bayley's naïve whiteness codes the slim, athletic, passive body of Poussey as violent merely because she is Black, this is not simply his character's 'fault', but indicative of systemic readings of violence as 'inherent to blackness'. Note my characterization of Bayley's innocence here is not in good faith, but reflects how the series positions him as a naïve, if somewhat rash young man who makes some bad decisions. This profoundly undermines the influence of institutionalized racism in perpetuating stereotypes of Black people as deserving of excessive force in policing.

From thinking about agency in relation to violence, I am also interested in how readings of agency as desire enable a fugitive reading on race and the institution. The range of narrative threads offered by focus on character-arcs allows for the development of characters' agency in flashbacks, dreams and desires in the present location of the prison, and for some characters, the stories transgress the locale of prison as they represent some women's experiences of leaving prison. Two storylines are cogent here, both of which offer important considerations of race, institutionalization and its implications beyond the sentence. These relate to Alieda Diaz' release from prison and job-hunting in Season 4; and the earlier release and recidivism of Tasha 'Taystee' Jefferson, whose storyline in Season 1 has her violate parole conditions to return to prison. In both storylines, the women depart from prison full of hopefulness for the return to the real world and their family lives; and in both cases, the realities of chaos, unpredictable living arrangements, the strictness of parole conditions and the pace of expectations seem unmanageable. In both of these examples, the women experience release as a further challenge, rather than the uncomplicated 'freedom' that seems so desirable from inside. Once outside Litchfield penitentiary, the implications of stigma, lack of work experience and the difficulties related to making sense of place are limitations for the women in their attempts to survive. By representing how narratives of desire (for different outcomes) are always returned to the contextual issues, *OITNB* promotes the wider problems of re-integration for people post-release. In particular, what is evident is the specific coalescence of race and the stigma of a criminal record when it comes to life outside.

This notion of carcerality extruding from the site of the prison itself is also evident in an episode when worsening employment conditions mean mistakes occur in the regime, and one of the long-term prisoners, Angie, is mistakenly released. When the beleaguered governor attempts to recover her himself he finds her sitting at the bus station, having spent her few dollars' release money on candy because she didn't know where to go. This is not only significant because she effectively performs institutionalization by allowing recapture but also because it signals how communities are themselves structured according to the institutionalized and systemic, as well as spatial logic of containment (as discussed by Alexander 2012). For Angie, the violence is not relegated to the punitive regime, but rather manifests as an extension of the mechanisms of the system that become internalized, in what Allspach calls the 'transportation of 'the carceral'' (2010: 718). She explores the ways neo-liberal governance re-regulates women's desires, behaviours and spatial locations.

The women's resistances are what form the narrative drive to the series. These range from interpersonal tactics to undermine individuals in authority that form the landscape of prison films and TV, through to scenes of bodies resisting the system. In the later seasons, the resistances are increased and form more urgent responses against the more brutal private company and the officers, whose own capacity to negotiate and de-escalate tensions is not well developed. One example that signals the growing use of force and the bullying of prisoners by officers is sited in the cafeteria. Blanca Flores is represented throughout as an unruly, Dominican woman, whose predominant use of Spanish even when spoken to in English means that she positions herself at the margins. In part, this is her tactic to avoid getting drawn into wider issues, but in 'Turn Table Turn' (Season 4, Episode 9), Flores deploys her forcefulness and single-mindedness by entering into a standing protest on the cafeteria tables. She is forced to spend several days standing on the table, not eating and without access to the bathroom by Officer Humphrey who finds her smell offensive. Women in prisons use this deliberate tactic of poor hygiene as a means of expressing agential control of their bodies, though this is also a common sign of depression. When Piper, as the white outsider, joins Flores in the protest, the situation escalates.

OFFICER:	You heard Piscatella, no food.
PIPER:	I am not gonna stand by while somebody starves to death. So give me four shots, or whatever, make me crawl back to my bunk.

(Season 4, Episode 10 'Bunny Skull, Bunny Skull')

This is one instance in which the central character of the series as the representative of the middle-class, white woman drives the action. Flores being forced to stand without food develops into wider action by Piper becoming involved. In the same episode, the couple Brook Soso and Poussey discuss the need for a wider resistance movement. The two characters have different expectations of what strikes can do. For Brook, socialized as a campus activist, her belief is that activism can lead to change. Poussey, although also raised in privileged circumstances as a military child, has a different experience of what resistance means for Black people in prison.

SOSO:	We'll just have to take down the prison administration first, and then we'll be able to take over the world.
POUSSEY:	Wait, you don't think that protest is going to work, do you?
SOSO:	Of course, I do. Why wouldn't I?
POUSSEY:	I don't know, you're excited to have a project.
SOSO:	A project? This isn't knitting. This is social change and justice. It's important.
POUSSEY:	Absolutely, it just ain't gonna happen in this place.
SOSO:	Well, I'm not willing to not try.
POUSSEY:	Brook, this isn't important, okay? Over there, outside all of this. That's what's important. Why waste your energy trying to get some dude who don't even matter fired, when they're gonna hire some other guy tomorrow who'll probably be worse?

(Season 4, Episode 10 'Bunny Skull, Bunny Skull')

This exchange prefigures the extent to which the later protest is doomed to fail. Poussey's logic is that the regime will prevail and the systemic nature of prison rules and regulations cannot be stopped by the prisoners' desire for justice. Nonetheless, she joins the group in solidarity. Yet, her understanding of the prison as inevitable and fixed in its punishment is then brought to bear when she becomes the victim of brutal restraint by Officer Bayley, and dies as a result of asphyxiation. Poussey's death is, as explored earlier, the symbol of necropolitics. The regime's policies mean prisoners are 'let live' in squalid conditions, and its operatives are destined to 'make die' (cf. Mbembe 2003). In Season 5, then, as a result of the worsening tensions and the death of Poussey a turning point, the prison faces riot conditions. After three days of looting, destruction of property, hostage-taking and attempts to negotiate for better conditions, the prisoners invested in acknowledgement of Poussey's death decide that TV celebrity Judy King should be used to deliver their demands.

The riot is a violent rupture of the logic of the institution that enables prisoners to air their demands in a way that makes their conditions visible. However, the genre shifts mean that this is not a straightforward message. Instead, it is one that relies on a racialized narrative that is mediated in the example of Judy who has been given preferential treatment in prison and who gets captured by the white supremacist trio to leverage some additional demands when they believe she can help them escape. However, their attempt to escape with her is to tie Judy to a pole in a manner similar to crucifixion, and their sojourn to the roof of the building has them wearing fabrics over their heads to obscure their identities. When footage of Judy and the white supremacists is mediated from recordings obtained by helicopter cameras, Judy's captors are discussed as Islamic terrorists.

Later, Judy is bartered in an excruciating comedic scene between the white supremacists and the Black women, both of whom wish to exploit the social capital of the middle-aged white celebrity. For Taystee, thinking about gaining ground for the demands, the mediated stakes for the wider public are higher if Judy delivers the demands about the conditions in prison than if an 'ordinary' prisoner does. It is of course notable that Judy's white privilege and her status as a TV star have meant that her own experiences of prison bear little resemblance to those of her fellow inmates. As they prepare the statement, the following exchange signals Judy's distance from daily prison life:

OFFICER [who is being held hostage but is helping the women prepare statement]: Oh, and I personally think it might be helpful if you shared some sort of, um, relatable tribulations from your time in here. Some painful experiences, uh, injustices. Uh. Um – We could also lie.

JUDY KING: [stutters] I am game to lie. All right, so now, ladies, what would you like me to say?

(Season 5, Episode 5 'Sing it, White Effie')

Women add to the list that the use of the SHU is arbitrary, that they are denied proper healthcare and dental care, that officers beat them for no reason, that cavity searches are undertaken for no reason.[11] They comment that they are living in overcrowded conditions and access to bathrooms means hygiene is an issue, and that the quality of food is poor. They continue to add to the list:

TAYSTEE: We don't get paid for our labor. We're denied education. We're denied the chance to breastfeed our babies. We're denied basic humanity. And we get killed in the cafeteria for no reason.
[…]
JANAE: You can't let this white woman speak for us. She needs to take our stories out her mouth.
(Season 5, Episode 5 'Sing it, White Effie')

Later, as the Black women face the media and Judy is about to make the statement, Taystee realizes that Janae's comment was correct, and takes the opportunity for self-representation.

TAYSTEE: Sorry. She will not be speaking for us because Judy King can't speak for the inmates of this prison. She was kept separate from us, held in a private room with better treatment and a seltzer-maker. And moments after our friend, Poussey Washington, was murdered by a guard for doing nothing wrong, Judy King was packing her bags to go home on early release. Because she's rich and white and powerful. Now, our fight is not with Judy King. Our fight is with a system that don't give a damn about poor people and brown people and poor brown people. [sobbing] Our fight is with the folks who hold our demands in their hands. Which you people need to read, by the way, and stop watching this fool shit comin' out of here online and get a hold of our demand list because those demands are fair and necessary, and show that we intend to keep this demonstration peaceful and focused on change.
(Season 5, Episode 5 'Sing it, White Effie')

Taystee's intervention interrupts the plan to let the white celebrity deliver the list of demands. Instead, she makes a plea to be heard, and demands that Poussey's death be acknowledged. In other words, she insists that, despite the necropolitics of the institution, Black death be considered grievable. Taystee's monologue highlights her need to articulate a desire that is beyond merely tangible or material improvements to conditions – namely the desire to be seen/to be made visible/to be recognized as human. Her speech highlights the problem that is endemic to Black people, and in this case specifically Black women in prison – the struggle to be represented, to appear at all. However, it must also be understood as operating within its popular form on mainstream TV, and her language in this speech does not fundamentally differ from a 'heroic' outburst of a male hero in a prison film such as *The Shawshank Redemption*. This kind of speech seems staged and predictable – addressing the presumed liberal white viewer, offering a very easy to consume image of justice.

The major plot point that performs race, space and violence is the revelation that Frieda, a middle-aged 'redneck' inmate, has been constructing a survivalist bunker in an abandoned indoor pool underneath the prison. This, coupled with the mediated riot device of armed officers, media and a crowd of worried supporters waiting outside, serves to demonstrate the dynamic that prison is predicated upon – the contested and protected threshold between inside/outside – and the perspective of viewer enables proximity and distance from the struggles of women.

If, as human geography would have it, space is a set of relations and not a container, then the scenes I have focused upon in *OITNB* offer a means of seeing prisons as dynamic negotiations of power, race relations and the effects of these negotiations (cf. Massey 2004). Momentary escapes – which are theorized often in arts in prisons as constituted (Cheliotis 2012a, 2012b) by creativity, collectivity and the imagination – are produced in the scenes of escape that signal the paradoxes of fugitivity. In the first example, the breach of the perimeter fence triggers the ever-tightening surveillance, segregation and punitive regime of the private company. The breach embodies what is ephemeral and elusive as a marker of paradoxical freedom. In the other example, we understand Frieda's construction as a time-intensive labour that is only possible as she has been incarcerated for such a long time. She has imagined a future in which freedom will mean ever diminishing space. Where survival is imagined as possible only underneath the existing structures of the prison. For Frieda, the decision to invite people she connects with into the bunker is one that signals solidarity, alliances and collective resistance. It is not an unproblematic resistance, however, as she reinforces segregationist ideas about who has the right to survive over others.

Breaches of prison imagine the women as resisting the carceral function of prison as impenetrable, monolithic and complete. While neither instance – the breach of the perimeter fence or the bunker – is entirely 'successful' in dismantling the regime, they offer productive moments of fugitivity. The swim and Frieda's bunker produce opportunities to defy the logic of containment; while demonstrating that carcerality extrudes, and ultimately, subsumes whatever freedoms are carved into its structures. In the case of the breach of the fence, the women are rounded up and return to their dorms having swum in the tainted reservoir waters. Although some of the women find momentary respite from the riot in Frieda's bunker, and they manage to capture a sadistic officer, the final moment of the most recent season includes a line-up of women being captured by riot police, signalling a return to the most punitive logic of carcerality – deadly force.

There are plenty of possible narratives in *OITNB* that merit further analysis in relation to both the prison TV series genre that blends comedy and tragic containment and issues related to media representations of women in prison. For the purposes of this chapter, however, the focus remains on the two core, interrelated analytic points: desire and resistance. The shift in the series from largely being constructed around personal narrative in the first three seasons to the wider prison culture in Seasons 4 and 5 is indicative of the limitations of individual narratives in the face of the system, and its structural racism. On the one hand, it is perhaps initially empowering to consider the agency of people in prison by having their backstories, prior traumas, motivations and complex issues made evident. On the other hand, to focus entirely on individuals and agency is to assume that 'strength', resilience or righteousness is sufficient to prevail. Instead, despite the often-uneven results in terms of genre and coherence of the series, *OITNB* provides a valuable representational critique of the individual narrative that is profoundly politicized. That is, the complex and seemingly intractable framing of the prison as field is determined by wider neo-liberal trends towards privatization and marketization.

A feminist analysis allows a specific engagement with how agency, desire and the body interrelate with spaces of incarceration. *OITNB* offers a visual culture of the domestic spaces of inhabitation in prison as well as reading those against the patriarchal, hegemonic structures of prison. Rather than attempt to analyse this across all storylines, I have focused on Suzanne Martin and the main plot point of protests for recognition that specifically affect the Black characters. In light of this, I revisit hooks' critical invitation to reassess how cultural representations need tropes that disrupt, unsettle and radically revision the status quo. In the context of a US prison narrative, the prevailing narratives of poverty, lack of choice, drug addiction and lives characterized by abuse and chaos are not sufficiently challenged. hooks argues for representations that

> transform our worldviews and move us away from dualistic thinking about good and bad. Making a space for the transgressive image, the outlaw rebel vision, is essential to any effort to create a context for transformation.
>
> (1992: 4)

Partly, this is due to the series' genesis as an adaptation of Kerman's memoir (2010). It straddles genres between the comedy of mainstream series in the Internet era (replete with one-liners and glib observances of the harms of prison) and the drama of the contexts of the characters' lives (represented largely through flashbacks to the backstories of the characters). Nevertheless, if, as the media visibility (McClelland 2015), awards and public discussions (hooks and Cox 2016) portend, the series has opened debates about the value, place and necessity of prison in society, then there is further important activist-aligned work to be done on developing the seasons to come. This correlates with Kohan's statement that writing the series is her contribution to prison abolition (cited in Householder and Trier-Bieniek 2016b: 17), which moves *OITNB* beyond an adaptation of a memoir (and the focus on individuals) to a more up-to-date sociopolitical critique in the later seasons.

I develop a fugitive reading of *OITNB* by conceiving of a methodology that reads representations of prison as valuable for understanding prison's daily rituals, effects and implications. I also consider how prison cultures are informed by tropes and narratives of race, space and violence. In certain scenes from *OITNB*, fugitive tactics of Blackness can be productive in thinking through how prisons institutionalize and perform race inequalities. In particular, a focus on resistance and the labour associated with race are explored via a range of thinkers in order to platform the importance of prison cultures in mainstream media. Representations of marginalization, intersectionality and criminalization in the examples from *OITNB* help to humanize the issues faced by women who are caught up in the criminal justice system, and how these are particularly acute for Black and Minority Ethnic people. The chapter signals the frame of genre as significant in the understanding of prisoners' narratives as inevitably informed by institutionalized racism. This is thus a particularly feminist reading of *OITNB* in which genre trouble, tropes and characterization can stage power, and draw attention to the lived conditions of institutions, prison labour and human rights.

Notes

1 Jenji Kohan claims that the central character Piper

> was my Trojan Horse. You're not going to go into a network and sell a show on really fascinating tales of black women, and Latina women, and old women and criminals. But if you take this white girl, this sort of fish out of water, and you follow her in, you can then expand your world and tell all of those other stories.
>
> (cited in Symes 2017: 31)

2 I am retaining the use of capitals in 'Black' to reflect what Mirzoeff claims as significant in recent work on Black Lives Matter: aware that it is 'against convention [but] in keeping with the practice of Black Lives Matter and my own conviction that a distinction between Black people, blackness, and black is structural under regimes of white supremacy' (2017: 17).

3 It is interesting to note that Netflix does not release data for viewing statistics (ratings), as other media channels do. However, the budget and the stature of the cast in mainstream popular culture (McClelland 2015) indicate the influence of the series. For more, see Artt and Schwan (2016); Belcher (2016); Cecil (2015, 2017); Enck and Morrissey (2015); Fernández-Morales and Menéndez-Menéndez (2016); Householder and Trier-Bieniek's volume of critical essays (2016a, 2016b); Kerman (2010); Schwan (2016); and Silverman and Ryalls (2016).

4 For more on transgender prisoners, Stanley and Smith's (2011) edited collection *Captive Genders* is instructive, including scholarly and experiential accounts of trans embodiment and the prison industrial complex.

5 This point is also discussed by Julia Sudbury (2002: 72):

> Increasingly, black women and women of color are the raw material that fuel the prison industrial complex: as scapegoats of tough-on-crime rhetoric, targets of drug busting operations that generate millions for police, customs and military budgets, or workers sewing and assembling electronics in prison workshops.

6 The obvious exception to this is in early seasons in which Sophia's offence is explained as fraud related to her need to pay for medical procedures for transition. In Season 1, Episode 3

'Lesbian Request Denied', Laverne Cox's real-life twin brother played her character pre-transition in a flashback scene.

7 Official use of restricted accommodation or solitary confinement varies considerably internationally. In the United Kingdom, for example, prison rule 45 specifies reasons people may be removed to segregation for Good Order and Discipline or for their own protection (see Shalev and Edgar [2015]). In the United States, SolitaryWatch.org publishes statistics from across the states demonstrating that in some cases solitary confinement has been used for decades (2017). The UN Human Rights Committee proposed that isolation should be abolished, suggesting that prolonged periods of isolation are in violation of international human rights law (solitaryconfinement.org 2017).

8 Wacquant says:

> By analogy with 'welfare,' I designate by 'prisonfare' the policy stream through which the state gives a penal response to festering urban ills and sociomoral disorders, as well as the imagery, discourses, and bodies of lay and expert knowledge that accrete around the rolling out of the police, the courts, jails, and prisons, and their extensions (probation, parole, computerized databanks of criminal files, and the schemes of remote profiling and surveillance they enable). Penalization joins socialization and medicalization as the three alternative strategies whereby the state can opt to treat undesirable conditions and conduct.
>
> (2009b: 16–17, cited in Wacquant 2010b: 202)

9 The far-reaching critique of the neo-liberal policies that result in workfare can also be brought to a critical understanding of the prison industrial complex. Private companies win contracts to incarcerate prisoners. These contracts mean that sentencing, processing and incarcerating people are monetized. Prisons are not paid for 'successful' results (such as rehabilitation), although most would include programmes that at least pay lip service to prisoners' readiness for work. The results when people are released show that people are likely to re-offend as their experiences of incarceration do not help with desistance. It is also not in the interests of private companies to release prisoners since their profits are driven by the number of people warehoused inside. Wacquant claims that after the focus on rehabilitation between the 1920s and 1990s, the 'function of punishment was downgraded to retribution and neutralization' (2010b: 203).

10 Aduba has won several major acting awards, including Emmys for best supporting performance in both comedy and drama categories and awards for Screen Actors' Guild as well as Golden Globe nominations.

11 Solitaryconfinement.org (2017) publishes valuable materials on how nations use solitary confinement in violation of international human rights laws.

Chapter Five

Prison Lesbians: Screening Intimacy and Desire

Lesbian Spectatorship and Criticism

Lesbian desire on stage and screen is consistently caught in a paradox – either accused of replicating the presumed male heterosexual spectator and thereby fetishizing same-sex love; or of appealing to a queer-identified viewer as a marginalized subject. I explore lesbian desire in screen and fictional examples that are about women in prison in particular, and consider how such desire is produced as a fundamental tactic of surviving in prison, forming a core element of prison culture that is not often studied. In turn, I propose same-sex desire as a challenge to the institutional habitus so that it becomes a feature of resistance, forming a series of tropes across a range of genres representing women in prison. The examples I analyse are from the novel *Affinity* by Sarah Waters (also a BBC adaptation), via exploitation films through to mainstream television series *Bad Girls* and Australian television drama *Wentworth*.[1] Although these representations emerge from containment, I demonstrate that a major feature of lesbian intimacy in prison is that it destabilizes that which is otherwise constrained and contained – the desiring and resistant body. To do so, I draw on established practices developed in media studies and performance studies about lesbian and queer spectatorship (Dolan 1989, 1990, 1993a, 1993b, 2007; Fuss 1991; Garber 2006; Hart 1994; Halberstam 1998, 2001, 2011) that in turn develops from feminist criticism (Case 2009; Case and Abbitt 2004; de Lauretis 1984, 1987, 1989a, 1989b, 2007; Goodman and de Gay 1998; Mulvey 1996, 1999).

I am invested in furthering the critical project of fictional representations in relation to feminist criminology (Cecil 2007a, 2007b, 2007c; Ciasullo 2008; Herman 2003; Millbank 2004; O'Neill and Seal 2012; Rafter 2000; Seal 2010). This chapter furthers the work of Hart (1994) and Seal (2010) by exploring what is specific about deviance and the transgression of prison lesbian representations. To do so, I draw impetus from feminist criminology and maintain my critique of taxonomies alongside the drive to develop queer strategies for analysing film and media (Case and Abbitt 2004; Dolan 1990, 1993a, 1993b; Halberstam 1998, 2001). Simultaneously, I avoid the tendency to explain lesbian sex and desire as *pseudo-families* as often characterized in criminology (Dirsuweit 1999; Giallombardo 1966; Hensley et al. 2002; Owen 1998; Ward and Kassebaum 2007), not least because it constitutes lesbian attachments as contingent, or performative rather than real.[2]

Gender and sexualities are often more complex than many of the formative thinkers in film and performance criticism that I have drawn upon warrant in their call for recognition of subjectivities and the specific erotics of queers on stage and screen (Davy 1993; Dolan 1990, 1993b; Harris and Aston 2006; Hart 1993, 1994). Nonetheless, in order to recuperate something of a queered response to prison, it might be valuable to start from the place of the simultaneous impossibility and inevitability of gay male sexuality in the context of prison – in which plotlines of men who have sex with men are most often deployed as a dark threat or even a distasteful joke that seems to lurk in many male prison narratives. In such work, gay desire is always already *not desire* in the context of prison, but another form of violence.[3] On the contrary, while working as an artist in prison, my experience of lesbian or bisexual identifications in prisons for women is that women's sexualities are presumed to be 'turned' by prison.

This chapter reflects Jill Dolan's politics of feminist spectatorship (1989, 2013) but stops short of offering examples of what she sees as the utopian possibilities of performance (2005). That is, although some of the material I discuss allows for a complex and nuanced understanding of desire and resistance in terms of sexuality, the frame of the institution is a rejoinder that these representations do not necessarily alter the ways in which lesbians or bisexual women experience incarceration. I am interested in the performativity of same-sex desire, and the trouble that produces for the prison, so I mainly use the term 'lesbian' even though many women who express same-sex desire in prison do not identify as such. I am aware this erases some of the important work in identity politics, and my aim is not to undermine the legitimacy of bisexual identities, but rather to concentrate specifically on the intersections between representations and the trouble of so-called 'deviant' genders/sexualities in the context of prison. The aim is to not so much to construct a sense of same-sex desire in prison as legitimate, but to consider how structures of representation attend to producing the prison lesbian as concomitant with prison. I hope to demonstrate how lesbian desire exists outside of the logic of prison and as such troubles the institution and its fixity.

Within popular culture, there are many tropes that perpetuate the imagery of 'caged heat' (Cecil 2007c), arguably drawing from the invisible status of women behind bars, resulting in partial representations of women as worthless, violent and inherently sexualized. Mediated and cultural representations of women in prison stand in for daily encounters that would inevitably challenge stereotypical tropes. I consider the nature of representations of women's sexuality in prison across a wide spectrum of desire including romantic intimacy, sexual innuendo and loving relationships. However, I would not like to romanticize or make claims that lesbian desire is transformative of contexts of violence, coercion and constraint, and so it is also important to consider how portrayals of lesbian narratives play into wider storylines endemic to prison cultures. I thus also consider coercion, inmate-rape and the issue of sex by analysing examples of officer/inmate 'consensual' relations as well as graphic depictions of assault and rape. This is valuable in relation to troubling the trope of prison lesbians in particular, especially since the performativity of lesbian desire in the context of prisons is so maligned and misunderstood (Dirsuweit 1999; Freedman 1996; Rusche and Kirchheimer 2003; Ward and Kassebaum 2007).

Lynda Hart and Peggy Phelan's important work (1993) on feminist performance provides some productive critical concerns for form, content and reception of work that explicitly produces a range of female subjectivities. In the more specific concern of lesbian subjectivities, contributors, Kate Davy, Jill Dolan (1993b) and Lynda Hart develop a sense of the significance of lesbian representations. But, rather than remain impressed that lesbian storylines, transgressive desires and non-hegemonic sexualities are featured on stage, they argue for a complex reading of genre, signification and impacts of the figure of the lesbian, and also of what 'lesbian' does to the form. Kate Davy calls this 'that refusal/resistance [that] lesbians perform [asking us to attend to] – the specificity of, if not lesbian desire, then lesbian desiring; if not lesbian sexuality, then lesbians as sexual' (1993: 63).

What I am interested in is how framing lesbian desire in this way reflects back on performance. Perhaps, to draw on the recent work of Sarah Mullan (2015), what is necessary is a 'post-lesbian' performance criticism that allows for queer readings of work that also acknowledges the often-complex relationships between feminism, lesbianism and issues of authorship and representation. In the context of this, then, I wondered whether attempting to understand the prison lesbian by engaging with mainstream popular media representations enabled me to think about 'Doing Bird'.[4] In particular, what is productive is how prison as context suggests a slippage between 'being lesbian' and 'doing lesbian'. In my examples, I am not therefore invested in highlighting that there *are* lesbian characters in prison TV shows. From this standpoint, that would be as ridiculous as being shocked that there are, in fact, gay men or lesbians in prison. Instead, as I proceed through the examples and how they interrelate with theories on female criminality and transgression, incarceration – *doing time* – becomes synonymous with *doing lesbian*.

Dawn Cecil says any cultural product that offers alternative stories helps to dismantle some of the inaccuracies of mainstream media (2007c: 305). Popular media tends to portray women as 'sex-crazed' to the extent that there is a sub-genre of prison films about women in prison that rely on narratives of dominance, submission, punishment and penitence underscored by women's positions as sexual objects.[5] Partly, these representations are carried through from the long history of fetishizing women's criminality as deviance. The reading of criminal women as distinct from 'normal, women is, as Lynda Hart outlines, starkly evident in the work of Cesare Lombroso, for whom the boundary produced is 'rigidly gender-dimorphic' (1994: 30). Early criminology thus produced the understanding of women's deviance as against nature. In her historiographic study of the links between violence and lesbians in culture, Hart says:

Women who were incapable of redemption simply were not women at all. The born offender, usually a murderess, was in the last analysis not even an aberration of femininity, but rather a man, albeit problematically in a woman's body, a close cousin to her newly constructed sister the invert.

(1994: 30)

Hart continues by considering how criminal deviance and social deviance in the form of same-sex desire are rhetorically linked as perversions, or limits of the boundaries of acceptable femininity.

> Crossing either one of those borders constituted a transgression from which there was no return. Women who killed, and women who loved other women, passed through the mirror of oppositional gender discourse and landed on the other side.
>
> (1994: 30)

This formulation from Hart strongly positions the understanding of both non-normative gender presentation and same-sex desire as deviant. This correlates with the historical framing of homosexual bodies as, in Foucault's *History of Sexuality* 'defective' and 'degenerate' (1990), which, according to criminologist Lizzie Seal 'established a template for perceiving lesbianism as abnormal and ultimately undesirable' (2010: 27).

Feminist criminology has developed against the backdrop of this biological essentialism, and seeks to undo some of the discursive assumptions about crime and gender that prevail. Nevertheless, there is a lot of value in these early attempts (Giallombardo 1966; Horn 1995; Lombroso and Ferrero 1895; Ward and Kassebaum 2007) to understand women's experiences of prison, despite replicating epistemological structures that are outdated in their misogyny. From these accounts, the overwhelming anxiety about lesbian practices and the desire to classify women's sexual transactions in prisons as temporary and deviant signals much about the prevailing homophobic social milieu. In the post-2000 era, criminological research displays less anxiety about these kinds of labels (Daly 2004; O'Neill and Seal 2012). This is not to say that the prison system is more accepting of 'deviant' sexualities, considering kinship ties are discouraged because they make alliances stronger (Freedman 1996; Potter 2004). Prison operates to sever ties and reduce alliances, and so any relationships (sexual or otherwise) are monitored (Schur 1984). To take this further, just like slaves, prisoners do not have control over their own bodies, and thus to express desire through consensual sexual activity (between inmates) is forbidden, while prisoner/staff sexual contact is understood as assault, and generally results in legal action if discovered. Consent is impossible if women are not understood to have agency over their own bodies. This framing from the criminological understandings of realities for incarcerated women is essential for the critical analysis of representations as it enables an understanding of prison cultures and the relationship to veracity.

Scholarly accounts of cultural tropes in genres of film and novels set in women's prisons suggest that there is a predominance of lesbian imagery (Cecil 2007b, 2007c, 2015; Carrabine 2012; Ciasullo 2008). This conflation between incarceration and desire is worth unpacking, both in order to understand better what lesbian desire can tell about prison, and to consider how popular cultural production focused on women's prisons operates to make lesbian desire visible.[6] Legal Studies scholar Jenni Millbank says:

> Lesbians, as symbols, are disruptive and highly charged. They evoke active, autonomous female sexuality; women as sexual subjects and sexual objects – desirous and desirable to each other.
>
> (Millbank 2004: 156)[7]

So pervasive is the imagery of the prison lesbian that this has become a metonym for almost any woman in prison, since criminal women are stereotypically understood as masculine, unfeminine and unruly (Carlen 1983, 2002; Smart 1977; Faith 2011). These descriptors conflate women's lack of adherence to the dominant performances of gender and sexuality with modes of criminal transgression (Dirsuweit 1999; Freedman 1996; Halberstam 2001; Rowe 2012, 2014; Scanlon and Lewis 2017).

In their account of female masculinity, queer theorist Jack Halberstam attends to how popular culture largely inscribes a conservative message 'namely, that female criminality must be contained because it erodes femininity' (1998: 202), going on to say that films can thus 'also make a hard-hitting critique of both class and gender politics' (1998: 202). Similarly, Karlene Faith's account of stereotypes in women-in-prison films also highlights this conservatism by designating women as bad, and offering prison as a cathartic return to 'normal' female behaviours through a series of challenges that offer 'salvation' (2011: 258–59). She says that in many screen representations

> the stereotypes of the madwoman or the criminal women are not challenged, but, rather, are grossly exploited so as to highlight and promote the image of a good, desirable woman. The monsters serve as the sick/bad backdrop for her potential normalcy.
>
> (2011: 259)

Faith's description of desire here presumes a heterosexual male gaze that is well rehearsed in film criticism (Mulvey 1984). From this perspective, the notion of a 'return' to normalcy indicates both the renouncement of transgressive criminal behaviour and a return to heterosexual desire. This – as I show in the analysis of *Bad Girls*, *Wentworth* and *Affinity* – sets up heterosexual norms as the cathartic resolution to the narratives that are otherwise characterized by tragic containment. Lesbian narratives are thus inextricably tragic, or otherwise doomed to serve a wider cultural story of how righteousness prevails.

Mulvey's formative work (1996, 1999) as well as criticism by de Lauretis (1984, 1989) is valuable in thinking about the effects and productions of various kinds of subjectivity for women in film. In relation to performance, I draw on Dolan's efforts at establishing a feminist spectatorship (1990, 2007), as well as Sue-Ellen Case's (2009) thinking on feminist and queer strategies for analysing performance. These exemplars establish a mode of analysis for lesbian subjectivities produced in performance that are productive in relation to popular media. For both scholars, what is important is a question of genre: how precisely does the staging experience (and by extension, film's framing) render certain relations and subjectivities possible? How do particular ways of viewing constitute the production of the lesbian subject? How do issues of norms in gender dynamics, such as butch/femme aesthetics (Case 1988) or BDSM in performance relate to how lesbian desire is staged (Dolan 2007)? While both scholars have focused on explicit performance, they are also invested in how lesbian subjects can shift into mainstream representations (Dolan 2011). In other words, performance is the object of study because it has the capacity to make visible, or present, the bodies of lesbians as desiring subjects (Case 2009; Dolan 1993). Following this, it is important to conceive of how cultural products that are not necessarily produced by lesbians, but that nevertheless contain narratives about lesbian desire, perpetuate tropes of visibility. To such an end, Dolan draws on de Lauretis' assertion that it is difficult to

> alter the standard of vision, the frame of reference of visibility, of what can be seen, [since] the conventions of seeing, and the relations of desire and meaning in spectatorship [remain] partially anchored or contained by a frame of visibility that is still heterosexual.
> (de Lauretis 1989, cited in Dolan 2007: 342)

Without rehearsing the history of feminist film criticism, what I am interested in is how the understanding of meanings produced through performance (and here I include film as a cultural production) circulate to create an understanding of lesbians in prison. This is distinct from the kinds of media analyses that engage with the effects of representations, such as Scanlon and Lewis (2017) who conducted focus groups with lesbian identified women to understand how lesbian meanings are produced for them. In this present study, I am invested in the forms and narratives that are evident in the figure of the prison lesbian.

Transgression and Sexuality: Prison Lesbian Tropes

Characterized by invisibility, prurience and confusion, discussions of prison lesbians and their effects in the prison system are usually framed as research problems to be addressed by a social science paradigm. Lesbianism is considered one of the deviant characteristics to be studied by psychologists (Severance 1996), practices to be analysed in relation to prison health (Maeve 1999), historiographies of deviants (Freedman 1996; Potter 2004) or a form of kinship to be understood by prison anthropologists (Ward and Kassebaum 2007). The form of desire in itself, sex and sexuality as a performance against the regime are rarely considered. Millbank's excellent work on representations in fiction further highlights how lesbianism often features as an 'aggravating factor' in sentencing (2004: 157).

In an unusually sensitive engagement with love and sexuality in women's prisons, Katherine Maeve's primary research explores how the three tropes of women 'turned on, turned out and turned over' form explanations for how women in prison come to 'participate' in love and sexual relationships with each other (1999: 48). This is a similar finding for Marsha Clowers, in the context of a prison education programme:

> Though prohibited by prison regulations, research suggests that approximately 50 percent of incarcerated women will adopt homosexual behavior during the length of their sentence for an array of reasons. In order to replicate the structure of the society from which they have been removed, women form couples. Women become partners

for the purposes of companionship and affection, just as they might on the outside and, occasionally, women trade sex for protection, for resources, or out of a need to belong to a group.

(2001: 24)

This is congruent with my own experiences working with women in prison, where there was a great deal more visible same-sex desire on a daily basis than in my experiences in men's prisons in South Africa and the United Kingdom. However, at the same time as being surrounded by women overtly engaged in affectionate touch, I noted an interesting perpetuation of what Adrienne Rich called a 'compulsory heterosexuality' (cited in Hart 1994) that I read as a performance for survival.[8] In other words, even though some women in the ten prisons I worked in over several years were engaging in consensual (although unsanctioned) sexual activities with each other, they would often insist on presenting themselves as heterosexual to their wider community of friends and family.[9] This consensual sex is distinct from sex between officers or staff and prisoners that is de-facto non-consensual. This is because, as discussed in relation to self-harm (Walsh 2018c), prison regulations deny bodily autonomy, which is part of contemporary prisons' remit to ensure safe custody. Just as prisoners do not have the right to choose to harm themselves, they cannot consent to sex (Faith 2011; Maeve 1999; Millbank 2004).

Performing according to the line of compulsory heterosexuality that prevails in prison aids women's face-saving. It is a tactic for navigating the system smoothly, seen in a clear example from *Orange Is the New Black*. The character Lorna Morello maintains a sexual relationship with Nicki Nichols across several seasons while consistently maintaining a presentation of herself as rampantly heterosexual, and even getting married whilst in prison to maintain that illusion. This is cogent with criminological research that demonstrates the complexities of navigating distinctive worlds and identities. Women may perceive the need to 'choose' between identities and behaviours they adopt inside and who they wish to be outside (Severance 2004: 55).[10] Theresa Severance considers how lesbianism may impact on women's re-integration into families, or bonds with children after release. This is distinct from the postfeminist assumption of sexual permissiveness that presumes fairness and equal treatment to all sexualities in the era of same-sex marriage and broadening cultural visibility for LGBTQ communities in many Western countries. Yet, it cannot be presumed that more permissive social mores mean that sexuality is not a stigmatizing factor for criminalized women. Partly, the anxiety about lesbianism as a stigma does little to disestablish assumptions about gender norms and sexuality, but it nevertheless demonstrates that desire outside of heterosexual norms may have consequences for women that are far beyond the pursuit of pleasure.

If lesbian love is not merely a salacious plot point, then this notion of consequence is also relevant for a criticism of screen representations for a mainstream audience. Drawing on de Lauretis (1984, 2007) for an extended argument about spectatorship of *OITNB*, Symes proposes that mainstream television can address straight-identified audiences through the creation of specific viewing positions – namely, voyeurism and identity or sexual tourism; however, this address does not solely determine the spectator's possibilities for identification and desire.

(2017: 35)

In her analysis of women who murder, Seal draws on feminist criminology to explore 'certain cultural anxieties pertaining to morality and correct behaviour' (2010: 30). Unlike Halberstam's version of female masculinity as moving beyond merely deviant, for Seal, the construction of lesbians and butch women, in particular, as related to criminal violence relies on anxieties that seek to restore women to adherence to normative femininity.[11] Seal notes that

> these anxieties circulate around femininity in particular as it symbolises cultural boundaries. The perceived assumption of masculinity by women, especially in relation to violence, is often constructed through conservative discourses as a worrying power grab, and as a symptom of cultural decline. This is frequently against a backdrop of shifting mores in terms of gender and sexual relations.
>
> (2010: 30)

Similarly Millbank's important discussion seeks to problematize how critical considerations of violent lesbians often reject how 'cultural texts [are presented] as if they contained and passed on simple "messages" about sex and sexuality' (2004: 157). Yet, it is necessary to maintain a critical focus on precisely how cultural production pathologizes lesbians, and also, without fetishizing sexuality, to understand violence, criminality and criminalization as also part of lesbian experience. This attendance to how stigma is at work may contribute to reading lesbians as deviants and criminals and criminals as lesbians. Millbank also highlights how critiques of lesbian representations must enable a wide spectrum of characteristics so as not to produce what she calls a 'tyranny of positive images' (2004: 157). Her approach signals the need to understand lesbian representations across the widest spectrum from survivor through to victim and hero.

> Opposing hetero-normative imagery of aggressive, pathologized lesbians through producing '*pro*-social' images of 'normal' feminine, devoutly monogamous lesbians arguably conforms to, and reinscribes, rather than undoes dominant cultural codes of gender and sexuality.
>
> (2004: 158, original emphasis)

I will return to Millbank's position to conceive of the values that are perpetuated in the representations of lesbian love in *Bad Girls*, *Wentworth* and *Affinity*.

Cultural criminologist Nicole Rafter's theorization on prison film focuses on male protagonists, offering a taxonomy of how representations correlate with four things, namely: to enable audiences to identify with 'perfect man', 'perfect relationships', 'fantasies of sex and rebellion' and 'insights into realities of prison life' (cited in Carrabine 2012: 66). For Rafter, these issues concern where the viewer is positioned in terms of empathy, and also is relevant in relation to the proximity to authenticity. As Carrabine notes, Rafter's perspective is that 'the genre insists on "heroic masculinity" to such an extent that it is incapable of delivering a genuinely realistic understanding of imprisonment, especially from a woman's perspective' (2012: 66). As my analysis of the examples in this chapter shows, these claims are troubled immediately when put into service of analysing representations of women in prison. This is, I propose, complex for several reasons: first, as men are the usual protagonists for heroic narratives, the notion of 'perfect woman' is already undone by women's crimes and transgressions. Heroism for women is bound up with prevailing assumptions about morality, strength and the ability to thrive. Rafter's imaginary of prison film as the conduit for perfect relationships between men is related to the kinds of solidarity and enduring friendship that survives the pains of imprisonment, stating

> [t]he supermen of standard prison films are perfect partly because they embody old-fashioned gender ideals. They prove that they are still real men, men who can lead without pettiness or manipulation.
>
> (2000: 124)

Rafter's perspective on homosexual desire relates to male bonding, but as Carrabine shows, she is 'largely dismissive of women-in-prison movies and regards them as exploitative soft porn, where lesbianism is offered as a spectacle to titillate male viewers' (2012: 16). Such dismissal is too easy, and doesn't sufficiently explore what the genre does by constructing women-in-prison stories in the manner they do. Without promoting a hierarchy of representations, more attention in relation to the examples I propose, which are not exploitation-style B-movies, but which, as mainstream TV series, nevertheless share some tropes.

The issues highlighted in criminological accounts reflects the importance of a feminist analysis, considering that the male prisoner is imagined to have agency in expressing desire or using sexuality to bond in legitimate ways against the prison authorities, while women's desire on screen is considered to be exploitative, and irrational. This is not to diminish Rafter's critique of the women-in-prison genre as largely exploitative, but to open the potential for debate about all representations of lesbian love (Millbank 2004) or homosocial desire (Sedgwick 1985, 1990). The final claim that is put forward by criminological accounts of prison film relates to authenticity, and is of course one important element of prison cultures that is threaded throughout the book; that is, the tension between fictional representations and the cultural work they might do in terms of raising awareness about prison.[12]

In an earlier chapter I refer to the problems of performance and representation, stating there is a propensity in much criminological literature to typologize. This can of course be understood as replicating the law, and the legibility of crime and criminals in certain ways according to the letter of the law. Types and tropes emerge as a function of groups and social dynamics, and therefore also are prevalent in prisons as microcosms of the social world. Film, television and performance representations adopt the tropes as a means of affording certain dramatic results, and also often to forge a construction of a prison culture. For women, however, to reduce experiences to tropes is to repudiate the complex, often messy and contradictory nature of criminal offending – and thus, character types such as pure 'villain' may too easily replicate the construction of transgression as 'un-female'. In any case, the problem of representing women's prisons is the issue that women who have been sentenced are already vilified in certain ways as antagonists (Chesney-Lind 1997, 1999; Chesney-Lind and Irwin 2008; Faith 2011).

Thus, women in prison are always already positioned as visible in opposition to the wider social norms of 'woman'. This lends itself, when we turn to representations, to characters that are immediately marked out as transgressive of such norms, which are, as ever, idealizations and norms that reflect desire and are inevitably coded as 'attractive' – usually feminine, white and sexually available (Whatling 1997). This is in opposition to analysis of men in prison, for whom crime is often explicable, and their character flaws are shown to be part of 'being a man' – characterized by hyper-masculinity, loyalty, quick to anger, but righteous, and often with a cause that the viewer can understand, such as exacting revenge for a perceived slight (Mason 2003a, 2003b; Wilson and O'Sullivan 2004). For women who are represented as having transgressed the law, tropes often also conflate the visual imagery as a rejection of conventions of femininity in ways that do not sufficiently account for class, poverty, drug abuse or as having access to choices outside of crime.

Regarding women-in-prison films, then, the prominent trope of an innocent, attractive 'outsider' entering the prison to be corrupted by its wantonness is often visually produced as a young, attractive white woman whose fall from grace is spectacular and often portrayed as a mistake, or a miscarriage of justice. The naïve femininity is immediately a trope to which the viewers can attach themselves – as they, alongside her – must learn about the harms and deprivations of the prison. She (and we as viewers) must come to understand prison culture, read the range of characters she comes across and keep herself safe. The ideal prison subject (in popular culture) is femme identified, and her offence is not one that transgresses her femininity, but upholds it as somewhat passive, perhaps by constructing her as a victim of circumstance. This description is easily applicable to Piper Kerman from *Orange Is the New Black*, Bea Smith from *Wentworth* or any number of protagonists from women-in-prison films. When we begin to consider how violence interpellates that, the image becomes more complex. For Walters,

> [t]heir violence is radically contextualized, so that the tough but innocent good girls are seen as violent toward men who have done (or who desire to do) violence unto them, whereas the embittered bad girls are generally *not* the victims of the male-dominant system but are rather the tools of that system (e.g., killer wardens). Female violence is thus not 'beyond the imagination,' but is rather positioned as the understandable result of systemic injustice.
>
> (2001: 122)

Added to this is the complication that is central to this chapter – that is, when lesbian desire is also a component of the narrative, then it is necessary to explore what is at work in the construction of how same-sex desire is made visible. As a result, it is necessary to consider some of the problems and possibilities afforded by a conception of same-sex desire as a trope specifically in the context of women in prison.

In prison films, tropes of lesbianism and sexualized representations often reproduce notions of transgression and weak-mindedness. On the one hand, they may perform an important function in constructing female characters that are active in pursuing their object of desire. On the other, they may also elide narratives of violence and power dynamics of institutions, and in exploitation movies, for example, may fetishize experiences of prison. The issue for film is the burden on representation – to have both villains and heroes as expressing lesbian desire, for example, speaks to the diversity of experiences of same-sex desire. Ann Ciasullo's important work on lesbian representations proposes 'the prison lesbian, in her various incarnations, both embodies and enacts a series of "promises" for straight readers/viewers' (2008: 196). This promise relates to the paranoia I mention above that seeks to 'correct' or return transgressive women to norms of femininity. Ciasullo offers a sense of how 'the cultural imaginary can project anxiety and ardor, loathing and lust, all with the ultimate promise that that which is dangerous and thrilling will be contained' (2008: 196).

For prison lesbians, sex can perform an important function for manipulation – to win favour, or get certain people on side. Sex can also be used as a means of violating women in acts of bullying. In other accounts, lesbian sex is represented as 'turning' any straight women (Maeve 1999; Mayne 2000). In popular culture, this is often what is represented as the ultimate fall – the feminine identified woman who may have made a mistake becomes coded as truly transgressive. The core of this is about legibility as women – what counts as being a woman, and also what can be 'salvaged' for women who transgress assumed norms of femininity. This is seen in the attitude of small-minded counsellor Mr Healy in *OITNB*, who attempts to 'save' Piper from what he perceives to be temporary, and misguided, lesbian tendencies. This narrative of 'corrections' is pronounced for women – and the purpose of incarceration remains to restore women to the norm of womanhood. A study by Severance depicts prison lesbians as a problem; temporary, and as troubling the systems and regimes (Severance 2004). For researchers on sexuality in prison there has been the tendency to develop typologies of prison lesbian as either a 'true' lesbian or a 'situational lesbian' or 'turnout' (Pardue et al. 2011: 283). In all instances, the research considers what the effects and implications are of same-sex desire for the regime – or in other words, to account for the ways lesbian sex affects the prison culture.

Ciasullo's perspective on prison film sets the scene for the 'problem' of lesbians:

As one of the most enduring genres in twentieth-century American popular culture, the women-in-prison narrative presents its readers/viewers with the opportunity to 'understand' – that is, to experience vicariously, to identify with, to enjoy – female homosexuality through the figure of the prison lesbian. But this enjoyment, like the instances of 'pseudo' lesbianism in prison, is necessarily temporary. After all, the narrative's primary obligation lies in the fortification of heterosexuality, not homosexuality; thus it demarcates the limits of lesbianism, encloses the 'true' lesbian behind prison walls, establishes the limits of desire, and above all, restores the (heterosexual) order.

(2008: 218)

For her, the distinction between the 'true' lesbian and the 'turnouts' offers a way of understanding the inherent homophobia and misogyny at play as the prison lesbian is considered to be

immoral and abnormal, the turnout is understood as simply reacting to her environment. In this taxonomy, only the true lesbian is worthy of the burden of abnormality, regardless of what 'deviant' activities the turnout might engage in while in prison.

(2008: 202)

The tropes I have explored here raise valuable points for critiquing how popular media portrays the figure of the prison lesbian. The notion of the turnout or prisoner who is 'gay till the gate' (a phrase used in UK prisons) does not destabilize the natural order, and perpetuates the understanding of how women's deviance can be corrected, provided she can return to 'normal' (presumably heterosexual, monogamous, family-orientated) relationship after release. Following the logic of tragic containment, the turnout might be able to return to a cathartic model in which her flaws can be overcome if they are acknowledged, whereas the prison lesbian cannot escape the inevitability of her transgression.[13]

Revisiting Salaciousness: *Bad Girls*

The British TV series *Bad Girls* maintains a reputation as the foremost series about women in prison. It ran for eight seasons, broadcast on ITV from 1999 to 2006. Subsequently, it was adapted into a stage musical called *Bad Girls: The Musical* (2007) by original writers Maureen Chadwick and Ann McManus. For the purposes of this introduction to prison lesbians on television, I refer to the original series. For criminologists Wilson and O'Sullivan, *Bad Girls* is a 'real prison drama' as it

develops an original and novel approach to dramatising prison so as to achieve its aim of delivering a wide range of inclusive viewing pleasures, to maintain public interest in a dramatic product that seeks to 'speak the truth'.

(2004: 123)

Their analysis of the series engages in typologizing the characters and formulating the centrality of the sexually charged relationship between lifer Nikki Wade and the reformist

Governor, Helen Stewart. The critical exploration of what *Bad Girls* offers to the understanding of prison cultures relates to how the series navigates seriousness of intent and moves beyond viewer pleasure to consider the force of the representations. However, in their efforts to take the series seriously in terms of its cultural importance in the representation of prisons, they seek to undermine the centrality and importance of lesbian desire in the narrative.

> The main reason for giving these two players higher status in the hierarchy of seriousness is to allow them to carry a 'message', with Nikki acting as articulator of legitimate grievances about the management of the prison and reform-minded Helen attempting to respond to these within the constraints of the authority structure.
> (Wilson and O'Sullivan 2004: 125)

While the power distinction between the prisoner and the authority is notable, the impact and implications of this central love story in the popular drama cannot be underestimated, and is, as Millbank demonstrates, 'necessary, important and desirable' (2004: 159). For her, 'the transgressive impact of lesbianism is deliberately centred as a *positive* force at the heart of the narrative' (2004: 159). Existing scholarship does little to problematize the relationships across positions of different power, and I will return to this problem later.

G-wing in HMP Larkhall is the setting for the show, in which a wide range of women across ages, class and ethnicities are incarcerated. From the first episode, the cinematography and style of the show allows for committed social commentary, as the resistance of prison officers to their working conditions and the range of social problems evidenced by women incarcerated at Larkhall. This is especially evident in the cinematographic depictions of the regime that punctuate the episodes – long shots of the cell windows at night and panning shots of the wing corridors during association remind the viewer of the scale of incarceration. While the cells are overcrowded and claustrophobic, and the officers are overworked, the sense of multiplication of the stories of women who are negotiating parenthood, allegiances, addictions and desires is notable.

For Wilson and O'Sullivan, the attention to diverse stories offers value in the form of 'eclectic juxtaposition' (2004: 124). What is novel about the show is the choice to align viewers with Helen/Nikki as central figures throughout Seasons 1 to 3. Their analysis of the show works on the 'pleasure/purpose bargain' (2004: 124) that both delivers plots that engage viewers and signal scenes with 'message'.

> Whereas virtually all prison dramas rhetorically take the side of the prisoners against the oppressions of the authorities, *Bad Girls* is probably the only one ever to uncompromisingly and consistently construct itself from the point of view that (women) prisoners understand and appreciate the irrationality and futility of (women's) prisons more than anyone else.
> (2004: 129)

Their reading of the series indicates its importance for prison drama. However, I am not convinced that Wilson and O'Sullivan offer enough problematization of the salaciousness of the lesbian portrayals in the story. First, at the time, there were very few mainstream TV representations of lesbian relationships, and indeed, few TV shows with a predominantly female cast. The 'pleasure/purpose bargain' (2004: 124) that they mention needs to be understood as revolving around how lesbian desire is made acceptable to a largely heterosexual viewing public. Unusually, the series doesn't entirely demonize lesbian love, but promotes it as one valid form of desire for the women in prison. Millbank's proposition is that lesbianism in this series is portrayed 'as a rupture that crosses, and thereby dissolves, the hierarchical lines of gaoler and prisoner – both literally and figuratively freeing the women imprisoned' (2004: 159). I would like to consider this in relation to claims from law scholar Didi Herman that *Bad Girls* is

> genre-less. This failure to conform to any particular genre facilitates its ability to convey non-dominant ideologies – in this case, a homonormativity that goes beyond the (re)production of positive images, or the conventional homosociality or 'situational lesbianism' of the prison context.
>
> (2003: 155)

It is significant beyond the virtues of genre-less-ness proposed by Herman, in the sense that sex and desire are offered as a legitimate and prevalent part of life in prison, rather than merely as secret or hidden. To that end, *Bad Girls* makes an important part of prison culture visible to a wider public who will probably never experience prison. Wilson and O'Sullivan take up Herman's claims for what *Bad Girls* did for a lesbian storyline on mainstream TV:

> *Bad Girls* provides a consistent comment on the problem of abuse and sees all sexual desire as having a potential to become abusive [...] The show is a plea for more caring interpersonal relationships and for higher standards of care in public institutions.
>
> (2004: 134)

Their view seeks to place the lesbian plot within wider conversations about the intentions of prisons as public institutions. Herman's view, however, seeks to characterize the show as producing what she calls 'lesbian homonormativity', saying 'the show not only takes lesbianism for granted, but also presents lesbian sexuality as commonsense desire' (2003: 143).[14] Herman's perspective is focused on the positive constructions of lesbianism, which I go on to demonstrate as limiting. Nonetheless, in addition to the range of desire (from lascivious and incidental to pure and loving), Herman's theorization of lesbian love and desire as homonormative is driven by this view of Nikki:

> Other inmates clearly respect Nikki as an important advocate and activist within the prison, and she is used by the program's writers to comment critically on a range of issues

affecting women in prison, including prison healthcare, the incarceration of women forced to abandon vulnerable children, and the treatment of non-English speaking inmates [...] In contrast to heteronormative genres where the lesbian is often portrayed as out to get something (sex, power, and so on), Nikki is presented as a thoroughly decent, caring, committed, and in many respects, selfless person.

(2003: 145)

However, *Bad Girls* also makes a point of lesbianism as one way of doing time, for example Shell in Season 1, Episode 3 stages the series' first same-sex kiss to provoke a new inmate who is a Christian. It also offers one of the only examples of (heterosexual) sex between uniformed officers and women in prison as framed by trajectories of sex work and intersections with addiction. Ultimately, although dated in style and much more focused on the serious business of prison reform (in Seasons 1 to 3 in particular), the series is formative in its range of lesbian representations. Its cinematography also signals its intent to place narratives in the political context. The closing frames of each episode in the first two seasons offer valuable visual trope of a panning shot of the outside of the prison building – setting the scene once again of the stories as contained in the urban prison building – but also always including women's voices shouting to one another, sending parcels to other floors and commenting on the days' events. This offers a consolidation of the sense of tensions and alliances in the prison community.

A work of fiction that has been adapted to a screen version that promotes lesbian desire as a central motif as the reader and viewer engage with a compelling tale of women's love and dreams of freedom – *Affinity* (Waters 1999).

Affinity: Transformation and Desire as Illusion

Sarah Waters' novel *Affinity* (1999) is constructed as a braid of two narratives in the context of Millbank prison in the 1870s. The novel was also adapted into a miniseries for the BBC (2008). The two protagonists are presented as symmetrical figures on opposite sides of Victorian social classes – Margaret Prior is a privileged spinster who is recovering from a suicide attempt after her father's death; and Selina Dawes, who made a living as a spirit medium prior to being convicted for fraud. Both women's actions would have been considered crimes against feminine norms: Margaret's transgression is her suicide attempt (which for women of a different class would have resulted in incarceration) (Llewellyn 2004: 207). Selina's crime relates to a series of events at séances. She is convicted for 'fraud and assault' (1999: 27), although in her reminiscence of the séance, the fraud is framed as the sexual assault of a young woman by Selina's spirit guide Peter Quick.

Although this example references an historic imagining of prison life, it nevertheless offers an interesting set of tropes for lesbianism, visibility and surveillance.[15] Mark Llewellyn's literary studies approach concerns the functioning of panopticon for females more generally in Victorian times as disciplinary. He considers Margaret's punishment in the context of her class as an educated spinster:

> [J]ust as Selina and the other inmates have had fixed terms set upon their imprisonment, so Margaret is informed by her mother that 'You wouldn't be ill like this [...] if you were married' (p. 263), implying that the punishment of the gaze would also not be present, were Margaret to conform to society's laws via a suitable union. Margaret's own 'criminality' and monstrosity is constructed solely in terms of her improper femininity.
>
> (2004: 207–08)

Waters' historical fiction depicts lesbians and desire in the form of first-person narrative that offers perspective on female oppression in the era. In the context of Margaret Prior's class, her salvation comes in the form of charitable works, which enable her to enter Millbank Prison, where she, in turn, perpetrates a disciplining surveillance on the less fortunate criminalized women. Llewellyn proposes:

> For Margaret, being a 'lady visitor' is an outlet for her lesbian desire. Although a victim of the gaze, Margaret is also an active participant in using the gaze for her own (sexual) satisfaction.
>
> (2004: 210)

Millbank also engages with the politics of visibility when she refers to Selina's 'demands to be treated as a subject not an object by asking Margaret to speak of herself before she will engage in conversation' (2004: 169). This can be seen in Selina's rejoinder to Margaret:

> You have come to Millbank to look upon women more wretched than yourself, in the hope that it will make you well again [...] Well, you may look at me, I am wretched enough. All the world may look at me, it is part of my punishment.
>
> (Waters 1999: 47)

The television miniseries makes much of the viewer's entry into the prison, in which the camera takes the viewpoint of the lady visitor as she navigates corridors and peers in through the metal doors to see glimpses of Selina. Writing in her diary, she observes:

> Seen close, of course, Millbank is not charming. Its scale is vast, and its lines and angles, when realised in walls and towers of yellow brick and shuttered windows, seem only wrong or perverse.
>
> (Waters 1999: 8)

Over the course of several visits, Margaret becomes infatuated with Selina, and forms an attachment to her that is described by Selina as 'affinity'. In Waters' characteristic style, the assumptions about power, dominance or passivity are consistently revealed to be constructs. Rather than Margaret's privilege equating to agency, Selina is portrayed as capable of transgressing the limitations of her position.

> Margaret's higher social status allows her to occupy both the role of observed and observer, and displace her punishment onto others, voyeuristically examining Selina through the cell door, and later watching her '[feeling] a rush of pity. [thinking]: *You are like me*' (1999: 82). Yet Margaret is utterly unknowing when it comes to her own imprisoned image; she is unmistakably shocked and unnerved when Selina turns the gaze back on her: 'she had thrust my own weak self at me again. She looked at me, and *her* eyes had pity in them!'.
>
> (1999: 88, cited in Llewellyn 2004: 211, original emphases)

The novel's force produces the lesbian desire as founded on transgression. Margaret's escalating emotional attachment to Selina means that she plans and executes a series of agential acts. Prior to imagining freedom with Selina, her depression had made resisting norms seemingly impossible. Yet, her encounters with Selina introduce her to directness that serves to nurture the sense of affinity. Several images that confound the fixity of the prison are taken by Margaret to mean she can trust Selina; for example, Margaret sees Selina holding a beautiful purple flower that is impossible in the context of the sterile environment of the prison cell. Margaret's willingness to believe Selina's capacity to conjure and to manifest the impossible is also a commentary on the fragility and impossibility of desire in the context of prison. Most of the novel concerns parallel struggles for Margaret – to transgress expectations and manifest her desires as legitimate. The plan she executes will enable Selina to escape prison through sheer will and with the help of the spirits. Margaret's obsessive desire for Selina means that she begins to imagine how a life together may look beyond the prison. The climax of the novel delivers a sudden cathartic resolution to the potential tragedy of Selina's escape and Margaret's departure from her life of privilege to live together abroad. In a return to the imagery of visibility, Waters exposes Selina's deception.

> I saw it all – I see it now, still, with a crisp and dreadful certainty. It was myself, a spinster, plain and pale and sweating and wild, and groping from a swaying prison ladder after the severed yellow tresses of a handsome girl.
>
> (Waters 1999: 240)

Although the love story had encouraged a means of thinking beyond prison and towards a transgression of norms and lifestyles of the time, Selina's betrayal of Margaret returns the notion of 'real' prison lesbian relationship as impossible. For Millbank, this does not reinforce the problem of lesbianism as tragic, but as transformative of how readers and viewers might engage with desire in the context of prison, particularly in relation to the power differential of visitor/prisoner.

The power imbalance and power structures are not reinscribed on each side of the dyad, or even simply inverted by reversing them. Rather, the women occupy mixed and contradictory positions, and the power structures that surround them are melted, rather than reinforced, by the rupture of transgressive lesbian desire.

(2004: 169)

What I should like to add to Millbank's observation is that these representations form interruptions and force visibility of lesbian love also evident in *Bad Girls*. Desire itself must be proven and translated into performance in the most unlikely of contexts. In *Affinity*, Selina's plan involves conjuring belief in and the detailed imagining of desire, such that Margaret is able to plan and execute a daring escape from her life as a lady visitor.

In all three examples, prison as a context for the transgressive desire is constitutive of the women's practices of lesbian love as contained, by necessity driven by a fantasy of impossible romance that must be revealed as a construct or fiction. This plot point ensures that it is not viable to imagine prison relationships as enduring – even if it seems possible that incarcerated women would have time together in confined spaces with little distraction.

Unlike Millbank's hopeful reading of love in *Bad Girls* and *Affinity*, prison love must fail. While representations of lesbians in prison may signal transgression and resistance to norms and values, the function of prison prevails. For Llewellyn (2004), this function is primarily predicated on a sense of visibility, a panoptic sense of surveillance that means the prevailing norms and values will always inform the meanings of lesbian couplings. This point is also taken up by Millbank, who says:

The presence of the panopticon and the deep complicity of women in perpetuating oppressive power structures sounds like a warning bell about the conclusions that I have drawn in the previous section. Is it ever really possible to transcend hierarchy? To transform a genre? To liberate? As Ruthann Robson (1992) says of the lesbian outlaw, 'we are always both inside and outside of the law, we are, 'always already' domesticated'.

(Llewellyn 2004: 19, cited in Millbank 2004: 176)

Sex, Assault and Trauma in *Wentworth*: Domesticating Desire and Tragic Containment[16]

While I outline the value of representations of sexual desire in prison, I would like to consider the importance of not assuming sexuality and sexual agency to be de facto positive in the context of prison. The imagery of prison lesbians has, as the discussion of the women-in-prison film genre has demonstrated, developed tropes of insatiable butch lesbians 'turning' sex-starved femmes. The examples I consider explore the imbrication between containment and desire in the context of prison, as I hope to draw attention to the problems and limitations of a purely 'heroic' (Herman 2003) depiction of desire.

Halberstam's (2011) *The Queer Art of Failure* theorizes about the tendency in Gay and Lesbian Studies to valorize certain kinds of queer visibility over others – in other words, to focus on heroics not victimization, even when the same visual cues might be used.[17] While their focus in this instance is on the link between fascism and tropes of AIDS activism, they aim to draw attention towards a sclerotic and ahistorical view of how tropes, visual cultures and popular imagery are produced and replicated. For them, 'the real struggle is about the context of contemporary claims that people want to make about the political rightness of their desires' (2011: 153). Rather than undermining that representations of queer desire in popular media are righteous, a critical consideration of how lesbian subjects are mediated allows us to contemplate Halberstam's drive to explore 'why we cannot tolerate the linking of our desires to politics that disturb us' (2011: 153). This links with Millbank's (2004) rejoinder to make allowance for *antisocial* in addition to co-opted or domesticated images of lesbianism that offer no threat to the patriarchal or hegemonic order.

In particular, the next section details the understanding of prison as inherently coercive and that the structures of sexuality and sex in prisons are not always a function of desire but fundamentally of power. *Wentworth* is the contemporary telling of the *Prisoner Cell Block H* backstory. Its examples of lesbian sex include depictions of a wide range of sex and desire, including romantic intimacy, sexual innuendo, coercion, inmate-rape and the issue of officer/inmate relations as well as the graphic gang rape of the fallen former Governor 'The Freak' by a group of lesbian prisoners. *Wentworth* shifts the visual pleasure in the lesbian subject that is endemic to many of the exploitation filmic tropes to a prison culture that exposes desire and coercion as fundamentally inflected by the impacts of surveillance, diminished agency and deprivation.

Some of the memorable prison lesbians in *Wentworth* are depicted as 'top dog'. This is a character type that maintains the power to define the rules of engagement in prison culture, and will often use desire as a means of manipulating the other women. In *Wentworth*, this position correlates with the character that is willing to mete violence, using aggression, dominance and threat to ensure she maintains the position of power. These conflations of characteristics are not of course endemic to lesbians, but in *Wentworth*, the shift between character types promotes a representation of the kinds of acts that are necessitated by the role of top dog as anathema to femininity. In early seasons, the top dog position is occupied by matriarch Jackie Holt. When Jackie is murdered by Bea Smith, the 'out' lesbian Franky Doyle takes the position largely to maintain drug operations in the wings. Much of the Seasons 2 and 3 focuses on power struggles between her and Bea, whose own experience of same-sex love unseats her from the position.

Wentworth is not immune to stereotypical representations of prison lesbians and yoking it to imagery of 'forbidden' love. By replicating the scenario of a lifer (Franky) pursuing and seducing a powerful woman – a governor or a prison psychologist – *Wentworth* imagines the prison lesbian as manipulative, cunning and active in her transgression of regulations. The power differential is critical in considering how the representation of prison lesbians forces viewers to imagine beyond crime, but may also reinforce lesbianism simply as deviance. This is particular to this pairing of the prison service professional and the long-term prisoner, who might otherwise be portrayed as violent and beyond redemption. Instead, the viewer can begin to see how the professional can be attracted to her in spite of the risk to her own position.

Troubling of the trope of 'turning' otherwise naïve prisoners lesbian, *Wentworth* imagines Bridget, and *Bad Girls* offers Helen as the well-educated professional, as 'turned' by the charismatic lesbian. Although both run the risk of being salacious examples, they also highlight the lesbian relationship as standing in for state care.[18] In *Wentworth*, prisoner Franky and Bridget garner a grudging acceptance of the relationship once on the outside. In the exemplar of lesbian love *as* tragic containment, Bea and Allie's relationship is forged after a long period of illegibility.

From her first scene in *Wentworth*, Franky is notable for her rebellious, energetic defiance of regulations and her outrageous flirtatiousness. Her characterization circulates on youthful violence as she rejects all forms of affection, choosing instead to nurture dependence and loyalty in women who are addicts. Franky's characterization gets more nuanced when she uses flirtation to manipulate the prison psychologist, and as such the construction of the prison lesbian shifts from a sub-plot to a core construction in the storyline. In this way, the trope of the prison lesbian as top dog who will devour her enemies through violence or seduction is perpetuated in *Wentworth*.

Interestingly, unlike the tropes from standard women-in-prison flicks, her character is not portrayed as particularly butch or masculine, though she is fit and strong. Her tendency to violence and her recourse to sex instead of resolving problems are explained away through flashbacks of surviving the abandonment of her father and a troubled childhood. At every opportunity, Franky is active in pursuing her desire, using sex and relationships as a distraction from her power struggles on the wing. When she ends up in sessions with the prison psychologist, Bridget, she initially uses flirtation and explicit sexual conversation to deflect attention from the aims of therapy. Instead, in an extended seduction, Franky and Bridget form a highly charged sexual relationship that survives Franky's parole. This relationship fulfils a valuable purpose for representations of lesbians in prison, in that the fact of Franky's incarceration does not stigmatize her or make her desire impossible. This is not to say that maintaining relationships post-release is simple, but merely that the purported seriousness of both this relationship, and Nikki and Helen's from *Bad Girl* are evident in the reunion of the couples outside the bounds of prison cultures. Franky's character is active and driven by desire, and several other characters also draw on a wider spectrum of gender presentation than is usually afforded by television drama.

Two antagonists that trouble the norms of female passivity are Joan 'The Freak' Ferguson and Kaz who is imprisoned for leading a misandrist vigilante group – 'The Red Right Hand' – that seeks revenge for women who have experienced abuse. Both women are unapologetically violent – Kaz is driven by empathy, but is unafraid of meting out violence, while Joan Ferguson rules with an iron fist in a leather glove. Halberstam promotes the importance of the range of representations of violent women:

The depiction of women committing acts of violence against men does not simply use 'male' tactics of aggression for other ends; in fact, female violence transforms the symbolic function of the feminine within popular narratives and simultaneously challenges the hegemonic insistence upon the linking of might and right under the sign of masculinity.

(2001: 251)

While Kaz is sentenced for her violent acts against men, Joan is depicted as being obsessive, cold and disgusted by most people. Her calculating violence is both corporeal and tactical – visualized in early seasons through her training in fencing. Joan's psychopathy allows an overarching narrative as the villain of villains. Initially the maligned governor of Wentworth Prison, she is a calculating and impressively intelligent, powerful woman whose notable weak spot appears to be an obsessive relationship with a young woman. In flashbacks, it becomes evident that she cared about Jeanna, who died tragically. *Wentworth* does not only produce a generous view of lesbian desire however, but in its focus on Ferguson, it also replicates the well-worn trope of lesbian desire as vampiric and deadly (as discussed by Creed 1999). By means of flashbacks in Seasons 2 and 3, we are introduced to the memories of Ferguson before she became governor of Wentworth. In her early years in the prison service, she became obsessed with a pregnant inmate and helped her. The implication, rather than exposition, is that this is a possessiveness related to a sociopathic lesbianism. When the unhealthy attention between the two is exposed, the baby is taken away, Jeanna commits suicide and then Ferguson's mission becomes about exacting revenge against the social worker who removed the child – revealed to be Wentworth's senior corrections officer Will Jackson.

For these characters, lesbian desire features as a background to their main action – although not usually the focus of the narrative – it is used as an excuse or justification for them holding the seat of power. For instance, in a climactic scene that highlight's Ferguson's continued power despite being incarcerated herself, Ferguson maintains her influence over a range of the prisoners by knowing precisely how to manipulate them. For instance, Ferguson has the following voiceover narration to Kaz just after she has seen Allie and Bea kiss for the first time: 'on this side of the bars it is so easy to lose yourself. In love, or lust or despair. Because the alternative is to wait and watch your life tick away' (Season 4, Episode 7 'Panic Button'). She is talking to Bea's enemy, Kaz, and is using the opportunity to encourage her to rail against Bea. Her characterization of lesbian love as 'losing herself' is a manipulation of Kaz's tendency to protect Allie, along with the remainder of her group. Joan's deliberate conflation of desire and weakness is a means of her narrating Bea as less capable of holding power, and also a veiled threat to Kaz that Allie's love for Bea is a betrayal that undermines her position as well as negating her maternal influence.

In Season 4, Episode 8 ('Plan Bea'), the relationship escalates, which allows for the disintegration of Bea's status as decisive and active. This is particularly notable when it comes to depicting her first lesbian experiences – when she is uncertain about this identity and insecure about what to 'do'. The leap from desiring to acting on sexual desire is somehow depicted as vaguely ridiculous or unimaginable. Bea's reaction is a reminder that lesbian visibility is about more than identity markers but about troubling what is taken for granted as 'normal' or natural sexual behaviour. Although it enables character development for Bea as someone who had never experienced sexual pleasure, the characterization does not signal lesbianism as a cure-all for post-traumatic stress or a sudden enjoyment of sex after systematic abuse by her husband. In this lesbian relationship there is no place beyond the prison as both Allie and Bea are serving long sentences and so the proxy 'family' that each creates as well as their positions within the prison culture are to be nurtured and maintained. For the duration of Season 4, what is questioned is how their support and care for one another is possible when the cynical wing-mates, opposition from crews and of course the regime work to delegitimize romantic contact. Their storylines show that love is not uncomplicated and nor does it occur outside of the systems, complexities and illogic of the prison. When Allie is accused of being involved in the plot to have Bea killed, Bea and her friends struggle to believe her. In these expositions of burgeoning lesbian affinities, the narrative of desire or the strength of love is not, in this genre of tragic containment, sufficiently convincing, as it might be in a romantic drama, for example. The overriding logic is the logic of prison, and that circulates on who is seen to be in charge and how women must perform to be in accordance with their rules.

Much of the pace of *Wentworth* relies on the momentum of the power struggles and the ongoing tensions between the officials and the plots and schemes of the prison population to navigate their domains – in terms of human capital, drugs or influence. In Season 4, however, *Wentworth*'s pace slows down to two main plots: first, Joan Ferguson's attempts to prevail while awaiting trial, and second, Allie and Bea's burgeoning relationship. Where these intersect is when Joan intervenes just after Bea and Allie's only sex scene (in Season 4, Episode 12 'Seeing Red'), to inject Allie rendering her in a coma. Bea recognizes Joan as the perpetrator, and begins to seek revenge, when she believes that Allie will not survive.

Cinematographically there is a strong focus on Bea and Ferguson in frames that allow for close-up characterization. This comes to a climactic point when Ferguson's trial is abandoned due to lack of evidence and she prepares for release. In a moment of extremely high stakes, Bea plans to attack Joan and goad her into admitting that she set Allie up by drugging her. However, Ferguson overpowers her, gaining hold of the weapon. The attack here could have been depicted as simply another physically demanding fight for power, but instead the camera is positioned in an intimate proximity, so that we see Bea's determination as she sets Ferguson up for more time inside by running herself through on the weapon. Ferguson is shown to be ecstatic, almost orgasmic in her pleasure at the demise of Bea Smith, before she realizes that she will be remanded once more and charged with her murder.

Although this season is of value for its depiction of nurturing love and growing bonds of solidarity between the women who accept Bea's relationship with Allie, the sudden shift from fully fledged lesbian love to both partners suffering punishing injuries does little to challenge the problem of lesbian representation in popular culture. Namely, one of the lovers will die or face a tragic end. Nonetheless, what the series promotes is the implications of lesbian love – as building alliances that reach beyond the prison or that change how the women are seen beyond the wings. This is especially the case with Franky and her relationship with Bridget, which survives Franky's release and the two maintain a relationship throughout Season 4. In this, we might consider that *Wentworth* depicts domestication and the notion of lesbian storyline as a closure rather than a rupture. As such, I hesitate to promote the mere fact of lesbian representation in these examples as resistance in and of itself – especially because in both *Wentworth* and *Affinity* the protagonists are severely punished for transgression, even if their desires are momentarily represented as legitimate. What I should like to consider next, then, is to what extent the frame of the prison (as conservative and normative in its hegemonic regimes of correction) highlights sex and the body in general as core problems of incarceration.

Sexual assault and victimization as well as rape are commonplace in prison films – in male prison they signal feminization of the victims while in female prisons coercive sex is used to teach women a lesson – arguably, a form of 'correction' that mimics the institution's power. A large percentage of women in prison would have experienced some form of sexual abuse and/or domestic abuse in their lives prior to incarceration (Chesney-Lind and Irwin 2008; Herman 1992). As a context for women's positions as always already victims of sexual violation, representations of prison sex must be understood as contributing towards a vision of women's desire and agency in addition to how these are violated further in the context of prison, the surveillance of bodies and the punishment of pleasure. By attending to the ways in which hetero-and homosexual prison sex on screen, and in particular, coercive sex, is portrayed, we might raise further questions about bodily autonomy, women's agency and the consequences of sexual intimidation, pregnancy or STIs for the prison service. This allows for a feminist reappraisal of how such representations demand that we consider the institutions' role in the duty of care to prisoners.

This is not to say that all prison rapes occur within the trope of the female prisoner as victim of a deranged power-crazy officer such as in *Chained Heat* (1983), *Caged Heat* (1974) and many more. Rape scenes can occur between inmates, and these are usually depicted as brutal gang violence rather than lone perpetrators. Across the range of women-in-prison representations, rape as a plot point is always situated to highlight women's vulnerabilities in the patriarchal system that does not adequately recognize their victimization, or manage it effectively (Halberstam 2001; Hart 1999; Walters 2001). Walters says that 'like the rape-revenge genre in which female violence is justified through a prior victimization, there is often a certain celebratory air about [women in prison] films' (2001: 120). She goes on to cite the cultural critic Halberstam, whose consideration of prison films is used to develop a theorization of female masculinity. Their perspective is that

> scenes of rebellious women in prison films always allow for the possibility of an overt feminist message that involves both a critique of male-dominated society and some notion of female community
>
> (1998: 201, cited in Walters 2001: 120)

Female virtue is often a plot point in mainstream films and television. In storylines that account for crime and morality, a woman being violated sexually is the most significant action that is used to shift consequences for her future, explain psychological damage and drive vengeance (often displaced onto a partner whose honour, by extension, is tainted). In both *Wentworth* and *Bad Girls*, sexual violence is prevalent as just another form of violence in prison. Having overseen the consequences of sexual violence as Governor, Ferguson is later subjected to a particularly brutal gang rape at the hands of 'Juice', whose crew use a broom handle to violently assault her. The plot point is notable in that Juice is a butch lesbian – represented as lascivious and vile in her attempts to own 'fresh meat' (Seasons 2 and 3). However, it is also obvious in the staging of the scene that Ferguson has set up this abuse in order to justify later actions, including building an alliance with Kaz. Ferguson's rape is a means of signalling the dual fear that is the basis of patriarchy's operation to uphold female virtue – namely that women must want to maintain their purity, and thus that violation signals moral degradation. It also reinforces women as manipulative and that they must by necessity be lying or manufacturing rape claims. This is of course a consistent trope in the legal system in which bodies, autonomy and the deviance of women are consistently centre stage.

In both *Wentworth* and *Affinity*, there is a sense that love transgresses the norms and containment of prison – for Bea Smith, the experience of intimacy and fulfilling sexual relationship is not maintained for longer than one episode while for Margaret Prior, what she believed to be authentic is revealed as an illusion. Punishment and containment are the contexts for desire but in which love seems impossible. Although in both examples, the love stories are represented as transformative, both storylines promote the dangers of such love affairs, and this 'return' to fear and insecurity is produced as cathartic and normative. Prison culture cannot accept love, only desire. Unlike *Bad Girls'* homonormative desire as articulated by Herman (2003), *Wentworth's* narratives return to prison structures as negating the possibility for lesbian attachments that are healthy.

It is tempting to laud any representations of prison lesbians as performing a valuable function by staging same-sex desire within and in spite of the structures of punishment. However, at the same time as signalling an important public visibility for lesbians, popular culture representations must also be enabled across nuanced, complex characterizations that are not over-burdened by the need to be truthful or representative of all lesbian love. On this score, the three examples of fictional representations are relevant in drawing on the drama of prison for lesbians and the particular implications of lesbians for the institution.

What I consider productive on this point is how the visual and narrative function of the prison lesbian produces certain kinds of criminological meaning. This is particularly the case in my claim throughout the chapter that desire and coercion are fundamentally inflected by the impacts of surveillance, diminished agency and deprivation. In the fictional representations, this is evident in figures such as Margaret Prior, whose situation in terms of era, class and privilege are one means of surveillance and control that is immediately recognizable as imbued by Victorian morals, including misogyny. For Selina, as a working-class lesbian, and her servant lover, successive crimes are inevitable as they attempt to escape poverty, stigma, class prejudice and homophobia. For these characters, control inflects how they relate to one another, and desire becomes emblematic of freedom and transgression.

Halberstam's reading of prison film discussed in both the prior chapter and this one demonstrates how the form 'makes clear links between poverty, female masculinity, female criminality, and the predatory butch' (1998: 202). This enables criticism of mainstream TV representations of how these issues are conflated visually and in plot points. Halberstam's point is directly related to the major drive in feminist criminology that is to decouple gendered assumptions about crime and offending with a simultaneous need for considering gender in the pursuit of appropriate services and care in custody. As Suzanne Bouclin argues in relation to film representations, they reflect

> some of the dominant socio-legal assumptions about women's 'criminality,' [they] also expose the women's prison as a contradictory space [...] rais[ing] jurisprudential questions around whether prisons can ever (re)form women.
>
> (2009: 21)

This necessitates a critical conception of whether the figure of a lesbian in film, fiction or stage representations does indeed offer a rupture or transgression of containment. Rather, as Millbank shows in *Bad Girls*, Season 3 signals Nikki and Helen's reunion as lovers outside of prison, with Nikki having been released, and Helen resigned. However, this is not the transcendent freedom offered by lesbian love that might otherwise be read, but signals the closure of the relationship in terms of the prison (as their storylines are largely absent thereafter). In this example, and in Sarah Waters' *Affinity*, the protagonists face impossible love that signals freedom when rehearsed inside the prison, but which appears materially different outside the context of the prison. For Margaret Prior, love is revealed as an illusion and she is returned to the position of unattached, unhinged and unhappy spinster, having been bewitched by her inappropriate desires for Selina.

In the analysis of three representations of prison lesbians, I demonstrate how lesbian desire is produced in service of conservative and limiting narratives that uphold prison's sticky moral function. Plots in *Wentworth* and *Affinity* set up heterosexual norms as the cathartic resolution to the narratives that are otherwise tragic containment. Instead of replicating the unhelpful binaries I note as problematic in feminist criminology between violent/reformed, heterosexual/lesbian or indeed inside/outside, a queer reading (Muñoz 2009) promotes or trouble the sense of closure I have identified in these examples. Such a project considers the resistance of desire as primary, rather than always already constrained by the frame of the institution. This necessitates, as discussed by Lisa Duggan and Muñoz (2009), a critical modality of hope in navigating these dialectical positions.

Thus, to return to my distinction between *being* and *doing* lesbian, the examples I have highlighted enable a sense of how lesbianism is constructed, perpetuated and produced by incarceration in these examples. What is recuperated in an examination of the tyranny of representation and the burden of 'true' reflections of lesbian desire is perhaps where the particular analysis from performance is valuable. Aside from cathartic relief about the uneasy situating of morally dubious characters whose lesbianism may then be foregrounded in viewers' perceptions, and a potentially liberating full spectrum of characters that are lesbian, there is also the need to consider what George Rodosthenous (2015) calls the pleasure of voyeurism. The sense of the wider public watching and participating in desiring inside and outside prisons is predicated on both pleasure and righteousness. This challenge is taken up by my analysis of three fictional screen representations of lesbians in order to further the critical project of feminist criminology – namely, as Cecil (2007b, 2007c) and Ciasullo (2008) propose – to expose the workings of the cultural imaginary when it comes to prison lesbians as deeply related to the understanding of deviance, transgression and desire.

Notes

1 Note that as in the prior chapter, I am largely working on representations beyond the women-in-prison (WIP) genre that is characterized by exploitation. These films usually follow predictable tropes that are about punishing transgressive women behind bars, by identifying striking oppositions between good and innocent girlish characters and unruly vixens. These are discussed in detail by scholars working across the disciplines of criminology and cultural and media studies (Brown 2009; Cecil 2007a, 2007b, 2007c, 2015, 2017; Ciasullo 2008; Clowers 2001; Faith 2011; Hart 1994; Herman 2003; Mason 2003a; Rafter 2000; Rafter and Brown 2011; Walters 2001; Wilson and O'Sullivan 2004).
2 For example, for some studies, lesbian pseudo-families are read as those women who form alliances with a compatible partner as a marriage unit. The inmates maintained that 'to engage in homosexuality as duplication of the outside world, makes times go by faster and (furthermore) that no one can do time alone' (Giallombardo 1966: 136).
3 See Gear and Ngubeni (2002), for more on sex and inmate violence, and for an important study of coercion in male South African prisons.
4 This is a phrase I encountered from prisoners describing doing time as 'doing bird'.
5 Cecil (2007c) cites a range of films in the genres otherwise referred to as 'babes-behind-bars' or 'vixens in chains' films, such as *Big Doll House* (1971), *Caged Heat* (1974). Television shows include Australian drama *Prisoner Cell Block H* (1979–86), and, from the United Kingdom, *Bad Girls* (1999–2006) (Cecil 2007c: 305–06). *Bad Girls* was also staged in the West End as a musical (2007). The Australian Channel 5 has created a prequel series to *Prisoner: Cell Block H* that develops backstories to popular characters in *Wentworth Prison* (2013–ongoing).
6 This draws on the work of Lynda Hart, who argues 'that one ghost in the machine of heterosexual patriarchy is the lesbian who shadows the entrance into representation of women's aggression'. Hart's book concentrates on the manoeuvres

> in which the production of violent women in representation depends on a dis-articulated threat of desire between women. It is not a matter, then, of looking for the lesbian *behind* representations of violent women, but rather of understanding how the lesbian functions

in a structural dialectic of appearance/disappearance where the aggressive woman is visible.

(1994: vii, original emphasis)

7   However, there have also been several examples of novels that do not re-inscribe dominant cultural codes of gender and sexuality in relation to criminal women (Hart 1996). Millbank (2004), for example, refers to Angela Carter's *Nights at the Circus* (2006) and Sarah Waters' *Affinity* (1999), both of which have been literary inspirations in my own theatre practice in prison (see also Carrabine 2012).

8   Hart's study of 'fatal women' (1994) in relation to lesbian performativity was formative reading. See Owen (1998: 134–48). My own participatory performance practice has developed over fifteen years of working in prisons in South Africa and the United Kingdom, with both men and women.

9   This is also discussed in Dirsuweit's excellent work on sexuality in South African prison system (1999).

10 Severance says that

> [w]hile same-sex relationships between inmates are assumed to be situational, accounts of women in this study suggest a more complicated pattern. Many women who had participated in same-sex relationships expressed uncertainty and confusion about their sexual identities and the impact these experiences would have on future relationships, not only with significant others but also with children and family. Considering that most of these women are mothers, the long-term implications for family structures post-release could be far-reaching.
>
> (2004: 54)

11 Seal says

> [t]he tendency to masculinise women who kill is exacerbated in cases of women perceived as being lesbian. In addition to criminological theories on the relationship between heightened masculinity in women and the propensity to offend, biological and psychological explanations of homosexuality in women have historically linked lesbianism to masculinity.
>
> (2010: 24)

12 This is obviously a distinction I am making between performance and popular media that are works of fiction and those that have a documentary purpose. For example, Pete Brook's photography project (2017); Ava duVernay's *13th* (Netflix 2016); Brett Story's *The Prison in Twelve Landscapes* (2016). Michelle Brown writes critically of how social documentary enables the 'ability to create chains of causality and accountability in chronicling the actions of the state […] [and] how governments should relate to their most vulnerable subjects' (2012: 101). Suzanne Bouclin's work on representations in film and jurisprudence is also instructive (2009).

13 This yoking of inevitable tragedy to lesbian identity is explored by Lynda Hart (1994) in *Fatal Women* – particularly in the figure of Aileen Wournos. Lisa Duggan also investigates the figure of the *Sapphic Slasher* (2000).

14 Didi Herman formulates a theory of lesbian homonormativity in *Bad Girls*.

> Although the intimate scenes between Nikki and Helen are not graphic or prolonged by any means, they are firmly located in the show's lesbian feminist perspective. These scenes are erotic, without being exploitative in the WIP sense, and when, at the end of the second season, Nikki and Helen finally have sex in Helen's home (again disrupting the conventional WIP containment of lesbianism within the prison) it is an 'amazing' experience for them both.
>
> (2003: 150)

15 Mark Llewellyn says:

> Both Selina and Margaret are 'queer' in society's eyes because of their unnameable desire. For Margaret, this desire can to some extent be enacted through the voyeuristic privileges of her class; for Selina, it is spiritualism that provides an outlet. Waters' use of the parallel is an exceedingly good one when one considers more deeply the 'ghostly' status of Victorian lesbian sexuality. Without a proper definition, lesbians were essentially spectres haunting a culture which would not acknowledge their crime, yet punished those suspected of practising it.
>
> (2004: 211)

16 Maeve, referring to her study with women in prison related to sexuality and health, notes that the state discussed in her article is

> under a permanent federal consent order to protect women prisoners from sexual abuse. In the past, corrections officers were accused of sexual coercion, sexual extortion, rape, and subsequent forced abortions. In an attempt to correct these egregious behaviors, corrections personnel are closely monitored with regard to all interactions with inmates. Any unusual kindness or appearance of closeness will cost an employee her or his job. Because of this, staff are constantly reminded to behold all female inmates as sexual predators bent on seduction for their own devious ends. Who women actually are, who they may have been, or who they might become, all become secondary to the potential dangers inherent in their sexuality.
>
> (1999: 55)

17 Referring to cultural depictions of homosexuality and fascism, Halberstam provides examples that offer 'powerful criticism of identity politics, made in terms that are different from many contemporary critiques of identity; [...] the presumption of stable and ethical identity in the present blocks out all evidence of contradictory and possibly politically objectionable identities in the past' (2011: 152).

18 I am grateful for discussion on the tyrannies of representation at the University of Roehampton that prompted this politicized reading.

Chapter Six

Performance through Prison: Institutional Ghosts and Traces of the Traumatic

The real [...] is always nostalgically or futuristically outside over there, on the other side of fantasy, recessing away from the viewer like the vanishing point of perspective.
(Schneider 1997: 95)

Representing Cycles of Re-offending between 'The Mix' and 'Churn'

In the 2008 French film *I have Loved you so Long (Il y a longtemps que je t'aime)*, written and directed by Philippe Claudel, the protagonist Juliette (played by Kristen Scott Thomas), a woman released after serving fifteen years in prison. Her award-winning performance characterizes the dual tensions of people released from prison. First, Juliette must navigate the ambiguities of freedom in an unfamiliar world; and second, the traces of prison itself are evident in her habitus. The film concentrates on her relationship with her estranged sister, who has taken her in, and who must work hard to build rapport, manage un-ease and establish communication in spite of her lack of memories of their past.

Claudel's choice in *I have Loved you so Long* is to focus on the present, without offering any explanation or flashbacks that may explain away Juliette's behaviours as she attempts to adjust to living with her estranged sister. Scenes are shot close-up to focus on nicotine stains on her hands, and the camera lingers on Juliette as she seems to hold her breath. This allows for the complex performance of tensions, regret and the readjustment of habitus to everyday rhythms. It also signals that time and its iterations are the substance but also the major challenge when considering representations of characters in prison, or post-release. By addressing the shifts in women's performance post-release, I attend to some of what has generally been little documented in terms of prison cultures. This choice expands how we might understand prison's relationship with time, narrative and habitus, and thus also returns to a consideration of the cycle of tragic containment. One element that is significant in that cycle is the sense of returns – with an emphasis on how one period of incarceration often and inevitably results in further convictions for people.

The preceding chapters explore performance tactics of incarcerated women by examining habitus they acquire in prison. In doing so, the object of study has largely remained focused on women's embodied acts of complicity and resistance within prison spaces. One of the profoundly performative elements of prison is its relationship with time as it separates out prisoners' sense of self through a promissory process of transformation. The 'successful' navigation of prison apparatus points towards potentiality of 'going clean', 'going straight' or getting out of what Barbara Owen calls 'the mix'. Owen refers to a slang term in US prisons that characterizes 'the mix' as the confusing, chaotic behaviour that results in conflicts, drug intrigues, petty thievery, illicit relationships and low-level 'drama' (1998: 178–83). To put it another way, prison explicitly stages the rehearsal of repertoires of how to become 'good women'. Such repertoires are tied to a patriarchal (neo-liberal) world order that ties particular value to gender norms.

My focus on performance and film representations here considers how prison exerts a continuing presence for women after release. Criminology is committed to researching the 'pains' (Sykes 1958; Crewe 2015) of imprisonment, and for feminist criminologists, this includes its gendered implications, but what gets less critical attention is how these pains, stigmas and repetitive 'hauntings' continue post-release. Women's pathways out of prison reflect how resettlement cycles always already retain the traces of prison as stigma, or ghostly haunting.[1] Institutionalization becomes a citational repetition for women, even as they seek to distantiate themselves from identities, affects and the stigma of lives 'before' incarceration. To this end, some additional theoretical concerns from feminist criminology are explored before engaging with the final stages of the cycle of tragic containment by mapping criminological concerns with performance models.

Following Carlton and Segrave, there is considerable importance in challenging the assumption that prison 'comprises a discrete episode in women's lives' (2011: 552).[2] Their research demonstrates the value in extending a gendered analysis beyond the walls of the institution to explore post-prison experiences. The function here is to examine the aesthetic 'release' of performance and its relationship to the political, ethical and social implications of women's release from prison. Whilst it is important to consider how different criminal justice contexts and state systems will mean distinctive experiences for women upon release, the focus here is not on the implications of particular criminal justice policies upon how women experience release.

Instead of universalizing claims, I use this stage of the cycle of offending to reflect back on specific theatrical representations. This approach to the pathways out of prison is a means of consolidating the frames of performance analysis in order to trace the impact of the 'spectacle' of punishment (inside) in relation to the everyday (outside). In doing so, we should consider prison theatre, performances in and of prison and plays and films about prison within a sociopolitical context. The argument demonstrates the potential for cycles of repetition or recidivism that form distinctive outcomes in the model of tragic containment; the steps beyond prison (with concomitant surveillance, governmentality, the threat of return to prison and the stigma associated with incarceration). Unlike other studies of theatre in prison, I draw attention to the role of performance in challenging the intersecting structures that criminalize women in the first instance, and then punish them in gender-specific ways, in order to release women into lives still characterized by marginality, chaos, uncertainty and inequality. To this end, my main focus is on the United Kingdom as a context.

Based in North-East England, theatre company Open Clasp's touring production *Key Change* (2014) signals the foregrounding of punishment and the cycles of victimization as inherent to women's slippage into crime. The characters are portrayed as understandably, and inevitably, sliding into chaotic situations in which domestic violence, abuse and drugs are factors in offending. Like many works about prison and offending, Catrina McHugh's relentless script was developed in collaboration with women in HMP Low Newton. It constructs the women's stories as surrounded by poverty and characterized by lack of choice. The inevitability, and the looming threat of prison even prior to incarceration, foreshadows some of the challenges identified by organizations working with women in the community. The performance by five actors in an empty space relies on building women's backstories and generating composite images that imbricate social contexts with their personal experiences that lead them all to their cells. The performers create prison spaces and shift across times and cities as they construct each of their narratives. In one section, they demonstrate how violence and domestic abuse have shaped their lives. In this scene, they are reflecting on how courses in prison helped them make sense of years of abuse:

KELLY:	I've turned a corner, got my eye on the prize. It was the courses and the gym that did it for me and the Freedom Programme. I learned about The Bully – he uses intimidation The Bad Father
KIM:	He uses the children to control you.
KELLY:	The Headworker – emotional abuse.
LUCY:	He tells you you're stupid, ugly and calls you a nag. He puts you down in front of others and he'll say it's a joke.
KELLY:	The Jailer – he isolates you, sulks if your friends come round, won't look after the kids,
ANGIE:	He charms your mam.
KELLY:	The Sexual Controller
ANGIE:	Demands sex, refuses it, rapes you.
KELLY:	The King of the Castle
KIM:	He treats you like a servant.
KELLY:	The Liar – He blames you
ANGIE:	Blames drink, drugs,
LUCY:	His work, his temper, low self-esteem and you believe him.
KELLY:	The Persuader – if you leave him, he'll threaten suicide, cry, say he has nowhere to go…
LUCY:	Threaten you, frighten you and you go back. The Dominator – he is one man but can change into any of the above. And if you ask me what would I say to this man, if this man was sittin' here today, I would tell him. 'I'm not a victim, I'm a survivor'.

(McHugh 2014: 29)

Figure 5: Keith Pattison, Open Clasp *Key Change*. Performers: Jessica Johnson and Christina Berriman Dawson.

Open Clasp's work illustrates the ways abusive relationships have performed a containing, punitive and demeaning function for women that foreshadows their time in prison. In this short scene, and throughout the play, prison is strangely characterized as preferable to the chaos, danger and anxiety of their lives prior to incarceration. Yet, this does not signal prison as a preferable locale for many of these women, who may have found security, safety and stability in other kinds of welfare provision, if social systems operated in ways that served vulnerable people. This dual tension is experienced by people exiting prison in a range of contexts, and is experienced particularly by women as a paradox. Release often signifies further marginalization, as intersecting issues are often exacerbated by time inside.

It is important to recognize here that these descriptors of life post-release are not universal, but rather the habitus required is specific to local contexts (Winfree et al. 2002). For instance, women leaving prison in Western contexts may be expected to survive alone and in homes they maintain through accessing welfare. There may be significant attention to gaining access to children and release may go along with the hopes of returning to work of some sort. In other contexts, life post-release may be more communal by necessity, even though resultant stigma may impact on women's life-chances differently, as depicted in the shattering documentary film *Zendan-e Zanan* (*Women's Prison*) by Manijet Hakmat on Iranian women trying to survive post-release (2002). However, in most of the examples from mainstream culture, release is represented differently for women than it is for men. Women's specific challenges are significant in the context of how they are able to narrate shifts from victim–survivor–hero. This set of challenges often forms tropes in films such as Laurie Collyer's 2006 film, *Sherrybaby*. In this film, and in many other Anglo-American representations, the protagonist is fixated upon restoring her own role as 'good mother'. This is distinct from film representations of male characters whose capacity to parent or be caregivers is not tied to their moral character in the same ways as for women. Further, when men are released from prisons, film representations routinely focus on restoring their place in the economic spheres and not in the domestic realm.

Themes of time, repetitious cycles, lead to the sense of the 'inevitable' churn of the prison population. 'Churn' is the criminological term for returning prison populace. These themes are examined by drawing on prison's performative presence in the lives of women ex-prisoner using literature that explores women's release, recidivism or desistance to consider how these are reflected in cultural representations.

There is comparatively little research on women's post-prison experiences, which suggests that the 'problem' of unruly women is only research-worthy when they are in the control of the state. The introductory section of the chapter is therefore not simply about providing context about probation (United Kingdom), parole (United States) or experiences in the community, but serves to model the precarious positioning of women exiting the scene of prison's stages onto the rather less spectacular stages of everyday life. From a methodological perspective, the current criminological understandings of women after release are deployed in relation to performance and popular culture examples. This serves empirical engagement with Clean Break's education programme as well as analysis of *This Wide Night* – another play by Chloë Moss (2008) commissioned by Clean Break that drew upon women's testimonies from a series of writing workshops in prison.

It is compelling, and indeed, fundamental to the Judeo-Christian ideology still underpinning criminal justice in Western countries to imagine that, once a prisoner is released from prison, the narratives of salvation kick in, and that they will desist from crime for the payoff of freedom. This narrative trope of redemption suggests that, having 'paid debts' to society by 'doing time', the 'tragic containment' of institutions can be set aside. But such a view draws on binaries that are more common in fictional narratives than in everyday examples. Instead of the exit from prison indicating a 'new life' with many possibilities, the pathways to re-integration into society are much more complex. Oft-cited data has shown that in the United Kingdom, of the women who are released from prison, up to 51 per cent are reconvicted within a year (Healy 2014; Wyld and Noble 2017).[3] These data indicate a need for much more structured and complex engagement with people as they leave incarceration, and are profoundly affected by the prison system that creates 'offenders', and survives by incarcerating masses of people.

Such a context indicates the value of engaging with the cycle of re-offending, and the threat of return to prison as a powerful trope in the lives of women. Furthering Foucault's views, for example, on the inescapability of the dominating order (Counsell 2009: 4), I see prison and its operations as processual. Such processes are not merely inflicted on the bodies of the ex-prisoners as punishing regimes, but rather as extensions of the mechanisms of the system that become internalized, or what Allspach has called the 'transportation of "the carceral"' (2010: 718). She explores the ways neo-liberal governance re-regulates women's desires, behaviours and spatial locations. Such regulation, she claims, 'operates through risk discourses that trigger a variety of practices spanning spaces, socio-economic fields and various actors, including the women themselves' (2010: 718). Segrave and Carlton's (2013) research on women's lived experiences of release characterizes it as fundamentally different from such simplistic narratives of redemptive release. They argue that women experience 'multiple episodes of release' that correspond with a lifetime of disadvantage, experiences of injustice and oppression, cycles of state intervention (often from an early age), criminalization and serial imprisonment (2013: 1). They go on to explore the ways in which

> [w]omen's post-release experiences are profoundly shaped and impacted by this broader context, along with myriad systemic and structural factors. Such complexities make drawing attention to women's post-release realities a significant, but not insurmountable, challenge.
>
> (2013: 1)

Offending and re-offending are tied in with value judgements about 'risk'; and such terminologies also extend to the ways women are expected to self-regulate their own multiple vulnerabilities and 'risk factors', such as alcohol or drug dependencies (Covington 2003). In other words, women become accustomed to monitoring themselves in relation to their 'licence' or probation or parole conditions.[4] We might read this as a set of tasks or obstacles in a performer's improvisation arsenal. And yet, as Allspach (2010) points out, many of the conditions women return to in the community perpetuate the conditions of risk. For example, many temporary hostels from which women are due to apply for more permanent housing (and which are monitored by probation) are also in poverty-stricken neighbourhoods, and can place women in 'dangerous' proximity to drug dealing and prostitution. This is evident in *Wentworth*'s depiction of maternal protagonist Liz who is released from prison and must stay in a hostel while she organizes herself a more permanent place to live (Season 2, Episode 10 'Jail Birds'). Often, temporary hostels cater to mixed genders, which may prove risky for some women. For Liz, this means that she must double lock the door to stop an unstable male resident entering her room, resulting in difficulty sleeping as she fears attacks. The surveillance of intimate associations, the control of bodies (through random urine samples, for example, used for drug testing) and the licence conditions stipulating times women should be indoors seem overly demonstrative as 'corrective' gestures when the geographies of control are sited in risky spaces. This argument pits individual women's agency against territories in which their intersecting vulnerabilities are foregrounded. For Liz, this ultimately means that she becomes embroiled in using alcohol and concealing a weapon. This leads to her parole conditions being violated, and she is returned to prison, where she feels more secure.

Such extensions of the terrains of surveillance and control sound unnecessarily punitive, although they may be perceived by women as paradoxically 'welcome', according to Wacquant (2002), who demonstrates that the pains and repressions of prison are contingent. An ethnography by Rosie Deedes cites a prisoner:

> In prison, although it's an alien situation which is distressing, you are still sheltered, you are kind of among a set, a set regime, you're among a set of people who are fully aware of you and you are of them, and they've got their role and you've got your role but out there is a whole different thing.
>
> (cited in Gelsthorpe et al. 2007: 26)

This interviewee uses terminologies familiar to social theories of performativity to discuss appropriate behaviours within the field of the institution. This chimes with how the prison may act, according to Wacquant, 'counterintuitively and within limits, as a stabilizing and restorative force for relations already deeply frayed by the pressures of life and labor at the bottom of the social edifice' (2002: 388). Connecting Wacquant's position with Allspach's, the underlying drive of prison's neo-liberal apparatus serves to uphold its own regimes – and to gloss Foucault's notion of biopolitics, becomes a means of producing and maintaining its own systems.

There are wider political implications to the maintenance of a vulnerable, under-skilled, poorly educated populace of ex-prisoners whose dependency on state mechanisms renders them subject to penal control even when they are out in the community. Nevertheless, dependency and the structure of prison or probation controls can seem important for women. Owen's ethnography about 'the mix' characterizes the cocktail of intrigues, experiences and petty excitements of prison life in opposition to the banality of the 'real' of the outside world. One of her interview participants makes the following claim:

> The majority of people who run things in here never had anything in their life […] These people have no values, no convictions. They run the street all their lives. Here they are big because they get $140 […]. Where else in the world can that be the top of life? They have it going on. Then they parole, and it is not so good anymore, and on the streets, they are not running shit. So then they get a case, come back and hey, they are big daddy now.
>
> (1998: 179)

In short, prison gives some women a frame of meaning – a sense of structure – against which to measure themselves. The performative paradox of prison is that it positions women as both convicted as guilty (victimizers) and as victims (by infantilizing them and reducing agency). Prison does not fundamentally challenge women's prior experiences of victimization, and, as criminological literature demonstrates, release from prison highlights women's vulnerability.

The state, through prison and probation services, creates a carceral network of furthering control through constant surveillance, the limitation of freedoms and the need for self-monitoring (Pasko 2017). This is also explored by Haney's (2010) ethnography of US halfway houses. Rather than a clear dichotomy between punishment 'inside' and freedom 'outside', it is clear that the mechanisms of enacting control are more pervasive, and more complex in their applications. This pervasive presence serves as a phantasmagoria, which from its Greek roots suggests a shifting and complex assemblage of images that could be both real and imagined. Thus, while in prison, women imagine freedom as a spatial and behavioural set of possibilities, and yet upon release, the repetitive flickering of the carceral apparatus of control serves to define and delimit such freedom. 'Real freedom' is an illusion that is always already the counterpoint of incarceration, drawing on Phelan's assertion (following Lacan) that the 'impossibility [of the real] maintains rather than cancels the desire for it' (1993: 14). This is also taken up in the epigraph to this chapter, by Schneider, which suggests:

> The real […] is always nostalgically or futuristically outside over there, on the other side of fantasy, recessing away from the viewer like the vanishing point of perspective.
> (1997: 95)

By articulating the real in this way using a spatial metaphor, Schneider's thinking shifts beyond only the temporal realm. In this view, the imagined impossible freedom of release performs a legitimizing function of the punitive present. Instead, freedom is the spatialized illusion of a 'somewhere else'. Its refusal is seen through the repetitive cycles of incarceration, surveillance and control. In prison fictions and representations, this is a core trope that needs critical attention. Such a view also contains the necessity of desire in this complex, iterative spacetime of cycles of incarceration/freedom.

Performance theories offer critical approaches for thinking through prison institutions theoretically. The institution's legacy is brought into focus by modelling it in relation to several key concerns in performance studies, particularly notions of time and repetition, presence and visibility, and mimetic presence. This means a shift from the contextualization of women exiting prison towards the function of performance representations. To do so takes Phelan's performance ontology further by suggesting that women's experiences post-release always already recuperate the power of the institution. This approach models the needs, desires and behaviours of women post-release by exploring them through the performative lens of the institution. Women's repertoires remain influenced and sometimes even dictated by institutional limitations well after release, such that even when ostensibly 'somewhere else', prison's traces are evident.

Performance 'Out of [the] Joint': Traces of the Institution after Release

In the internal lives of women ex-prisoners the institution takes on magnified proportions, casting a long shadow in their lives, as Abigail Rowe (2011) demonstrates. Rowe's findings show that

> [i]mprisonment challenged, developed or confirmed identities in ways that were variously welcome or distressing. This reflexive management of self-meanings is a technology of the self, employed in response to the dislocation of imprisonment in order to cope with its painful and stigmatizing meanings.
>
> (2011: 587)

Rowe demonstrates that prison processes and the impacts on self-narratives are not always negative, but can be associated with recovery, growth or renewal. This is associated with 'having time to reflect, taking up opportunities to address personal problems, or experiencing respite from problematic personal circumstance or the attritional effects of active addiction' (2011: 579). Further, it is through the repetition and citation of 'being' an ex-prisoner that maintains the powerful force of the institution once women are in the community, through what Goffman names the 'mortification' rituals of the total institution – leading to what he calls a 'spoiled identity' (1963).[5] This is often in spite of – and indeed because of – interventions by charitable organizations dedicated to helping women. Labelling women 'vulnerable', 'marginalized' and ex-offenders often perpetuates the feelings of stigmatization. Goffman and women's performances of 'spoiled identities' (1963) are discussed later in particular relation to *This Wide Night*. At the same time self-help discourses, as well as the characterization of women prisoners and ex-prisoners as 'victims', are pervasive.

At this point I would also point towards a caveat that in the United Kingdom, agencies are beginning to recognize the difficulties of victimizing language and have made claims for a 'post-Corston' narrative that allows interpretation in 'terms of women's inequality' (Clinks 2013). The Corston Report highlights the need for gender-specific sentencing, prison regimes and alternatives to custody (also explored in reports from a series of events around Women's 'Offending' in Clinks, 2013; Gelsthorpe et al. 2007; Women in Prison 2013a).

One of the lobbying phrases used to characterize resettlement resources and services is 'wrap around' and 'through the gate'. This suggests an omnipresent set of multiple agencies poised to comfort, support and hold women's hands out of prison and into security in the community, which is not only unlikely, but also patronizing. This sets up the state as paternalistic and describes a relationship characterized by dependency. Seen in relation to discourses of so-called 'dependency culture' powerfully addressed by Haney (2010), the ex-prisoner as 'victim' has been largely adopted and absorbed by liberal media.[6] Feminist criminology shows that the same women who are vilified for 'abandoning' their children through unruly behaviour are then characterized as powerless against the might of the state post-release (Jewkes 2007; Rowe 2011; Schen 2005; Townsend 2012a, 2012b;

Vallely and Cassidy 2012a, 2012b). Their powerlessness is exacerbated by awareness that children in care are not always able to maintain contact with the ex-prisoner (Brooks-Gordon and Bainham 2004). That such a system punishes women at both ends of prison sentencing in relation to family ties suggests, see Haney (2010), that the state does not have the best interests of (working-class/poor) women and their families at heart. Gilfus says the

> process of criminalization for women is indeed intricately connected to women's subordinate position in society where victimization coupled with economic marginality related to race, class, and gender all too often blur the boundaries between victims and offenders.
>
> (2012: 27)

In both the United States and the United Kingdom, women living in poverty are often impacted harder than middle-class women, who may have better access to childcare provision and more stable support networks while they are incarcerated. It is important to note, too, that intersections of ethnicity, race, class and gender coagulate in these narrative structures. They often serve to reinforce typologies of ex-prisoner, in which race and class intersect. These typologies and tropes position the most 'acceptable' ex-prisoners as a white, middle-class woman, and the least acceptable a foreign national woman from a minority ethnic background (Vallely and Cassidy 2012a, 2012b; Warr 2016). In the United States, this is equally stratified according to race and class, and arguably even more starkly drawn for women in relation to resettlement rules and parole/probation governance that are encircled by a punitive carceral geography (Wacquant 2009a, 2009b). In that context, women experience further marginalization and the vulnerability of familial bonds as 'failures', and often articulate frustration at victimization they experience as mothers (Brink 2003; Golden 2005). This is often related to how families are separated, with children ending up in state care due to (even short-term) incarceration. Many women leaving prison face extraordinary struggles to maintain contact with children, and especially to regain custody of their children, after time inside.

The effect of this is that public perspectives on women ex-prisoners – particularly in response to theatrical representations – and also personal memoir (Graney 2003, 2004, 2006; Lamb 2007; Levi and Waldman 2011) become sedimented in a particular range of affectual responses – predominantly pity, shame and outrage. What is of interest here is how the norms and values of incarceration are repeated citationally long after women have left prison. It is necessary then, to return to the notion of engendered habitus as I introduce, and then unpack, some of the performance implications of prison's repetitive presence as traumatic trope in the lives of ex-prisoners.

Criminological literature demonstrates that, upon release from prison, most women return to impoverished neighbourhoods, with little chance of sufficient access to services and resources (Leverentz 2010: 651). Often, they must navigate the difficulties of remaining isolated from criminal activities since (generally) women's criminal activities are networked in relation to intimate partners, family and friends (Allspach 2010; Leverentz 2010). Key factors in women's cycles of re-offending relate to intersecting issues related to poor educational attainment, low-quality training in prison, little access to training outside prison and few job opportunities in a risk-averse employment landscape. In addition, the criminal 'licence' is used (often with extreme implications), to delimit and contain the repertoire of behaviours of women. For example, being in 'the wrong place' or drinking alcohol (even if not intoxicated) could mean a woman ex-prisoner 'violates' licence/parole conditions, and is returned to prison. We can see this in instances from *Wentworth*, when Liz Birdsworth returns to prison due to being caught up in helping a friend, and unwittingly violates the terms of her conditions. A similar example from *OITNB* is when Taystee leaves but finds a way to get back inside quite quickly, as she reflects that she feels 'at home' in prison. As noted by Allspach, this suggests that women must become self-monitoring to the degree of risk posed by their surroundings. They learn to adopt a set of strategies and tactics related to identifying and avoiding risk. In other words, they need to engage in complex re-inscriptions of their own status as survivors/victims – particularly since, in many cases, women's criminal activities stem from addiction and association with violent men (Allspach 2010; Gelsthorpe et al. 2007), seen in the *Key Change* scene extracts from Open Clasp. Thus, women intending to maintain 'successful' pathways out of prison necessarily replicate pre-determined terminologies, and a sanctioned habitus that remains focused on their presumed victimhood and vulnerability.

The limen between inside/outside, incarceration/freedom becomes a site of negotiation in which women must confront the distance between their current situation and imagined future situation. Much of the time women's re-entry into society coincides with painful negotiation of practical problems relating to housing, access to children and, in some cases, the ability to get a job, or access to welfare. Almost all women leaving prison would face significant worries about surviving – especially since, in order to justify their 'freedom', they need to refuse involvement in what may have been a lucrative 'career' from the proceeds of crime (through sex work or involvement in drug and gang culture, for example).[7]

Carlton and Segrave's important study on women's survival post-release demonstrates that 'experience of imprisonment can emulate and magnify pre-existing traumas, placing women at risk upon release' (2011: 558). Their investigation draws attention to the prison as extension of trauma that has circulated in their lives in complex and intersecting ways prior to incarceration. Yet, in this consideration of prison itself as traumatic, the functions of the institution mimetically reproduce the dynamics of abusive relationships. They see 'prison as punishing women in a way that emulates and entrenches their experiences of control and victimization on the outside' (2011: 558).

This is what happens to the title character in the Clean Break show *Joanne* (Bruce et al. 2015), which is a series of monologues commissioned by female playwrights for a single actor. Each short play is about a central (unseen) protagonist, with the different characters highlighting the professional interventions that serve criminalized women throughout the cycle of offending and re-offending (including educators, social workers, peer support workers, hostel night shift staff, for example).

> She looks cold. And she's just sitting there counting the money over and over. Ten pounds, twenty pounds, thirty pounds, forty. Forty-six pounds, that's what she gets for making it out. I give her the mobile phone which I've brought for her. With credit.
> (Odimba in Bruce et al. 2015: 6)

All of the characters reflect on Joanne and how their interactions relate to her navigation of these cycles. 'And I want to be honest with Joanne. And she looks like the type they might scare so I tell her how it's going to be. First stop, probation […]' (2015: 6). The support worker narrates the steps she takes to get Joanne linked up with services as she attempts to get her 'through the gate'.

> I get her well prepared and by the time we get to them, it's easy. After 10 months inside, she can hardly string a sentence together. She could say it herself but somehow she is silenced by all of this. Lost. Cat not only got her tongue but bloody refused to give it back! But before we leave there I have her saying all the right things. That's what I'm here to do isn't it?
> (Odimba in Bruce et al. 2015: 7)

The innovative monologue form about the same character from different times and contexts enables the playwrights to approach women's interactions with criminal justice professionals in more detailed ways than are usually afforded in plays about prison, where the focus inevitably becomes polarized into 'us' and 'them'. In *Joanne*, what is staged is the wider context and conditions faced by women, and this situates re-integration beyond personal responsibilities. The play's structure thus initially appears to avoid some of the pitfalls I highlight in relation to tragic containment. The unseen protagonist, however, in being represented through the eyes of the professionals remains caught in the terminologies and spectacle of criminal justice.

By contrast, research for the Fawcett Society on resource provision for women in the community suggests that women who were 'successful' desisters 'crafted highly traditional "replacement selves" (namely as a child of God, good wife, involved mother) that they associated with their pathways out of crime' (Gelsthorpe et al. 2007: 22).[8] In other words, women need to develop a post-institutional habitus that can 'pass' in the day-to-day struggle to survive outside of institutional constraints (and comforts). Joanne characterizes this struggle by being unable to articulate herself in the face of professional support services. While audiences do not get presented with exactly what fate meets Joanne, it is obvious that she faces alienation, marginality and enduring stigma.

Most women significantly underestimate the challenges of re-entry in relation to how a new 'performance' may conflict with/contradict or undermine the 'place' they may have occupied prior to incarceration. However, most women do not factor in the enduring stigma of prison in their imagining of life outside, because, for women who have led 'criminal lives' before going to prison, stigma, deviance and 'spoiled identities' are often important identity markers, forming a codified and accepted habitus. The stigma may not feel devastating to their own identity in this case, since the prior habitus had already incorporated danger or risk. If they attempt to remove themselves from this kind of group or 'association', then they need to develop new repertoires of living. The analysis of women's experiences post-release involves their abilities to face uncertainty, the willingness and capacity to adapt to the expected normative role. In addition, successful desistance requires that women's achievements (such as staying 'clean' from drugs or alcohol) are recognized and validated; in other words, audienced.

For those women who have been in prison without having had the kinds of experience mentioned above (in terms of risk or dangerous criminal habitus prior to imprisonment), re-entry may be a shock, because they experience the stigma of having been a prisoner as a visible marker. Women mention how factors such as appearance, for example their skin, weight, as well as ways of walking, and ability to cope with everyday things such as traffic have been affected by institutionalization. Women's prison habitus has been so structured, limited and controlled that the unpredictability of the flows and tensions of everyday obstacles can seem insurmountable. There is an assumption, noted by Goffman (1963) that everyone 'can see', or read what he calls the 'mortification' through their bodies – perhaps more relevant in the past when women wore the scarlet letter, for example, or had heads shaved during incarceration.

Unlike Nathaniel Hawthorne's character Hester Prynne, however, contemporary women leaving prison do not have 'real' stigmatizing symbols, but feel marked by traces of incarceration. Hawthorne's treatment of Hester in the novel *A Scarlet Letter* is an obvious literary analogy adopted in scholarly accounts of stigma. A short extract that is indicative of the scarlet letter as stigma is instructive:

> On the breast of her gown, in fine red cloth, surrounded with an elaborate embroidery and fantastic flourishes of gold thread, appeared the letter A. It was so artistically done, and with so much fertility and gorgeous luxuriance of fancy, that it had all the effect of a last and fitting decoration to the apparel which she wore; and which was of a splendor in accordance with the taste of the age, but greatly beyond what was allowed by the sumptuary regulations of the colony […] But the point which drew all eyes, and, as it were, transfigured the wearer, – so that both men and women, who had been familiarly acquainted with Hester Prynne, were now impressed as if they beheld her for the first time, – was that SCARLET LETTER, so fantastically embroidered and illuminated upon her bosom. It had the effect of a spell, taking her out of the ordinary relations with humanity, and inclosing her in a sphere by herself.
>
> (2010: 30, original emphasis)

This 'marking' is experienced as embodied, in the sense that the body becomes accustomed to restricted distances, for example, or that sight is reduced due to lack of stimulus.[9] The women negotiate an interrelated set of stigmas – social judgements related to physical or psychological 'appearance' – alongside the constant presence of the prison's function of increased self-surveillance. Such stigmatization leads to women's excessive shame, anxiety and struggle to release prison's grip on their self-image. As Goffman suggests, however, stigmatized people can develop a capacity for improvising in the everyday. That is, women are required to engage with a wider set of survival skills that are fundamentally about successful performance. I do not agree with Goffman's characterization of stigmatized people in opposition to what he calls 'normals' (1963), nor do I advocate his repertoires of surviving stigma, which he does not necessarily contest. Yet, his explorations of how stigmatized persons present various 'symbols' is valuable to this argument in terms of representation. Goffman's insistence on the development of normative performances that help to 'pass' in the 'real' world outside of the institution raises some important questions with which performance studies has been concerned. Such questions are useful to consider in relation to trauma theory in order to revisit the implications of the 'tragic-containment' model.

The argument that the institution maintains a disciplinary function is, of course, not new. Foucault argued this in *Discipline and Punish* (1977), though my argument here draws more on the notion that there is a wide frame through which to understand the means by which (criminal) bodies continue to experience stigma, erasure and invisibility after release. The seeming impossibility of 'transformation' discourses is evident in light of the structural inequalities that continue to perform exclusionary functions against women whose race, ethnicity, habitus and gender performances do not conform to societal norms. In light of the tension between narratives of transformation, the probation-related imperative to perform successful re-integration and the affects related to carceral traces, I return to the importance of performance studies in order to unpack some of the complexities raised by women leaving prison.

For a range of reasons, including ex-prisoners being denied voting rights in the United States, for example, release from prison can suggest a severing of meaning, rather than a return to a full 'normal' life.[10] Rather than experiencing coherence associated with a return to the 'real' world, women's narratives are fragmented, and rendered less connected to civic life. Such fragmentation of meaning is a logical conclusion to the pains of imprisonment. Yet, the fragmentation is not merely the women's ontological experience, but relates to the dynamic of stories played out in the public sphere.

The publicness of punishment has been explored elsewhere in the book, but it is the specificity of what is publicly visible as women leave prison that is important here. Writing about the death penalty in the United States, Conquergood demonstrates that the spectacle of public executions was historically driven by audience fascination with the 'fate of the prisoner's immortal soul' (2002a: 345–46). By contrast, there is very little spectacle remaining in relation to women leaving prison. However, despite being able to depart from the physical site of incarceration under the illusion of freedom, women are nevertheless drawn into a series of performative reckonings that are as much about attempting to live 'by the letter' as staking a claim to a place in society.

Women are required to follow a script after release that has been determined by probation or parole officers in relation to their sentence. Whilst in prison, they are monitored, surveilled and subject to 'writing up'. In the community too, the women are inscribed by probation reports that, instead of reflecting their complex and chaotic lives, often reduce their stories to bullet points about how they served their sentences. Probation reports are thus not only about how women survive on a day-to-day basis, but underscored by how they 'do time'. The wider context of crime and justice, and how they are represented, is upheld by the symbolism of women's recidivism. The inevitable story of hopelessness, melancholia and loss is an argument that supports the existence of the institution as curative. Prison's 'failure', when played out on the stages of women's everyday domestic settings after release, paradoxically becomes its justification: women must be incarcerated again because the first time did not 'work', returning ex-prisoners to the cycle of tragic containment.

Performance, Trauma and Witnessing: Prison's Presence

Performance research is not merely about describing events that are considered 'performance', but can pose problems about embodied experiences of doing, acting, being and witnessing. What is foregrounded is the mimetic repetition of the theatrical presence of the prison and its implication for how women perform. The complicity and reciprocity of meaning-making emerges through women performing the cycles from prison to the community and onward – either by returning to prison or by treading a pathway out of a life of crime. Prison's performance in the lives of women leaves a trace or scar of its presence. In doing so, the repetition of prison (through memory, mimesis, stigma and nightmares) is aligned with the performativity of trauma as outlined by Douglass and Vogler (2003). Modes of trauma and how it plays out in artforms inflect my reading of instances of women's return to the community as scarred by the mimetic repetition of the presence of prison.

Links between trauma and narrative have gained prominence in recent scholarship (Ball 2003; Caruth 1995; Vogler 2003; Wade 2009), and yet, as Diana Taylor argues (2002: 154), traumatic memories often rely on live, interactive performance for transmission. Several studies have concentrated on the demand for testimony and witnessing promoted by trauma narratives (Felman and Laub 2002; Salverson 2001).[11] Taylor says that 'bearing witness is a live process, a doing, an event that takes place in real time, in the presence of a listener' (2002: 154). According to Felman and Laub, the listener 'comes to be a participant and a co-owner of the traumatic event' (2002: 57). However, trauma narratives do not turn on their truth claims, but on their aesthetic qualities. As Ball suggests, there is a necessity to recall the difficulties of validating experience of trauma: 'it would be impossible to validate survivor experience on moral grounds that require consensus about its status as a referent in relation to the law' (2003: 261). In fictional representations, the women's status as unruly, criminal and stigmatized always already positions their narratives or testimonies of surviving trauma (including in the institution) as suspicious, partial and unreliable. Perhaps it is in this frame that organizations dedicated to staging women's concerns tend towards positioning women's experiences firmly as survivor-victims. This demands a particular kind of moral/ethical witnessing from audiences/listeners whose own positions in relation to the law are called into question by virtue of the moral obligation of testimony.

Thinking alongside what trauma studies offers aligns with my consideration of performative pathways out of prison. How these correlate with the cycle of tragic containment in the ways women tread the pathways or expectations of 'success' (desistance) or 'failure' (re-offending). What is not accounted for is the vast spectrum of possibilities that exist in the performance of everyday life that slip between success and failure. However, probation systems are called to characterize women's adaptation and resilience to the community in bold, quantifiable measurable outcomes rather than reflecting the more nuanced possibilities of expression related to the self, identification, work and leisure. The measurement of women in these limited terms suggests that they need to adopt the language and performance register in which they are being judged (Merrill and Frigon 2015). It is this citational adoption of 'cheer' or 'strength' or 'resilience' that I propose is a drag act. In interventionist programmes it is worth considering to what extent these myths of transformation are an obvious 'drag act' (Butler 1993b), in the sense that it is deployed against and through the image of women as survivor-victim/s. In other words, 'transformation' is painted on top of the victimized women in bold and brash strokes – a citation (cf. Diamond 1997).

'I want you to look like a mum': Gender Norms and Institutional Haunting in *This Wide Night*

In order to explore this further I engage with another play text by Moss. This performance of *This Wide Night* is one of the most well-known of Clean Break's plays (Walsh 2018a). I have mentioned this play in passing in other chapters as emblematic of performance about women in prison. It was produced in the United Kingdom in 2008 and 2010, was recipient of the Susan Smith Blackburn award for writing in 2009 and has been staged in Australia and the United States. In the play, the two characters, Marie and Lorraine are reunited when Lorraine is released from prison. They are unlikely friends: Lorraine is a cheery yet medicated older woman whose immediate action on release is to look for her old cellmate, Marie. The younger woman, Marie, has been housed in a dreary studio flat. She is consistently on edge, masking something from Lorraine. As Dolan notes in her review of the Broadway staging of the play, the women's backstories remain murky, 'as if Moss insists that the details of their histories, their crimes, and their rehabilitation don't really matter to how they'll go forward in their lives' (2010: online). Moss's play raises important questions and obstacles faced by women who re-enter society after time in prison. It stages concerns relating to the mask

Figure 6: Production shot: *This Wide Night*, Moss, 2009. Produced by Clean Break.

adopted by women who feel they must 'present' themselves as coping because by definition being 'free' is understood to be better than prison in an unspoken hierarchy of contexts.[12]

The play's setting within Marie's studio flat presents the contingent and precarious placing of these women as adumbrated by the carceral geographies of limited mobility, restricted opportunities and modest aspirational horizons. Both women leave the flat (never together), but the audience experiences them within the confines of the four walls of the studio. The fact that they never leave this precarious 'home' suggests that even when women do manage to obtain housing, it does not indicate the beginning of a cycle to desistance, but rather, the possibility that failure/re-offending are very likely. This is suggested through the play's action in the isolation, marginalization, poverty and lack of social ties evident in the two characters' narratives. Running throughout the play is the condition of the relationship between the two women.

Criminologists demonstrate that support networks and relationships are one of the important factors in resettlement (Gelsthorpe et al. 2007: 22). The analysis of this play also examines the intersections of trauma studies with thematics of family reparations as the two women attempt to reassert their positions in structures that have been strained (or broken) by crime and incarceration.

Dolan's reflection on a New York production of *This Wide Night* highlights the impossible ties between the women as constitutive of a mimetic repetition of prison's operations.

> Because the women don't have the emotional or social or financial resources to propel themselves elsewhere, the room becomes an existential 'no exit', in which they're bound to one another through fear as well as through longing for a future neither one of them can really imagine.
>
> (Dolan 2010: online)

In her reflection on Lorraine's institutionalized habitus, Dolan mentions that for the character, her biological functions have continued to be governed by the timings and logistics of the prison. This is seen in Lorraine's dependence on regularity and routine – such as mealtimes or medication times (also notable in Suzanne's character in *Orange Is the New Black*).

> Lorraine, whose awkward, jerking movements represent a woman desperately trying to embody what she thinks freedom means, hasn't a clue how to remake her life. Lorraine is so accustomed to the regimentation of prison life that she gets hungry precisely at 5:30, when dinner was served inside.
>
> (Dolan 2010: online)

In related work on trauma and prison's performativity, I consider how Lorraine's body continues to be overshadowed by prison (Walsh 2018a), particularly in relation to how Moss depicts Lorraine as dependent on Marie. Although she has been out of prison for a few months, she is also not yet 'free' of prison's hold. Dolan characterizes them both as 'among the forgotten, formerly institutionalized women for whom a world not bound by four confining walls is impenetrable, unreadable, and utterly uninhabitable' (2010: online). The play does not merely demonstrate the impact of the institution on their bodies, but positions the remains or traces of institutional expectations in the form of probation as infantilizing.

The sense of the cyclical, repetitive dialogue that reinforces the characters' sense of hopelessness means it has been necessary to include fairly long interchanges between the women. Here, Marie is narrating how she navigated the support worker she was allocated after release.

MARIE: I don't have to see her no more. That Suzanne. She got right on my tits. She used to put her arm round me when I sneezed like somethin' bad had just happened. If we were sat next to each other. In the park. On the bus. I'd sneeze and her fuckin' arm'd come round and give a little…

LORRAINE: Jesus, I wouldn't want none of that. I just wanna bit of help getting some money, somewhere proper to stay. I wouldn't want none of that fuckin'… shit.

MARIE:	You haven't got no choice sometimes. S'what you gotta do. Prove you're good enough. Show them.
LORRAINE:	I'm not a performing monkey. What you supposed to do?
MARIE:	Talk. Only I never said nothing. She did all the talking and I pretended I was listenin'. She used to say stuff like 'value'. Not like 'value for money', like 'personal value'.

(2008: 10–11)

Marie's disgust at the suggestion that she performs 'strength' is at odds with her bravado in this scene. It is also undermined by a later scene, in which she reveals herself to be afraid, and unable to cope with the minutiae of everyday life on the outside. In the early sections of the play, Marie engages in tutelage, giving advice for how to remove the visible traces of prison – in other words how to survive her release. She is defensive, buffered by her months 'outside', and thus puts on a face of courage; partly, we suspect, to entertain Lorraine, and partly to convince herself that she is managing. Marie buys Lorraine a gift of a blouse, so that she can appear more 'like a mother' when she meets her adult son for the first time since he was adopted, aged seven. Marie scrutinizes Lorraine while she changes into the blouse, which is too small for her.

LORRAINE:	[…] How about that?
MARIE:	I want you to look nice.
LORRAINE:	Well, this is it, I wanna look nice but it isn't a fashion parade.
Pause.	
MARIE:	I want you to look like a mum.
LORRAINE:	What's that meant to mean?
MARIE:	You wore that jumper inside all the time.
Beat.	
LORRAINE:	So.
MARIE:	So I just think… you can tell. (*Beat.*) You have an idea in your head. He might have an idea in his head. Of something, I dunno… what.

(2008: 32)

Marie goes on to tell Lorraine how she imagines her mother. The scene demonstrates a performance of gender norms as Marie offers to 'make' Lorraine over into a more effective, more believable woman, rather than appear to be a 'lifer'. For Marie, the jumper 'prisonifies' Lorraine's appearance. The younger woman attempts to dress Lorraine 'as if' she were a 'real mother'. She implies that the prison jumper she criticizes negates this element of Lorraine's identity, as if the costume of a 'mum' will be convincing enough for Lorraine's now-grown boy to see her as such. Marie's actions suggest she is projecting her own desires for her mother to be something particular onto Lorraine. However, Lorraine says she wants to 'be herself' (2008: 34).

The older woman rejects Marie's explicit suggestion that prison traces can be seen, and instead remembers a specific duffel coat her little boy wore when he was taken into care years previously. This memory – described through the sensory traces it has repeated over the years – is what has nurtured her identity of motherhood during her life sentence. While we experience this story of loss from Lorraine's perspective, the image of the 7-year-old boy being removed from his home suggests a traumatizing cycle of abandonment, loss and guilt. While Moss never explicitly states Lorraine's motives for crime, we are led to assume she murdered a long-time abuser (presumably her partner). Some readings of the play suggest the abuse was targeting her child, Ben. This understanding reveals a different mode of the cycle of tragic containment – whereby Lorraine's violent (self) defence is justified, and therefore the trauma of incarceration and its impacts on her identity as a mother in particular, as well as on the son (who is himself a survivor/victim), is the core of the play's impact.

Later, Marie turns on Lorraine for settling into a comfortable routine after Lorraine chastises her for coming home late. The audience is not given precise information about what she was doing outside of the studio. Depending on the direction of this scene, it could seem she is involved in prostitution again, or another nefarious activity she needs to keep secret from Lorraine, who, it seems, has internalized the institutional narratives about 'sanctioned' and 'unsanctioned' behaviours. Marie tries to deflect attention away from her nocturnal activities by telling Lorraine they should go away on holiday (something she mocked her for in an earlier scene as unrealistic). Lorraine is unwilling.

LORRAINE:	Why the rush?
MARIE:	Why Not?
LORRAINE:	It's a bit… unexpected.
MARIE:	What, your affairs not in order or something? You not finished highlighting the rest of the week's telly in the TV Quick? (*Beat.*) Just stick a pair of knickers in a bag. Get a B&B. Go and sit on the beach –
LORRAINE:	It's raining.
MARIE:	Go and sit in a fucking pub, then. This was your idea, Lorraine.
LORRAINE:	I know.
MARIE:	Right then. Get ready.
LORRAINE:	Not… now though. Not straight away.
MARIE:	Why not?
LORRAINE:	I just need a bit of time. Get me head round it. Feels a bit… sudden.
MARIE:	I'm talking about going to Brighton for two nights not emigrating to Australia. (*Beat.*) When was the last time you did something spontaneous, Lorraine?
LORRAINE:	I'm not s'posed to go on holiday yet, am I?
MARIE:	Oh fuck them, Lol. You're a free woman now. What about the sand between your toes… all that?

LORRAINE: I do want to. I'd love it, Marie. More than anything. Just need to get geared up first, that's all.

(2008: 48)[13]

Having become settled into a housing arrangement, having her personal networks, and a promise that Marie will approach her employers for a job, Lorraine feels somewhat secure in the studio flat. Dolan's understanding of their predicament is that their intimacy

> comes from being forced to share space, which fostered a connection between them that they can't even describe or name. On the outside, Marie wields the power of the space and the lease, but Lorraine holds the power to care, an obscure notion on which Marie clearly can't depend. She's waiting to be abandoned again, as it appears her mother left her earlier in her life.

(2010: online)

Tensions between Marie and Lorraine grow more visceral after Marie returns in the early hours of the morning having been beaten in some way that remains unexplained. Lorraine attempts to comfort her:

LORRAINE: We'll be alright, you and me, Marie. We will.
MARIE: Why d'you keep doin' that, Lorraine? Why d'you keep sayin' 'we' and 'you and me'? There is no fuckin' 'you and me'.
LORRAINE: Course there is… what you saying that for? I love you.
MARIE: Oh Lorraine, stop it, you make me feel fuckin' – you creep me out when you say you love me. You don't even fucking know me.
LORRAINE: Don't say that, Marie, don't say that.
MARIE: Love. You aren't my fucking mother, Lorraine, or my fucking… girlfriend.
LORRAINE: Marie, stop it don't say stuff like – we're mates –
MARIE: Yeah, well, 'mates' don't spend every fucking second of every fucking day together, Lorraine. They don't sleep in the same fucking room night after endless night, talking about everything under the sun apart from what the fuck they're gonna do with their miserable fucking lives.
LORRAINE: There's things to look forward to. Things to hope for.

(2008: 54)

This scene demonstrates the effects of a temporal lag in their experiences. Marie's cynicism about what 'freedom' means is connected to her sensation of having no reliable connections, and a lack of security – financial and bodily – even though she has been out of prison for more than six months. On the other hand, while Marie is concerned with the fear of tangible and practical loss, Lorraine is holding on to their connection from prison, where trust and proximity meant that being 'mates' could survive because of ties of solidarity or kinship. Marie's reaction reveals the need for the re-working of prison habitus for life outside.

For both women, the dramaturgy emphasizes the traps and pitfalls of idealized imaginaries – either of what 'care' or kinship might mean, or of what 'freedom' might mean. The play highlights the practicalities of surviving in a hostile world that operates on financial and skills-based capital rather than the capacity for care, patience and generosity demonstrated in different ways by the two characters. Yet, while it is both warm and empathetic in tone, the play conforms to a rigid understanding of gendered habitus that demonstrates the poverty of the role spectrum for women who leave prison. More than any of the other plays I have discussed, *This Wide Night* positions gender norms very specifically as a set of internalized and disciplinary functions that, in particular, have traumatic consequences for children when the norms of family, care and protection from harm are spoiled. Indeed, the very gender of women criminals results in a 'spoiled' identity – to gloss Goffman's (1963) concept.[14] In this view, women who commit crime call their legitimacy as women into question. Furthermore, the processes of prison and the legacy of its operations serve to further erode the notion of a coherent pathway or narrative potential that conforms to gendered expectations.

In the final sequence, Marie explains why she seemed to have abandoned Lorraine in her final months of the sentence. She conflates the prison with her relationship with Lorraine. Her yearning for the intimacy of their friendship or nurturing relationship became located in the spatial dimension of the institution.

MARIE: I'm so sorry I stopped coming in. I hated it.
LORRAINE: That's alright... Jesus, that's okay. Fuckin' hell, you've just got shot of the place, you don't wanna be back in there every five minutes, do yer? Gotta get on with things.
MARIE: I hated it mostly because I sort of missed it. (*Beat.*) Or I missed you.

(2008: 58)

It is as if she could not imagine their connection outside of that space, and therefore the plan to move in together was an attempt to hold on to, or map across their connection – bridging the chasm between inside and outside. Yet, Marie's temporal and emotional distance from prison as she navigated her everyday life threw a new perspective on that intimacy. Rather than the legacy of prison casting the negative shadow on 'real life', for Marie, the everyday casts a pall on the prison reality. Each space makes the other unbearable. In each space, the other becomes a phantasmagoria of impossibility and loss. This points towards the inevitable repetition of inside/outside as a scopic field, not only for representations of women post-release, but in their own performative reflections of their time inside.

Clean Break often toured productions to prisons after staging them in professional theatres. In 2009, I was on tour with this play, and I facilitated workshops in many of the women's prisons across the United Kingdom through theatre activities after the performance by professional performers. In workshops with groups of women after watching this play, the women always wanted to piece together the backstories of the characters. While Moss is deliberately obfuscatory about biographical specifics, women always seemed to want to define what was happening outside the studio flat, reading into the blocking, body language and hidden codes of performance narrative details that resonated from their experiences. For instance, many of the women accessing drug treatment were quick to recognize Marie as a 'junkie' who was 'turning tricks' with her landlord, for example, whenever she left the studio. Most of the women in workshops were sympathetic to Marie, although they would always challenge her on her lies – suggesting that the code on the outside should be about rebuilding broken trust, and attentiveness to the triggers of criminal behaviour. The women's focus on actions outside the studio also raises the importance of an imagined 'elsewhere' upon which the spectators can project their desires, hopes and experiences. Rather than a concentration on the containment of the flat, their focus on spatialization is what these women brought to the understanding of the characters and their futures.

In these workshops, many women wanted to believe in the possibility for care and affection post-release, but were often cynical about the possibilities for friendships mapping across from inside/outside. Many women claimed that prison time was about being alone, which seemed to contradict the empirical evidence of community and intimacy in workshops and between prison buildings. Nevertheless, these perspectives testified to the schism – both spatially and emotionally described – in relation to trust and togetherness. Also, importantly, they attest to how prison produces certain kinds of relations that are not 'real' but are deployed as part of a prison culture. They function because the representation of prison kinship, friendship, intimacies of various kinds serve a function in getting women through their sentences. In a way, these forms of relating are a representation of intimacy that, through repetition, become a prison habitus. In terms of desire, we can see in this play how the desire to maintain such kinship across time and space is problematized by pressures and marginalization.

For women in prisons watching *This Wide Night*, there is an important exchange that may be considered mimetic-cathartic. While they are currently incarcerated, they are reflecting on the pathways out of prison and their own potential (and archival) experiences of release. For the audience, there is catharsis in the shared witnessing of what Peschel outlines as affect, time, social space and contested power (2012: 163). Together, women witness the characters' new relationships to prior shared experiences that were institutional but nevertheless experienced as personal and embodied. They also encounter the ways prison continues to function as a touchstone – both spatial and temporal – to which women refer as they testify to their experiences of incarceration.

The notion of catharsis in relation to the expectation of the purging of fear demands that an audience feel sufficiently able to identify themselves in relation to the protagonists' struggles. However, this kind of sentimental assumption suggests that a theatre-going audience would identify with women whose stories reflect intersections of poverty, marginalization and a lack of choice. More interesting for this argument is the suggestion that audiences comprising of women in prison may experience a cathartic moment in mimetic empathy with the two protagonists. A reflection from a performance of *This Wide Night* in HMP

Morton Hall demonstrates the potency of mimetic collapse. The women had gathered in the early morning and were waiting outside the gymnasium in order to enter as audience for *This Wide Night*. During the performance, I was aware of the many mutterings that accompanied scenes women 'recognized'. They seemed to be making a commentary (as they would in front of the TV) about whether the characters were authentic enough. One woman made quite a lot of noise rustling through her bag of snacks, in order to locate a pen and paper. Rather than being alienated, she was aroused by the emotions relating to her experience of the play. She was, she told me afterwards, inspired to write a poem to one of the women.

Later, in the workshop, it did not take very long for the women to begin to give advice to the two women about how to handle their re-integration better. One woman told us proudly that she had noticed Marie coming in with some money and hiding it, which is what she used to do when 'on the game' (doing sex work). She shifted in and out of character – speaking as both Marie and herself – as she narrated the difficulties of staying off drugs, and away from abusive relationships. Other women stepped into role as Lorraine or Marie and questioned their peers about what survival strategies they would recommend – many of them giving advice gained from their own experiences of release (and re-offending). As facilitator, it struck me that the women were quick to judge themselves, conflating the character's stories with their own.

Moss demonstrates through Marie and Lorraine that hope and inspiration can indeed be gained whilst in prison through forging caring friendships, through a sense of achievement in education programmes or workplace training, and through the space and time offered for self-contemplation. Yet, these hopes and desires are all too often revealed to be phantasms, as the incessant temporal churn of everyday life outside does not allow for reflexivity, instead requiring practical action. Moss's play provides glimpses of the ways in which prison continues to victimize women who have survived incarceration.

The cycle of tragic containment positions the re-integration stage as cathartic. This relies on evidence that criminal habitus can be transformed through 'correction' such that women exiting prison can adapt to an everyday or acceptable habitus. This, however, rests on the assumption that the external environment is conducive to 'straight' behaviour, and that wider structural inequalities would not be responsible for women's 'choice' to re-offend. Rather than operate as a productive mode in the cycle I outline, catharsis becomes a means of reducing women to 'rightful' places – in which economics, education, relationships and addictions are subservient to a moral righteousness that is somehow presumed to be restored through incarceration.

This is particularly evident in the production of *Pests* (Franzmann, 2014), a later Clean Break commission. Two sisters – Pink and Rolly – appear to be squatting in a diabolical room in an unknown place. The play circulates around 'the mix'. The duo reunite, fight, cajole one another, lie and deceive. Rolly's pregnancy merits as much conversation as the latest round of shoplifting or their adventures including sex work. When Rolly tries to get a different type of job, their conversation reveals a series of abuses, workplace discrimination and the endless despair of poverty. Neither feels able to escape poverty by 'going straight',

Figure 7: Production shot: *Pests*, Franzmann, 2014. Produced by Clean Break.

so shoplifting, pawnshops and drugs appear to be a viable alternative. Throughout the performance, spaces of possibility are closed to the women; yet they tell imaginative stories to one another. Outside of their room, however, they are excluded – through their dialect and through discrimination – as they are refused access to jobs, other living arrangements and more stable lives within society.

This staging, seen in the image, draws on magic realism to shift outside the bounds of the real space of the squat. Its aesthetic expansion does not transcend the hopelessness of their situation, but does illuminate how in scenography, narratives of possibility might need to be excessive or impossible set against the gritty mess of lived experience. Within this excessive aesthetic, this sets up a contingent morality where the protagonists justify and perpetuate the conditions that criminalized them in the first place. When one batters a potential employer who sexually harasses her, it is acceptable to the other. The final act of violence relates to a young girl who is battered till she loses an eye. Pink's violence circulates around the loss of a pair of shoes that, for her, signal freedom and imagination. *Pests*' scenography is decidedly not aiming for verisimilitude but situates criminalized women within ambiguous landscapes hewn from narcotics, violence and loss.

Thinking through theatrical representations has produced a sense of how tragic containment continues to function beyond prison gates. While such theatrical representations in general (and the tragic form I outline in particular) tend to rely on cathartic neat representations (Jürs-Munby 2009; Lehmann 2006), the daily real-life stories of ex-prisoners' re-integration into society expose the insidiousness of gendered expectations. These social scripts do not make allowance for the embodied experiences of chaos that securitization, survival obstacles and state bureaucracy produce in their lives. These institutional factors, coupled with the 'softer' weaknesses of addictive behaviours and destructive life choices, are not simple choices to be made and enacted. Rather, they are messy processes that are inherently contradictory. In theatrical form, and popular culture, this can mean that narratives could perpetuate misogynist victimization and depict the inevitable failure of women exiting prison. This is precisely what feminist criminological critiques propose: that the majority of systems designed to do so are not equipped for the specificities and collectivities of criminalized women.

Throughout, I argue for ways we may begin to view performance strategies as potential knowledge that may have practical, embodied, political force. I work through the concerns of prison habitus as simultaneously archival (in the sense that they are fixed and scripted by regimes of punishment and correction), and repertoires, in the ways that past issues and scenarios may be understood in the present. But, Taylor says, 'performance does more than that. The physical mechanics of staging can also keep alive an organizational infrastructure, a practice or know-how, an episteme, and a politics that goes beyond the explicit topic' (2006: 68). While Taylor's concern is explicitly on the interrelationship of national/transnational histories, her formulation of the ways performance paradigms can provide models for understanding and working through their often traumatic histories can also be applied to specific individual narratives, as seen in the extract from *Key Change* (McHugh 2014). Taylor refers to the ways the past is 'used' as

> a repository for strategies in carrying on their lives, confronting contemporary struggles, and envisioning futures. The repertoire, this often overlooked system of storage, makes these resources of the past available, useable over time, both through [...] repetitions and in moments of crisis.
>
> (2006: 72)

To reiterate, this is not a unique factor to prisons and release, but may be applied to any of Goffman's total institutions (2007). On a wider scale, however, if we view social and cultural practices that circumscribe women released from prison, it is evident that the repetition of unhelpful structures of deprivation and punishment outside has a negative effect on the 'transformation' of the tragic cycles of inevitable return to offending behaviour. Taylor's argument provides a means of seeing how strategies and tactics (see de Certeau) developed through incarceration, and in response to surviving chaotic contexts can be transposed to everyday performances once women are released from prison. The traces of prison as visible and perceived stigma serve as performative warnings to the wider public of the consequences of crime by forming a residue of institutionalization.

By modelling women as survivor-victims of the institution, it demonstrates the institutional interests prevalent in the maintenance of restricted performance repertoires. Women's performances of post-incarceration stigma are constituted by the disciplinary imperative of the prison. As well as making reference to Open Clasp's *Key Change* (McHugh 2014), two Clean Break commissions Franzmann's *Pests* (2014), Bruce et al.'s *Joanne* (2015), I argue that the choice between recidivism and desistance is not in a social/economic vacuum. Women are not judged as performing as moral agents, but as defined and limited by prevailing socio-economic conditions (particularly in the United Kingdom's ongoing milieu of cuts to social services post 2010 (Prison Reform Trust 2010; Women in Prison 2013a, 2013b). The close reading of Clean Break's *This Wide Night* by Moss (2008) considers the implications of a mimetic relationship to cycles of tragic containment. The collapse of selves evident in this mimetic-cathartic moment of witnessing in the prison workshop returns women prisoners to the limited spectrum of possibilities of victim–survivor. This critique points towards the need for other postdramatic representational strategies in contemporary performance (Lehmann 2006). These points collectively set the ground for a consideration of how performance *of* prison results in a set of performative functions post-release as an epistemological crisis of representation.

Notes

1. Marvin Carlson (2003) considers the apparatus of the theatre as replete with hauntings. I am attending to this conception here as well as acknowledging the Derridean influence of haunting (Derrida 1993).
2. Their research looks at women's survival rates (as well as suicides) post-release that can be directly attributable to traumatic experiences of both incarceration and release into unsupported, unmanageable living conditions (Carlton and Segrave 2011).
3. Women in Prison (2013) collated statistics from The Bromley Briefing and the Ministry of Justice from 2012. In addition to the 51 per cent reconviction rate mentioned above, 'for those serving sentences of less than 12 months this increases to 62%. For those women who have served more than 10 previous custodial sentences the re-offending rate rises to 88%'. In the United States, the Sentencing Project offers the following statistics: 'Between 1980 and 2014, the number of incarcerated women increased by more than 700%, rising from a total of 26,378 in 1980 to 215,332 in 2014' (2015: 1). 'Though many more men are in prison than women, the rate of growth for female imprisonment has outpaced men by more than 50% between 1980 and 2014. There are 1.2 million women under the supervision of the criminal justice system' (2015: 1). Note, this is different from averages per year that reflect sentencing trends as well as the wider political climate.
4. All prisoners receive licence conditions upon release that are determined in relation to their risk to the public, and meant to reflect their specific criminogenic histories and patterns of offending.
5. As highlighted in Chapters One and Two, Goffman's 'total institutions' are not only prisons, but all institutions that serve to separate people from a wider community – for reasons as

diverse as education, mental health incapacitation, the need for health quarantine or for punishment. Readers might make connections with boarding schools, asylums or hospitals. The focus of this argument is on prisons, although I am not arguing that these factors are unique to prison.
6   For a sense of how 'victimizing discourse' is replicated in media, see reports in *The Independent* by Guinness (2011); Peachey (2012); Vallely (2012a, 2012b); and *The Guardian* by Roberts (2013); Roberts (2008); as well as an evaluation report by Thorn (2013).
7   Feminist criminologists have engaged with the gender specific issues in criminal justice policy and practice that could increase women's opportunity for desistance. Desistance is the criminological term for not re-offending. See Cheliotis (2012b) and McNeil et al. (2010).
8   Their findings also indicate that 'work was not a key factor. This may be partly explained by a shift in the market economy and the fact that women are frequently marginalized in unstable service sector jobs. However, this may also be to do with how women see themselves' (Gelsthorpe et al. 2007: 22).
9   These points are often noted in relation to activism concerning babies in prison and the babies' biological and psychological development being hindered by incarceration (Vallely 2012a).
10 Women's emergence out of what Nina Billone refers to as the 'civil death' (2009) of incarceration is singular in its lack of ritual and its paradoxical refusal of continuity of meaning. Billone outlines the function of incarceration as effectively characterizing women as 'dead' in the civic realm, since they are unable to function as citizens (i.e. have the right to vote). In other words, for Billone, the women's existence is circumscribed by civic sphere in which they have no agency or participation in democratic functioning.
11 Performance studies scholars have developed further explorations on the potential of the live encounter in performance as a participatory, shared moment of telling and listening (Harris 1999; Peschel 2012; Rokem 2000; Stuart Fisher 2011; Wake 2009b, 2013; Walsh 2018a).
12 I discuss this production in an article on performativity and painful pasts (Walsh, 2018a).
13 'Lol' is Marie's nickname for Lorraine.
14 Goffman's notes on the management of spoiled identities relate to stigmatization discussed briefly in Chapters Two and Six. The stigma arises from individuals living with (real or perceived) undesirable or adverse characteristics that make them 'less worthy' than so-called 'normal' members of society. As mentioned previously, I do not agree with this distinction between 'normal' and 'spoiled' identities, but see the value in Goffman's explanation of how stigma can serve to performatively repeat the undesirable qualities, thereby externalizing the internalized stigma.

Conclusion

Paradoxes of Prison Cultures

Between 2012 and 2016, The Donmar Warehouse staged a trilogy of Shakespeare's tragedies with an all-female cast, set in prison, with the protagonist in all three shows played by Dame Harriet Walter. Directed by Phyllida Lloyd, the version of *Julius Caesar* framed the cast as a company of prisoners staging plays. Their performances of loyalties, betrayals, love and despair are all understood as playing out within the wider imaginary of the prison. The spitting paranoia of Walter's portrayal of Brutus exemplifies the theorization of containment and desire that I put forward in *Prison Cultures*. If, in stage or screen representations of prisons, female characters break apart the usual images as survivors or victims in particular, then their capacity to challenge the institution is foregrounded. Feminist readings of this work, in particular, would highlight the choice to have cross-gender casting – so that while this indeed augments the usual understandings of women in prison to also include Brutus as a troubled 'hero', the theatrical frame relies on a woman cast in Shakespeare's male role. Thus, although the performance successfully draws attention to key forces in the lives of women prisoners, the knowledge that the women are 'playing men' could undermine whatever radical possibilities are opened up by Lloyd's dramatic conceit. For this reason, most of the works I have focused on here are contemporary new writing rather than innovations in staging classical drama.

Problems and Paradoxes in Prison and Performance

Baz Kershaw (1999) highlights the intention of radical performance as to expose the interrelationship between structural hierarchies in theatrical representation. In this book, that means as well as analysing cultural, social and political reproduction of who and what women in prison *are*, I have considered what they *mean*. When Joe Kelleher (2009: 59) points out the limitations of political theatre, he demonstrates that when the radical is invoked in relation to performance that it is necessary to unpack its limitations and consider what lies beyond the scope of performance. Certainly, heeding Kershaw's reticence, I do not propose that a performance *of* or *about* prison could dismantle the power structures and hegemonic positions such as the state vs women in prison. Rather, *Prison Cultures* rehearses the shift in perspective from a range of received carceral meanings to ones that are produced by artists and circulated to the public.

Having spent several years making performance in prisons, and having reflected on institutions and performance in relation to one another, it has become clear that there is no single everyday performance that adequately resists the institution; no performance practice that sufficiently challenges the structures of power; and no theatre that authentically manifests its operations outside of the reach of the prison industrial complex. Despite seemingly radical intentions of various performance interventions, and abolitionist activism, prisons still incarcerate too many people in the United Kingdom and the United States, and the prison service still continues to fail women incarcerated in male-focused regimes. In light of this, critical approaches from the intersections of performance studies and feminist criminology can hardly claim to dismantle these concerns. That state apparatus performs a function of protecting the public is inevitably not fundamentally challenged by critique from the humanities. Arguably, there is no single discipline that could present findings that challenge civic institutions. The conclusions I arrive at via performance studies are unfortunately not going to be read as convincing to policy-makers, for whom criminal women are still a 'problem'. In this rehearsal of the limitations of my research field, I am, of course, aping the epistemological hierarchies of what constitutes relevant knowledge claims. Nonetheless, the very paradox of performance (and other arts) *in* and *of* criminal justice settings demands critical attention. I have demonstrated that performance provides both methodological and epistemological possibilities for disentangling the relations between power/institution/bodies and witnesses. Throughout the book, I work against a heroics epistemology, which can be beset by what Sedgwick calls the presumption of liberatory 'righteousness' (2003: 10). Instead, I seek new critical analytic models that attend to multiple perspectives on the issues in criminal justice and how they relate to representations. For instance, I consider the production of women's resistant subjectivities in relation to gender, space and power. Second, I problematize the authenticity claims of 'the cage' and consider that performance in and of prison replicates and perpetuates its operations – even when its manifestation is ostensibly about freedom and creativity. Performance, then, is a particularly relevant mode of enquiry, accustomed as it is (in theory and practice) to navigating contradictions and conflict.

There are limitations related to the dismantling of bricks, mortar and fences of the prisons that incarcerate women. Despite the tendency of criticism to be 'pessimistic' (Sedgwick 2003: 12), this book nevertheless points towards utopian possibilities. An abolitionist approach is required, and must be articulated in a range of disciplinary perspectives, and not relegated to a singular practice of revolt (Davis and Dent 2001; Davis 2012; Kandaswamy 2016; Rustbelt Abolition Radio 2017; Sudbury 2005a, 2005b). Critical, abolitionist, feminist scholarship about prison cultures contributes towards understanding how institutions are replicated in the popular imagination. By examining performance through the imagery, spaces and experiences of prisons, I propose that performance can allow for the consideration of the problems of institutions, power and bodies in relation to aesthetics and ethics. Furthermore, performance practices *in* and *of* prisons can promote creative possibilities for women whose adoption of coping tactics would serve them well as they transition from inside to outside the institutional frame.

The broad concern throughout the book is 'what does performance offer to the subject of women in prison to challenge stereotypes of "the cage"?'. In particular, I have investigated

Figure 8: Ensemble in *Julius Caesar* (Donmar Warehouse Shakespeare Trilogy). Photographer: Helen Maybanks. Reproduced with permission.

how the dyads public/private, inside/outside become troubled by performance. By focusing on performance, I concentrated on the centrality of the body in experiences of incarceration, and in particular, the relationship with gender as both constitutive of, and constituting, victimization. In order to push through such positionality, *Prison Cultures* invests in exploring what tactics women in prison perform that helps them cope with the strategic punishment of the institution. Beyond merely coping, I explore how performance moves towards articulating women's survival of incarceration. The core of the book considers what precise mechanisms performance offers that challenge/subvert/augment/transform the imaginary of prison. Ultimately, these questions braided together to argue that there are significant challenges related to aesthetics and ethics concerning representation in performance and popular culture.

In methodological terms, what is significant is the interplay of examples and analysis with the theoretical modelling of the cycle of tragic containment. This was chosen in order to augment the literature in the applied theatre realm that often relies on reportage of particular practice models or aesthetics that often subsume the ideological positioning of the work (Prentki and Preston 2009: 14). While compelling in fervour, such research does not always result in critically reflexive findings. In such work, the findings tend to be normative, rather than problematized. Therefore, instead of defending a chosen aesthetic model (which is the approach of much of the literature in performance), my approach has developed a dialogue between praxis and the chosen theories. This resulted in a necessarily complex approach to engaging with the field and performance manifestations that provoke critical questions about institutions and representation.

This intention to provoke and problematize the understanding of the relationship between performance tactics and the institution also led me to engage with a wide, interdisciplinary set of literature. My theoretical framework seeks to position performance in relation to both sociological and criminological analyses of space as well as the relationship between women, victimization and crime. In particular, the theories I draw on help to position the research in an explicitly feminist project in which the women as objects of study are re-positioned through methodological engagement as participants in the investigation. My argument highlights the implications, rewards and maintenance of the patriarchal status quo if and when theatrical representations uphold the model of victim–survivor. For this reason, I proposed the addition of the third vector in the triad – hero. The results offer an explication of a feminist structure of feeling in relation to representations in prison culture and contemporary performance about prison.

The introduction outlined the initial context of the study as everyday performances of women in prison. The argument progressed from the evidence that punishment limits the spectrum of performance possibilities. I demonstrated the paradox that women's crimes mean they are victimizers but often portrayed as victims. This central concern is braided throughout the argument, through a multivalent adoption of theoretical positions. Although it draws on feminist criminology, sociology and criticism of dramatic literature, the informing discourse is from performance studies. Victimhood, particularly, is exposed as a category that denies agency and political force. Thus, although I have attended to the ways women in prison are unjustly victimized, I propose that it is necessary to develop more productive categories that account for confidence, decision-making and the ability to articulate choices. This degree of performative participation is central to the concept of agency that some might argue is what is denied to women when they commit crimes and are punished. It is necessary to consider the entire journey of incarceration as one that includes release, and thus there is the need to consider how ex-prisoners are expected to relate to their social and civic roles post-release.

The journey of *Prison Cultures* is argued as a series of perspectives that relate to the spatial, behavioural and spectral presence of prison's power in the lives of women currently incarcerated and/or post-release. The argument engaged with these perspectives in order to present the wide range of performance paradigms deployed by women. I have positioned these as tactics that correspond with the need for developing or adopting institutional norms and values or alternatively, to resist them. Performing (both conscious, aesthetic performance and everyday performance or habitus) becomes necessary to cope with the prison itself. The issue of 'survival' relates to women's self-esteem, capacity to engage in imagining and planning for a future outside of prison and to remain connected to community support structures. The argument here does not explicitly suggest that women's performances stand in for survival, but that they point towards the meaningfulness of tactics in relation to coping with the strategic omniscience of the law in their lives.

Throughout, I have attended to the two key vectors of desire and resistance in relation to performance. Rather than being understood only in terms of a psychoanalytic approach as explored by Muñoz (1999), for example, I position desire and resistance and multiple, embodied, performed as tactics for different ends. By suggesting this, I understand them as significant potentialities for transforming the otherwise stultifying conditions of prison. Both desire and resistance are at play in Franzmann's *Pests* (2014) when the sisters imagine, role-play and use narcotics to imagine their way out of the ongoing prison of criminalization. In the popular culture TV series that are discussed, characters imagine their way across prison boundaries, deploying resistance and desire in socially productive ways – for example when Sophia Bursett makes plans to keep in touch with her family in *OITNB*. Depictions of the more negative side of resistance and desire can be replete with drama, and of course, have confluence with the cycle of tragic containment. When Franky gets sent back to prison for violating parole conditions in *Wentworth*; or when *Affinity*'s Margaret is lulled into offending behaviour by allowing her sexual desire for Selina to challenge her moral fortitude, they are characters that face the cathartic resolution of what is inevitable for offending women. Tragic containment returns such offending women to prison, or ramps up punishment, or reverts to stripping them of dignity – often visually achieved by rendering her less feminine, as in the proliferation of scenes in which women's heads are shaved to shame them into repentance.

Much of the book circles on the value of the models I put forward in *Prison Cultures*. The spectrum of victim–survivor–hero is evidently useful for modelling how aesthetic representations and performance methodologies conform to or expand upon the limitations inherent to such categories. This is particularly important for applied theatre practices, in which practitioners could consider the extent to which their methods perpetuate victimhood or indeed fetishize trauma narratives.

Dramaturgically, the model of tragic containment allows for the exploration of the wider possibilities of pathways into and out of crime. As a result of the conceptual basis of this research, writers and directors would be able to engage with understanding the extent to which plays with criminal justice themes conflate 'offending' with tragic inevitability. As such, the results are a broadening of the potential narratives to reflect the ongoing difficulties of 'surviving' post-release, and the need to platform the political and social importance of community-based support. Prison would not then be seen as a discrete term or presence in the institutional frame. The cultural representations of prison would thus incorporate the effects and implications of incarceration and the reasons for criminalization in the first instance. In other words, the implication is that prison tropes ought to be deployed more politically, rather than sensationally. This, and the subsequent points are relevant for the field of feminist criminology. The value here is in the capacity of cultural productions to engage the wider public in witnessing and responding to the debates related to criminal justice. What is noteworthy is that I aim not merely to return the tragic object to its 'rightful place', as the Aristotelian logic of tragedy would have it, but to open up debates about the insistence of the women as 'tragic', and the institution as the 'rightful place'. I am aware, however, that a single monograph, like a single performance, or one popular culture representation, cannot hope to provide definitive answers, particularly in relation to the multiple fields and disciplines informing this study. Rather, interdisciplinary scholarship in arts in criminal justice is enriched by the positioning of these questions, rather than foreclosed by them.

The argument throughout explores the performative framing of the separation of 'criminal' bodies from civil society. I explore how incarceration, removal, programmes of rehabilitation and re-entry cycles perpetuate distinctions between 'us' and 'them', both in relation to psycho-social barriers, but more explicitly, in the cultural representations of prison and prisoners. I consider the staging of this distinction in relation to spatial, aesthetic and affectual relationships. By grounding the study in feminist criminology, I am offering an argument about the functions of prison that systemically contribute to a moral/ethical and aesthetic separation of certain types of bodies. I have concentrated on the intersecting marginalities of poverty, class, and race as well as the criminalization of certain women. The argument is predicated on the understanding that prison's successful 'performance' demands a particular repetition of the restoration of norms. I propose that these normative presumptions relate to the assumption of a linear progression of the cycles of incarceration – modelled by the cycle of tragic containment. The rigid cycle is disrupted by agential performance. These can be either performances of resistance that are against the institution, or performances against the fixed inevitable pathways that presuppose vulnerable women would return to crime. Both views challenge assumptions about women's bodies, agency and the relationship with social and civic institutions.

Prison as Pedagogy

I realized, soon after I stepped into the stinking corridors of Modderbee prison in Johannesburg's East Rand in 2002, that prison would teach me something. I couldn't have anticipated that I would spend quite so much time learning its intricate choreography of paranoia and power dynamics. At the end of this project, I am humbled by its pedagogic function. Most particularly, I am grateful for the reflexive space. At the tail end of this investigation, one thing is clear: prison still smells like regret.

(Research Diary, December 2013)

In almost every prison story (and scholarly account of arts practice), there is always a sense of the 'could have' or the 'should have'. For convicted women, these promissory acknowledgements of possibility are both frustrating and rewarding. They remind of the possibility of a different 'there and then' that relates mimetically to the 'here and now'. For those strangers entering prisons as outsider researchers or arts practitioners, the regrets can relate to seemingly insignificant moments of attention. Throughout *Prison Cultures*, I have deliberately avoided the simplistic juxtaposition of institution and patriarchy, even though there are obvious comparisons. For prisoners across the spectrum of genders, the institutional frame operates to foreground their gender in limiting, punitive reinforcement of heteronormative values.

I have shown that the institution is predicated on, and perpetuates, sedimented performances from women whose sentences are constructed around rehearsal and repetition of what appears to be 'good'. The frisson in the fabric of institutions in the event of resistance, non-compliance or improvisation is palpable. Women find they progress through the system by playing the role of docile prisoner; and yet, contrary to the somewhat playful mockery of 'good behaviour' evident in characters such as Liz Birdsworth in *Wentworth*, there are real consequences for vulnerable women whose 'successful' performances do not carve possibilities for re-integration within communities. This is because institutional norms do not map neatly onto everyday life, although they continue to assert their dominance.

While effective improvisation in prison plays to the watchful audience of officers, probation teams and security cameras, there is less chance of women's attempts to survive post-release being spectated by empathic viewers. What occurs is a self-referential, almost mythic mimetic reflection of prison/prisoner. Each reflects and refracts the injury, shame and pity of the other. Each, in its reflections, becomes weaker, more vulnerable to criticism. The very idea of prison flickers. Its ideological dominance and certainty is as unmistakeable as patriarchy. This mythic, mimetic chimera of prison is positioned as a construct, and, in order for its mechanisms to be questioned, research and practice must attend to the position of the body. Performance reasserts embodied affect into the reckoning of power, institution and society. There ought to be no excuse for replicating lazy tropes in contemporary performance, or in popular media. Prison, the performance of prisoners and the representations of carceral subjectivities in contemporary performance ought to be inflected with the complexities, contradictions and quandaries that are shown to be playing out daily behind walls, perimeter fences and electric gates.

Bibliography

Abraham, N. and Busby, S. (2014), *Celebrating Success*, London: Clean Break and Central School of Speech and Drama.

Adebayo, M. (2015), 'Revolutionary beauty out of homophobic hate: A reflection on I Stand Corrected', in G. White (ed.), *Applied Theatre: Aesthetics*, London: Bloomsbury Methuen, pp. 123–55.

Adkins, L. (2004), 'Introduction: Feminism, Bourdieu and after', in L. Adkins and B. Skeggs (eds), *Feminism after Bourdieu*, Oxford: Blackwell, pp. 3–18.

Agamben, G. (1998), *Homo Sacer: Sovereign Power and Bare Life* (trans. D. Heller-Roazen), Stanford, CA: Stanford University Press.

——— (2005), *State of Exception* (trans. Kevin Attell), Chicago, IL: University of Chicago Press.

Ahmed, S. (2004), 'Affective economies', *Social Text*, 22:2, pp. 117–39.

——— (2014), *The Cultural Politics of Emotion*, 2nd ed., Edinburgh: Edinburgh University Press.

Ahmed, S. and Stacey, J. (eds) (2001), *Thinking Through the Skin*, London: Routledge.

Ahrens, L. (ed.) (2008), *The Real Cost of Prisons Comix*, Oakland, CA: PM Press.

Alcoff, L. (1991), 'The problem of speaking for others', *Cultural Critique*, 20, pp. 5–32.

Alexander, B. K. (2005), 'Performance ethnography: The re-enacting and inciting of culture', in N. K. Denzin and Y. S. Lincoln (eds), *Handbook of Qualitative Inquiry*, Thousand Oaks, CA: Sage, pp. 411–41.

Alexander, J. C. (2012a), *Trauma: A Social Theory*, Cambridge, MA: Polity Press.

Alexander, M. (2012b), *The New Jim Crow: Mass Incarceration in the Age of Colorblindness*, rev. ed., New York, NY: The New Press.

Alli, S. (2016), *Brett Story: The Prison in 12 Landscapes*, Guernica, https://www.guernicamag.com/brett-story-12-landscapes/. Accessed 23 February 2018.

Allison, E. (2016), 'Women are dying in jails they should not have been sent to', *The Guardian*, https://www.theguardian.com/society/2016/aug/09/women-dying-in-jails-they-should-not-be-sent-to. Accessed 23 February 2018.

Allspach, A. (2010), 'Landscapes of (neo-)liberal control: The transcarceral spaces of federally sentenced women in Canada', *Gender, Place and Culture: A Journal of Feminist Geography*, 17:6, pp. 705–23.

Amkpa, A. (2003), *Theatre and Postcolonial Desires*, London: Routledge.

—— (2008), 'Postcolonial theatre and the ethics of emancipatory becoming', in *Teatro do Mundo: Teatro e Justiça – Afinidades Electivas*, Porto: Centro de Estudos Teatrale di Universidade de Porto, pp. 27–75.

Amoore, L. (ed.) (2005), 'Introduction: Global resistance/Global politics', in L. Amoore, *The Global Resistance Reader*, London: Routledge, pp. 1–12.

Anderson, P. (2004), '"To lie down to death for days": The Turkish hunger strike, 2000–2003', *Cultural Studies*, 18:6, pp. 816–46.

—— (2009), 'There will be no Bobby sands in Guantanamo Bay', *PMLA*, 124:5, pp. 1729–36.

—— (2010), *So Much Wasted: Hunger, Performance, and the Morbidity of Resistance*, Durham, NC: Duke University Press.

Anderson, P. and Menon, J. (eds) (2009), *Violence Performed: Local Roots and Global Routes of Conflict*, Basingstoke: Palgrave Macmillan.

Anonymous Prison Officer (2012), Post-show interview, HMP Askham Grange, interviewed by A. Walsh, 30 November.

Aran, I. (2017), '*Orange Is the New Black*'s new season is scattered, tone-deaf, and often agonizing to watch', http://splinternews.com/orange-is-the-new-blacks-new-season-is-scattered-tone-1796037851. Accessed 23 February 2018.

Archer, N. (2014), 'Security blankets: Uniforms, hoods, and the textures of terror', *Women & Performance: A Journal of Feminist Theory*, 24:2–3, pp. 186–202.

Arendt, H. (1969), *On Violence*, San Diego, CA: Harcourt Brace.

Arendt, J. (2011), '[In]Subordination: Inmate photography and narrative elicitation in a youth incarceration facility', *Cultural Studies <=> Critical Methodologies*, 11, pp. 265–73.

Arts Alliance (2011), *Breaking the Cycle – Arts Alliance Response to the Green Paper*, London: Arts Alliance.

Artt, A. and Schwan, A. (2016), 'Screening women's imprisonment: Agency and exploitation in *Orange Is the New Black*', *Television and New Media*, 17:6, pp. 1–6.

Ashe, F. (2007), *The New Politics of Masculinity: Men, Power, and Resistance*, London: Routledge.

Aston, E. (1995), *An Introduction to Feminism and Theatre*, Routledge: London.

—— (2003), *Feminist Views on the English Stage: Women Playwrights, 1990–2000*, Cambridge: Cambridge University Press.

—— (2006), '"Bad girls" and "Sick boys": New women playwrights and the future of feminism', in G. Harris and E. Aston (eds), *Feminist Futures? Theatre, Performance, Theory*, Basingstoke: Palgrave, pp. 71–87.

Athanasiou, A. (2016), 'Nonsovereign agonism (or, beyond affirmation versus vulnerability)', in J. Butler, Z. Gambetti and L. Sabsay (eds), *Vulnerability in Resistance*, Durham, NC: Duke University Press, pp. 256–77.

Atwood, M (2017), *Hag-Seed: Shakespeare's Tempest Retold*, London: Penguin/Random House.

Babetto, C. and Scandurra, A. (eds) (2012), *Art and Culture in Prison Project*, Fiesole: Fondazione Giovanni Michelucci.

Bago, I., Linn, O. M. and Pekić, M. (2016), 'Art at the edge of the law', *Extravagant Bodies: Crime and Punishment*, Zagreb: Kontejner, pp. 6–17.

Baim, C., Brookes, S. and Mountford, A. (eds) (2002), *The Geese Theatre Handbook: Drama with Offenders and People at Risk*, Winchester: Waterside Press.

Balfour, M. (2001), *Theatre and War: Performance in Extremis, 1933–1945,* New York, NY: Berghahn Books.

—— (2003), *The Use of Drama in the Rehabilitation of Violent Male Offenders*, Lewiston: Edwin Mellon Press.

—— (ed.) (2004), *Theatre in Prison: Theory and Practice*, Bristol: Intellect Books.

—— (2007), 'Performing war: "Military Theatre" and the possibilities of resistance', *Performance Paradigm*, 3, n.pag.

—— (2009), 'The politics of intention: Looking for a theatre of little changes', *Research in Drama Education: The Journal of Applied Theatre and Performance*, 14:3, pp. 347–59.

Ball, K. (2000a), 'Introduction: Trauma and its institutional destinies', *Cultural Critique*, 46, pp. 1–44.

—— (2000b), 'Disciplining traumatic history: Goldhagen's impropriety', *Cultural Critique*, 46, pp. 124–52.

—— (2003), 'Ex/propriating survivor experience. Or Auschwitz 'after' Lyotard', in A. Douglass and T. A. Vogler (eds), *Witness and Memory: The Discourse of Trauma*, London: Routledge, pp. 249–74.

—— (ed.) (2007), *Traumatizing Theory: The Cultural Politics of Affect in and Beyond Psychoanalysis*, New York, NY: The Other Press.

Balme, C. (2012), 'Public sphere and contemporary performance', *Critical Stages*, 7, http://www.criticalstages.org/criticalstages7/entry/Public-Sphere-and-Contemporary-Performance?category=2#sthash.lyRqs7Wr.dpbs. Accessed 30 December 2012.

Bamford, A. and Skipper, H. (2007), *'Every Time You Have this Conversation you Move Forward a Little Bit': An Evaluative Report of Arts in Prison*, London: Anne Peaker Centre for Arts in Criminal Justice.

Barak, K. S. (2016), 'Jenji Kohan's Trojan horse: Subversive uses of whiteness', in A. K. Householder and A. Trier-Bieniek (eds), *Feminist Perspectives on Orange Is the New Black: Thirteen Critical Essays*, Jefferson, NC: McFarland and Co, pp. 55–72.

Barish, J. A. (1985), *The Anti-Theatrical Prejudice*, Berkeley, CA: University of California Press.

Baroody-Hart, C. (1987), 'The subculture of serious artists in a maximum security prison', *Journal of Contemporary Ethnography*, 15, pp. 421–48.

Bartley, S. (2017), 'Hard labour and punitive welfare: The unemployed body at work in participatory performance', *Research in Drama Education: The Journal of Applied Theatre and Performance*, 22:1, pp. 62–75.

Belcher, C. (2016), 'There is no such thing as a post-racial prison: Neoliberal multiculturalism and the white savior complex on *Orange Is the New Black*', *Television and New Media*, 17:6, pp. 491–503.

Belfiore, E. (2002), 'Art as a means of alleviating social exclusion: Does it really work? A critique of instrumental cultural policies and social impact studies in the UK', *International Journal of Cultural Policy*, 8, pp. 91–106.

Bell, D. and Valentine, G. (1995), 'Introduction: Orientations', in D. Bell and G. Valentine (eds), *Mapping Desire: Geographies of Sexualities*, London: Routledge, pp. 1–30.

Bergstrom, A. (2013), '"Untamed she-cats in a jungle behind bars": Lesbian prison pulp fiction and the threat of female sexuality, 1950–1965', *Clio's Scroll*, https://www.ocf.berkeley.edu/~clios/abergstrom/. Accessed 23 February 2018.

Berry, K. (2000), *Dramatic Arts and Cultural Studies: Acting Against the Grain*, New York, NY: Taylor & Francis.

Bhabha, H. (1984), 'Of mimicry and man: The ambivalence of colonial discourse', *October,* 28, pp. 125–33.

—— (1994), *The Location of Culture*, London: Routledge.

Bharucha, R. (2007), 'Envisioning ethics anew: Rustom Bharucha talks with *Performance Paradigm*', *Performance Paradigm,* 3, pp. 1–6.

Billone, N. (2009), 'Performing civil death: The Medea Project and Theater for Incarcerated Women', *Text and Performance Quarterly,* 29:3, pp. 260–75.

Bliss, E., Chen, K. B., Dickison, S., Johnson, M. D. and Rodriguez, R. (2009), *Prison Culture*, San Francisco, CA: City Lights.

Bloom, B. E. (ed.) (2003), *Gendered Justice: Addressing Female Offenders*, Durham, NC: Carolina Academic Press.

Bosworth, M. (1999), *Engendering Resistance: Agency and Power in Women's Prisons*, Aldershot: Ashgate.

—— (2000), 'Confining femininity: A history of gender, power and imprisonment', *Theoretical Criminology*, 4:3, pp. 265–84.

—— (2008), 'Border control and the limits of the sovereign state', *Social and Legal Studies*, 17:2, pp. 199–215.

—— (2012), 'Subjectivity and identity in detention: Punishment and society in a global age', *Theoretical Criminology*, 16:2, pp. 123–40.

Bosworth, M. and Carrabine, E. (2001), 'Reassessing resistance: Race, gender and sexuality in prison', *Punishment and Society*, 3:4, pp. 501–15.

Bosworth, M. and Flavin, J. (eds) (2007), *Race, Gender and Punishment: From Colonialism to the War on Terror*, New Brunswick, NJ: Rutgers University Press.

Bottoms, S. (2010), 'Silent partners: Actor and audience in Geese Theatre's *Journey Woman*', *Research in Drama Education: The Journal of Applied Theatre and Performance*, 15:4, pp. 477–96.

—— (2014), 'Timeless cruelty: Performing the Stanford Prison Experiment', *Performance Research*, 19:3, pp. 162–75.

Bouclin, S. (2009), 'Women in prison movies as feminist jurisprudence', *Canadian Journal of Women and the Law*, 21:1, pp. 19–34.

Bourdieu, P. (1984), *Distinction: A Social Critique of the Judgment of Taste* (trans. R. Nice), Cambridge, MA: Harvard University Press.

—— (1987), 'The force of law: Toward a sociology of the juridical field' (trans. R. Terdiman), *The Hastings Law Journal*, 38:5, pp. 805–53.

—— (1990), *The Logic of Practice* (trans. R. Nice), New York, NY: Columbia University Press.

—— (1998), *Acts of Resistance: Against the New Myths of the Time* (trans. R. Nice), Cambridge, MA: Polity Press.

Bourdillon, R. (2017), 'Love is not about gender: It's about the needs we have inside', Divamag.co.uk, http://www.divamag.co.uk/Diva-Magazine/Culture/Love-is-not-about-gender-its-about-the-needs-we-have-inside/. Accessed 23 February 2018.

Bibliography

Boyle, M. S. and Bogad, L. (2015), 'Irresistible images: Michael Shane Boyle in conversation with Larry Bogad', *Contemporary Theatre Review*, https://www.contemporarytheatrereview.org/2015/irresistible-images/. Accessed 23 February 2018.

Branco, P. (2010), 'On prisons and theatres: Santo Stefano and San Carlo', *Law Text Culture*, 14:1, pp. 277–85.

Brink, J. (2003), 'You don't see us doin' time', *Contemporary Justice Review*, 6:4, pp. 393–96.

Brooks, P. (2017), 'Prison photography', https://prisonphotography.org/pete-brook/. Accessed 23 February 2018.

Brook, P. and Estienne, M. H. (2018), *The Prisoner*, London: Nick Hern Books.

Brooks-Gordon, B. and Bainham, A. (2004), 'Prisoners' families and the regulation of contact', *Journal of Social Welfare and Family Law*, 26:3, pp. 263–80.

Brown, K. (2016), 'Season four of *Orange Is the New Black* has a race problem', https://theestablishment.co/season-four-of-orange-is-the-new-black-has-a-race-problem-159a999dc66c. Accessed 23 February 2018.

Brown, M. (2009), *The Culture of Punishment: Prison, Culture, and Spectacle*, New York, NY: New York University Press.

—— (2012), 'Social documentary in prison: The art of catching the state in the act of punishment', in L. Cheliotis (ed.), *The Arts of Imprisonment: Control, Resistance and Empowerment*, Ashgate: Farnham, pp. 101–18.

—— (2014), 'Visual criminology and carceral studies: Counter-images in the Carceral Age', *Theoretical Criminology*, 18:2, pp. 176–97.

Brown, P. (2017), 'No license plates here: Using art to transcend prison walls', https://www.nytimes.com/2017/04/02/arts/design/california-prison-arts.html. Accessed 23 February 2018.

Brown, S. A. and Silverstone, C. (2007), *Tragedy in Transition*, Blackwell: Oxford.

Brubaker, R. (1993), 'Social theory as habitus', in C. Calhoun, E. Lipuma and M. Postoma (eds), *Bourdieu: Critical Perspectives*, Chicago, IL: University of Chicago Press, pp. 212–34.

Bruce, D., Ikoko, T., Lomas, L. Odimba, C. and Sarma, U. S. (2015), *Joanne: Five Monologues*, London: Nick Hern Books.

Burbach, R. (2001), *Globalisation and Postmodern Politics*, London: Pluto Press.

Burfoot, A. and Lord, S. (eds) (2006), *Killing Women: The Visual Culture of Gender and Violence*, Waterloo: Wilfred Laurier University Press.

Butler, J. (1993a), *Bodies that Matter: On the Discursive Limits of 'Sex'*, New York, NY: Routledge.

—— (1993b), 'Critically queer', *GLQ: Journal of Lesbian and Gay Studies*, 1, pp. 17–32.

—— (1999), 'Performativity's social magic', in R. Shusterman (ed.), *Bourdieu: A Critical Reader*, Oxford: Blackwell, pp. 113–28.

—— (2004), *Precarious Life: The Powers of Mourning and Violence*, London: Verso.

—— (2007), 'Subversive bodily acts', in S. During (ed.), *The Cultural Studies Reader*, 3rd ed., London: Routledge, pp. 371–82.

—— (2009), *Frames of War: When is Life Grievable?*, New York, NY: Verso.

—— (2016), 'Rethinking vulnerability in resistance', in J. Butler, Z. Gambetti and L. Sabsay (eds), *Vulnerability in Resistance*, Durham, NC: Duke University Press, pp. 12–27.

Butler, J. and Athanasiou, A. (2013), *Dispossession: The Performative in the Political*, Cambridge, MA: Polity Press.

Butler, J., Gambetti, Z. and Sabsay, L. (eds) (2016), *Vulnerability in Resistance*, Durham, NC: Duke University Press.

Cabinet Office Social Exclusion Task Force (2009), 'Short study on women offenders', http://www.ccrm.org.uk/images/docs/womenoffenders.pdf. Accessed 23 February 2018.

Calvino, I. (2002), *The Complete Cosmicomics* (trans. M. McLaughlin, T. Parks and W. Weaver), Penguin: London.

—— (2006), *Six Memos for the New Millennium* (trans. P. Creagh), London: Vintage.

Campt, T. (2015), 'Black feminist futures and the practice of fugitivity', talk at Barnard Centre for Research on Women, http://bcrw.barnard.edu/bcrw-blog/black-feminist-futures-and-the-practice-of-fugitivity/. Accessed 23 February 2018.

Carlen, P. (1983), *Women's Imprisonment: A Study of Social Control*, London: Routledge.

—— (ed.) (2002), *Women and Punishment: The Struggle for Justice*, Portland, OR: Willan Publishing.

Carlen, P. and Tchaikovsky, C. (1985), 'Women in prison', in P. Carlen, J. Hicks, J. O'Dwyer, D. Christiana and C. Tchaikovsky (eds), *Criminal Women: Autobiographical Accounts*, Oxford: Basil Blackwell, n.pag.

Carlson, M. (2003), *The Haunted Stage: The Theatre as Memory Machine*, Ann Arbor, MI: University of Michigan Press.

Carlton, B. and Segrave, M. (2011), 'Women's survival post-imprisonment: Connecting imprisonment with pains past and present', *Punishment and Society*, 13:5, pp. 551–70.

—— (eds) (2013), *Women Exiting Prison: Critical Essays on Gender, Post-Release Support and Survival*, London: Routledge.

Carrabine, E. (2010), 'Imagining prison: Culture, history and space', *Prison Service Journal*, 187, pp. 15–22.

—— (2011), 'Images of torture: Culture, politics and power', *Crime, Media, Culture: An International Journal*, 7:1, pp. 5–30.

—— (2012), 'Telling prison stories: The spectacle of punishment and the criminological imagination', in L. Cheliotis (ed.), *The Arts of Imprisonment: Control, Resistance and Empowerment*, Farnham: Ashgate, pp. 47–72.

—— (2014), 'Seeing things: Violence, voyeurism and the camera', *Theoretical Criminology*, 18:2, pp. 134–58.

—— (2015), 'Contemporary criminology and the sociological imagination', in J. Frauley (ed.), *C. Wright Mills and the Criminological Imagination: Prospects for Creative Inquiry*, Farnham: Ashgate, pp. 73–99.

—— (2016), 'Picture this: Criminology, image and narrative', *Crime Media Culture*, 12:2, pp. 253–70.

Carter, A. (2006), *Nights at the Circus*, London: Vintage.

Caruth, C. (1995), 'Traumatic awakenings', in E. K. Sedgwick and A. Parker (eds), *Performativity and Performance*, London: Routledge, pp. 89–109.

—— (1996), *Unclaimed Experience: Trauma, Narrative and History*, Baltimore, MD: Johns Hopkins University Press.

Case, S. E. (1988), 'Towards a butch-femme aesthetic', *Discourse*, 11:1, pp. 55–73.
—— (1993), 'Toward a butch-femme aesthetic', in H. Abelove, M. Barale and D. Halperin (eds), *The Lesbian and Gay Studies Reader*, London and New York: Routledge, pp. 294–306.
—— (2009), *Feminist and Queer Performance: Critical Strategies*, Basingstoke: Palgrave.
Case, S. E. and Abbitt, E. S. (2004), 'Disidentifications, diaspora, and desire: Questions on the future of the feminist critique of performance', *Signs: Journal of Women in Culture and Society*, 29:3, pp. 925–38.
Caster, P. (2004), 'Staging prisons: Performance, activism and social bodies', *TDR: The Drama Review*, 48:3, pp. 107–16.
Caulfield, L. S. (2010), 'The role of the arts in prisons: The Howard League for penal reform', *ECAN Bulletin*, 4, London: The Howard League.
—— (2011), *Interim Report: An Evaluation of the Artist in Residence at HMP Grendon*, Grant Report to the Motesiczky Charitable Trust, London: Motesiczky Trust.
Caulfield, L. S. and Wilson, D. (2010), 'Female offenders' experiences of the arts in criminal justice', *Journal of Social Criminology*, 3, pp. 67–90.
Cavendish, D. (2008), 'Her naked skin: Rapture and pain among the suffragettes', *The Telegraph*, 4 August, http://www.telegraph.co.uk/culture/theatre/drama/3557832/Her-Naked-Skin-rapture-and-pain-among-the-Suffragettes.html. Accessed 23 February 2018.
—— (2012), 'A tender subject, Bloomberg Space, London EC2', review, *The Telegraph*, 20 March, http://www.telegraph.co.uk/culture/theatre/theatre-reviews/9155041/a-tender-subject-Bloomberg-Space-London-EC2-review.html. Accessed 23 February 2018.
Cecchetto, D., Cuthbert, N., Lassonde, J. and Robinson, D. (eds) (2008), *Collision: Interarts Practice and Research*, Newcastle: Cambridge Scholars Publishing.
Cecil, D. K. (2007a), 'Doing time in "Camp Cupcake": Lessons learned from newspaper accounts of Martha Stewart's incarceration', *Journal of Criminal Justice and Popular Culture*, 14:2, pp. 142–60.
—— (2007b), 'Dramatic portrayals of violent women: Female offenders on prime time crime dramas', *Journal of Criminal Justice and Popular Culture*, 14:3, pp. 243–58.
—— (2007c), 'Looking beyond caged heat: Media images of women in prison', *Feminist Criminology*, 2:4, pp. 304–26.
—— (2015), *Prison Life in Popular Culture: From The Big House to Orange Is the New Black*, Boulder, CO: Lynne Rienner Publishers.
—— (2017), 'Prisons in popular culture', *Oxford Research Encyclopedia of Criminology*, http://criminology.oxfordre.com/view/10.1093/acrefore/9780190264079.001.0001/acrefore-9780190264079-e-194. Accessed 23 February 2018.
Chan, W., Chunn, D. E. and Menzies, R. (eds) (2005), *Women, Madness and the Law: A Feminist Reader*, London: The GlassHouse Press.
Chalmers, S. (2009), 'Work of art or monstrous cynicism?: Paedophile creates extraordinary paper sculpture in a bid to win freedom', *Daily Mail*, 11 April, http://www.dailymail.co.uk/news/article-1169119/Work-art-monstrous-cynicism-Convicted-paedophile-creates-extraordinary-paper-sculpture-bid-win-freedom.html. Accessed 23 February 2018.
Chanter, T. and Plonowska, Z. (eds) (2005), *Revolt, Affect, Collectivity: The Unstable Boundaries of Kristeva's Polis*, Albany, NY: State University of New York Press.

Cheliotis, L. K. (2010), 'The ambivalent consequences of visibility: Crime and prisons in the mass media', *Crime Media Culture*, 6:2, pp. 169–84.

—— (ed.) (2012a), *The Arts of Imprisonment: Control, Resistance and Empowerment*, Farnham: Ashgate.

—— (2012b), 'Theatre states: Probing the politics of arts-in-prisons programmes', *Criminal Justice Matters*, 89:1, pp. 32–34.

—— (2014), 'Decorative justice: Deconstructing the relationship between the arts and imprisonment', *International Journal for Crime, Justice and Social Democracy*, 3:1, pp. 16–34.

Cherukuri, S. (2008), *Women in Prison: An Insight into Captivity and Crime*, New Delhi: Foundation Books.

Chesney-Lind, M. (1997), *The Female Offender: Girls, Women, and Crime*, Thousand Oaks, CA: Sage.

—— (1999), 'Media misogyny: Demonizing "violent" girls and women', in J. Ferrell and N. Websdale (eds), *Making Trouble: Cultural Constructions of Crime, Deviance, and Control*, New York, NY: Aldine De Gruyter, pp. 115–40.

Chesney-Lind, M. and Irwin, K. (2008), *Beyond Bad Girls: Gender, Violence and Hype*, Routledge: London.

Chesney-Lind, M. and Pasko, L. (eds) (2004), *Girls, Women and Crime: Selected Readings*, Thousand Oaks, CA: Sage.

Chesney-Lind, M. and Rodriguez, N. (2012), 'Women under lock and key: A view from the inside', in S. Walklate (ed.), *Gender and Crime Volume IV: Gender, Crime and Punishment*, London: Routledge, pp. 221–39.

Chouliaraki, L. (2008), *The Spectatorship of Suffering*, London: Sage.

Churchill, C. (1990), *Plays: 2 Softcops, Top Girls, Fen, Serious Money*, London: Methuen Drama.

Ciasullo, A. (2008), 'Containing "deviant" desire: Lesbianism, heterosexuality, and the women-in-prison narrative', *The Journal of Popular Culture*, 41:2, pp. 195–223.

Clark, M. (2004), 'Somebody's Daughter Theatre: Celebrating difference with women in prison', in M. Balfour (ed.), *Theatre in Prisons: Theory and Practice*, Bristol: Intellect, pp. 101–06.

Cleveland, W. (2003), 'Common sense and common ground: Survival skills for artists working in correctional institutions', in R. M. C. Williams (ed.), *Teaching the Arts Behind Bars*, Boston, MA: Northeastern University Press, pp. 28–39.

Clinks (2013), 'Breaking the Cycle of Women's Offending: Where Next?', *Clinks Women's Conference Report*, http://www.womensbreakout.org.uk/wp-content/uploads/downloads/2013/04/Clinks-Womens-Conference-report.pdf. Accessed 23 February 2018.

Clowers, M. (2001), 'Dykes, gangs, and danger: Debunking popular myths about maximum-security life', *Journal of Criminal Justice and Popular Culture*, 9:1, pp. 22–30.

Cohen, S. (1985), *Visions of Social Control: Crime, Punishment and Classification*, Cambridge, MA: Polity Press.

—— (2001), *States of Denial: Knowing about Atrocities and Suffering*, Cambridge, MA: Polity Press.

—— (2002), *Moral Panics and Folk Devils: The Creation of the Mods and Rockers*, 3rd ed., London: Routledge.

Cole, S. (2009), 'Enchantment, disenchantment, war, literature', *PMLA*, 124:5, pp. 1632–47.

Collins, P. H. (1986), 'Learning from the outsider within: The sociological significance of black feminist thought', *Social Problems*, 33:6, pp. 14–32.

Colvin, S. (2015), 'Why should criminology care about literary fiction? Literature, life narratives and telling untellable stories', *Punishment & Society*, 17:2, pp. 211–29.

Conquergood, D. (1989), 'Poetics, play, process, and power: The performative turn in anthropology', *Text and Performance Quarterly*, 9, pp. 82–88.

—— (1991), 'Rethinking ethnography: Towards a critical cultural politics', *Communication Monographs*, 58, pp. 179–94.

—— (1995), 'Of caravans and carnivals: Performance studies in motion', *TDR: The Drama Review*, 39:4, pp. 137–41.

—— (2002a), 'Performance studies: Interventions and radical research', *TDR: The Drama Review*, 46:2, pp. 145–56.

—— (2002b), 'Lethal Theatre: Performance, punishment, and the death penalty', *Theatre Journal*, 54:3, pp. 339–67.

—— (2007), 'Performing as a moral act: Ethical dimensions of the ethnography of performance', in P. Kuppers and G. Robertson (eds), *The Community Performance Reader*, London: Routledge, pp. 57–70.

Corston, J. (2007), *A Report by Baroness Jean Corston of a Review of Women with Particular Vulnerabilities in the Criminal Justice System*, London: Howard League for Penal Reform.

—— (2011), *Women in the Penal System: Second Report on Women with Particular Vulnerabilities in the Criminal Justice System*, London: Howard League for Penal Reform.

Costa, M. (2010), 'Charged – review', *The Guardian*, 15 November, http://www.guardian.co.uk/stage/2010/nov/15/charged-review. Accessed 23 February 2018.

Counsell, C. (2009), 'Introduction', in C. Counsell and R. Mock (eds), *Performance, Embodiment and Cultural Memory*, Cambridge: Cambridge Scholars Publishing, pp. 1–15.

Covington, S. (2003), 'A woman's journey home: Challenges for female offenders', in J. Travis and M. Waul (eds), *Prisoners Once Removed: The Impact of Incarceration and Reentry on Children, Families, and Communities*, Washington: Urban Institute, pp. 67–103.

Cox, E. (2008), 'The intersubjective witness: Trauma testimony in Towfiq Al-Qady's *Nothing But Nothing: One Refugee's Story*', *Research in Drama Education: The Journal of Applied Theatre and Performance*, 13:2, pp. 193–98.

Crawley, E. (2004), 'Emotion and performance: Prison officers and the presentation of self in prisons', *Punishment & Society*, 6:4, pp. 411–27.

Creed, B. (1999), 'Lesbian bodies: Tribades, tomboys and tarts', in J. Price and M. Shildrick (eds), *Feminist Theory and the Body: A Reader*, New York, NY: Routledge, pp. 111–24.

Crémieux, A., Lemoine, X. and Rocchi, J. P. (eds) (2013), *Understanding Blackness through Performance: Contemporary Arts and the Representation of Identity*, Basingstoke: Palgrave.

Crenshaw, K. (1993), 'Mapping the margins: Intersectionality, identity politics and violence against women of color', *Stanford Law Review*, 43, pp. 241–98.

Crenshaw, K., Richie, A. J., Anspach, R., Gilmer, R. and Harris, J. (2015), *Say Her Name: Resisting Police Brutality Against Black Women*, New York, NY: African American Policy Forum.

Crewe, B. (2015), '"Inside the Belly of the Beast": Understanding and conceptualising the experience of imprisonment', in H. Tubex and A. Eriksson (eds), *The International Journal for Crime, Justice and Social Democracy*, 4:1, pp. 50–65.

Cvetkovich, A. (2003), *An Archive of Feelings: Trauma, Sexuality, and Lesbian Public Cultures*, Durham, NC: Duke University Press.

Dalton, D. (2000), 'The deviant gaze: Imagining the homosexual as criminal through cinematic and legal discourses', in C. Stychin and D. Herman (eds), *Sexuality in the Legal Arena*, London: Athlone Press, pp. 69–83.

Daly, K. (2004), 'Different ways of conceptualizing sex/gender in feminist theory and their implications for criminology', in M. Chesney-Lind and L. Pasko (eds), *The Female Offender: Girls, Women, and Crime*, Thousand Oaks, CA: Sage, pp. 42–60.

Damon, M. (1989), 'Tell them about us', *Cultural Critique*, 14, pp. 231–57.

Davey, K. (2017), 'Open Clasp Performance of Key Change at the Houses of Parliament', National Criminal Justice Arts Alliance, https://www.artsincriminaljustice.org.uk/open-clasp-performance-of-key-change-at-the-houses-of-parliament/. Accessed 29 September 2017.

Davies, P. (2011), *Gender, Crime and Victimisation*, London: Sage.

Davis, A. (2004), 'On teaching women's prison writing: A feminist approach to women, crime, and incarceration', *Women's Studies Quarterly*, 3/4, pp. 261–79.

—— (2012), *The Meaning of Freedom and Other Difficult Dialogues*, San Francisco, CA: City Lights Publishers.

Davis, A. Y. (1981), *Women, Race and Class*, New York, NY: Random House.

—— (2003), *Are Prisons Obsolete?*, New York, NY: Seven Stories Press.

Davis, A. Y. (2008), 'Locked up: Racism in the era of neoliberalism', *The Drum*, 19 March, http://www.abc.net.au/news/2008-03-19/locked-up-racism-in-the-era-of-neoliberalism/1077518. Accessed 11 August 2016.

Davis, A. Y. and Dent, G. (2001), 'Prison as a border: A conversation on gender, globalization, and punishment', *Signs*, 26:4, pp. 1235–41.

Davis, T. (2003), 'Theatricality and civil society', in T. C. Davis and T. Postlewait (eds), *Theatricality*, Cambridge: Cambridge University Press, pp. 127–55.

Davy, K. (1993), 'From lady dick to ladylike: The work of Holly Hughes', in L. Hart and P. Phelan (eds), *Acting Out: Feminist Performance*, Ann Arbor, MI: University of Michigan Press, pp. 55–84.

De Certeau, M. (1984), *The Practice of Everyday Life* (trans. S. Randall), Berkeley, CA: University of California Press.

De Lauretis, T. (1984), *Alice Doesn't: Feminism, Semiotics, Cinema*, Bloomington, IN: Indiana University Press.

—— (1987), *Technologies of Gender: Essays on Theory, Film and Fiction*, Bloomington, IN: Indiana University Press.

—— (1989a), 'Sexual indifference and lesbian representation', *Theatre Journal*, 40:2, pp. 155–77.

—— (1989b), 'The violence of rhetoric: Consideration on representation and gender', in N. Armstrong and L. Tennenhouse (eds), *The Violence of Representation: Literature and the History of Violence*, London: Routledge, pp. 239–58.

—— (1994), *The Practice of Love: Lesbian Sexuality and Perverse Desire*, Bloomington, IN: Indiana University Press.

—— (2007), *Figures of Resistance: Essays in Feminist Theory* (ed. P. White), Urbana and Chicago, IL: University of Illinois Press.

Dehart, D. and Lynch, S. M. (2013), 'Gendered pathways to crime: The relationship between victimization and offending', in C. M. Renzetti et al. (eds), *Routledge International Handbook of Crime and Gender Studies*, London: Routledge, pp. 120–38.

Denzin, N. K. and Giardina, M. D. (2007), *Contesting Empire/Globalizing Dissent: Cultural Studies after 9/11*, Boulder, CO: Paradigm.

Derrida, J. (1993), *Specters of Marx* (trans. P. Kamuf), New York, NY: Routledge.

—— (1998), *Of Grammatology* (trans. G. C. Spivak), Baltimore, MD: Johns Hopkins University Press.

Diamond, E. (1989), 'Mimesis, mimicry, and the "true-real"', *Modern Drama*, 32:1, pp. 58–72.

—— (1991), 'The violence of "we": Politicizing identification', in J. G. Reinelt and J. R. Roach (eds), *Critical Theory and Performance*, Ann Arbor, MI: University of Michigan Press, pp. 390–98.

—— (1995), 'The shudder of catharsis in twentieth century performance', in E. K. Sedgwick and A. Parker (eds), *Performativity and Performance*, London: Routledge, pp. 152–72.

—— (ed.) (1996), *Performance and Cultural Politics*, London: Routledge.

—— (1997), *Unmaking Mimesis: Essays on Feminism and Theater*, London: Routledge.

—— (2003), 'Modern drama/Modernity's drama', in R. Knowles, J. Tompkins and W. B. Worthen (eds), *Modern Drama: Defining the Field*, Toronto: University of Toronto Press, pp. 3–14.

Digard, L. and Liebling, A. (2012), 'Harmony behind bars: Evaluating the therapeutic potential of a prison-based music programme', in L. Cheliotis (ed.), *The Arts of Imprisonment: Control, Resistance and Empowerment*, Farnham: Ashgate, pp. 277–302.

Dillon, S. (2013), '"It's here, it's that time": Race, queer futurity, and the temporality of violence in Born in Flames', *Women and Performance: A Journal of Feminist Theory*, 23:1, pp. 38–51.

Dirsuweit, T. (1999), 'Carceral spaces in South Africa: A case study of institutional power, sexuality and transgression in a women's prison', *Geoforum*, 30, pp. 71–83.

Dissel, A. (1996), 'South Africa's prison conditions: The inmates talk', *Imbizo*, 2, pp. 4–10.

Dixon, A. and Jones, E. (2013), *Learning for Women in Prison*, Cardiff: National Institute of Adult Continuing Education.

Doane, M. A. (1987), *The Desire to Desire: The Women's Films of the 1940s*, Bloomington, IN: Indiana University Press.

Dodds, S. (2011), *Dancing on the Canon: Embodiments of Value in Popular Dance*, Basingstoke: Palgrave MacMillan.

Dolan, J. (1989), *The Feminist Spectator as Critic*, Ann Arbor, MI: University of Michigan Press.

—— (1990), '"Lesbian" subjectivity in realism: Dragging at the margins of structure and ideology', in S. E. Case (ed.), *Performing Feminisms: Feminist Critical Theory and Theatre*, London: Johns Hopkins University Press, pp. 40–53.

—— (1993a), *Presence and Desire: Essays on Gender, Sexuality and Performance*, Ann Arbor, MI: University of Michigan Press.

—— (1993b), 'Desire cloaked in a trenchcoat', in L. Hart and P. Phelan (eds), *Acting Out: Feminist Performance*, Ann Arbor, MI: University of Michigan Press, pp. 105–18.

—— (2005), *Utopia in Performance: Finding Hope at the Theatre*, Ann Arbor, MI: University of Michigan Press.

—— (2007), 'Practicing cultural disruption: Gay and lesbian representation and sexuality', in J. Reinelt and J. Roach (eds), *Critical Theory and Performance*, 2nd ed., Ann Arbor, MI: University of Michigan Press, pp. 334–54.

—— (2010), 'Review *This Wide Night*', *The Feminist Spectator*, 30 May, http://feministspectator.princeton.edu/2010/05/30/this-wide-night/. Accessed 22 October 2016.

—— (2011), 'On "Publics": A feminist constellation of key words', *Performance Research*, 16:2, pp. 182–85.

—— (2013), *Feminist Spectator in Action: Feminist Criticism for the Stage and Screen*, London: Macmillan.

Donaldson, S. (2001), 'A million jockers, punks, and queens', in D. Sabo, T. A. Kupers and W. London (eds), *Prison Masculinities*, Philadelphia, PA: Temple University Press, pp. 118–27.

Douglas, M. (1966), *Purity and Danger*, London: Routledge.

Douglass, A. and Vogler, T. A. (eds) (2003), *Witness and Memory: The Discourse of Trauma*, London: Routledge.

Drake, D. (2012), *Prisons, Punishment and the Pursuit of Security*, Basingstoke: Palgrave.

Drake, D. H., Darke, S. and Earle, R. (2015), 'Sociology of prison life: Recent perspectives from the United Kingdom', in J. Wright (ed.), *International Encyclopaedia of Social and Behavioural Sciences,* 2nd ed., Oxford: Elsevier, pp. 924–29.

Drinkwater, N. (2017), *The State of the Sector: Key Trends for Voluntary Sector Organisations Working with Offenders and their Families*, London: Clinks.

Duggan, L. (2000), *Sapphic Slashers: Sex, Violence, and American Modernity*, Durham, NC: Duke University Press.

Duggan, L. and Muñoz, J. (2009), 'Hope and hopelessness: A dialogue', *Women and Performance: A Journal of Feminist Theory*, 19:2, pp. 275–83.

Duggan, P. (2012), *Trauma-Tragedy: Symptoms of Contemporary Performance,* Manchester: Manchester University Press.

Duggan, P. and Wallis, M. (2011), 'Trauma and performance: Maps, narratives and folds', *Performance Research: A Journal of the Performing Arts*, 16:1, pp. 4–17.

Duncan, M. (1996), *Romantic Outlaws, Beloved Prisons: The Unconscious Meanings of Crime and Punishment*, New York, NY: New York University Press.

Duncan, N. (ed.) (1996), *BodySpace: Destabilizing Geographies of Gender and Sexuality*, London: Routledge.

During, S. (ed.) (2007), *The Cultural Studies Reader,* 3rd ed., London: Routledge.

Eagleton, T. (2003), *Sweet Violence: The Idea of the Tragic*, Oxford: Blackwell.

Earle, R. (2013), 'What do ethnographers do in prison?', *Criminal Justice Matters*, 91:1, pp. 18–19.

—— (2014), 'Inside white – Racism, social relations and ethnicity in an English prison', in C. Phillips and C. Webster (eds), *New Directions in Race, Ethnicity and Crime*, Oxfordshire: Routledge, pp. 160–77.

—— (2014), 'Insider and out: Making sense of a prison experience and a research experience', *Qualitative Inquiry*, 20:4, pp. 429–38.

Economist, The (2012), 'Reaching for the stars: Another way to reduce reoffending', *The Economist,* 8 December, http://www.economist.com/news/britain/21567975-another-way-reduce-reoffending-reaching-stars/print. Accessed 28 December 2012.

—— (2017), 'Too many prisons make bad people worse: There is a better way', *The Economist*, https://www.economist.com/news/international/21722654-world-can-learn-how-norway-treats-its-offenders-too-many-prisons-make-bad-people. Accessed 23 February 2018.

Ellis, J. and Gregory, T. (2011), *Demonstrating the Value of Arts in Criminal Justice*, Report for Arts Alliance, London: Arts Alliance.

Emck, K. (2017), *Rehabilitating Prisoners with Needlework*, https://www.youtube.com/watch?v=jlpLtjEbBJQ&app=desktop. Accessed 23 February 2018.

Enck, S. M. and Morrissey, M. E. (2015), 'If "Orange Is the New Black", I must be color blind: Comic framings of post-racism in the prison-industrial-complex', *Critical Studies in Media Communication*, 32:5, pp. 303–17.

Erez, E., Adelman, M. and Gregory, C. (2009), 'Intersections of immigration and domestic violence: Voices of battered immigrant women', *Feminist Criminology*, 4:1, pp. 32–56.

Escape Artists (2006), *Barred Voices: Perspectives on Theatre in Prison in the UK*, London: Escape Artists.

Evans, B. and Giroux, H. (2015), *Disposable Futures: The Seduction of Violence in the Age of Spectacle*, San Francisco, CA: City Lights Books.

Fahy, T. and King, K. (eds) (2003), *Captive Audiences: Prison and Captivity in Contemporary Theatre*, New York, NY: Routledge.

Faith, K. (2011), *Unruly Women: The Politics of Confinement and Resistance*, 2nd ed., New York, NY: Seven Stories Press.

Fanon, F. (2008), *Black Skin, White Masks* (trans. Richard Philcox), New York: Grove Press.

Farrell, K. (2000), 'The berserk style in American culture', *Cultural Critique*, 46, pp. 179–209.

Fassin, D. (2017), *Prison Worlds: An Ethnography of the Carceral Condition* (trans. R. Gomme), Cambridge, MA: Polity Press.

Fassin, D. and Rechtman, R. (2007), *The Empire of Trauma: An Inquiry into the Condition of Victimhood* (trans. R. Gomme), Princeton, NJ: Princeton University Press.

Fawcett Society (2006), *Justice and Equality: Second Annual Review of the Commission on Women and the Criminal Justice System*, London: Fawcett Society.

—— (2007), *Women and Justice: Third Annual Review of the Commission on Women and the Criminal Justice System*, London: Fawcett Society.

—— (2009), *Engendering Justice from Policy to Practice: Final Report from the Commission on Women and the Criminal Justice System*, London: Fawcett Society.

Feldman, A. (2004), 'Memory theaters, virtual witnessing, and the trauma-aesthetic', *Biography*, 27:1, pp. 163–202.

Felman, S. and Laub, D. (2002), *Testimony: Crises of Witnessing in Literature, Psychoanalysis, and History*, New York, NY: Routledge.

Fernández-Morales, M. and Menéndez-Menéndez, M. I. (2016), '"When in Rome, use what you've got": A discussion of female agency through *Orange Is the New Black*', *Television and New Media*, 17:6, pp. 534–46.

Ferraro, K. J. and Moe, A. M. (2003), 'Mothering, crime, and incarceration', *Journal of Contemporary Ethnography*, 32:1, pp. 9–40.

Ferrell, J. (2004), 'Strange city', in J. Ferrell, K. Hayward, W. Morrison and M. Presdee (eds), *Cultural Criminology Unleashed*, London: Glasshouse Press, pp. 167–80.

—— (2009), 'Kill method: A provocation', *Journal of Theoretical and Philosophical Criminology*, 1:1, pp. 1–22.

Ferrell, J. and Sanders, C. R. (eds) (1995), *Cultural Criminology*, 3rd ed., Boston, MA: Northeastern University Press.

Ferrell, J. and Wensdale, N. (eds) (1999), *Making Trouble: Cultural Constructions of Crime, Deviance, and Control*, New York, NY: Aldine de Gruyter.

Ferrell, J., Hayward, K., Morrison, W. and Presdee, M. (eds) (2004), *Cultural Criminology Unleashed*, London: Grasshouse Press.

Ferrell, J., Hayward, K. and Young, J. (2008), *Cultural Criminology: An Invitation*, Thousand Oaks, CA: Sage.

Fili, A. (2013), 'Women in prison: Victims or resisters? Representations of agency in women's prisons in Greece', *Signs: Journal of Women in Culture and Society*, 39:1, pp. 1–26.

Firmin, C. (2010), *Female Voice in Violence Project: A Study into the Impact of Serious Youth and Gang Violence on Women and Girls*, Race On The Agenda Final Report, http://www.childrenscommissioner.gov.uk/force_download.php?fp=%2Fclient_assets%2Fcp%2Fpublication%2F478%2FFemale_voice_in_violence_final_report.pdf. Accessed 23 February 2018.

Fitzpatrick, L. (2011), 'The performance of violence and the ethics of spectatorship', *Performance Research: A Journal of the Performing Arts*, 16:1, pp. 59–67.

Flanders, L. (2017), 'No single-issue politics, only intersectionality: An interview with Kimberlé Crenshaw', *Truthout*, http://www.truth-out.org/opinion/item/40498-no-single-issue-politics-only-intersectionality-an-interview-with-kimberle-crenshaw. Accessed 23 February 2018.

Ford, A. (1995), '*Katharsis*: The ancient problem', in E. K. Sedgwick and A. Parker (eds), *Performativity and Performance*, London: Routledge, pp. 109–32.

Forsyth, A. and Megson, C. (eds) (2009), *Get Real: Documentary Theatre Past and Present*, New York, NY: Palgrave.

Foucault, M. (1977), *Discipline and Punish: The Birth of the Prison* (trans. Alan Sheridan), London: Penguin.

—— (1986), 'Of other spaces' (trans. J. Miskowiec), *Diacritics*, 16, pp. 22–27.

—— (1990), *The History of Sexuality*, vol. 1 (trans. Robert Hurley), London: Penguin.

—— (2003), *The Birth of the Clinic: An Archaeology of Medical Perception* (trans. A. M. Sheridan), London: Routledge.

Fowler, N. (2017), *New Drama Unfolds in Vandalia Women's Facility Thanks to Expanded Prison Performing Arts*, News.stlpublicradio.org, http://news.stlpublicradio.org/post/new-drama-unfolds-vandalia-womens-facility-thanks-expanded-prison-performing-arts#stream/0. Accessed 23 February 2018.

Fox, H. (2017), 'Cooking in confinement: Inside the kitchen at Chino Prison', *L.A. Weekly*, http://www.laweekly.com/restaurants/how-prison-kitchens-feed-inmates-for-about-one-dollar-per-meal-8258237. Accessed 23 February 2018.

Fox, K. (2012), 'A tender subject – Review', *The Observer*, 25 March, http://www.guardian.co.uk/stage/2012/mar/25/tender-subject-mark-storor-review. Accessed 23 February 2018.

Fraden, R. (2001), *Imagining Medea: Rhodessa Jones and Theatre for Incarcerated Women*, Chapel Hill, NC: University of North Carolina Press.

Frank, A. W. (1995), *The Wounded Storyteller: Body, Illness and Ethics*, Chicago, IL: University of Chicago Press.

Franzmann, V. (2014), *Pests*, London: Nick Hern Books.

Frauley, J. (ed.) (2015), *C. Wright Mills and the Criminological Imagination: Prospects for Creative Inquiry*, Farnham: Ashgate.

Freedman, E. B. (1996), 'The prison lesbian: Race, class and the construction of the aggressive female homosexual, 1915–1965', *Feminist Studies*, 22:2, pp. 397–423.

Freshwater, H. (2009), *Theatre and Audience*, Basingstoke: Palgrave.

Fryett, S. E. (2016), '"Chocolate and Vanilla Swirl, Swi-irl": Race and lesbian identity politics', in A. K. Householder and A. Trier-Bieniek (eds), *Feminist Perspectives on Orange Is the New Black: Thirteen Critical Essays*, Jefferson, NC: McFarland and Co, pp. 26–42.

Fugard, A., Kani, J. and Ntshona, W. (1974), *Statements: Three Plays*, London: Oxford University Press.

Fusco, C. (2000), 'The other history of intercultural performance', in L. Goodman and J. de Gay (eds), *The Routledge Reader in Politics and Performance*, London: Routledge, pp. 130–42.

—— (2001), *The Bodies That Were Not Ours: And Other Writings*, London: Routledge.

Fuss, D. (ed.) (1991), *Inside/Out: Lesbian Theories, Gay Theories*, London: Routledge.

Garber, L. (2006), 'On the evolution of queer studies: Lesbian feminism, queer theory and globalization', in D. Richardson, J. McLaughlin and M. E. Casey (eds), *Intersections between Feminist and Queer Theory*, Basingstoke: Palgrave, pp. 78–96.

Gardner, L. (2012), '66 minutes in Damascus – Review', *The Guardian*, 21 June, http://www.guardian.co.uk/stage/2012/jun/21/66-minutes-damascus-review. Accessed 23 February 2018.

Gear, S. and Ngubeni, K. (2002), *Daai Ding: Sex, Sexual Violence and Coercion in Men's Prisons*, Johannesburg: Centre for the Study of Violence and Reconciliation.

Gelsthorpe, L. (2006), 'Women and criminal justice: Saying it again, again and again', *Howard Journal of Criminal Justice*, 45:4, pp. 421–24.

—— (2010), 'Women, crime and control', *Criminology and Criminal Justice*, 10:4, pp. 375–86.

Gelsthorpe, L. and Morris, A. (2002), 'Women's imprisonment in England and Wales: A penal paradox', *Criminology and Criminal Justice*, 2:3, pp. 277–301.

Gelsthorpe, L., Sharpe, G. and Roberts, J. (2007), *Provision for Women Offenders in the Community*, Fawcett Society Research Report, London: Fawcett Society.

George, D. (1996), 'Performance epistemology', *Performance Research: A Journal of the Performing Arts*, 1:1, pp. 16–25.

Giallombardo, R. (1966), 'Social roles in a prison for women', *Social Problems*, 19:3, pp. 268–88.

Giardina, M. D. and Denzin, N. K. (2011), 'Acts of activism ↔ Politics of possibility: Toward a new performative cultural politics', *Cultural Studies ↔ Critical Methodologies*, 11:4, pp. 319–27.

Gibbons, J. A. (1997), 'Struggle and catharsis: Art in women's prisons', *The Journal of Arts Management, Law and Society*, 27:1, pp. 72–80.

Gilfus, M. E. (2012), 'From victims to survivors to offenders: Women's routes of entry and immersion into street crime', in S. Walklate (ed.), *Gender and Crime Volume IV: Gender, Crime and Punishment*, London: Routledge, pp. 9–29.

Gilman-Opalsky, R. (2016), *Specters of Revolt: On the Intellect of Insurrection and Philosophy from Below*, London: Repeater Books.

Gilroy, P. (1993), *The Black Atlantic: Modernity and Double Consciousness*, London: Verso.
Giroux, H. (1996), *Fugitive Cultures: Race, Violence and Youth*, New York, NY: Routledge.
—— (2003), 'Spectacles of Race and Pedagogies of Denial: AntiBlack Racist Pedagogy Under the Reign of Neoliberalism', *Communication Education,* 52:3, pp. 191–211.
—— (2015), *The Violence of Organized Forgetting: Thinking beyond America's Disimagination Machine*, San Francisco, CA: City Lights Publishers.
Giordano, M. (1999), *Das Experiment: Black Box,* Berlin: Rowohlt Taschenbuch Verlag.
Giorgio, G. (2009), 'Traumatic truths and the gift of telling', *Qualitative Inquiry*, 15:1, pp. 149–67.
Gluhovic, M. (2012), *Performing European Memories: Trauma, Ethics, Politics*, Basingstoke: Palgrave Macmillan.
Goddard, L. (2007), *Staging Black Feminisms: Identity, Politics, Performance*, Basingstoke: Palgrave Macmillan.
Goffman, E. (1963), *Stigma: Notes on the Management of a Spoiled Identity*, New York, NY: Simon & Schuster.
—— (1990), *The Presentation of Self in Everyday Life*, London: Penguin.
—— (1997), *The Goffman Reader* (ed. C. Lemert. and A. Branaman), Oxford: Blackwell.
—— (2005), *Interaction Ritual: Essays in Face-to-Face Behaviour*, New Brunswick: Transaction Publishers.
—— (2007), *Asylums: Essays on the Social Situation of Mental Patients and Other Inmates,* New Brunswick: Aldine Transaction.
Golden, R. (2005), *War on the Family: Mothers in Prison and the Families They Leave Behind,* London: Routledge.
Gómez-Peña, G. (2000), *Dangerous Border Crossers: The Artist Talks Back*, London: Routledge.
—— (2005), *Ethno-Techno: Writings of Performance, Activism, and Pedagogy*, New York, NY: Routledge.
—— (2008), 'Border hysteria and the war against difference', *TDR: The Drama Review,* 52:1, pp. 196–203.
Gómez-Peña, G. and Wolford, L. (2002), 'Navigating the minefields of Utopia: A conversation', *TDR: The Drama Review*, 46:2, pp. 66–96.
Goodman, L. and de Gay, J. (eds) (1998), *The Routledge Reader in Gender and Performance*, London: Routledge.
—— (eds) (2000), *The Routledge Reader in Politics and Performance*, London: Routledge.
Gordon, A. F. (2008), *Ghostly Matters: Haunting and the Sociological Imagination*, Minneapolis, MN: University of Minnesota Press.
Gormley, J. and Monzani, K. (2016), 'Patti Smith reads from Oscar Wilde in HM prison reading', *The Guardian*, https://www.theguardian.com/global/video/2016/nov/03/patti-smith-reads-from-oscar-wilde-in-hm-prison-reading. Accessed 23 February 2018.
Government Equalities Office (2008), *Women's Changing Lives: Priorities for the Ministers for Women, One Year On,* Progress Report, http://www.official-documents.gov.uk/document/cm74/7455/7455.pdf. Accessed 12 April 2011.
gov.uk (2013), *What Works: Evidence Centres for Social Policy,* https://www.gov.uk/government/publications/what-works-evidence-centres-for-social-policy. Accessed 11 May 2016.

Gramsci, A. (1971), *Selections from the Prison Notebooks* (trans. and ed. Q. Hoare and G. Nowell-Smith), New York, NY: International Publishers.

Graney, P. (2003), *2003 Anthology: Writings from Women on the Inside*, Seattle, WA: Pat Graney Company.

—— (2004), *Prison Project Anthology 2004: Writings from Women on the Inside*, Seattle, WA: Pat Graney Company.

—— (ed.) (2006), *Keeping the Faith 2006: Writings from Women on the Inside*, Seattle, WA: Pat Graney Company.

Grant, D. and Crossan, J. M. (2012), 'Freedom to Fail: The Unintended Consequences of a Prison Drama', *Performance Research: A Journal of the Performing Arts,* 17:1, pp. 97–100.

Groskop, V. (2008), 'Sex and the suffragette', *The Guardian*, 26 August, http://www.guardian.co.uk/stage/2008/aug/26/theatre.women. Accessed 23 February 2018.

Grossman, J. (2009), *Rethinking the Femme Fatale in Film Noir: Ready for her Close Up*, Basingstoke: Palgrave.

Guinness, M. (2011), 'Force-fed and Beaten – Life for women in jail', *The Independent*, Sunday, 18 December, http://www.independent.co.uk/news/world/politics/forcefed-and-beaten--life-for-women-in-jail-6278849.html. Accessed 23 February 2018.

Gullberg, S. (2013), *State of the Estate: Women in Prison's Report on the Women's Custodial Estate 2011–2012,* http://www.womeninprison.org.uk/userfiles/file/StateoftheEstateReport.pdf. Accessed 23 February 2018.

—— (2017), *The Corston Report 10 Years On*, London: Women in Prison.

Hahn-Rafter, N. and Heidensohn, F. (eds) (1995), *International Feminist Perspectives in Criminology: Engendering a Discipline,* Buckingham: Open University Press.

Halberstam, J. (1998), *Female Masculinity*, Durham, NC: Duke University Press.

—— (2001), 'Imagined violence/queer violence: Representations of rage and resistance', in M. McCaughey and N. King (eds), *Reel Knockouts: Violent Women in the Movies*, Austin, TX: University of Texas Press, pp. 244–66.

—— (2005), *In a Queer Time and Place: Transgender Bodies, Subcultural Lives,* New York: New York University Press.

—— (2011), *The Queer Art of Failure*, Durham, NC: Duke University Press.

—— (2013), 'The wild beyond: With and for the undercommons', in S. Harney and F. Moten (eds), *The Undercommons: Fugitive Planning and Black Study,* Wivenhoe: Minor Compositions, pp. 2–13.

Hall, S. (1996a), 'New ethnicities', in D. Morley and K. H. Chen (eds), *Stuart Hall: Critical Dialogues in Cultural Studies*, New York, NY: Routledge, pp. 441–49.

—— (1996b), 'What is this "Black" in Black popular culture?', in D. Morley and K. H. Chen (eds), *Stuart Hall: Critical Dialogues in Cultural Studies*, New York, NY: Routledge, pp. 468–78.

—— (2009), 'Old and new identities, old and new ethnicities', in L. Back and J. Solomos (eds), *Theories of Race and Racism: A Reader,* 2nd ed., pp. 199–208.

Haslam, S. A. and Reicher, S. D. (2012), 'When prisoners take over the prison: A social psychology of resistance', *Personality and Social Psychology Review,* 16:2, pp. 154–79.

Haney, C., Banks, W. C. and Zimbardo, P. G. (1973), 'Interpersonal dynamics in a simulated prison', *International Journal of Criminology and Penology,* 1, pp. 69–97.

Haney, L. A. (2010), *Offending Women: Power, Punishment, and the Regulation of Desire,* Berkeley, CA: University of California Press.

Haraway, D. (1988), 'Situated knowledges: The science question in feminism and the privilege of partial perspective', *Feminist Studies*, 14:3, pp. 575–99.

Harden, J. and Hill, M. (eds) (1998), *Breaking the Rules: Women in Prison and Feminist Therapy*, New York, NY: Harrington Park Press.

Harney, S. and Moten, F. (2013), *The Undercommons: Fugitive Planning and Black Study,* Wivenhoe: Minor Compositions.

Harris, G. (1999), *Staging Femininities: Performance and Performativity*, Manchester: Manchester University Press.

Harris, G. and Aston, E. (eds) (2006), *Feminist Futures? Theatre, Performance, Theory,* Basingstoke: Palgrave.

Hart, L. (1993), 'Identity and seduction: Lesbians in the mainstream', in L. Hart and P. Phelan (eds), *Acting Out: Feminist Performance,* Ann Arbor, MI: University of Michigan Press, pp. 119–40.

—— (1994), *Fatal Women: Lesbian Sexuality and the Mark of Aggression*, Oxford: Taylor & Francis.

—— (1996), 'Doing it anyway: Lesbian sado-masochism and performance', in E. Diamond (ed.), *Performance and Cultural Politics*, London: Routledge, pp. 48–64.

Hawthorne, N. (2010), *The Scarlet Letter,* Dover: Dover Thrift.

Hayes, C. (2011), *Clinks Response to Breaking the Cycle: Effective Punishment, Rehabilitation and Sentencing of Offenders*, http://www.clinks.org/publications/responses. Accessed 23 February 2018.

Hayward, K. (2004), 'Space – The final frontier: Criminology, the city and the spatial dynamics of exclusion', in J. Ferrell, K. Hayward, W. Morrison and M. Presdee (eds), *Cultural Criminology Unleashed*, London: Glasshouse Press, pp. 155–66.

—— (2010), 'Opening the lens: Cultural criminology and the image', in K. Hayward and M. Presdee (eds), *Framing Crime: Cultural Criminology and the Image*, London: Routledge, pp. 1–16.

Hayward, K. and Presdee, M. (eds) (2010), *Framing Crime: Cultural Criminology and the Image,* Abingdon: Routledge.

Healey, A. and Gormley, J. (2017), 'How a German prison is using theatre to de-radicalise young ISIS volunteers – Video', *The Guardian*, https://www.theguardian.com/stage/video/2017/mar/06/german-youth-prison-theatre-isis-volunteers-video. Accessed 23 February 2018.

Healy, D. (2014), 'Becoming a desister: Exploring the role of agency, coping and imagination in the construction of a new self', *British Journal of Criminology*, 54:5, pp. 873–91.

Heathfield, A. and Hsieh, T. (2015), *Out of Now: The Lifeworks of Tehching Hsieh*, updated ed., London: Live Art Development Agency and MIT Press.

Hedderman, C., Palmer, E. and Hollin, C. (2008), *Implementing Services for Women Offenders and Those 'At Risk' of Offending: Action Research with Together Women,* Ministry of Justice Research Series 12/08, London: National Offender Management Services.

Hedderman, C., Gunby, C. and Shelton, N. (2011), 'What women want: The importance of qualitative approaches in evaluating work with women offenders', *Criminology and Criminal Justice,* 11:1, pp. 3–19.

Heidensohn, F. (1986), 'Models of justice: Portia or persephone? Some thoughts on equality, fairness and gender in the field of criminal justice', *International Journal of the Sociology of Law*, 14:3–4, pp. 287–98.

—— (1996), *Women and Crime*, 2nd ed., Basingstoke: Macmillan Press.

—— (2000), *Sexual Politics and Social Control*, Buckingham: Open University Press.

—— (2012), 'The future of feminist criminology', *Crime Media Culture*, 8:2, pp. 123–34.

Helmreich, W. B. (2007), 'Introduction', in E. Goffman (ed.), *Asylums: Essays on the Social Situation of Mental Patients and Other Inmates*, New Brunswick: Aldine Transaction, pp. i–xiv.

Henderson, M (ed.) (1995), *Borders, Boundaries, and Frames: Cultural Criticism and Cultural Studies*, London: Routledge.

Henne, K. and Shah, R. (2016), 'Feminist criminology and the visual', *Oxford Research Encyclopedia of Criminology*, doi:10.1093/acrefore/9780190264079.013.56. Accessed 23 February 2018.

Hensley, C., Tewkesbury, R. and Koscheski, M. (2002), 'The characteristics and motivations behind female prison sex', *Women & Criminal Justice*, 13:2&3, pp. 125–39.

Heritage, P. (1998), 'Rebellion and theatre in Brazilian prisons: An historical footnote', in J. Thompson (ed.), *Prison Theatre: Perspectives and Practices*, London: Jessica Kingsley Publishers, pp. 231–38.

—— (2002), 'Stealing kisses', in M. Delgado and C. Svich (eds), *Theatre in Crisis?: Performance Manifestos for a New Century*, Manchester: Manchester University Press, pp. 166–78.

—— (2004), 'Real social ties: The ins and outs of making theatre in Brazilian prisons', in M. Balfour (ed.), *Theatre in Prison: Theory and Practice*, Bristol: Intellect, pp. 189–202.

Herman, D. (2003), '*Bad Girls* changed my life: Homonormativity in women's prison drama', *Critical Studies in Media Communication*, 20:2, pp. 141–59.

Herman, J. L. (1992), *Trauma and Recovery: The Aftermath of Violence – From Domestic Abuse to Political Terror*, New York, NY: Basic Books.

Herrmann, A. (2009), '"The mothership": Sustainability and transformation in the work of clean break', in T. Prentki and S. Preston (eds), *The Applied Theatre Reader*, London: Routledge, pp. 328–35.

Heyman, P. (2011), 'Reflection on *gotojail* Project', Personal Interview, Southbank, interviewed by A. Walsh, 20 October.

Heywood, L. (2012), interview on Geese Theatre, Telephone Interview, interviewed by A. Walsh, 30 July.

Hitchings, H. (2012), 'Mark Storor: A tender subject, secret venue – Review', *Evening Standard*, 16 March, http://www.thisislondon.co.uk/arts/theatre/mark-storor-a-tender-subject-secret-venue--review-7574857.html. Accessed 23 February 2018.

hooks, b. (1990), *Yearning: Race, Gender, and Cultural Politics*, Boston, MA: South End Press.

—— (1992), *Black Looks: Race and Representation*, Boston, MA: South End Press.

—— (1994), *Outlaw Culture: Resisting Representations*, London: Routledge.

hooks b. and Cox, L. (2014), 'bell hooks and Laverne Cox in a public dialogue at the new school', 13 October, https://www.youtube.com/watch?v=9oMmZIJijgY. Accessed 23 February 2018.

Horn, D. G. (1995), '"This norm which is not one": Reading the female body in Lombroso's anthropology', in J. Terry and J. Urla (eds), *Deviant Bodies: Critical Perspectives on Difference in Science and Popular Culture*, Bloomington, IN: Indiana University Press, pp. 109–28.

Householder, A. K. and Trier-Bieniek, A. (eds) (2016a), *Feminist Perspectives on* Orange Is the New Black: *Thirteen Critical Essays,* Jefferson, NC: McFarland and Co.
―――― (eds) (2016b), 'Introduction: Is *Orange* the New Black?', in A. K. Householder and A. Trier-Bieniek (eds), *Feminist Perspectives on* Orange Is the New Black: *Thirteen Critical Essays,* Jefferson, NC: McFarland and Co, pp. 12–25.
Hughes, J. (1998), 'Resistance and expression: Working with women prisoners and drama', in J. Thompson (ed.), *Prison Theatre: Perspectives and Practices,* London: Jessica Kingsley Publishers, pp. 43–64.
―――― (2005a), *Doing the Arts Justice: A Review of Research Literature, Practice and Theory*, Canterbury: The Unit for Arts and Offenders.
―――― (2005b), 'Ethical cleansing? The process of gaining ethical approval for a new research project exploring performance in place of war', *Research in Drama Education*, 10:2, pp. 229–32.
―――― (2007), 'Theatre, performance and the "War on Terror": Ethical and political questions arising from British theatrical responses to war and terrorism', *Contemporary Theatre Review*, 17:2, pp. 149–64.
Hughes, J. and Parry, S. (eds) (2015), 'Celebrating Margaretta D'Arcy's theatrical activism', *Contemporary Theatre Review*, https://www.contemporarytheatrereview.org/2015/margaretta-darcy/. Accessed 23 February 2018.
Hunting, K. (2016), 'All in the (prison) family: Genre mixing and queer representation', in A. K. Householder and A. Trier-Bieniek (eds), *Feminist Perspectives on* Orange Is the New Black: *Thirteen Critical Essays,* Jefferson, NC: McFarland and Co, pp. 122–38.
Inchley, M. (2013), 'Hearing the unhearable: The representation of women who kill children', *Contemporary Theatre Review*, 23:2, pp. 192–205.
Jackman, J. (2017), *How Do you Make a Film about Detained Women that your Government Doesn't Want You to See?*, https://i-d.vice.com/en_uk/article/7xb3wb/how-do-you-make-a-film-about-detained-women-that-your-government-doesnt-want-you-to-see. Accessed 23 February 2018.
Jackson, J. L. (2011), 'Situational lesbians and the daddy tank: Women prisoners negotiating queer identity and space, 1970–80', *Genders Archive 1998–2013*, https://www.colorado.edu/gendersarchive1998-2013/2011/02/01/situational-lesbians-daddy-tank-women-prisoners-negotiating-queer-identity-and-space-1970. Accessed 9 August 2018.
Jacobs, S., Jacobson, R. and Marchbank, J. (eds) (2000), *States of Conflict: Gender, Violence and Resistance*, London: Zed Books.
James, E. (2003), *A Life Inside: A Prisoner's Notebook*, London: Atlantic Books.
Jeffreys, T. (2012), 'Artangel presents: Mark Storor – A tender subject', *ThisisLondon*, http://www.thisislondon.co.uk/arts/theatre/mark-storor-a-tender-subject-secret-venue--review-7574857.html. Accessed 23 February 2018.
Jenks, C. (2003), *Transgression*, London: Routledge.
―――― (2011), 'The context of an emergent and enduring concept', *Crime, Media, Culture*, 7:3, pp. 229–36.
Jenness, V. (2010), 'From policy to prisoners to people: A "Soft Mixed Methods" approach to studying transgender prisoners', *Journal of Contemporary Ethnography*, 39, pp. 517–53.

Jensen, G. F. and Jones, D. (1976), 'Perspectives on inmate culture: A study of women in prison', *Social Forces*, 54:3, pp. 590–603.

Jewkes, Y. (2007), 'Prisons and the media: The shaping of public opinion and penal policy in a mediated society', in Y. Jewkes (ed.), *Handbook on Prisons,* Cullompton: Willan, pp. 447–66.

Johnston, C. and Hewish, S. (2010), *Criminal Justice: An Artist's Guide*, Report for Arts Alliance, London: Arts Alliance.

Jolie, R. A. and Hoffman, M. (2017), '*Orange Is the New Black* chooses fandom over social justice', *Bitch Media,* https://www.bitchmedia.org/article/orange-is-the-new-black/instagram-mocks-prisoners. Accessed 23 February 2018.

Jones, A. (ed.) (2001), *The Feminism and Visual Culture Reader*, London: Routledge.

Jürs-Munby, K. (2009), '"Did you mean *Post-Traumatic Theatre*?": The vicissitudes of traumatic memory in contemporary postdramatic performances, *Performance Paradigm,* 5:2, n.pag.

Kaba, M. (2017), 'Free us all', *The New Inquiry,* https://thenewinquiry.com/free-us-all/. Accessed 23 February 2018.

Kandaswamy, P. (2016), 'Centering prison abolition in women's, gender, and sexuality studies', *SandF Online,* 13:2, http://sfonline.barnard.edu/navigating-neoliberalism-in-the-academy-nonprofits-and-beyond/priya-kandaswamy-centering-prison-abolition-in-womens-gender-and-sexuality-studies/. Accessed 23 February 2018.

Kanter, J. (2007a), 'Disciplined bodies at play: Improvisation in a federal prison', *Cultural Studies <=> Critical Methodologies,* 7, pp. 378–96.

⸺ (2007b), *Performing Loss: Rebuilding Community through Theater and Writing,* Carbondale, IL: Southern Illinois University Press.

Kara, S. A. (2009), *Sex Trafficking: Inside the Business of Modern Slavery*, New York, NY: Columbia University Press.

Kellaway, K. (2008), 'Turning the tables: Interview with Rebecca Lenkiewicz', *The Observer,* 29 June, http://www.guardian.co.uk/stage/2008/jun/29/theatre.features. Accessed 23 February 2018.

Kelleher, J. (2009), *Theatre and Politics*, Basingstoke: Palgrave.

Kelleher, J. and Rideout, N. (eds) (2006), *Contemporary Theatres in Europe: A Critical Companion*, London: Routledge.

Kempadoo, K. (2005), 'Victims and agents of crime: The new crusade against trafficking', in J. Sudbury (ed.), *Global Lockdown: Race, Gender, and the Prison-Industrial Complex*, New York, NY: Routledge, pp. 35–56.

Kendall, K. (2005), 'Beyond reason: Social constructions of mentally disordered female offenders', in W. Chan, D. E. Chunn and R. Menzies (eds), *Women, Madness and the Law: A Feminist Reader*, London: The GlassHouse Press, pp. 41–58.

Kennedy, H. (2005), *Eve Was Framed: Women and British Justice*, London: Vintage.

Kerman, P. (2010), *Orange Is the New Black: My Year in a Women's Prison*, London: Abacus.

Kershaw, B. (1992), *The Politics of Performance: Radical Theatre as Cultural Intervention*, London: Routledge.

⸺ (1995), 'The politics of performance in a postmodern age', in P. Campbell (ed.), *Analysing Performance: A Critical Reader*, Manchester: Manchester University Press, pp. 133–52.

⸺ (1999), *The Radical in Performance: Between Brecht and Baudrillard*, London: Routledge.

—— (2003), 'Curiosity or contempt: On spectacle, the human, and activism', *Theatre Journal*, 55:4, pp. 591–611.

—— (2004), 'Pathologies of hope in drama and theatre', in M. Balfour (ed.), *Theatre in Prison: Theory and Practice,* Bristol: Intellect Books, pp. 35–51.

Khan, P. (2006), 'Legal performance and the imagination of sovereignty', *E-Misférica*, 3:1, http://hemisphericinstitute.org/journal/3.1/eng/en31_pg_kahn.html. Accessed 23 February 2018.

Kilby, J. (2001), 'Carved in skin: Bearing witness to self-harm', in S. Ahmed and J. Stacey (eds), *Thinking Through the Skin*, London: Routledge, pp. 124–41.

Kirkwood, L. (2009), *It Felt Empty When the Heart Went at First but It is Alright Now*, London: Nick Hern Books.

Koshal, E. (2010), '"Some Exceptions" and the "Normal Thing": Reconsidering *Waiting for Godot*'s theatrical form through its prison performances', *Modern Drama,* 53:2, pp. 187–210.

Kruger, L. (2007), '"White Cities", "Diamond Zulus" and "The African Contribution to Human Advancement": African modernities and the world fairs', *TDR The Drama Review*, 51:3, pp. 19–45.

Kruttschnitt, C. and Gartner, R. (2008), 'Female violent offenders: Moral panics or more serious offenders?', *Australian and New Zealand Journal of Criminology*, 41:9, pp. 9–35.

Kunzel, R. (2008), *Criminal Intimacy: Prison and the Uneven History of Modern American Sexuality*, Chicago, IL: University of Chicago Press.

Kupers, T. A. (2001), 'Rape and the prison code', in D. Sabo, T. A. Kupers and W. London (eds), *Prison Masculinities*, Philadelphia, PA: Temple University Press, pp. 111–17.

Lamb, W. (2007), *I'll Fly Away: Further Testimonies from the Women of York Prison*, New York, NY: HarperCollins.

Lamb, W. and The Women of York Correctional Institution (2003), *Couldn't Keep it to Myself: Testimonies from Our Imprisoned Sisters*, New York, NY: Harper Collins.

Lamble, S. (2009), 'Unknowable bodies, unthinkable sexualities: Lesbian and transgender legal invisibility in the Toronto women's bathhouse raid', *Social and Legal Studies,* 18:1, pp. 111–29.

—— (2013), 'Queer necropolitics and the expanding carceral state: Interrogating sexual investments in punishment', *Law Critique*, 24:3, pp. 229–53.

Larlham, D. (2009), 'Brett Bailey and third world bunfight: Journeys into the South African psyche', *Theater*, 39:1, pp. 7–27.

Laughlin, S. (2017), *The Scariest Part Of Working In A Prison Isn't The Inmates*, https://thoughtcatalog.com/sarah-laughlin/2017/03/the-scariest-part-of-working-in-a-prison-isnt-the-inmates/. Accessed 23 February 2018.

Law, V. (2014), 'Against carceral feminism', *Prison Books Collective*, https://prisonbooks.info/2014/10/17/against-carceral-feminism/. Accessed 23 February 2018.

—— (2017), Orange Is the New Black *Overlooks the Rich, Real-Life History of Resistance in Prison*, https://rewire.news/article/2017/06/14/orange-new-black-overlooks-rich-real-life-history-resistance-prison/. Accessed 23 February 2018.

Lawston, J. M. (2008), 'Women, the Criminal Justice System, and incarceration: Processes of power, silence, and resistance', *NWSA Journal*, 20:2, pp. 1–18.

Lawston, J. M. and Lucas, A. E. (eds) (2011), *Razor Wire Women: Prisoners, Activists, Scholars, and Artists*, New York, NY: SUNY Press.

Lazare, S. (2015), 'Say her name: In expression of vulnerability and power, black women stage direct action with chests bared', *Common Dreams*, 22 May, http://www.commondreams.org/news/2015/05/22/say-her-name-expression-vulnerability-and-power-black-women-stage-direct-action. Accessed 23 February 2018.

—— (2016), 'What you Need to Know about the DOJ's Claim it is ending private prisons', *Truthout*, 19 August, http://www.truth-out.org/news/item/37297-what-you-need-to-know-about-the-doj-s-claim-it-is-ending-private-prisons. Accessed 23 February 2018.

Lees, P. (2017), *Facts, Not Opinions, Matter When It Comes to Transgender Prisoners*, https://inews.co.uk/opinion/paris-lees-transgender-prisoners-isnt-time-talked-facts/. Accessed 23 February 2018.

Lefait, S. (2012), 'Dystopian villages: Surveillance and re-mediation in the prisoner', *TV/Series*, 2, pp. 78–92.

Lehmann, H. T. (2006), *Postdramatic Theatre* (trans. K. Jürs-Munby), Abingdon: Routledge.

Leiboff, M. (2010), 'Law, muteness and the theatrical', *Law Text Culture*, 14:1, pp. 384–91.

Leiboff, M. and Nield, S. (2010), 'Introduction: Law's theatrical presence', *Law Text Culture*, 14:1, pp. 1–2.

Lenkiewicz, R. (2008), *Her Naked Skin*, London: Faber.

—— (2011), 'An almost unnameable lust', in R. Lenkiewicz, *Charged*, London: Nick Hern Books, pp. 115–36.

Lemert, C. and Branaman, A. (eds) (1997), *The Goffman Reader*, Blackwell: Oxford.

Leverentz, A. (2010), 'People, places, and things: How female ex-prisoners negotiate their neighbourhood context', *Journal of Contemporary Ethnography*, 39, pp. 646–81.

Levi, R. and Waldman, A. (eds) (2011), *Inside This Place, Not of It: Narratives from Women's Prisons*, San Francisco, CA: Voice of Witness.

Leys, R. (2000), *Trauma: A Genealogy*, Chicago, IL: University of Chicago Press.

Liebling, A. (1999), 'Doing research in prison: Breaking the silence?', *Theoretical Criminology*, 3:2, pp. 147–73.

—— (2004), *Prisons and their Moral Performance: A Study of Values, Quality, and Prison Life*, Oxford: Oxford University Press.

Lindfors, B. (2003), 'Ethnological show business: Footlighting the dark continent', in E. Striff (ed.), *Performance Studies*, Palgrave: Basingstoke, pp. 29–40.

Lingis, A. (2004), 'Love junkies', *Performance Research*, 9:4, pp. 45–53.

Llewellyn, M. (2004), '"Queer? I should say it is criminal!": Sarah Waters' *Affinity*', *Journal of Gender Studies*, 13:3, pp. 203–14.

Lombroso, C. and Ferrero, W. (1895), *The Female Offender*, London: T. Fisher Unwin.

Lopez, T. A. (2003), 'Emotional contraband: Prison as metaphor and meaning in U.S. Latina Drama', in T. Fahy and K. King (eds), *Captive Audience: Prison and Captivity in Contemporary Theater*, New York: Routledge, pp. 25–40.

Lorde, A. (1993), *Zami; Sister Outsider; Undersong*, New York, NY: Book of the Month Club.

—— (2013), 'Uses of the erotic: The erotic as power', in A. Lorde, *Sister Outsider*, Freedom, CA: The Crossing Press, pp. 53–59.

Loucks, N. (2000), 'Prison rules: A working guide', Millennium Edition, *Prison Reform Trust*, http://www.prisonreformtrust.org.uk/Portals/0/Documents/prisonrulesworkingguide.pdf. Accessed 23 February 2018.

Lovell, T. (2000), 'Thinking feminism with and against Bourdieu', *Feminist Theory*, 1:1, pp. 11–32.

Loyd, J. M., Mitchelson, M. and Burridge, A. (eds) (2012), *Beyond Walls and Cages: Prisons, Borders and Global Crisis*, Athens, GA: University of Georgia Press.

Lucas, V. (2007), 'There is no justice – Just "us": Black Britons, British Asians, and the Criminal Justice System in verbatim drama', in R. Arana (ed.), *'Black' British Aesthetics Today*, Newcastle: Cambridge Scholars Publishing, pp. 262–71.

Luckhurst, R. (2008), *The Trauma Question*, London: Routledge.

Lukenchuk, A. (2006), 'Traversing the chasms of lived experiences: Phenomenological illuminations for practitioner research', *Educational Action Research*, 14:3, pp. 423–35.

Lyng, S. (2004), 'Crime, edgework and corporeal transaction', *Theoretical Criminology*, 8, pp. 359–75.

—— (ed.) (2005), *Edgework: The Sociology of Risk-Taking*, London: Routledge.

Madison, D. S. (2012), *Critical Ethnography: Methods, Ethics, and Performance*, 2nd ed., Los Angeles, CA: Sage.

Maeve, M. K. (1999), 'The social construction of love and sexuality in a women's prison', *Advances in Nursing Science*, 21:3, pp. 46–65.

Martin, C. (ed.) (2002), *A Sourcebook on Feminist Theatre and Performance: On and Beyond the Stage*, London: Routledge.

Mason, P. (ed.) (2003a), *Criminal Visions: Media Representations of Crime and Justice*, Cullompton: Willan Publishers.

—— (2003b), 'The screen machine: Cinematic representations of prison', in P. Mason (ed.), *Criminal Visions: Media Representations of Crime and Justice*, Cullompton: Willan Publishers, pp. 278–97.

Massey, D. (1994), *Space, Place, and Gender*, Minneapolis, MN: University of Minnesota Press.

—— (2004), 'Geographies of responsibility', *Geografiska Annaler: Series B, Human Geography*, 86:1, pp. 5–18.

Matarasso, F. (1997), *Use or Ornament: The Social Impact of Participation in the Arts*, London: Comedia.

Matthews, R. (1999), *Doing Time: An Introduction to the Sociology of Imprisonment*, New York, NY: Palgrave.

Mattsson, E. (2017), 'Governing by proximity', *Performance Research*, 22:3, pp. 42–48.

Mayne, J. (2000), *Framed: Lesbians, Feminists, and Media Culture*, Minneapolis, MN: University of Minnesota Press.

Mazzei, J. and O'Brien, E. E. (2009), 'You got it so when do you flaunt it?: Building rapport, intersectionality, and the strategic deployment of gender in the field', *Journal of Contemporary Ethnography*, 38:3, pp. 358–83.

Mbembe, A. (2003), 'Necropolitics' (trans. L. Meintjies), *Public Culture*, 15:1, pp. 11–40.

McAndrew, S. and Warne, T. (2005), 'Cutting across boundaries: A case study using feminist praxis to understand the meanings of self-harm', *International Journal of Mental Health Nursing*, 14, pp. 172–80.

McAvinchey, C. (2006a), 'Unexpected acts: Women, prison and performance', in J. Somers and M. Balfour (eds), *Drama as Social Intervention*, Ontario: Captus Press, pp. 216–27.

—— (2006b), 'Possible fictions: The testimony of applied performance with women in prisons in England and Brazil', unpublished Ph.D. thesis, Queen Mary University.

—— (2009), '"Is this the play?": Applied performance in pupil referral units', in T. Prentki and S. Preston (eds), *The Applied Theatre Reader*, London: Routledge, pp. 276–82.

—— (2011a), *Theatre and Prison*, Basingstoke: Palgrave Macmillan.

—— (2011b), 'Review: *Performance Affects: Applied Theatre and the End of Effect*', *Contemporary Theatre Review*, 21:2, pp. 233–34.

McCaughey, M. and King, N. (eds) (2001), *Reel Knockouts: Violent Women in the Movies*, Austin, TX: University of Texas Press.

McClelland, M. (2015), '*Orange Is the New Black*: Caged heat', *Rolling Stone*, http://www.rollingstone.com/tv/features/orange-is-the-new-black-cover-story-caged-heat-20150612. Accessed 23 February 2018.

McConachie, B. (2007), 'Falsifiable theories for theatre and performance studies', *Theatre Journal*, 59:4, pp. 553–77.

McCorkel, J. A. (2003), 'Embodied surveillance and the gendering of punishment', *Journal of Contemporary Ethnography*, 32:1, pp. 41–76.

McGuinness, C. M. (2016), 'Protesting *Exhibit B* in London: Reconfiguring antagonism as the claiming of theatrical space', *Contemporary Theatre Review*, 26:2, pp. 211–26.

McHugh, C. (2014), 'Key change', unpublished script by Open Clasp Theatre Company, Newcastle.

McKean, A. (2006), 'Playing for time in "The Dolls House": Issues of community and collaboration in the devising of theatre in women's prison', *Research in Drama Education*, 11:3, pp. 313–27.

—— (2011), 'Five years on and the audience still shout "Encore"', *Capture*, pp. 6–10.

McKenzie, J. (1998), 'Genre trouble: (The) Butler did it', in P. Phelan and J. Lane (eds), *The Ends of Performance*, New York, NY: New York University Press, pp. 217–35.

—— (2001), *Perform or Else: From Discipline to Performance*, London: Routledge.

McKinnon, S. L. (2009), 'Citizenship and the performance of credibility: Audiencing gender-based asylum seekers in U.S. immigration courts', *Text and Performance Quarterly*, 29:3, pp. 205–21.

McLaughlin, C. (2006), 'Inside stories, memories from the Maze and Long Kesh prison', *Journal of Media Practice*, 7:2, pp. 123–33.

McLean, A. and Liebing, A. (eds) (2007), *The Shadow Side of Fieldwork: Exploring the Blurred Borders Between Ethnography and Life,* Blackwell: Oxford.

McLeod, J. (2005), 'Feminists re-reading Bourdieu: Old debates and new questions about gender habitus and gender change', *Theory and Research in Education,* 3:11, pp. 11–30.

McNay, L. (1992), *Foucault and Feminism: Power, Gender and the Self*, Boston, MA: Northeastern University Press.

—— (1994), *Foucault: A Critical Introduction*, Cambridge, MA: Polity Press.

—— (1999), 'Gender, habitus and the field', *Theory, Culture and Society,* 16:1, pp. 95–117.

—— (2000), *Gender and Agency: Reconfiguring the Subject in Feminist and Social Theory*, Cambridge, MA: Polity Press.

McNeill, F., Anderson, K., Colvin, S., Overy, K., Sparks, R. and Tett, L. (2010), 'Inspiring desistance? Arts projects and "What Works"', *Justitiele Verkenningen*, 37:5, pp. 80–101.

McRobbie, A. (2006), 'Vulnerability, violence and (cosmopolitan) ethics: Butler's *Precarious Life*', *The British Journal of Sociology*, 57:1, pp. 69–86.

McWatters, M. (2013), 'Poetic testimonies of incarceration: Towards a vision of prison as manifold space', in D. Moran, N. Gill and D. Conlon (eds), *Carceral Spaces: Mobility and Agency in Imprisonment and Migrant Detention*, Farnham: Ashgate, pp. 199–218.

Megson, C. and Forsythe, A. (eds) (2009), *Get Real: Documentary Theatre Past, Present and Future*, Basingstoke: Palgrave Macmillan.

Mercer, C. (2016), 'Never mind a second chance: Our incarcerated women need a first one', *The Guardian*, 17 August, https://www.theguardian.com/commentisfree/2016/aug/17/us-women-prison-population-crime-rates. Accessed 23 February 2018.

Merrill, E. and Frigon, S. (2015), 'Performative criminology and the "State of Play" for theatre with criminalized women', *Societies*, 5, pp. 295–313.

Miles, A. and Clarke, R. (2006), *The Arts in Criminal Justice: A Study of Research Feasibility*, Manchester: Centre for Research on Socio-Cultural Change, University of Manchester.

Millbank, J. (2004), 'It's about *this*: Lesbians, prison, desire', *Social and Legal Studies*, 13:2, pp. 155–90.

Miller, J. H. (2007), 'Performativity as performance/ performativity as speech act: Derrida's special theory of performativity', *South Atlantic Quarterly*, 106:2, pp. 219–35.

Mills, Wright C. (2000), *The Sociological Imagination: Fortieth Anniversary Edition*, Oxford: Oxford University Press.

Minh-ha, T. (1989), *Woman, Native, Other*, Indianapolis, IN: Indiana University Press.

—— (2011), *Elsewhere, Within Here: Immigration, Refugeeism, and the Boundary Event*, New York, NY: Routledge.

Ministry of Justice (2009), *A Report on the Government's Strategy for Diverting Women Away from Crime*, http://www.justice.gov.uk/publications/docs/report-women-in-criminal-justice-system.pdf. Accessed 23 February 2018.

—— (2010a), 'Breaking the Cycle: Effective Punishment, Rehabilitation and Sentencing of Offenders', Green Paper Evidence Report, http://www.justice.gov.uk/consultations/docs/breaking-the-cycle.pdf. Accessed 23 February 2018.

—— (2010b), *Women in Focus: Promoting Equality and Positive Practice: Government Strategy to Divert Women Away from Crime*, London: Government Equalities Office.

—— (2011), *Prison Service Instruction PSI 54/2011: Mother and Baby Units*, London: Government Equalities Office.

—— (2013a), *About Her Majesty's Inspectorate of Prisons*, http://www.justice.gov.uk/about/hmi-prisons. Accessed 23 February 2018.

—— (2013b), *Strategic Objectives for Female Offenders*, London: Government Equalities Office.

—— (2016), *Types of Offender: Women Prisoners*, http://www.justice.gov.uk/offenders/types-of-offender/women. Accessed 23 February 2018.

—— (2017), *Population and Capacity Briefing for Friday 24 November 2017*, London: Ministry of Justice.

Mirzoeff, N. (2011), 'The right to look', *Critical Inquiry*, 37:3, pp. 473–96.

—— (ed.) (2013), *The Visual Culture Reader*, 3rd ed., London: Routledge.

—— (2017), *The Appearance of Black Lives Matter*, Miami: [Name] Publications.

Moi, T. (1991), 'Appropriating Bourdieu: Feminist theory and Pierre Bourdieu's sociology of culture', *New Literary History*, 22:4, pp. 1017–49.

Moore, L. and Scraton, P. (2014), *The Incarceration of Women: Punishing Bodies, Breaking Sprits*, Basingstoke: Palgrave.

Moraga, C. and Anzaldúa, G. (eds) (1981), *This Bridge Called My Back: Writings by Radical Women of Color*, San Francisco, CA: Kitchentable Press.

Moran, D. (2012a), '"Doing time" in Carceral Space: TimeSpace and Carceral Geography', *Geografiska Annaler: Series B, Human Geography*, 94:4, pp. 305–316.

—— (2012b), 'Pseudo carceral spaces: Replica prison cells', *Carceral Geography Weblog*, http://carceralgeography.com/2012/05/22/pseudo-carceral-spaces-replica-prison-cells/. Accessed 23 February 2018.

—— (2013), 'Carceral geography and the spatialities of prison visiting: Visitation, recidivism, and hyperincarceration', *Environment and Planning D: Society and Space*, 31, pp. 174–90.

—— (2015), *Carceral Geography: Spaces and Practices of Incarceration*, Farnham: Ashgate.

Moran, D., Gill, N. and Conlon, D. (eds) (2013a), *Carceral Spaces: Mobility and Agency in Imprisonment and Migrant Detention*, Farnham: Ashgate.

Moran, D., Piacentini, L. and Pallot, J. (2013b), 'Liminal transcarceral space: Prison transportation for women in the Russian Federation', in D. Moran, N. Gill and D. Conlon (eds), *Carceral Spaces: Mobility and Agency in Imprisonment and Migrant Detention*, Farnham: Ashgate, pp. 109–26.

Moreau, J. (2017), '"Overwhelming" number of lesbians and bisexual women are incarcerated', https://www.nbcnews.com/feature/nbc-out/overwhelming-number-lesbians-bisexual-women-incarcerated-n728666?cid=eml_onsite. Accessed 23 February 2018.

Morris, A. (1984), *Women, Crime and Criminal Justice*, Oxford: Basil Blackwell.

Morris, R. C. (2010), *Can the Subaltern Speak? Reflections on the History of an Idea*, New York, NY: Columbia University Press.

Morton, S. (2007), *Gayatri Spivak: Ethics, Subalternity and the Critique of Postcolonial Reason*, Malden, MA: Polity Press.

Moss, C. (2008), *This Wide Night*, London: Nick Hern Books.

—— (2011), 'Fatal light', in C. Moss, *Charged*, London: Nick Hern Books, pp. 29–56.

Mountford, A. and Farrall, M. (1998), 'The house of four rooms: Theatre, violence and the cycle of change', in J. Thompson (ed.), *Prison Theatre: Perspectives and Practices*, London: Jessica Kingsley Publishers, pp. 109–26.

Möbius, J. (2017), 'Die Krux mit dem Kreuz: Passionsspiele im Jugendgefängnis San Fernando in Mexiko-Stadt', in F. Evers, K. Flade, F. Lempa, L. K. Seuberling and M. Warstat (eds), *Applied Theatre: Rahmen und Positionen*, Berlin: Theater der Zeit, pp. 137–53.

Mullan, S. (2015), 'Post-Lesbian? Gendering queer performance research', *Theatre Research International*, 40:1, pp. 100–03.

Mulvey, L. (1996), *Fetishism and Curiosity*, Bloomington, IN: Indiana University Press.

—— (1999), 'Visual pleasure and narrative cinema', in L. Braudy and M. Cohen (eds), *Film Theory and Criticism: Introductory Readings*, New York, NY: Oxford University Press, pp. 833–44.

Munro, R. (2003), *Iron*, London: Nick Hern Books.
Muñoz, J. E. (1999), *Disidentifications: Queers of Color and the Performance of Politics*, Minneapolis, MN: University of Minnesota Press.
—— (2009), *Cruising Utopia: The Then and There of Queer Futurity*, New York, NY: New York University Press.
Museums Association. (2017), *Museums and Prisons*, http://www.museumsassociation.org/museum-practice/museums-and-prisons. Accessed 29 September 2017.
Naffine, N. (1987), *Female Crime: The Construction of Women in Criminology*, London: Allen & Unwin.
—— (1996), *Feminism and Criminology*, Philadelphia, PA: Temple University Press.
Nancy, J. L. (1991), *The Inoperative Community*, Minneapolis, MN: University of Minnesota Press.
National Offender Management Service (2011), *NOMS Vision and Values: NOMS Homepage*, http://www.justice.gov.uk/about/noms/noms-vision-and-values.htm. Accessed 23 February 2018.
Needham, A. (2012), 'Gay prisoners to get jail tales shown in Artangel Installation', *The Guardian*, 5 March, http://www.guardian.co.uk/society/2012/mar/05/gay-prisoners-artangel-installation?INTCMP=ILCNETTXT3487. Accessed 23 February 2018.
Neelands, J. (2004), 'Miracles are happening: beyond the rhetoric of transformation in the Western traditions of drama education', *Research in Drama Education*, 9, pp. 47–56.
Neve, L. and Pate, K. (2005), 'Challenging the criminalization of women who resist', in J. Sudbury (ed.), *Global Lockdown: Race, Gender, and the Prison-Industrial Complex*, New York, NY: Routledge, pp. 19–34.
Nevitt, L. (2013), *Theatre and Violence*, Basingstoke: Palgrave Macmillan.
New Philanthropy Capital (2011), *Unlocking Value: The Economic Benefit of the Arts in Criminal Justice*, London: Arts Alliance.
Nguyen, M. T. (2001), 'Punk Planet 42', Threads and Circuits blog, https://threadandcircuits.wordpress.com/2010/04/12/punk-planet-42-marchapril-2001/. Accessed 23 February 2018.
—— (2010), 'Carceral chic', blogpost, https://iheartthreadbared.wordpress.com/tag/prison/. Accessed 23 February 2018.
Nicholson, H. (2005), *Applied Drama: The Gift of Theatre*, London: Palgrave.
Nield, S. (2006a), 'On the border as theatrical space: Appearance, dis-location and the production of the refugee', in J. Kelleher and N. Rideout (eds), *Contemporary Theatres in Europe: A Critical Companion*, London: Routledge, pp. 61–72.
—— (2006b), 'There is another world: Space, theatre and global anti-capitalism', *Contemporary Theatre Review*, 16:1, pp. 51–61.
—— (2008), 'The proteus cabinet, or "We are Here but not Here"', *Research in Drama Education: The Journal of Applied Theatre and Performance*, 13:2, pp. 137–45.
—— (2010a), 'Galileo's finger and the perspiring waxwork: On death, appearance and the promise of flesh', *Performance Research: A Journal of the Performing Arts*, 15:2, pp. 39–43.
—— (2010b), 'On St Margaret Street', *Law Text Culture*, 14:1, pp. 3–11.
Ogletree, C. J., Jr. and Sarat, A. (eds) (2015), *Punishment in Popular Culture*, New York, NY: New York University Press.

Oliver, K. (2001), *Witnessing: Beyond Recognition*, Minneapolis, MN: University of Minnesota Press.

O'Neill, M. (2004), 'Crime, culture and visual methodologies: Ethno-mimesis as performative praxis', in J. Ferrell, K. Hayward, W. Morrison and M. Presdee (eds), *Cultural Criminology Unleashed*, London: Glasshouse Press, pp. 219–30.

O'Neill, M. and Seal, L. (2012), *Transgressive Imaginations: Crime, Deviance and Culture*, Basingstoke: Palgrave.

Opsal, T. D. (2011), 'Women disrupting a marginalized identity: Subverting the parolee identity through narrative', *Journal of Contemporary Ethnography*, 40:2, pp. 135–67.

Ostheimer, R. T. (2015), *On Working with Offenders: Opening Minds, Awakening Emotions*, Cambridge: MuseumsEtc.

Owen, B. (1998), *In the Mix: Struggle and Survival in a Women's Prison*, Albany, NY: SUNY Press.

Pardue, A., Arrigo, B. A. and Murphy, D. S. (2011), 'Sex and sexuality in women's prisons: A preliminary typological investigation', *The Prison Journal*, 91:3, pp. 279–304.

Pasko, L. (2017), 'Beyond confinement: The regulation of girl offenders' bodies, sexual choices, and behavior', *Women & Criminal Justice*, 27:1, pp. 4–20.

Peachey, P. (2012), 'State of women's jails shames Britain, says prisons inspector', *The Independent*, 1 March, http://www.independent.co.uk/news/uk/crime/state-of-womens-jails-shames-britain-says-prisons-inspector-7466989.html. Accessed 23 February 2018.

Peaker, A. (1998), 'Drama and the institution', in J. Thompson (ed.), *Prison Theatre: Perspectives and Practices*, London: Jessica Kingsley Publishers, pp. 197–208.

Peaker, A. and Johnston, C. (2007), *Handbook for Artists: Working in Arts in Criminal Justice and Crime Prevention Settings*, 5th ed., London: Anne Peaker Centre.

Peaker, A. and Vincent, J. (1990), *Arts in Prisons: Towards a Sense of Achievement*, London: Home Office, Research and Planning Unit.

People's Palace Projects (2013), *Projects: Staging Human Rights People's Palace Projects*, http://www.peoplespalaceprojects.org.uk/projects/staging-human-rights/. Accessed 23 February 2018.

Perman, L. (2009), 'Chained to the kitchen sink drama', *The Stage*, 31 July, http://blogs.thestage.co.uk/newsblog/2009/07/chained-to-the-kitchen-sink-drama/#comments. Accessed 23 February 2018.

—— (2013), 'Restorative theatre: Working inside out with prisons and offenders', *The Guardian*, http://www.theguardian.com/culture-professionals-network/culture-professionals-blog/2013/mar/13/restorative-theatre-clean-break-offenders. Accessed 23 February 2018.

Peschel, L. (2012), 'Structures of feeling' as methodology and the re-emergence of Holocaust Survivor Testimony in 1960s Czechoslovakia', *Journal of Dramatic Theory and Criticism*, 26:2, pp. 161–72.

Peschel, L. and Duggan, P. (eds) (2016), *Performing (For) Survival: Theatre, Crisis, Extremity*, Basingstoke: Palgrave.

Phelan, P. (1993), *Unmarked: The Politics of Performance*, London: Routledge.

—— (1997), *Mourning Sex: Performing Public Memories*, London: Routledge.

—— (1998), 'Introduction', in P. Phelan and J. Lane (eds), *The Ends of Performance*, New York, NY: New York University Press, pp. 1–22.

——— (2009), 'Afterword: "In the Valley of the Shadow of Death": The photographs of Abu Ghraib', in P. Anderson and J. Menon (eds), *Violence Performed: Local Roots and Global Routes of Conflict*, Basingstoke: Palgrave, pp. 372–84.

Phelan, P. and Lane, J. (eds) (1998), *The Ends of Performance*, New York, NY: New York University Press.

Phillips, C. and Earle, R. (2010), 'Reading difference differently?: Identity, epistemology and prison ethnography', *British Journal of Criminology*, 50:2, pp. 360–78.

Pimlico Opera (2013), 'Homepage', http://www.pimlicoopera.co.uk. Accessed 23 February 2018.

Pollock, D. (1998), 'Performing writing', in P. Phelan and J. Lane (eds), *The Ends of Performance*, New York, NY: New York University Press, pp. 73–103.

Poole, S. (2007), 'Voicing the non-place: Precarious Theatre in a women's prison', *Feminist Review*, 87, pp. 141–52.

Potter, S. (2004), '"Undesirable Relations": Same-sex relationships and the meaning of sexual desire at a women's reformatory during the Progressive Era', *Feminist Studies*, 30:2, pp. 394–415.

Pramaggiore, M. (2015), 'Privatization is the new black: Quality television and the refashioning of the U.S. Prison Industrial Complex', in T. Miller (ed.), *Routledge Companion to Global Popular Culture*, New York, NY: Routledge, pp. 187–96.

Prentki, T. and Preston, S. (eds) (2009), *The Applied Theatre Reader*, London: Routledge.

Presdee, M. (2000), *Cultural Criminology and the Carnival of Crime*, London: Routledge.

Preston, S. (2009), 'Introduction to participation', in T. Prentki and S. Preston (eds), *The Applied Theatre Reader*, London: Routledge, pp. 127–29.

——— (2011), 'Back on whose track? Reframing ideologies of inclusion and misrecognition in a Participatory Theatre Project with young people in London', *RiDE: The Journal of Applied Theatre and Performance*, 16:2, pp. 251–64.

Prichard, R. (2011), *Dream Pill: Charged*, London: Nick Hern Books.

Prison Photography (2017), '*The Prison in Twelve Landscapes* is the best film of 2016 not to win an Oscar', https://prisonphotography.org/2017/01/24/the-prison-in-twelve-landscapes-is-the-best-film-of-2016-not-to-win-an-oscar/. Accessed 23 February 2018.

Prison Reform Trust (2010), *'No Way Out': Briefing Paper*, London: Prison Reform Trust.

——— (2011a), *Smart Justice for Women Project Overview*, London: Prison Reform Trust.

——— (2011b), *Bromley Briefings Prison Factfile*, London: Prison Reform Trust.

——— (2013a), *Government has Six Months to Overturn Prisoners' Voting Ban*, London: Prison Reform Trust.

——— (2013b), *Why Focus on Reducing Women's Imprisonment?*, London: Prison Reform Trust.

——— (2015), *Bromley Briefings Prison Factfile*, London: Prison Reform Trust.

——— (2016), *Bromley Briefings Prison Factfile*, London: Prison Reform Trust.

——— (2017), *Bromley Briefings Prison Factfile*, London: Prison Reform Trust.

Probyn, E. (2004), 'Eating for a living: A rhizo-ethology of bodies', in H. Thomas and J. Ahmed (eds), *Cultural Bodies: Ethnography and Theory*, Malden, MA: Blackwell, pp. 215–40.

Publications.parliament.uk (2017), *Prison Reform: Governor Empowerment and Prison Performance – Justice Committee – House of Commons*, https://publications.parliament.uk/pa/cm201617/cmselect/cmjust/1123/112305.htm. Accessed 23 February 2018.

Bibliography

Pussy Riot (2013), *Pussy Riot: A Punk Prayer for Freedom*, New York, NY: Feminist Press.

Quinn, P. (2017), 'Theatre review: Through the gap – York Theatre Royal', *Prison Service Journal*, 231, pp. 47–48.

Rae, P. (2009), *Theatre and Human Rights*, Basingstoke: Palgrave Macmillan.

Rafter, N. (2000), *Shots in the Mirror: Crime Films and Society*, New York, NY: Oxford University Press.

—— (2014), 'Introduction to special issue on *Visual Culture and the Iconography of Crime and Punishment*', *Theoretical Criminology*, 18:2, pp. 127–33.

Rafter, N. and Brown, M. (2011), *Criminology Goes to the Movies: Crime Theory and Popular Culture*, New York, NY: New York University Press.

Rajah, V. (2006), 'Respecting boundaries: The symbolic and material concerns of drug-involved women employing violence against violent male partners', *British Journal of Criminology*, 46, pp. 837–58.

Ramsbotham, D. (2003), *Prisongate: The Shocking State of Britain's Prisons and the Need for Visionary Change*, London: Free Press.

Rancière, J. (2009), *The Emancipated Spectator* (trans. Gregory Elliot), London: Verso.

Read, A. (1993), *Theatre and Everyday Life: An Ethics of Performance*, London: Routledge.

Reinelt, J. (1998), 'Notes for a radical democratic theater: Productive crises and the challenge of indeterminacy', in J. Colleran and J. S. Spencer (eds), *Staging Resistance: Essays on Political Theatre*, Ann Arbor, MI: University of Michigan Press, pp. 283–300.

Reinelt, J. and Roach, J. (eds) (2007), *Critical Theory and Performance*, 2nd ed., Ann Arbor, MI: University of Michigan Press.

Reiter, K. (2014), 'Making windows in walls: Strategies for prison research', *Qualitative Inquiry*, 20:4, pp. 417–28.

Renzetti, C. M. (2013), *Feminist Criminology*, London: Routledge.

Renzetti, C. M., Miller, S. L. and Gover, A. R. (eds) (2013), *Routledge International Handbook of Crime and Gender Studies*, London: Routledge.

Rhodes, L. A. (2001), 'Toward an anthropology of prisons', *Annual Review of Anthropology*, 30, pp. 65–83.

—— (2005), 'Changing the subject: Conversation in Supermax', *Cultural Anthropology*, 20:3, pp. 388–411.

—— (2009), 'Ethnography in sites of total confinement', *Anthropology News*, 50:1, p. 6.

—— (2013), 'Ethnographic imagination in the field of the prison', *Criminal Justice Matters*, 91:1, pp. 16–17.

Rich, A. (1996), 'Compulsory heterosexuality and lesbian existence', in S. Jackson and S. Scott (eds), *Feminism and Sexuality: A Reader*, New York, NY: Columbia University Press, pp. 130–41.

Richardson, D., McLaughlin, J. and Casey, M. E. (eds) (2006), *Intersections between Feminist and Queer Theory*, Basingstoke: Palgrave.

Richie, B. (2004), 'Feminist ethnographies of women in prison', *Feminist Studies*, 30:2, pp. 438–50.

—— (2012), *Arrested Justice: Black Women, Violence, and America's Prison Nation*, New York, NY: New York University Press.

Rickford, D. (2011), *Troubled Inside: Responding to the Mental Health Needs of Women in Prison*, London: Prison Reform Trust.

Rideout (2011), *Gotojail project homepage,* http://www.gotojail.info/. Accessed 20 August 2018.

Roach, J. (1996), *Cities of the Dead: Circum-Atlantic Performance*, New York, NY: Columbia University Press.

Roberts, J. (2008), 'Ofcom Report on the cost of telephone calls made by prisoners', *Inside Time*, http://www.insidetime.org/articleview.asp?a=299. Accessed 23 February 2018.

Roberts, Y. (2013), 'Women's centres give vital help to ex-convicts: So why cut them?', *The Guardian,* http://www.guardian.co.uk/society/2013/jan/27/women-in-prison-rehabilitation-chris-grayling. Accessed 23 February 2018.

Robson, R. (1992), *Lesbian Outlaw: Survival Under the Rule of Law*, Ithaca, NY: Firebrand Books.

Rocchi, J. P., Crémieux, A. and Lemoine, X. (2013), 'Introduction: Black beings, black embodyings: Notes on contemporary artistic performances and their cultural interpretations', in A. Crémieux, X. Lemoine and J. P. Rocchi (eds), *Understanding Blackness through Performance: Contemporary Arts and the Representation of Identity*, Basingstoke: Palgrave, pp. 1–22.

Rodosthenous, G. (ed.) (2015), *Theatre as Voyeurism: The Pleasures of Watching*, Basingstoke: Palgrave Macmillan.

Rokem, F. (2000), *Performing History: Theatrical Representations of the Past in Contemporary Theatre,* Iowa City, IA: University of Iowa Press.

Routledge, P. (2009), 'Toward a relational ethics of struggle: Embodiment, affinity, and affect', in R. Amster, A. DeLean, L. A. Fernandez, A. J. Nocella II and D. Shannon (eds), *Contemporary Anarchist Studies: An Introductory Anthology of Anarchy in the Academy*, New York, NY: Routledge, pp. 82–92.

Rowe, A. (2011), 'Narratives of self and identity in women's prisons: Stigma and the struggle for self-definition in penal regimes', *Punishment and Society*, 13:5, pp. 571–91.

—— (2012), 'Sexuality, criminality and the women's prison: Pat Arrowsmith's "Somewhere Like This"', *Prison Service Journal*, 199, pp. 32–34.

—— (2014), 'Situating the self in prison research: Power, identity, and epistemology', *Qualitative Inquiry*, 20:4, pp. 404–16.

Ruding, S. (2012), 'Review: Performing new lives: Prison theatre', *Research in Drama Education: The Journal of Applied Theatre and Performance*, 17:1, pp. 140–43.

Rudkin, H. (2012), 'Book review: Self-starvation as performance', *Cultural Studies Review,* 18:1, pp. 308–13.

Rumgay, J. (2012), 'Scripts for safer survival: Pathways out of female crime', in S. Walklate (ed.), *Gender and Crime Volume IV: Gender, Crime and Punishment*, London: Routledge, pp. 94–110.

Rusche, G. and Kirchheimer, O. (2003), *Punishment and Social Structure*, London: Transaction Publishers.

Rustbelt Abolition Radio (2017), *Episode 4: Survival and Resistance: Women Organizing towards Abolition*, https://rustbeltradio.org/2017/04/10/ep04/. Accessed 23 February 2018.

Rymhs, D. (2012), 'In this inverted garden: Masculinities in Canadian prison writing', *Journal of Gender Studies*, 21:1, pp. 77–89.

Sabo, D., Kupers, T. A. and James, W. (eds) (2001), *Prison Masculinities*, Philadelphia, PA: Temple University Press.

Sabo, D., Kupers, T. A. and London, W. (2001a), 'Gender and the politics of punishment', in D. Sabo, T. A. Kupers and W. London (eds), *Prison Masculinities*, Philadelphia, PA: Temple University Press, pp. 3–18.

—— (2001b), 'Sexualities, sexual violence, and intimacy in prison', in D. Sabo, T. A. Kupers and W. London (eds), *Prison Masculinities,* Philadelphia, PA: Temple University Press, pp. 109–10.

Salih, S. and Butler, J. (2004), *The Judith Butler Reader*, Oxford: Blackwell.

Salverson, J. (2001), 'Change on whose terms? Testimony and an erotics of injury', *Theater*, 31, pp. 119–25.

Scanlon, J. and Lewis, R. (2017), 'Whose sexuality is it anyway? Women's experiences of viewing lesbians on screen', *Feminist Media Studies*, 17:6, pp. 1–17.

Scarry, E. (1985), *The Body in Pain: The Making and Unmaking of the World*, Oxford: Oxford University Press.

Schechner, R. (1974), 'From ritual to theatre and back: The structure/process of the efficacy/entertainment dyad', *Educational Theatre Journal*, 26:4, pp. 455–81.

—— (1988), *Performance Theory*, London: Routledge.

—— (2006), *Performance Studies: An Introduction*, 2nd ed., New York, NY: Routledge.

Schen, C. (2005), 'When mothers leave their children behind', *Harvard Review of Psychiatry*, 13:4, pp. 233–43.

Scheper-Hughes, N. (2007), 'The gray zone: Small wars, peacetime crimes and invisible genocides', in A. McLean and A. Liebing (eds), *The Shadow Side of Fieldwork: Exploring the Blurred Borders Between Ethnography and Life*, Oxford: Blackwell, pp. 159–84.

Schept, J. (2013), '"A lockdown facility with the feel of a small, private college": Liberal politics, jail expansion, and the carceral habitus', *Theoretical Criminology*, 17:1, pp. 71–88.

Schmid, A. (2017), 'Crafting the perfect woman: How gynecology, obstetrics and American prisons operate to construct and control women', *Abolition Journal*, https://abolitionjournal.org/crafting-the-perfect-woman-how-gynecology-obstetrics-and-american-prisons-operate-to-construct-and-control-women/. Accessed 23 February 2018.

Schmidt, T. (2010), '"We say sorry": Apology, the law and theatricality', *Law Text Culture*, 14:1, pp. 55–78.

Schneider, R. (1997), *The Explicit Body in Performance*, London: Routledge.

—— (2010), 'Protest now and again', *TDR: The Drama Review*, 54:2, pp. 7–11.

—— (2011), *Performing Remains: Art and War in Times of Theatrical Reenactment*, London: Routledge.

—— (2012), '"It Seems As If… I am Dead": Zombie capitalism and theatrical labor', *TDR: The Drama Review*, 56:4, pp. 150–62.

Schuler, C. (2013), 'Reinventing the show trial: Putin and pussy riot', *TDR: The Drama Review*, 57:1, pp. 7–17.

Schur, E. M. (1984), *Labeling Women Deviant: Gender, Stigma, and Social Control*, New York, NY: Random House.

Schwan, A. (2016), 'Postfeminism meets the women in prison genre: Privilege and spectatorship in *Orange Is the New Black*', *Television and New Media*, 17:6, pp. 473–90.

Scott, J. C. (1992), *Domination and the Arts of Resistance: Hidden Transcripts*, New Haven, CT: Yale University Press.

Scullion, P. (2011), 'Prison wages cut to help victims', 26 September, http://www.politics.co.uk/news/2011/09/26/prison-wage-cuts-to-benefit-victims. Accessed 23 February 2018.

Seal, L. (2010), *Women, Murder and Femininity: Gender Representations of Women who Kill*, Basingstoke: Palgrave.

—— (2014), 'Imagined communities and the death penalty in Britain, 1930–65', *British Journal of Criminology*, 54:5, pp. 908–27.

Sedgwick, E. K. (1985), *Between Men: English Literature and Male Homosocial Desire*, New York, NY: Columbia University Press.

—— (1990), *Epistemology of the Closet*, Berkeley, CA: University of California Press.

—— (2003), *Touching Feeling: Affect, Pedagogy, Performativity*, Durham, NC: Duke University Press.

—— (2007), 'Axiomatic', in S. During (ed.), *The Cultural Studies Reader*, 3rd ed., London: Routledge, pp. 383–402.

Sedgwick, E. K. and Parker, A. (eds) (1995), *Performativity and Performance*, London: Routledge.

Segrave, M. and Carlton, B. (2010), 'Women, trauma, criminalisation and imprisonment', *Current Issues in Criminal Justice*, 22:2, pp. 287–306.

—— (2013), 'Introduction: Gendered transcarceral realities', in B. Carlton and M. Segrave (eds), *Women Exiting Prison: Critical Essays on Gender, Post-release Support and Survival*, London: Routledge, pp. 1–13.

Seitz, S. (2017), 'Beyond the bars: Arts and humanities education in prison', http://carceral-complex.com/2017/03/beyond-the-bars-arts-and-humanities-education-in-prison/. Accessed 23 February 2018.

Sentencing Project, The (2015), *Fact Sheet: Incarcerated Women and Girls*, Washington, DC: The Sentencing Project.

Sered, S. and Norton-Hawk, M. (2011), 'Gender overdetermination and resistance: The case of criminalised women', *Feminist Theory*, 12:3, pp. 317–33.

Severance, T. (2004), 'The prison lesbian revisited', *Journal of Gay and Lesbian Social Services*, 17:3, pp. 39–57.

Shailor, J. (ed.) (2011), *Performing New Lives: Prison Theatre*, London: Jessica Kingsley Publishers.

Shalev, S. and Edgar, K. (2015), *Deep Custody: Segregation Units and Close Supervision Centres in England and Wales*, London: Prison Reform Trust.

Shaughnessy, N. (2012), *Applying Performance: Live Art, Socially Engaged Theatre and Affective Practice*, Basingstoke: Palgrave.

Shevtsova, M. (2002), 'Appropriating Pierre Bourdieu's Champ and Habitus for a sociology of stage productions', *Contemporary Theatre Review*, 12:3, pp. 35–66.

Siede, C. (2015), '2015 was the year cinematic women broke out of prison', *AV Film*, https://film.avclub.com/2015-was-the-year-cinematic-women-broke-out-of-prison-1798244709. Accessed 23 February 2018.

Siegal, C. (1995), 'Compulsory heterophobia: The aesthetics of seriousness and the production of homophobia', *Genders*, 21, pp. 319–39.

Silverman, R. E. and Ryalls, E. D. (2016), '"Everything is Different the Second Time Around": The stigma of temporality on *Orange Is the New Black*', *Television and New Media*, 17:6, pp. 520–33.

Sim, K. (2017), 'Who gets sick from Yellow Fever? What carceral feminism does not see', http://novaramedia.com/2017/03/12/who-gets-sick-from-yellow-fever-what-carceral-feminism-does-not-see/. Accessed 23 February 2018.

Sloan, J. and Drake, D. H. (2013), 'Emotional engagements: On sinking and swimming in prison research and ethnography', *Criminal Justice Matters*, 91:1, pp. 24–25.

Sloan, J. and Wright, S. (2015), 'Going in green: Reflections on the challenges of "Getting In, Getting On, and Getting Out" for doctoral prison researchers', in D. Drake, R. Earle and J. Sloan (eds), *Palgrave Handbook of Prison Ethnography*, Basingstoke: Palgrave, pp. 143–63.

Smart, C. (1977), *Women, Crime and Criminology: A Feminist Critique*, London: Routledge.

Smoyer, A. B. (2016), 'Making fatty girl cakes: Food and resistance in a women's prison', *The Prison Journal*, 96:2, pp. 192–209.

Snitow, A., Stansell, C. and Thompson, S. (eds) (1983), *Powers of Desire: the Politics of Sexuality*, New York, NY: Monthly Review Press.

So Different So Appealing (2012), 'A tender subject review', 18 March, http://www.sodifferentsoappealing.com/2012/03/tender-subject.html#more>. Accessed 23 February 2018.

Solga, K. (2008), 'The line, the crack, and the possibility of architecture: Figure, ground, feminist performance', *Theatre Research in Canada*, 29:1, n.pag.

Solitaryconfinement.org (2017), *The Istanbul Statement on the Use and Effects of Solitary Confinement*, http://www.solitaryconfinement.org/uploads/Istanbul_expert_statement_on_sc.pdf. Accessed 23 February 2018.

Somers, J. and Balfour, M. (eds) (2006), *Drama as Social Intervention*, Concord, ON: Captus Press.

Son, E. (2006), 'The spaces of engagement of the Medea Project, Theatre for Incarcerated Women', *E-Misférica*, 3:1, http://hemisphericinstitute.org/journal/3.1/eng/en31_pg_son.html. Accessed 23 February 2018.

Sontag, S. (2003), *Regarding the Pain of Others*, London: Penguin.

—— (2004), 'Regarding the torture of others', *New York Times*, 23 May, http://www.nytimes.com/2004/05/23/magazine/regarding-the-torture-of-others.html?pagewanted=printandsrc=pm. Accessed 23 February 2018.

Spivak, G. C. (1988), 'Can the subaltern speak?', in C. Nelson and L. Grossberg (eds), *Marxism and the Interpretation of Culture*, Urbana, IL: University of Illinois Press, pp. 271–313.

Stacey, J. (1994), *Star Gazing: Hollywood Cinema and Female Spectatorship*, New York, NY: Routledge.

Stallybrass, P. and White, A. (1995), *The Politics and Poetics of Transgression*, Ithaca, NY: Cornell University Press.

Stanley, E. A. and Smith, N. (eds) (2011), *Captive Genders: Trans Embodiment and the Prison Industrial Complex*, Oakland, CA: AK Press.

States, B. O. (1985), *Great Reckonings in Little Rooms: On the Phenomenology of Theater*, Berkeley, CA: University of California Press.

Steck, R. (2010), 'Laughing lesbians: Camp, spectatorship, and citizenship', Ph.D. dissertation, Eugene, OR: University of Oregon.

Stephan, M. J. and Chenoweth, E. (2008), 'Why civil resistance works: The strategic logic of nonviolent conflict', *International Security*, 33:1, pp. 1–44.

Stern, V. (1989), *Bricks of Shame: Britain's Prisons*, 2nd ed., London: Penguin.

Stewart, L. and Gobell, R. (2015), *Effective Interventions for Women Offenders: A Rapid Evidence Assessment*, London: National Offender Management Service.

Steyerl, H. (2000), 'Culture and crime', *Transversal*, http://eipcp.net/transversal/0101/steyerl/en. Accessed 13 August 2018.

Story, B., Brown, M. and Carrabine, E. (2016), 'The prison in twelve landscapes: An interview with film producer and director Brett Story', *Crime, Media, Culture*, 13:1, pp. 107–13.

Stuart Fisher, A. (2011), 'Trauma, authenticity and the limits of verbatim', *Performance Research: A Journal of the Performing Arts*, 16:1, pp. 112–22.

Stychin, C. (1995), *Law's Desire: Sexuality and the Limits of Justice*, London: Routledge.

Subramanian, R., Delaney, R., Roberts, S., Fishman, N. and McGarry, P. (2015), *Incarceration's Front Door: The Misuse of Jails in America*, The Vera Institute of Justice, http://www.safetyandjusticechallenge.org/wp-content/uploads/2015/01/incarcerations-front-door-report.pdf. Accessed 23 February 2018.

Sudbury, J. (2002), 'Celling black bodies: Black women in the global prison industrial complex', *Feminist Review*, 70, pp. 57–74.

—— (ed.) (2005a), *Global Lockdown: Race, Gender, and the Prison-Industrial Complex*, New York, NY: Routledge.

—— (2005b), 'Introduction: Feminist critiques, transnational landscapes, abolitionist visions', in J. Sudbury (ed.), *Global Lockdown: Race, Gender, and the Prison-Industrial Complex*, New York, NY: Routledge, pp. xi–xxviii.

—— (2011), 'From women prisoners to people in women's prisons: Challenging the gender binary in antiprison work', in J. M. Lawston and A. E. Lucas (eds), *Razor Wire Women: Prisoners, Activists, Scholars, and Artists*, New York, NY: SUNY Press, pp. 169–83.

Sudbury, J. and Okazawa-Rey, M. (eds) (2009), *Activist Scholarship: Antiracism, Feminism and Social Change*, Boulder, CO: Paradigm Publishers.

Susen, S. (2011), 'Afterword: Concluding Reflections on the Legacy of Pierre Bourdieu', in S. Susen and B. S. Turner (eds), *The Legacy of Pierre Bourdieu: Critical Essays*, London: Anthem Press, pp. 367–410.

Susen, S. and Turner, B. S. (eds) (2011), *The Legacy of Pierre Bourdieu: Critical Essays*, London: Anthem Press.

Sutherland, A. (2013), '"Now We are Real Women": Playing with gender in a male prison programme in South Africa', *Research in Drama Education: The Journal of Applied Theatre and Performance*, 18:2, pp. 120–32.

—— (2015), 'Disturbing masculinity: Gender, performance and "violent" men', *South African Theatre Journal*, 28:1, pp. 68–77.

—— (2017), 'Method and madness: De/colonising scholarship and theatre research with participants labelled mad', *Research in Drama Education: The Journal of Applied Theatre and Performance*, 22:3, pp. 427–35.

Swavola, E., Riley, K. and Subramanian, R. (2016), *Overlooked: Women and Jails in the Era of Reform*, Vera Institute of Justice, http://www.safetyandjusticechallenge.org/

wp-content/uploads/2016/08/overlooked-women-in-jails-report-web.pdf. Accessed 23 February 2018.
Sweeney, G. (1993), 'Self-immolation in Ireland: Hunger strikes and political confrontation', *Anthropology Today*, 9:5, pp. 10–14.
Sweeney, M. (2004), 'Prison narratives, narrative prisons: Incarcerated women reading Gayl Jones's "Eva's Man"', *Feminist Studies*, 30:2, pp. 456–82.
—— (2010), *Reading is My Window: Books and the Art of Reading in Women's Prisons*, Chapel Hill, NC: University of North Carolina Press.
Sykes, G. M. (1958), *The Society of Captives: A Study of a Maximum Security Prison*, Princeton, NJ: Princeton University Press.
Symes, K. (2017), '*Orange Is the New Black*: The popularization of lesbian sexuality and heterosexual modes of viewing', *Feminist Media Studies*, 17:1, pp. 29–41.
Talking Birds (2017a), *Disorder Contained: A Theatrical Examination of Madness, Prison and Solitary Confinement*, https://histprisonhealth.com/arts-projects/disorder-contained-a-theatrical-examination-of-madness-prison-and-solitary-confinement/. Accessed 23 February 2018.
—— (2017b), *Disorder Contained Post-Show Expert Panel Discussion*, http://mixlr.com/talkingbirds/showreel/disorder-contained-post-show-expert-panel-discussion-2/. Accessed 23 February 2018.
Taylor, D. (1997), *The Archive and the Repertoire: Performing Cultural Memory in the Americas*, Durham, NC: Duke University Press.
—— (1998), 'A savage performance: Guillermo Gómez-Peña and Coco Fusco's "Couple in the Cage"', *TDR: The Drama Review*, 42:2, pp. 160–75.
—— (2001), 'Staging social memory: Yuyachkani', in P. Campbell and A. Kear (eds), *Psychoanalysis and Performance*, London: Routledge, pp. 218–35.
—— (2002), '"You are here": The DNA of performance', *TDR: The Drama Review*, 46:1, pp. 149–69.
—— (2006), 'Performance and/as history', *TDR: The Drama Review*, 50:1, pp. 67–86.
—— (2009), 'Afterword: War play', *PMLA*, 124:5, pp. 1886–95.
Taylor, D., Chaudhuri, U. and Worthen, W. (2002), 'A forum on theatre and tragedy: A response to September 11, 2001', *Theatre Journal*, 54:1, pp. 95–138.
Taylor, J. M. (2001), 'Desdemona's lament', *TDR: The Drama Review*, 45:4, pp. 106–24.
Taylor, P. (1996a), 'Rebellion, reflective turning and arts education research', in P. Taylor (ed.), *Researching Drama and Arts Education*, London: Falmer Press, pp. 1–22.
—— (ed.) (1996b), *Researching Drama and Arts Education*, London: Falmer Press.
Terry, A. (2016), 'Surveying issues that arise in women's prisons: A content critique of *Orange Is the New Black*', *Sociology Compass*, 10:7, pp. 553–66.
Terry, J. and Urla, J. (eds) (1995), *Deviant Bodies: Critical Perspectives on Difference in Science and Popular Culture*, Bloomington, IN: Indiana University Press.
Third World Bunfight (2012), '*Exhibit B* Programme Information', http://www.thirdworldbunfight.co.za/productions/exhibit-b.html. Accessed 23 February 2018.
Thompson, H. A. (2017), 'What's hidden behind the walls of America's prisons', The Conversation, https://theconversation.com/whats-hidden-behind-the-walls-of-americas-prisons-77282. Accessed 23 February 2018.

Thompson, J. (ed.) (1998), *Prison Theatre: Perspectives and Practices*, London: Jessica Kingsley Publishers.
—— (1999), *Drama Workshops for Anger Management and Offending Behaviour*, London: Jessica Kingsley.
—— (2000), 'Bewilderment: Preparing prisoners for "real" work in the fictional world of prison', *Community, Work & Family*, 3:3, pp. 242–59.
—— (2001), 'Making a break for it: Discourse and theatre in prisons', *Applied Theatre Research*, 2, pp. 1–4.
—— (2003), 'Doubtful principles in arts in prisons', in R. M. C. Williams (ed.), *Teaching the Arts Behind Bars*, Boston, MA: Northeastern University Press, pp. 40–61.
—— (2004a), 'From the stocks to the stage: Prison theatre and the theatre of prison', in M. Balfour (ed.), *Theatre in Prison: Theory and Practice*, Bristol: Intellect Books, pp. 57–76.
—— (2004b), 'Review: *Imagining Medea: Rhodessa Jones and Theater for Incarcerated Women*', *NTQ: New Theatre Quarterly*, 20:3, pp. 295–96.
—— (2005), 'Review: *Captive Audience: Prison and Captivity in Contemporary Theatre*', *Modern Drama*, 48:2, pp. 465–68.
—— (2006a), *Applied Theatre: Bewilderment and Beyond*, Oxford: Peter Lang.
—— (2006b), 'Performance of pain, performance of beauty', *RiDE: Research in Drama Education*, 11:1, pp. 47–58.
—— (2011a), *Performance Affects: Applied Theatre and the End of Effect*, Basingstoke: Palgrave.
—— (2011b), 'Humanitarian performance and the Asian tsunami', *TDR: The Drama Review*, 55:1, pp. 70–83.
Thompson, J. and Schechner, R. (2004), 'Why "Social Theatre"?', *TDR: The Drama Review*, 48:3, pp. 11–16.
Thompson, J., Hughes, J. and Balfour, M. (2009), *Performance in Place of War*, London: Seagull Books.
Thorn, L. (2013), *Naked State: Creativity and Empowerment of Incarcerated Women and Girls*, A Winston Churchill Travel Fellowship Report, http://www.wcmt.org.uk/reports/1102_1.pdf. Accessed 23 February 2018.
Townsend, M. (2012a), 'Women's prisons in desperate need of reform, says former governor', *The Guardian*, 11 February, http://www.guardian.co.uk/society/2012/feb/11/women-prisons-urgent-reform-needed. Accessed 23 February 2018.
—— (2012b), 'Women prisoners: Self-harm, suicide attempts and the struggle for survival', *The Guardian*, 11 February, http://www.guardian.co.uk/society/2012/feb/11/women-prisoners-suffering-mental-health. Accessed 23 February 2018.
Travis, A. (2010), 'Reoffending rates top 70% in some prisons, figures reveal', *The Guardian*, http://www.guardian.co.uk/uk/2010/nov/04/jail-less-effective-community-service. Accessed 23 February 2018.
Trounstine, J. (2004), *Shakespeare Behind Bars: One Teacher's Story of the Power of Drama in Women's Prison*, Ann Arbor, MI: University of Michigan Press.
Turner, J. (2013), 'The politics of carceral spectacle: Televising prison life', in D. Moran, N. Gill and D. Conlon (eds), *Carceral Spaces: Mobility and Agency in Imprisonment and Migrant Detention*, Farnham: Ashgate, pp. 219–38.

—— (2016), *The Prison Boundary: Between Society and Carceral Space*, London: Palgrave.

—— (2017), 'Power and resistance in prison: Doing Time, Doing Freedom by Thomas Ugelvik', *British Journal of Criminology,* 57:2, pp. 502–04.

Twersky, C. (2017), 'Chelsea Manning, artist, will show collaborative self-portraits at New York Gallery', *ARTnews,* http://www.artnews.com/2017/06/28/chelsea-manning-artist-will-show-collaborative-self-portraits-at-new-york-gallery/. Accessed 23 February 2018.

Ugelvik, T. (2014), *Power and Resistance in Prison: Doing Time, Doing Freedom*, London: Palgrave.

Valier, C. (2004), *Crime and Punishment in Contemporary Culture,* London: Routledge.

Vallely, P. (2012a), 'Mothers and prison: Babies behind bars', *The Independent*, http://www.independent.co.uk/news/uk/home-news/mothers--prison-babies-behind-bars-8143296.html#. Accessed 23 February 2018.

—— (2012b), 'Mothers and prison: The lost generation', *The Independent*, http://www.independent.co.uk/news/uk/crime/mothers--prison-the-lost-generation-8157387.html. Accessed 23 February 2018.

Vallely, P. and Cassidy, S. (2012a), 'Mothers and prison: The alternatives', *The Independent*, http://www.independent.co.uk/news/uk/crime/mothers--prison-the-alternatives-8160836.html. Accessed 23 February 2018.

—— (2012b), 'Mothers and prison: Thousands of children being brought up by their grandparents', *The Independent*, http://www.independent.co.uk/news/uk/crime/mothers-prison-thousands-of-children-being-brought-up-by-their-grandparents-8153540.html. Accessed 23 February 2018.

Van Hoven, B. and Sibley, D. (2008), '"Just Duck": The role of vision in the production of prison spaces', *Environment and Planning D: Society and Space,* 26, pp. 1001–17.

Villa, M. (2017), 'The mental health crisis facing women in prison', *The Marshall Project*, https://www.themarshallproject.org/2017/06/22/the-mental-health-crisis-facing-women-in-prison?utm_medium=social&utm_campaign=sprout&utm_source=facebook#.GXVIu2CG4. Accessed 23 February 2018.

Vogler, T. A. (2003), 'Poetic witness: Writing the real', in A. Douglass and T. A. Vogler (eds), *Witness and Memory: The Discourse of Trauma*, London: Routledge, pp. 173–206.

Wacquant, L. (2002), 'The curious eclipse of prison ethnography in the Age of Mass Incarceration', *Ethnography,* 3:4, pp. 371–97.

—— (2004), 'Habitus', in J. Beckert and M. Zafirovski (eds), *International Encyclopedia of Economic Sociology*, London: Routledge, pp. 315–19.

—— (2005), 'Carnal connections: On embodiment, membership, and apprenticeship: Response to special issue on "Body and Soul"', *Qualitative Sociology*, 28:4, pp. 445–71.

—— (2008a), 'Pierre Bourdieu', in R. Stones (ed.), *Key Sociological Thinkers*, 2nd ed., Basingstoke: Palgrave Macmillan, pp. 261–77.

—— (2008b), *Urban Outcasts: A Comparative Sociology of Advanced Marginality*, Cambridge, MA: Polity Press.

—— (2009a), 'The body, the ghetto and the penal state', *Qualitative Sociology,* 32:1, pp. 101–29.

—— (2009b), *Punishing the Poor: The Neoliberal Government of Social Insecurity*, Durham, NC: Duke University Press.

―― (2010a), 'Prisoner reentry as myth and ceremony', *Dialectical Anthropology,* 34:4, pp. 604–20.

―― (2010b), 'Crafting the neoliberal state: Workfare, prisonfare and social insecurity', *Sociological Forum,* 25:2, pp. 197–220.

―― (2011), 'Habitus as topic and tool: Reflections on becoming a prizefighter', *Qualitative Research in Psychology,* 8, pp. 81–92.

Wacquant, L. and Bourdieu, H. (1992), *An Invitation to Reflective Sociology,* Cambridge, MA: Polity Press.

Wade, L. A. (2009), 'Sublime trauma: The violence of the ethical encounter', in P. Anderson and J. Menon (eds), *Violence Performed: Local Roots and Global Routes of Conflict,* Basingstoke: Palgrave Macmillan, pp. 15–30.

Wake, C. (2009a), 'After effects: Performing the ends of memory. An Introduction to Volume 1', *Performance Paradigm,* 5:1, n.pag.

―― (2009b), 'The accident and the account: Towards a taxonomy of spectatorial witness in Theatre and Performance Studies', *Performance Paradigm,* 5:1, n.pag.

―― (2010), 'Caveat spectator: Juridical, political and ontological false witnessing in CMI (A Certain Maritime Incident)', *Law, Text, Culture,* 14:1, pp. 160–87.

―― (2013), 'To witness mimesis: The politics, ethics, and aesthetics of testimonial theatre in through the wire', *Modern Drama,* 56:1, pp. 102–25.

Walklate, S. (2004), *Gender, Crime and Criminal Justice,* 2nd ed., Portland, OR: Willan Publishing.

―― (ed.) (2012a), *Gender and Crime Volume III: Gendered Experiences of the Criminal Justice Process,* London: Routledge.

―― (ed.) (2012b), *Gender and Crime Volume IV: Gender, Crime and Punishment,* London: Routledge.

Wallis, M. and Duggan, P. (2011), 'Editorial: On trauma', *Performance Research: A Journal of the Performing Arts,* 16:1, pp. 1–3.

Walsh, A. (2011), 'Book review: *Offending Women: Power, Punishment, and the Regulation of Desire,* by Lynne A Haney', *Prison Service Journal,* 198, p. 54.

―― (2012a), 'Performing prisons, performing punishment: The banality of the cell in Contemporary Theatre', *Total Theatre Magazine,* Summer, pp. 32–33.

―― (2012b), 'Performing for survival', *Women in Prison Magazine,* Spring, pp. 34–37.

―― (2012c), 'Negotiating values of theatre in prison: Navigating arts vs. institution in research', *Ethics, Aesthetics, Society: TaPRA PG Conference,* London, February, unpublished.

―― (2012d), 'Space-making in women's prisons: Personal performance testimonies of "Doing Bird"', *Northampton PG Arts Conference,* Northampton, September, unpublished.

―― (2013a), 'The wound and the salve: Critical perspectives on applied theatre in prison', Trauma, Narrative and Performance Panel, *Northampton PG Arts Conference,* September, unpublished.

―― (2013b), 'Creating change, imagining futures: Participatory arts and young people "at risk"', Report for Ovalhouse and CUCR Creating Change Network, London: CUCR.

―― (2014), '(En)gendering habitus: Women, prison, resistance', *Contemporary Theatre Review,* 24:1, pp. 40–52.

—— (2016), 'Staging women in prison: Clean Break Theatre Company's dramaturgy of the cage', *Crime, Media, Culture*, 12:3, pp. 309–26.

—— (2017), 'Critical introduction to the arts behind bars', *The Oxford Encyclopedia of Criminology*, New York, NY: Oxford University Press.

—— (2018a), '"I've Stood at so Many Windows": Women in prison, performativity and survival', in T. Schult (ed.), 'Performativity and painful pasts', special issue, *Liminalities*, 14:3, http://liminalities.net/14-3/windows.pdf. Accessed 8 August 2018.

—— (2018b), 'Performing punishment, transporting audiences: Clean Break Theatre Company's *Sweatbox*', *Prison Service Journal*, 239, pp. 22–25.

—— (2019), 'What works? Prison, gender, and the affective labour of applied theatre in prison', in C. McAvinchey (ed.), *Applied Theatre: Women and the Criminal Justice System*, London: Methuen, n.pag.

Walsh, A. and Tsilimpounidi, T. (2016), 'Dear TINA: Protesting institutions in times of crisis', *Qualitative Inquiry*, 23:2, pp. 137–48.

Walsh, F. (2010), *Male Trouble: Masculinity and the Performance of Crisis*, Basingstoke: Palgrave.

Walters, S. D. (2001), 'Caged heat: The (R)evolution of women-in-prison films', in M. McCaughey and N. King (eds), *Reel Knockouts: Violent Women in the Movies*, Austin, TX: University of Texas Press, pp. 106–23.

Ward, D. and Kassebaum, G. (2007), *Women's Prison: Sex and Social Structure*, Chicago, IL: Aldine.

Warner, S. (2001), '"Do You Know What Bitch Is Backwards?": Mythic revision and ritual reversal in The Medea Project: Theater for Incarcerated Women', *Dialectical Anthropology*, 26, pp. 159–79.

—— (2004), 'The Medea Project: Mythic Theater for Incarcerated Women', *Feminist Studies*, 30:2, pp. 483–500.

—— (2011), 'Restorytive justice: Theater as a redressive mechanism for incarcerated women', in J. M. Lawston and A. E. Lucas (eds), *Razor Wire Women: Prisoners, Activists, Scholars, and Artists*, New York, NY: SUNY Press, pp. 229–45.

Warr, J. (2016), 'The deprivation of certitude, legitimacy and hope: Foreign national prisoners and the pains of imprisonment', *Criminology and Criminal Justice*, 16:3, pp. 301–18.

Waters, S. (1999), *Affinity*, Virago: London.

Watson, A. (2009), '"Lift Your Mask": Geese Theatre Company in performance', in T. Prentki and S. Preston (eds), *The Applied Theatre Reader*, London: Routledge, pp. 47–54.

Watterson, K. (1996), *Women in Prison: Inside the Concrete Womb*, Boston, MA: Northeastern University Press.

Weaver, L. (2009), 'Doing time: A personal and practical account of making performance work in prisons', in T. Prentki and S. Preston (eds), *The Applied Theatre Reader*, London: Routledge, pp. 55–62.

Weheliye, A. (2014), *Habeas Viscus: Racializing Assemblages, Biopolitics and Black Feminist Theories of the Human*, Durham, NC: Duke University Press.

Weil-Davis, S. (2011), 'Inside-out: The reaches and limits of a prison program', in J. M. Lawston and A. E. Lucas (eds), *Razor Wire Women: Prisoners, Activists, Scholars, and Artists*, New York, NY: SUNY Press, pp. 203–23.

Whatling, C. (1997), *Screen Dreams: Fantasising Lesbians in Film*, Manchester: Manchester University Press.

White, G. (2013), *Audience Participation in Theatre: Aesthetics of the Invitation*, Basingstoke: Palgrave.

White, G. (ed.) (2015), *Applied Theatre: Aesthetics*, London: Bloomsbury Methuen.

White, J. (1998), 'The prisoner's voice', in J. Thompson (ed.), *Prison Theatre: Perspectives and Practices*, London: Jessica Kingsley Publishers, pp. 183–96.

Whitehead, J. C. (2007), 'Feminist prison activism: An assessment of empowerment', *Feminist Theory*, 8:3, pp. 299–314.

Whybrow, N. (2010), *Performance and the Contemporary City: An Interdisciplinary Reader*, London: Palgrave.

Wilcox, P. and D'Artrey, M. (2008), 'Constructing the victim and perpetrator of domestic violence', in M. D'Artrey (ed.), *Media, Representation and Society,* Chester: Chester Academic Press, pp. 76–98.

Williams, R. (1966), *Modern Tragedy*, London: Chatto & Windus.

—— (1977), *Marxism and Literature,* Oxford: Oxford University Press.

—— (1987), *Drama from Ibsen to Brecht*, London: Hogarth Press.

—— (2006), *Culture and Materialism*, London: Verso.

Williams, R. M. C. (ed.) (2003), *Teaching the Arts Behind Bars*, Boston, MA: Northeastern University Press.

Williams, T. (2016), 'Number of women in jail has grown faster than that of men, study says', *The New York Times*, http://www.nytimes.com/2016/08/18/us/number-of-women-in-jail-has-grown-far-faster-than-that-of-men-study-says.html. Accessed 23 February 2018.

Wilson, A. (2010), 'Interrupted life: The criminal justice system as a disruptive force on the lives of young offenders', *Prison Service Journal*, 189, pp. 2–8.

Wilson, D. and O'Sullivan, S. (2004), *Images of Incarceration: Representations of Prison in Film and Television*, Winchester: Waterside Press.

Winfree, L., Jr, Newbold, G. and Tubb, S., III (2002), 'Prisoner perspectives on inmate culture in New Mexico and New Zealand: A descriptive case study', *The Prison Journal*, 82:2, pp. 213–33.

Winfrey, M. and Stinson, E. (2016), 'Pulses from the multitude: Virtuosity and black feminist discourse', *Women and Performance: A Journal of Feminist Theory*, 26:2–3, pp. 208–21.

Winston, J. (1998), *Drama, Narrative and Moral Education*, London: Falmer Press.

Women in Prison (2013), 'State of the Estate: Women in prison's report on the Women's Custodial Estate 2011–12', http://www.womeninprison.org.uk/ userfiles/file/StateoftheEstateReport.pdf. Accessed 23 February 2018.

—— (2016), 'Key Facts', http://www.womeninprison.org.uk/research/key-facts.php. Accessed 23 February 2018.

Women Moving Forward (2011), 'Women Breaking the Cycle: A Response to Breaking the Cycle from Women with Direct Experience of the Criminal Justice System', Women in Prison, http://www.womeninprison.org.uk/Greenpaper-womensvoices.php. Accessed 23 February 2018.

Women's Breakout (2013), 'Women's Community Solutions', Women's Breakout Website, http://www.womensbreakout.org.uk/about-us/womens-community-services/. Accessed 23 February 2018.

Woodland, S. (2013), '"Magic mothers and wicked criminals": Exploring narrative and role in a drama programme with women prisoners', *Applied Theatre Research*, 1:1, pp. 77–89.

Worrall, A. and Gelsthorpe, L. (2009), '"What works" with women offenders: The past 30 years', *Probation Journal: The Journal of Community and Criminal Justice*, 56:4, pp. 329–45.

Wyld, G. and Noble, J. (2017), *Beyond Bars: Maximising the Voluntary Sector's Contribution in Criminal Justice*, London: New Philanthropy Capital.

Yar, M. (2003), 'Panoptic power and the pathologisation of vision: Critical reflections on the Foucauldian thesis', *Surveillance and Society*, 1:3, pp. 254–71.

—— (2010), 'Screening crime: Cultural criminology goes to the movies', in K. Hayward and M. Presdee (eds), *Framing Crime: Cultural Criminology and the Image*, Abingdon: Routledge, pp. 68–82.

Young, J. (2011), *The Criminological Imagination*, Cambridge, MA: Polity Press.

Young, K. Y. (2016), 'We will survive: Race and gender-based trauma as cultural truth-telling', in A. K. Householder and A. Trier-Bieniek (eds), *Feminist Perspectives on Orange Is the New Black: Thirteen Critical Essays*, Jefferson, NC: McFarland and Co, pp. 43–55.

Young-Jahangeer, M. (2013), '"Less than a Dog": Interrogating theatre for debate in Westville Female Correctional Centre, Durban, South Africa', *Research in Drama Education: The Journal of Applied Theatre and Performance*, 18:2, pp. 200–03.

—— (2015), 'A cell called home: Reflections on the politics of containment and emancipation in Westville Female Correctional Centre', *Agenda*, 29:4, pp. 45–55.

Zimbardo, P. G., Haney, C., Banks, W. C. and Jaffe, D. (1973), 'The mind is a formidable jailer: A Pirandellian Prison', *The New York Times Magazine*, Section 6, p. 36.

Zoukis, C. (2017), 'Book review: Graphic novel helps prisoners navigate grievance system', *Huffington Post*, http://www.huffingtonpost.com/entry/book-review-graphic-novel-helps-prisoners-navigate_us_58dbe9ede4b0487a198a566c. Accessed 23 February 2018.

Filmography

Affinity, dir. Tim Fywell (BBC, UK, 2008).
Bad Girls (ITV, UK, 1999–2006).
Bad Girls: The Musical, dir. Maggie Norris (UK, 2007).
The Big Doll House, dir. Jack Hill (USA, 1971).
Buffalo 66, dir. Vincent Gallo (USA, 1998).
Caged Heat, dir. Jonathan Demme (USA, 1974).
Carandiru, dir. Hector Babenco (Brazil, 2003).
Cell 211, dir. Daniel Monzon (Spain, 2009).
Chained Heat, dir. Paul Nicholas (USA, 1983).
Das Experiment, dir. Oliver Hirschbiegel (Germany, 2001).
Dyke Jail (Carceles Bollefas), dir. Cecilia Montagut (Spain, 2017).
Hunger, dir. Steve McQueen (UK/Ireland, 2008).
I am a Fugitive from a Chain Gang, dir. Mervyn LeRoy (USA, 1932).
I Have Loved You So Long, dir. Philippe Claudel (France/Germany, 2009).
Locked up (Vis a Vis), dir. Jesus Comenar (and colleagues) (Spain, 2015–18).
Midnight Express, dir. Alan Parker (UK/USA, 1978).
Notes from the Field, written by Anna Deavere Smith (HBO, USA, 2018).
Orange Is the New Black, dir. Jenji Kohan (Netflix, USA, 2013–ongoing).
Papillon, dir. Franklin J. Schaffner (USA, 1973).
Prisoner: Cell Block H (Network 10, Australia, 1979–86).
Sherrybaby, dir. Laury Collyer (USA, 2006).
Stranger Inside, dir. Cheryl Dunye (USA, 2001).
The 13th, dir. Ava duVernay (Netflix, USA, 2016).
The Experiment, dir. Paul Scheuring (USA, 2010).
The Prison in 12 Landscapes, dir. Brett Story (USA, 2017).
The Shawshank Redemption, dir. Fram Darabont (USA, 1994).
Wentworth Prison (Channel 5, Australia, 2013–ongoing).
Women's Prison (Zendan-e Zanan), dir. Manijeh Hakmat (Iran, 2002).

Live Performances

66 Minutes in Damascus, dir. Lucien Bourjeilly (LIFT, Shoreditch Town Hall, London 2012).
An Almost Unnameable Lust, dir. Caroline Steinbeis. Writer, Rebecca Lenkiewicz (Clean Break, Soho Theatre, London, 2011).
a tender subject, dir. Mark Storor/Artangel (Smithfield Meat Market, London, 2012).
Bad Girls: The Musical, by Maureen Chadwick and Ann McManus (West Yorkshire Playhouse, Leeds, 2006).
De Profundis, HM Prison Reading (Artangel, Reading, 2016).
Dream Pill, dir. Tessa Walker. Writer Rebecca Prichard (Clean Break, Soho Theatre, London, 2011).
Fatal Light, dir. Lucy Morrison. Writer Chloë Moss (Clean Break, Soho Theatre, London, 2011).
Her Naked Skin, dir. Howard Barker. Writer Rebecca Lenkiewicz (National Theatre, London, 2008).
Hopelessly Devoted, dir. James Grieve. Writer Kate Tempest (Paines Plough, London, 2013).
it felt empty when the heart went at first but it is alright now, dir. Lucy Morrison. Writer Lucy Kirkwood (Clean Break, Arcola Theatre, London, 2009).
Journey Woman. Produced by Geese Theatre (Geese Theatre, Foston Hall, Derbyshire, 2009).
Julius Caesar, The Tempest and *Henry V,* dir. Phyllida Lloyd. Produced by Donmar Warehouse (Donmar, London, 2013–16).
Key Change. Produced by Open Clasp (Summerhall, Edinburgh, 2015).
Missing Out. Produced by Clean Break and Action for Prisoners' Families, Writer Mary Cooper (UK Tour, 2009).
Notes from the Field, written and performed by Anna Deavere Smith (Royal Court, London, 2018).
Riot Days. Produced by Pussy Riot (UK Tour, 2017/2018).
Sweatbox. Produced by Clean Break, Writer Chloë Moss (Tour, 2014).
The Cell: gotojail Project. Produced by Rideout (Southbank Centre as part of *Art by Offenders*, London, 2010).
The Factory, dir. Steve Lambert (Badac Theatre, Edinburgh, 2008).
The New World Order, dir. Ellie Jones (Hydrocracker, Brighton Festival, 2011).
There are Mountains, dir. Imogen Ashby (Clean Break, Askham Grange, 2012).
This is Camp X-Ray, dir. Jai Redman (Ultimate Holding Company, Manchester, 2003).
This Wide Night, dir. Lucy Morrison. Writer, Chloë Moss (Clean Break, Soho Theatre, 2008).
Two Undiscovered Amerindians Visit… Creators, Guillermo Gòmez-Peña and Coco Fusco (various locations, 1992).

Index

A

abolition 19, 20, 42, 106, 115, 137, 204
abuse 5, 28, 40, 60, 64, 66, 98, 103, 137, 152, 156, 162, 164–66, 170, 175, 192, 196
addiction 11, 40, 83, 130, 137, 155, 157, 181, 183, 196
aesthetic/s 8, 13–4, 28, 40, 45, 51, 54, 56, 57, 59, 60, 62, 67, 72–73, 76, 77, 78, 82, 83, 84, 89, 90, 93, 96, 99–100, 102–4, 107–8, 111, 117, 147, 174, 187, 197, 204, 205–8
affect 3,4, 5, 9, 38, 41, 45, 47, 51–52, 54, 57, 64, 70, 78, 88–89, 91, 99, 101, 103, 105–107, 109, 137, 149, 153, 157, 174, 182, 186, 195, 208–9
agency 6, 7, 12, 18, 26, 28, 30, 33, 36, 39, 41, 57, 59, 72–73, 77, 82, 106, 109, 117, 119, 122, 123, 125–8, 130, 132, 137, 146, 151, 159–61, 165, 166, 179, 180, 200, 206, 208
Affinity 18, 143, 147, 150, 157–60, 165–7, 169, 207
Ahrens, Lois 4, 55, 110
Alexander, Michelle 29, 116, 125, 132
Allspach, Anke 51, 132, 178, 179, 183
applied theatre 8, 10, 12, 14, 15, 17, 18, 20, 27, 31, 36, 45, 47, 51, 61, 70, 73, 75, 78, 82–5, 88–9, 93, 96, 99–108, 111, 205, 207
Artangel 3
authenticity 13, 20, 53, 64, 66, 67–71, 78, 100, 151, 204

B

Bad Girls 18, 143, 147, 150, 152, 154–7, 160, 162, 166–8, 170
Balfour, Michael 11, 61, 82, 86, 89, 90, 100, 107, 109
bare life 78, 119, 123
Black Lives Matter 5, 102, 121, 124, 128, 138
Bosworth, Mary 6, 12, 26, 34, 47
Bourdieu, Pierre 8, 14, 16, 17, 25, 28, 29, 31–4, 46, 63, 65, 84, 107
Brown, Michelle 4, 6, 9, 51, 52, 53, 59, 62, 69, 70–1, 78, 123, 129, 168, 169
bunker 136
Butler, Judith 26, 33, 36, 75, 76, 78, 119, 120, 188

C

cage 3, 14, 15, 17, 55–7, 62, 65–8, 72, 73, 76, 130, 144, 165, 168, 204
carceral 4, 5, 7, 11, 13, 43, 51, 53–4, 56–8, 60, 63, 68, 70, 72–5, 118, 120, 128, 132, 136, 178, 180, 186, 203, 209
carceral geography 51, 182, 189
Carrabine, Eamonn 5, 7, 12, 26, 51, 52, 62, 71, 74, 76, 78, 82, 126, 146, 151, 169
Caruth, Cathy 45, 111, 187
catharsis 43, 44, 72, 73, 84, 90, 108, 195–6
Cecil, Dawn 6, 52, 78, 117, 138, 143–6, 168
cell 17, 25, 52, 55–6, 62, 65, 68–73, 75, 122, 155, 159, 175, 188
Chesney, Lind, Meda 6, 40, 78, 152, 265

Clean Break 18, 19, 30, 40, 43, 45, 81, 82, 84, 87, 93, 95, 104–6, 109, 110, 111, 177, 183, 188–9, 194, 196–199
coercion 26, 82, 144, 161, 166, 168, 170
containment 3, 6, 11, 13, 15, 17, 19, 27, 38, 42–6, 65, 74, 106, 107, 115, 117, 118, 127, 129, 132, 136, 143, 147, 154, 160, 162, 164, 166–7, 170, 174, 177, 184, 186–8, 192, 195, 196, 197, 199, 203, 205, 207, 208
Conquergood, Dwight 57, 59, 75, 111, 186
Corston report 27, 36–7, 83, 110, 181
Couple in the Cage 17, 62, 65, 66–8, 76
criminological imagination 52, 76, 78
cultural criminology 4, 5, 6, 9, 15, 17, 29, 51–3, 78, 82
cycle of tragic containment 44, 107, 174, 187–8, 192, 196

D
Davis, Angela 18, 19, 103, 115, 122, 204
Deavere Smith, Anna 5
de Certeau, Michel 18, 91–2, 105, 107, 198,
de Lauretis, Teresa 35, 36, 48, 106, 143, 147, 148, 149
desire 3, 5, 7, 9, 13, 14, 15, 18, 19, 27, 28, 31, 32, 35, 38, 42, 46, 62, 67, 73, 78, 82, 84, 86, 91, 99, 104, 105, 108, 116, 117, 119, 122, 123, 128, 129, 132, 134–7, 143, 152, 178, 180, 191, 195, 196, 203, 207
desire, lesbian 144–9, 151, 153–68, 170, 207
desistance 14, 107, 109, 139, 177, 185, 188, 189, 199, 200
deviant 32, 37, 85, 144, 146, 148, 150, 154
disposition 14, 17, 32–5, 37, 46, 82, 84, 95, 97, 108
drugs 31, 40, 98, 103, 129, 130, 137, 138, 152, 161, 164, 174, 175, 178, 183, 185, 195, 196, 197
Dolan, Jill 6, 7, 41, 143, 144–5, 147–8, 188, 190, 193
Duggan, Patrick 27, 28, 43, 99, 101–2, 104

E
effect/ effective 4, 12, 27, 28, 34, 42, 53, 55, 58, 61, 63, 64, 70, 73, 74, 75, 86, 89, 96, 100, 104, 106–8, 109, 111, 115, 120, 121, 126, 127, 132, 136, 137, 147, 148, 153, 165, 185, 191, 193, 198, 200, 207, 209
ethics 8, 57, 63, 68, 73, 87, 96, 102, 107, 204, 205

F
failure 27, 31, 96, 97, 99, 106, 156, 161, 182, 187, 188, 189, 198
feminist criminology 6, 8, 12, 15, 17, 18, 19, 27, 32, 34, 36, 37, 38, 40, 41, 46, 74, 126, 143, 146, 150, 167, 168, 174, 181, 204, 206, 207, 208
fiction 3, 9, 10, 18, 32, 51, 66, 71, 74, 117, 129, 143, 148, 151, 157, 158, 160, 166–98, 169, 170, 177, 180, 188
Foucault, Michel 17, 25, 28, 33, 36, 43, 55–58, 73, 75, 77, 87, 119, 146, 178, 179, 186
front 25, 30, 31, 46, 47, 48, 90, 97
Fugitivity 118, 136
Fusco, Coco 17, 51, 62, 66–68, 76, 77, 78

G
Geese Theatre 18, 19, 30, 40, 47, 82, 84, 90, 100–6, 110
Gelsthorpe, Loraine 6, 30, 36, 37, 48, 101, 179, 181, 183, 184, 189, 200
Ghosts 101, 168, 170, 174, 200
Goffman, Erving 17, 25, 27, 29–31, 46, 47, 61, 65, 77, 96, 181, 185, 186, 194, 198, 199 200
Gómez-Peña, Guillermo 17, 51, 62, 66, 68, 76, 77, 78
gotojail project (The Cell) 68, 69, 70, 72

H
Halberstam, Jack 7, 124–6, 143, 147, 150, 161–2, 165, 167, 170
habitus 13, 4, 16, 17, 18, 25, 28, 29, 31, 32–36, 39, 41, 42, 43, 46, 48, 58, 65, 84, 85,

97–9, 106, 107, 120, 143, 173, 176, 182, 183, 184, 185–6, 190, 193, 194, 195, 196, 206
Hall, Stuart 118, 121
Hart, Lynda 12, 21, 41, 99, 143–6, 149, 165, 168, 169
Heritage, Paul 11, 14, 48, 83, 87–88, 90, 91, 109
Herman, Didi 143, 156, 160, 165, 166, 168, 170
Herrmann, Anna 12, 93
Hsieh, Tehching 3
homosocial 151, 156
hooks, bell 116, 117, 118, 119, 137
Hughes, Jenny 11, 26, 31, 82, 84–6, 91, 111

I
institution 3, 5, 6, 7, 8, 10, 11, 12, 13, 15, 16, 18, 20, 29–37, 39, 41, 42, 43, 45–6, 47, 48, 52, 54, 56, 57, 59–63, 65–7, 69, 72, 74–8, 81–4, 86–93, 95–9, 105, 106–10, 115, 116, 118–20, 123, 125, 126, 127, 134–5, 138, 143, 144, 153, 156, 165, 166, 167, 174, 177, 179–81, 183, 184, 185, 186, 188, 189, 194, 195, 198, 199, 203, 204, 205, 206, 207, 208, 209
institutionalized 3, 5, 19, 30, 116, 121, 132, 137, 174, 190, 198
intersectionality 83, 118, 138
intervention 7, 11, 12, 20, 26, 29, 30, 40, 69, 83, 85, 86, 88, 89, 99, 100, 102, 105, 107, 108, 111, 135, 178, 184, 188, 204
intimacy 18, 69, 143, 144, 161, 166, 193, 194–5
invisible 71, 82, 144

J
Journey Woman 84, 100–4

K
Kershaw, Baz 14, 25, 41, 43, 55, 57, 73, 75, 82, 90, 91, 109, 203
Key Change 175–176, 183, 198, 199
Kirkwood, Lucy 40
Koestler Trust 4, 69

L
labour 47, 52, 72, 78, 88, 96, 105, 106, 107, 109, 120, 130, 136, 137, 138
Lombroso, Cesar 41, 85–6, 107, 145–6
legibility 85, 151, 153, 162
Lenkiewicz, Rebecca 28, 40, 48
lesbian 18, 26, 38, 127, 139, 143–70

M
Massey, Doreen 92, 93, 106, 136
Mbembe, Achille 78, 119–20, 121, 134
McAvinchey, Caoimhe 7, 12, 32, 48, 59, 62, 69, 71, 74, 75, 78, 89, 91, 110, 111
McNay, Lois 33, 34
Medea Project for Incarcerated Women 36, 48, 83, 104
mental health 11, 38, 42, 81, 129, 130, 200
mimesis 99, 100–2, 187
Ministry of Justice 12, 20, 21, 47, 199
Moran, Dominique 9, 15, 51, 52, 54, 72, 73, 75
Moss, Chloë 30, 40, 93, 94, 177, 188–91, 194, 196, 199
Mulvey, Laura 125, 143, 147
Muñoz, José Estéban 7, 41, 76, 167, 207

N
National Criminal Justice Arts Alliance (NCJAA) 47, 78, 88, 104, 109
Necropolitics 78, 119–20, 121, 134, 135

O
offender 20, 28–9, 40, 43, 47, 69, 85, 86, 145, 177, 181, 182
officers 25, 35, 38, 58, 63, 64, 65, 68, 70, 72–3, 94, 98, 110, 115, 120, 121, 127, 128, 129, 131–6, 144, 149, 155, 157, 161, 163, 165, 170, 187, 209
O'Neill, Maggie 6, 9, 52, 143, 146
Open Clasp Theatre 45, 175, 176, 183, 199
Orange is the New Black (OITNB) 4, 18, 19, 58, 115, 117, 119–23, 125–38, 149, 153, 183, 207

P

panopticon 10, 17, 25, 54–8, 61, 73, 75, 157, 160
Peaker, Anne 11, 14, 61, 86, 88, 91, 109, 169, 179, 187, 190
penal 59, 69, 70, 71, 74, 84, 85, 101, 110, 125, 139, 179
performativity 8, 18, 28, 29, 34, 39, 53, 75, 102, 103, 111, 144, 187, 190, 200
photography 4, 5, 76, 169
poverty 12, 16, 40, 58, 115, 125, 137, 152, 167, 175, 178, 182, 189, 194, 195, 196, 208
power 4, 7, 8, 10, 12–17, 20, 26, 30, 34, 35, 36, 37, 40, 42, 53–7, 59, 62–5, 71, 73, 74, 75, 76, 82, 87–92, 97, 98, 102, 105, 106, 108, 119, 120, 124, 126, 127, 135–138, 150, 153, 155, 157–70, 178, 180–1, 193, 195, 203, 204, 206, 209
Post Traumatic Stress Disorder (PTSD) 45
Prichard, Rebecca 40
prison industrial complex 20, 91, 115, 118, 119, 120, 125, 138, 139, 204
Prisoner Cell Block H 161, 168
private/public 34, 95
punishment 4, 5, 6, 7, 15–19, 22–37, 40–4, 47, 51, 54–60, 63, 64, 65, 68, 69, 70–78, 87, 88, 90, 126, 131, 134, 139, 145, 158, 165–6, 174, 178, 180, 186, 198, 200, 205, 206, 207

Q

queer 13, 38, 124, 143–5, 147, 161, 167, 170

R

race 3, 5, 12, 18, 32, 58, 62, 77, 90, 109, 115–20, 125, 127, 128, 132, 136, 137, 182, 186, 208
racism 5, 64, 65, 77, 115, 116, 125, 130, 132, 136, 138
Rafter, Nicole 6, 52, 78, 123, 143, 150, 151, 168
realism 63, 197
Real Cost of Prisons Comix, The 4, 55

recidivism 88, 93, 98, 107, 109, 132, 174, 177, 187, 199
refusal 97, 106, 108, 126, 145, 180, 200
regime 5, 9, 19, 33, 38, 42, 46, 57, 67, 81, 88, 96, 107, 115, 101, 122, 123, 128–32, 134, 136, 138, 148, 153, 155, 164, 165, 178, 179, 181, 198
rehabilitation 4, 14, 16, 17, 19, 21, 29, 33, 36, 44, 45, 47, 52–3, 60, 75, 84, 93, 96–8, 101, 139, 188
re-offending 45, 60, 199
representation 3–9, 13, 14, 15, 17–21, 27, 28, 32, 40, 41, 51, 52, 53, 55, 57, 58, 60, 66, 68, 70, 73, 74, 76, 77, 78, 85, 87, 92, 98, 102, 103, 108, 110, 111, 116–9, 121–31, 135–8, 143–62, 164–70, 173, 174, 177, 180, 182, 186, 188, 194, 195, 197–9
resistance 3, 5, 7, 9, 12–19, 26–9, 32–5, 38, 41–4, 45–7, 53, 58, 73, 74, 84, 89, 91, 102, 105, 108, 118, 119, 121, 124–33, 136–7, 143–5, 155, 160, 165–7, 173
revolt 126, 204
Rideout 17, 51, 62, 68–70
riot 121, 126, 128, 134, 136
Rowe, Abigail 147, 181

S

secure housing units (SHU) 97, 122, 123, 134
Sedgwick, Eve Kosofsky 8, 53, 151, 204
self-harm 42, 46, 149
sex 38, 40, 66, 85, 127, 129, 143–53, 156–70, 175, 183, 196, 207
simulate/ simulation 17, 54, 59, 62–74
Smart, Carol 37, 101, 147
Solidarity 13, 77, 97, 124, 134, 136, 151, 164, 193
spectacle 51–59, 63, 65, 66, 72, 73, 75, 78, 87, 100, 120, 128, 130, 151, 174, 184, 186
spectatorship 4–6, 13, 53, 55, 68, 73, 75, 143, 144, 147, 148, 149
Staging Human Rights 48, 83, 109

Index

Stanford Prison Experiment 17, 51, 62–5, 70, 77
stigma 30, 125, 132, 149, 150, 162, 167, 174, 176, 181, 184–8, 198, 199, 200
structure of feeling 21, 25, 44, 99, 206
success 3, 7, 11, 19, 33, 39, 52, 53, 75, 95–9, 105, 106, 136, 139, 173, 183, 184, 185, 186, 188, 208, 209
surveillance 14, 25, 30, 51, 55, 57, 75, 85, 90, 91, 98, 105, 131, 136, 139, 157, 158, 160, 161, 165, 166, 174, 178, 179, 180, 186
survival 6, 34, 39, 40, 91, 98, 103, 123, 128, 136, 149, 183, 186, 196, 198, 199, 205, 206, 207
Sutherland, Alexandra 20, 82
Synergy Theatre Company 71

T

tactics 13, 15, 18, 20, 26, 33, 46, 81, 91–93, 101, 103, 105, 106, 107, 126, 127, 129, 131, 132, 137, 163, 173, 183, 198, 204–7
Taylor, Diana 7, 17, 27, 66, 187
testimony 84, 89, 103, 104, 187, 188
theatrical 7, 26, 40, 41, 51, 53, 55, 63, 64, 74, 77, 90, 86, 174, 182, 187, 197, 198, 203, 206
Thompson, James 7, 8, 11, 47, 61, 69, 72, 75, 82, 84, 87, 89, 90, 92, 93, 96, 98, 101–3, 108, 111
TIPP 90
total institutions 17, 29, 30, 47, 61, 65, 77, 86, 97, 181, 198, 199
traces 8, 10, 18, 32, 43, 45, 128, 173, 174, 180, 181, 185–7, 190, 191, 192, 198
transformation 12, 18, 25, 28, 30, 33, 35, 45, 46, 53, 75, 82, 84, 90, 102, 103, 107, 111, 117, 123, 137, 157, 173, 186, 188, 198

transgender 116, 119, 121, 122, 138
transgression 28, 42, 82, 106, 115, 143, 145–8, 151–4, 157–61, 165, 167, 168
trauma 10, 18, 27, 28, 39, 40, 43, 45, 64, 75, 84, 89, 90, 86, 100–4, 107, 108, 111, 128, 137, 160, 164, 182, 183, 186–90, 192, 194, 198, 199

V

victim-survivor-hero 14, 20, 27, 38–41, 46, 84, 97, 98, 107, 177, 199, 206, 207
violence 5, 7, 18, 28, 35, 40, 45, 53, 57, 62, 86, 94, 117–39, 144, 145, 150, 152, 153, 162, 163, 165, 166, 168, 175, 197
visibility 4, 8, 17, 26, 27, 30, 54, 55, 57, 62, 72, 73, 87, 117, 118, 137, 148, 149, 157–61, 164, 166, 180, 186
visual 3, 4, 5, 7, 9, 51, 52, 118, 119, 120, 123, 131, 137, 152, 157, 161, 163, 166, 167, 207
voice 75, 84, 100, 108, 124

W

Wacquant, Loïc 32, 52, 59, 76, 77, 98, 99, 108, 115, 119, 125–6, 130, 139, 179, 182
Waters, Sarah 18, 143, 157–60, 167, 169, 170
Watson, Andy 11, 48, 61, 90, 100
Wentworth 18, 19, 143, 147, 150, 152, 160–8, 178, 183, 207, 209
'what works' 78, 88, 107
Workfare 119, 125, 126, 130, 139

Z

Zimbardo, Phillip 17, 63–5, 68

Milton Keynes UK
Ingram Content Group UK Ltd.
UKHW051106120923
428513UK00010B/360